CONSTITUTIONAL DEMOCRACY IN AFRICA

Volume 2

Nigerian Law of Torts – *Kodilinye and Aluko*

Nigerian Legal System – *Obilade*

An Introduction to Equity in Nigeria – *Kodilinye*

Nigerian Law of Contract – *Sagay*

Criminal Law in Nigeria – *Okonkwo* and *Naish*

The Law of Evidence – *Aguda*

Nigerian Tax Law – *Ayua*

Introduction to International Law – *Umozurike*

History and Sources of Nigerian Criminal Law – *Karibi-Whyte*

Law of Judicial Immunities in Nigeria – *Olowofoyeku*

Military Rule and Constitutionalism in Nigeria – *Ben Nwabueze*

Military Rule and Social Justice in Nigeria – *Ben Nwabueze*

Democratisation – *Ben Nwabueze*

The Making of the 1989 Constitution of Nigeria – *Aniagolu*

Jurisprudence – *Elegido*

Sharia Law Reports of Nigeria Vol. 1 – *Mahmood*

A Compendium of Notable Pronouncements of our Jurists Through Cases – *Sanda*

Justice Delayed is Justice Denied – *Sanda*

Customary Law in Nigeria through the Cases – *Kolajo*

Layman's Guide to Criminal Law and Anti-Corruption Law – *Kolajo*

Modern Digest of Case Law – *Aderemi*

Law for the Layman – *Kolajo*

Family Law – *Onokah*

All-Nigeria Judges' Conference 2001 – *National Judicial Institute*

Constitutional Democracy in Africa Vol. I – *Ben Nwabueze*

Law of Consumer Protection – *Monye*

CONSTITUTIONAL DEMOCRACY IN AFRICA

Volume 2

CONSTITUTIONALISM, AUTHORITARIANISM AND STATISM

by

Ben Nwabueze

Foreword by

Julius Nyerere, *Former President of Tanzania*

and

Introduction by

Chief F. R. A. Williams SAN

Spectrum Books Limited

Ibadan

Abuja •Benin City •Lagos •Owerri

Spectrum titles can be purchased on line at

www.spectrumbooksonline.com

Published by
Spectrum Books Limited
Spectrum House
Ring Road
P.M.B. 5612
Ibadan, Nigeria
e-mail: admin1@spectrumbooksonline.com

in association with
Safari Books (Export) Limited
1st Floor
17 Bond Street
St. Helier
Jersey JE2 3NP
Channel Islands
United Kingdom

Europe and USA Distributor
African Books Collective Ltd.
The Jam Factory
27 Park End Street
Oxford OX1, 1HU, UK

ISBN: 978-029-461-9

Printed by Printmarks Ventures, Ososami, Ibadan

To
Nelson Mandela,
in admiration for his
unsurpassed heroism

CONTENTS

Table of Cases

Table of Statutes

Foreword

This seven-volume work now being presented is the culmination of an ambitious project of an illustrious Nigerian jurist who has already made his mark in the field of constitutional law and jurisprudence. It comes at a most appropriate time when ethnic nationalism is tearing apart the superstructure of states even in the old Western world and now brutally in the Balkans. Exploring the evolution of the state system transplanted to Africa by European colonialism, the author analyses the nature of this sophisticated organism and the failure of African leaders since independence to domesticate it. Professor Nwabueze argues that this **alien state** system had all but destroyed the mind, culture and personality of the African, eroded the indigenous bases of authority without establishing any roots in African culture, deconstructed the traditional African political institutions and offices and generated social violence, unrest and incompatibilities among the plural societies that make up each African state. He goes further to explore the differences between the more recent Western European colonial heritage with that of the ancient and medieval colonialism in North Africa and the subsequent Arab and Islamic religious and cultural colonialism in Africa south of the Sahara. In the author's view, one of the most serious problems haunting the post-independence African governments is the **national question,** that is: how to weld together harmoniously into one nation in each African territory, the peoples of different culture, language and sometimes even of race forcibly brought together by the colonial regimes.

Professor Nwabueze puts forward the thesis that a pre-condition for the evolution of true African states in the post colonial era, is the **decolonisation** of the African mind, culture, society and state in a conscious, slow but sympathetic effort. Without such a process of decolonisation, the endemic chaos that has set in everywhere cannot be dislodged nor can the plural societies forcibly patched together in the so–called post colonial African states cohere for long.

Professor Nwabueze's book does not merely fill a gap or a void in the literature of African history, law, economy, politics and society; rather, it creates a novel and significant niche that will, for many years to come, serve as a quarry for scholars and researchers seeking the explanation for the disorder and trauma that have followed the nominal transfer of power from the old colonialists to the native inheritors.

In its sweep and its formidable scholarship, its historicism and its underlying jurisprudence, this study is comparable to two projects of a similar nature by United Nations Educational Scientific, and Cultural Organization (UNESCO): *A Scientific and Cultural History of Mankind* and the companion volume, *General History of Africa*. Professor Nwabueze's work is at once magisterial and authoritative; it is learned and erudite without being pedantic; critical, incisive and perceptive without being carping; informative and comprehensive without being tedious. It will place the author securely in the gallery of Africa's great scholars.

These volumes are warmly recommended to all serious students of African politics, law, culture and society and to all those interested in restructuring African states into lasting and orderly societies and polities.

Julius K. Nyerere

Julius Nyerere

Postscript: Since this Foreword was written by Julius Nyerere who died not long after writing it, the work has been restructured into two sets of volumes under the titles *Colonialism in Africa* (two volumes of 831 pages) and *Constitutional Democracy in Africa* (five volumes of more than 2,500 pages)

Introduction

This volume (the second) lies at the heart of Professor Nwabueze's monumental five-volume study. It seeks to demonstrate the author's central thesis in the study, namely, that no other system of rule so far devised is more suitable and viable for the government of society or conduces more to the realization of the ends of human existence upon this earth than one in which the rulers are freely chosen by the people and are limited in their powers by a guarantee of the rights and freedom of the individual under a constitution that has the force of a supreme, overriding law. The book seeks to demonstrate the validity of the author's thesis by setting out, in the way of a contrast, the virtues of constitutional democracy against the evils of authoritarian rule.

The concept of human rights, being the core of constitutional democracy, is taken as the starting point. "Human rights," the author tells us, is a concept, a device, invented by philosophers for the protection of the dignity of the human person against the growing and menacing power of the state. The human being is endowed with certain inherent attributes – the faculty to think, to believe or disbelieve, to judge between right and wrong, to feel and to act. These faculties confer on him a dignity, a spiritual and moral integrity, that sets him apart from non-human beings, and which require to be respected by the state. To ensure the necessary respect for human dignity and to bestow efficacy upon it, the concept of human rights was invented as legal claims enforceable against the state by the individual. The innate faculties of rational thought, conscience, belief, emotions, feelings and choice are manifested in speech, movement, religious practices, association with others, processions and other overt ways. The ability to manifest the individual's innate faculties in the ways just mentioned also require protection by law, subject however to suitably framed qualifications in favour of the state for the maintenance of public order, state security, public safety, public morality and the general well-being of society.

Given that the territorial community, both national and international, is made up of individual human beings, it is clear that, unless the inherent faculties of the individual that confer dignity on him and his ability to manifest them in overt ways are protected by law against encroachment by the state, there can be no happiness, contentment or the good life in society, and consequently no peace, no progress and no development. Thus, "recognition of the inalienable rights of all members of the human family" is proclaimed by the United Nations Universal Declaration of Human Rights (1948), and is reaffirmed by the two International Covenants on the matter (1976), as "the foundation of freedom, justice and peace in the world," and disregard of them as the cause of "the barbarous acts which have outraged the conscience of mankind;" their protection under the rule of law is accordingly affirmed as "an essential guarantee against tyranny and oppression," and against a consequent uprising by the people in revolt to rid themselves of such tyranny.

The affirmation above of the value and importance of human rights relates in the main to civil rights. Political rights too have great value and importance, which has been greatly enhanced in our modern democratic age. I should, for greater effect, let the author speak directly by quoting his beautiful summation of the value and importance of political rights.

> The democratisation of government has, by tempering the arrogance of power, had the effect, to some extent, of bringing rulers and the ruled closer together in terms of equality. The degree of equality between the various members of society which came in the wake of popular power, the liberation of the masses of the people from subjugation to the hereditary power of the aristocratic class, has brought greater fulfilment, contentment and harmony by eliminating the injustice and tyranny associated with monarchical, aristocratic and oligarchic rule and the envy and jealousy aroused by inequality in rank and privileges between the classes... Participation creates for the individual citizen a sense of self-esteem, and a mechanism for obliging the government to take proper cognisance of his importance. With the authority bestowed by his vote, the individual is wooed and canvassed by a multitude of political office-seekers, and thereby acquires a certain degree of importance and respect. The notion of political rights is thus brought down to the level of the humblest citizen, making it the common property of all, rather than the exclusive prerogative of a privileged few... In Africa where the state lacks legitimacy because it originated in colonisation by means of conquest or treaties of cession obtained through undue influence, the value of popular participation in government goes beyond what is stated above; it serves also as a means of trying to legitimise the state and the form of government. A referendum to adopt or approve a constitution bestows upon it the stamp of public recognition of its suitability for the government of the community, and therefore as worthy of respect and obedience. And while popular elections are primarily a means to enable the people choose the persons to conduct public affairs on their behalf, they are also a circumstance

from which, over a period of time, public acceptance of both the form of government and the title of the state to govern may grow.

The author acknowledges, however, the prevalence in Africa of certain factors working against the full realisation of the value and importance of popular participation in government. Notable among them are illiteracy, ignorance and poverty; the non-existence or weakness of "civil society;" the absence of a tradition of respect for accountability, probity and for democratic behaviour; and massive rigging of elections. The impact of these inhibiting factors is examined with an incisiveness characteristic of the author's treatment of issues.

A critical question in the development of the concept of human rights concerns the form which legal protection should take to make it really effective in checking encroachment by the state. In response to this question, a bill of rights enshrined in the supreme law of the constitution of a country has been evolved as a mechanism whereby human rights are given recognition as legal claims enforceable against the state. But this must be taken with the reservation, as Sir Shridath Ramphal, former Secretary-General of the Commonwealth, maintains, that human rights, being a derivation from the inherent dignity of the human person, are not, by reason of such recognition, to be regarded as having been "conferred by constitutions, conventions or governments. These are the instruments, the testaments, of their recognition; they are important, sometimes essential elements of the machinery for their protection and enforcement, but they do not give rise to them." What these observations seem to indicate is that human rights have two dimensions: as rights derived directly from the inherent dignity of the human person they can be nothing more than moral rights, but their status as legal rights enforceable against the state must derive from their recognition by the law of the state, and the effective form of such recognition is a bill of rights enshrined in the law of the constitution of the state.

A bill of rights enshrined in the constitution is an invention of comparatively recent origin dating only from the American Revolution of 1776-87. England's **Magna Carta** of 1215, the earliest legal instrument of protection, has been described as a charter, not of "popular liberty" but of "feudal reaction," and as "tending to the restoration of feudal privileges and feudal jurisdictions; inimical alike to the Crown and to the growth of really popular liberties." Nor is its Bill of Rights of 1688 a bill of rights strictly so-called, both because it was concerned principally to assert and secure, not the rights of the individual, but the supremacy of parliament over the Crown, and because the few individual rights protected – the right to bear arms, the prohibition of forfeiture before conviction – were not legally binding on parliament. It is true that before 1215, the rights of the individual were recognised and protected by the common law of England, but again the protection availed only against the executive but not against parliament. The distinctive achievement of the American revolutionaries' invention of a bill of rights enshrined as part of the supreme law of the constitution is to make the protection enforceable equally against the sovereign law-making organ of the state.

From its origin as a by-product of the revolution in America in 1776-87, a bill of rights as a device for giving recognition to human rights and for enforcing them as legal claims against the state, in both its legislative and executive capacities, has been adopted, in its full-blown form, in the constitutions of most countries of the world: some 130 countries, at least, as at 2002. The next significant step in the development of legal protection and enforcement of human rights was the adoption of the Universal Declaration of Human Rights by the United Nations in 1948, which was given the force of a binding treaty in international law by the International Covenant of Civil and Political Rights (1976) and the International Covenant on Economic, Social and Cultural Rights (1976). This development is historic as marking the incorporation of a bill of rights into international law. Following the UN lead, a number of bills of rights at the regional level have been created, among them the African Charter of Human and Peoples' Rights adopted by the Organisation of African Unity (OAU) in 1981 (it entered into force on 21 October, 1986). The author has provided us with an in-depth exposition of the Charter that is both penetrating and masterly (chapter 4)

The great significance of the protection of human rights by international law by means of a bill of rights lies in the fact that, by involving the machinery of international law for the purpose and thus carrying the process beyond the domestic frontiers, the state binds itself to other states by means of a treaty to respect and secure the fundamental rights of its citizens, a treaty being a contractual engagement based on mutual consent of the contracting states and deriving its obligatory force from the good faith due to agreements in international law by the inviolable principle of *pacta sunt servanda*. A state-party to such a treaty is thereby enabled to complain, using the procedure provided in the treaty, about human rights violation by another state-party without rendering itself open to accusation of breaching the principle of non-interference in the internal affairs of other states. But the matter does not stop with merely binding the state to other states in contract. International protection of human rights has brought about a remarkable expansion in the traditional frontiers of international law itself through the use of a treaty not only to bind a state to other contracting states but also to confer upon the citizens of the state a right to redress against it at both the domestic and international levels for violations of their rights in contravention of the treaty stipulations. The individual has thus gained recognition, albeit limited to this purpose only, as a subject of international law.

Yet, in spite of its growing universality, a certain scepticism still persists concerning the usefulness and effectiveness of a bill of rights in checking human rights abuses by the state, which still continue more or less unabated as a menacing feature of life in many parts of the world, especially in developing countries. In the view of the author, the scepticism is misplaced or at least exaggerated. No well-constructed bill of rights backed by enforcement machinery with power to grant appropriate reliefs against human rights violations can fail to check the incidence of such violations. At the very least, it constitutes "the outer bulwarks of defence," serving, in the words of the Nigerian Minorities Commission (1985), to prevent "a steady deterioration of standards of freedom and the unobtrusive encroachment of government on individual rights."

The alleged irreconcilability of democracy with human rights is the subject dealt with in chapter 5. The uninformed might find the title of the chapter intriguing, but the discussion shows the author at his best in terms of scholarship, incisiveness and masterly presentation. It makes fascinating reading. The same qualities are exhibited in the discussion in the next chapter (chapter 6) about the cruciality of maintaining in a constitutional democracy an acceptable balance between it and the competing object of effective government. The bogey of national security used by African rulers as a cover to perpetrate enormities of all sorts is examined with rare insight.

In Part II of the volume, we are given a heart-rending but illuminating account of the evils of authoritarian rule that leaves us in no doubt that it is a form of rule to be avoided by all means just as a plague is to be avoided. Its evils are pervasive, ranging from atrocious repressions, bloody reign of terror, to the privatisation of the state. The repressions, as exemplified by the regimes of Kwame Nkrumah in Ghana (1958-1966), Kamuzu Banda in Malawi (1964-1994), and Mobutu Sese Seko in Zaire (1964-1997), have taken the form of detention without trial for long, indefinite periods of time, up to 25 years in some cases (27 years in one case in Malawi); repression of freedom of speech; interference with the due process of law in the courts; subordination of the legislative assembly to a point where it became totally subservient to the president, and other kinds of ruthless oppression.

The regimes of Jean-Bedel in the Central African Empire (later renamed Republic) (1965-1979), Macias Nguema in Equatorial Guinea (1968-1979), Idi Amin Dada in Uganda (1971-1979), and Mengistu Haile Mariam in Ethiopia (1977 -1991) epitomised a bloody reign of terror of heart-chilling proportions, involving widespread state-organised violence, savage brutality, sadistic torture and mass killing of hundreds of thousands of people, with millions forced to flee into exile and millions more subjected to threat of death by starvation. By the end of Idi Amin's $7^1/_2$ years reign of terror in Uganda the final death toll from the massacres, murders; "disappearances" and tortures had been put at 300,000 according to informed estimates by Amnesty International.

More de-humanising than the physical annihilation and torture is the terror, fear, tension, nightmare and feeling of insecurity created among the population. The pervasive atmosphere of terror, fear, tension and insecurity had deprived the people of the capacity to resist; it had cowed them, and induced in them a mood of cautiousness in order not to incur any risk to their lives or liberty: an attitude of resignation, submissiveness and timidity. Absolute power corrupts a people and its cherished values and civic virtues, one of its worst tragedies being the large number of people it turns into fawning, obsequious sycophants and praise-singers, and the eagerness with which hero-worshipping, which is not a bad thing in itself, is turned into the deification of the ruler.

The privatisation of the state under an absolute one-man dictatorship is perhaps the worst of the evils of authoritarian rule — it is of course almost invariably accompanied by the other evils noted above. It refers to an extreme form of one-man rule, in which the state is treated by the ruler as if it were his private estate — as if he owned it, with state affairs becoming practically indistinguishable from the strictly personal affairs of the ruler — with all institutions and powers of government being absorbed in him, and with impromptu decisions and actions based on his personal whims and caprices being substituted for regularised government decisions-taking procedures and processes. What is more, state money and other property are treated as if they were his personally to dispose of and be dealt with as he likes, with little or no restrictions, no obligation of accountability and with scant regard to laid-down financial regulations or budgetary controls, breeding in the process utter indiscipline in the expenditure of public funds and of course unbridled corruption.

Because governmental decisions and actions under the system are usually based, not on "the society's critical faculties and collective brain power," but rather on the ruler's supposed infallible wisdom, his ever-changing whims and caprices, his misperceptions and miscalculations, the system leads to sterility in leadership and in the administration of government, to political, institutional, intellectual and moral decay in the nation. But the decay accompanying the privatisation of the state may (as in the case of Mobutu Sese Seko's one-man rule in Zaire) go beyond political, institutional, intellectual and moral decay, and become general, permeating the very existence of the state itself, culminating in its atrophy through its inability to discharge its essential functions. It (the state) continues to exist of course, but only as "an idea without an existential content," or, putting it differently, it continues to exist only in a formal, symbolic and ritualistic sense; that is to say, its existence is marked only by rituals, symbols, state ceremonies and by certain banal artifacts like coins, banknotes and stamps — with the head of the ruler embossed on them — and official uniforms. Such was the state to which the Zairean state had been reduced under Mobutu's one-man rule.

The apartheid system — a form of fascism — under which the black majority of 24.1 million (1984 figures) in South Africa was ruled by a white minority of 4.8 million was characterised by tyranny of the most acute type. A chilling account of the atrocious repressions and oppressions under the system is given in chapter 10, which is a strongly recommended reading.

Socialist totalitarian rule, a form of rule in which anything that subserves the will of the leader is law — "socialist legality," as it is euphemistically called — is examined in chapter 11. It is there described as a despotism with a vengeance in that it magnifies the evils of "autocracy to their farthest limits" — to the point of despotism. It seeks to regiment and control "so many aspects of human existence: family life, friendship, work, leisure, production, exchange, worship, art, manners, travel, dress — even that final assertion of human privacy, death."

Part II ends with a penetrating discussion of the factors contributing to the authoritarianism of African rulers. The discussion is so fascinating and delightful, the style so engaging, such as to make it appealing to a generalist reader.

Part III, 'Statism and the Evils Associated with It", is simply a work of immense scholarship, profound intellectual stimulation and beautiful craftsmanship. The analysis of the notion of the state, its nature, origins and development can stand on its own as a treatise. The crowning piece of the entire volume is probably the final chapter (chapter 14), titled 'The Character of the State Inherited from Colonialism", where the author deals with the illegitimacy of the state and its constitution, its evils as an instrument of arbitrary, dictatorial power and of organised violence and oppression in the hands of the rulers, both Africans and their colonial predecessors, as well as an instrument of exploitation and discrimination based on race, ethnicity and political affiliation.

I congratulate Professor Nwabueze for what is, by any standards, an outstanding work, and recommend it warmly to all interested in learning something about constitutionalism, authoritarianism and statism.

I also warmly recommend it equally to statesmen and political activists who are concerned to ensure that their vision is rooted in well founded and rational ideas.

F.R.A. Williams
Lagos
June 2003

Preface

Statism and constitutional democracy may be said to be European colonialism's great, and seemingly enduring legacies to Africa. But what is the nature of these two complex and sophisticated notions brought to Africa by European colonialism? In the sophisticated form in which it was transplanted to Africa by European colonialism, the state, with its institutions, principles and processes, notably legislated law regularly enforced by courts with compulsive jurisdiction, was certainly unknown to the continent before colonisation and was, consequently, without roots in its culture, political system and way of life. So was constitutional democracy which is defined in the study as a government freely elected by the people on a universal adult franchise (one person, one vote) and limited in its power by a written constitution (a written constitution was unknown in Africa before European colonisation) having the force of a supreme law overriding all inconsistent legislative and executive acts of government and whose provisions are observed and respected **in practice** by the rulers and the ruled as the active, governing rules of government administration and of the game of politics generally. The question that arises is whether statism and constitutional democracy are a blessing or curse or a mixture of both. And what is the nature of colonialism itself? How did Africa come to be colonised by Europe? How did it regain its sovereignty seized from it during the period of colonisation? Apart from the alien state system and constitutional democracy, what are the other legacies of European colonialism to Africa?

These are the central issues examined in this seven volume work, *Colonialism in Africa: Ancient and Modern* in two volumes of 831 pages (a third volume is projected on the inheritance of social violence – civil wars and wars of secession) and *Constitutional Democracy in Africa* in five volumes of over 2,500 pages.

It has been an exciting, though exacting, task, which has left me thoroughly exhausted as well as broken health-wise. Studying the constitutions of African countries from independence to date, with the ever-frequent changes, is a most daunting task indeed. But I am pleased to have accomplished it.

Acknowledgements

I wish now to acknowledge my heavy debt of gratitude to the following people: the late Julius Nyerere, former President of Tanzania, for writing the Foreword; the late Dr. Pius Okigbo, for writing the Introduction to both volumes of *Colonialism in Africa: Ancient and Modern;* Hon. Justice Mohammed Bello, former Chief Justice of Nigeria; Chief F.R.A. Williams SAN, Hon. Justice Chukwudifu Oputa, former Justice of the Supreme Court of Nigeria, General (Dr) Yakubu Gowon, former Head of State of Nigeria and Chief Emeka Anyaoku, former Secretary-General of the Commonwealth, for writing the Introductions to volumes 1,2,3,4 and 5 respectively of *Constitutional Democracy in Africa.* My debt to them is all the heavier because of the enormous sacrifice of having to squeeze out the time amidst their extremely crowded programmes. My Secretary, Damian Obiefule, has been as untiring as ever in typing the manuscripts.

To my wife, Ngozi, and my sweet little daughter, Sarafina, I owe more than I can acknowledge for their perseverance, support, and encouragement during the long years that I was working on the volumes. Only they know what it meant. I am by nature an irritable and hot-tempered person, but my work on the volumes had made me infinitely more so.

To my good friend, Chief Joop Berkhout, the Chairman/Managing Director of Spectrum Books, Tony Igboekwe, Publishing Director, M.J. Achinike, Editorial Controller, and other staff of Spectrum Books, I am eternally grateful for their unfailing support and co-operation.

PART I

VIRTUES OF CONSTITUTIONAL DEMOCRACY

CHAPTER 1

The Concept of Human Rights

In this part of the volume, it seems appropriate to begin with an examination of the nature of human rights: respect for and protection of human rights being the core of constitutional democracy.

Human Dignity and Human Rights

The concept of rights (i.e. legal rights) bristles with difficulty, but the difficulty is infinitely greater in relation to human rights. The peculiar difficulty about the concept of human rights springs from their very nature. Human rights may be defined as the rights one holds by virtue, solely, of being a human person, that is to say, rights naturally inhering in the human being.[1] They are not "the result of one's actions," but rather

> arise from no special undertaking beyond membership in the human race. To have human rights, one does not have to be anything other than a human being. Neither must one do anything other than be born a human being.[2]

This definition shows at once that "not all rights held by human beings are human rights." Rights created by contract between two human beings arise otherwise than by virtue purely of their humanity, and are therefore not human rights; they differ from the latter for the further reason that they can be held by non-human persons like corporations; as such, they are "rights of persons without being among the rights of man."[3]

The respect and primacy accorded to human rights is because, in the

---

[1] Jack Donnelly, "Human Rights and Human Dignity: An Analytic Critique of Non-Western Conceptions of Human Rights," 76 *The American Political Science Review* (1982), p. 305.
[2] Jack Donnelly, *op. cit.*, pp. 305-306
[3] *ibid*, p. 305.

words of the preamble to the two International Covenants of 1976, they "derive from the inherent dignity of the human person." The human being everywhere is endowed, whether by God or by nature, with innate spiritual attributes, not possessed by non-human beings — the faculty of rational thought, the faculty of inner spiritual feelings and emotions, and the faculty of judging right and wrong and of belief. The human soul is the divine nature of God implanted in the human being. These spiritual attributes of the human being are encased by the human body, which therefore imparts inherent dignity to the human being as an entity whole and entire, a dignity which, because it is inherent in man's humanity, is universal to all human beings everywhere.

To say that human rights "derive from the inherent dignity of the human person" seems apt to imply that the two (human rights and human dignity) are equivalent or synonymous things. Herein indeed lies the source of the peculiar difficulty about the concept of human rights. To begin with, human rights are not a spiritual or physical attribute of the human being, but simply a concept invented by philosophers for the realisation of the inherent dignity of the human being; man is not born with human rights. Being innate in man, human dignity is coeval with him; he is born with it; not so the concept of human rights.

In the third place, human rights are a concept, a device, invented in response to the growth of the power of the state and the danger it posed to the liberty of the individual, a development originating in Western Europe in comparatively modern times. It is a device invented to counter the growing encroachment of state power upon the private domain of the individual. But man, with his in-born dignity, existed before the state, and could not have had human rights (i.e. legal claim on or against the state) from his inception and before the advent of the state. Surely, the individual could have no human rights "independent from and even prior to participation in any social or political collective."[4]

In the fourth place, the concept of human rights and the protection it affords is only one of several means used by human societies to try to protect and realise human dignity. One such other means is the family system in many

---

[4] Elaine Pagels, "The Roots and Origins of Human Rights," in Alice H. Henkin (ed.), *Human Dignity* (1979), p. 4.

traditional societies under which the extended family, rather than the individual, is the primary unit of social life, a system in which status and rights are determined not so much by virtue of being an autonomous human being as by virtue of membership of an extended family or other social unit. As Jack Donnelly pertinently observed, the individual in a traditional society so arranged and structured "has a secure and significant place in his society and has available a wide range of intense personal and social relationships which provide him important material and non-material support. He also has available regularised social protections"[5] of a nature altogether different from the protection sought to be provided through the concept of human rights in non-traditional societies that grew up in the West. To quote Jack Donnelly again, "there are conceptions of human dignity which do not imply human rights, and societies and institutions which aim to realise human dignity entirely independent of human rights."[6]

In the fifth place, as a concept connoting essentially a relationship between the individual and the state, as rights "conceived as being held primarily in relation ... to society in the form of the state,"[7] human rights as legal claim can only derive their legal force and efficacy, not from the inherent dignity of the human being, nor from the divine law of God or so-called law of nature, but from recognition by the law of the state. This point is crucially important and deserves to be specially noticed. Just as a contractual transaction based on mutual agreement between two or more competent persons does not derive its legal force and binding character from the fact of agreement alone unless agreements are recognised by the law of the state as having such force and binding character, so also human rights do not derive their legal force as claims on or against the state from the inherent dignity of the human person unless they are recognised as legal claims by the law of the state.

And since the force possessed by human rights as legal claims derives from recognition by the law of the state, the state can also withdraw the recognition in consequence of which human rights will lose their force as legal claims on or against the state. There is thus nothing imprescriptible about human rights as legal claims.

---

[5] Jack Donnelly, *op. cit.,* p. 312.
[6] Jack Donnelly, *ibid* at p. 303.
[7] Jack Donnelly, *op. cit.,* p. 306.

Yet the picture of human rights as resting for their legal force upon recognition by the law of the state is a somewhat partial picture. It fails to bring out the significance of the moral dimension of human rights, which distinguishes them from contractual or other legal rights. Unlike in the case of the latter, the moral dimension of human rights, predicated as it is upon the inherent dignity of the human person, imposes upon the state a duty — an inescapable moral duty — to recognise them in some way or other. This moral dimension of human rights is well articulated by Jack Donnelly. As he puts it:

> Since they are grounded in human nature, human rights are generally viewed as inalienable, at least in the way in which one's nature is inalienable. Inalienability is a particularly difficult concept to analyse. However, at the minimum, what is suggested is that in some moral sense one cannot fully renounce, transfer or otherwise alienate one's human rights. To do so would be to destroy one's humanity, to denature oneself, to become other (less) than a human being and thus it is viewed as a moral impossibility.[8]

Also making the point about the inalienability of human rights as a quality derived from their moral dimension, Sir Shridath Ramphal, former Secretary-General of the Commonwealth, has described them as deriving from

> every person's need to realise his essential humanity. They are not ephemeral, not alterable with time and place and circumstance. They are not the product of philosophical whim or political fashion ... They are fundamental and inalienable.[9]

The implication of the moral dimension of human rights is that, whilst their force as legal claims rests on recognition by the law of the state, they are not conferred or granted by the state, as are some other legal rights. The fact that recognition by the law of the state is necessary to give legal force to human rights as legal claims on or against the state in no way implies that they are conferred or granted by the state. Sir Shridath Ramphal is also most illuminating upon the point. Human rights, he said:

> are not conferred by constitutions, conventions or governments. These are the instruments, the testaments, of their recognition; they are important, sometimes essential, elements of the machinery for their protection and enforcement, but they do not give rise to them.[10]

---

[8] Jack Donnelly, *op. cit.*, p. 306.
[9] Shridath Ramphal, Keynote Address in Report of the ICJ Conference on Development, Human Rights and the Rule of Law.
[10] *loc. cit.*

The Concept of Human Rights in Africa: A Colonial Heritage

Before the birth of modern constitutionalism, the notion that the individual should be free from coercion by government — except such coercion as is necessary for the maintenance of peace and order in society, the preservation of the security of the state and the protection of life and property — did exist, but it did so only as a political (as distinct from legal) concept, as a political duty imposed on the ruler, in most cases by divine law. Donald Treadgold traces it as far back as the ancient Hebrews, to the reigns of David and Solomon.[11] "Judaism," writes Professor Louis Henkin, "knows not rights but duties, and at bottom, all duties are to God."[12]

In a global historical survey, entitled "The Roots and Origins of Human Rights," the historian, Elaine Pagels, has convincingly shown that the concept of human rights as a legal claim was nowhere known in antiquity. In all antiquity, she affirms, the notion that the individual had claims on society was unknown; only society had claims or could confer rights on its individual members.[13] According to her, the concept of human rights is only a modern development, dating back no further than modern times in Europe, nor has it been fully realised today even in American society.[14] We also read from Professor Sir Isaiah Berlin that "the notion of individual rights was absent from the legal conceptions of the Romans and Greeks; this seems to hold equally of the Jewish, Chinese, and all other ancient civilisations that have since come to light."[15]

In the light of Elaine Pagel's careful survey of the position upon this point in all ancient and traditional societies, African, American, Asian, Australian, Chinese, European, Jewish and Japanese, Jack Donnelly must be right when he says that human rights were not recognised in traditional African societies.[16] The contrary view adumbrated by Asante and others, namely, that "the African

---

[11] Donald Treadgold, *Freedom: A History* (1990), pp. 12, 23-33.
[12] Louis Henkin, "Judaism and Human Rights," in *Judaism: A Quarterly Journal of Jewish Life and Thought*, vol. 25, No. 4, p. 436.
[13] Elaine Pagels, in Alice H. Henkin (ed.), *Human Dignity* (1979), p. 2.
[14] *ibid*, p. 6.
[15] Isaiah Berlin, *Four Essays on Liberty* (1969), p. 129.
[16] Jack Donnelly, *op. cit.*, p. 308; also Jack Donnelly, in Claude E. Welch and Ronald I. Meltzer (eds.), *Human Rights and Development in Africa* (1984), pp. 269-270.

conception of human rights was an essential aspect of African humanism"[17] or that "traditional African societies supported and practised human rights,"[18] seems clearly untenable. Besides, with but few exceptions, the African polity before the advent of European colonialism was not a state in the true sense of the term, and the notion of the individual having a legal claim on or against it was hardly applicable. The concept of human rights as a legal claim of the individual on or against society in its formal character as a state is simply among Africa's heritage from European colonialism.

Legal protection of human rights by means of a Bill of Rights or in other forms is of even more recent origin still. England's *Magna Carta*, the earliest legal instrument of protection, has been described as a charter, not of "popular liberty" but of "feudal reaction," and as "tending to the restoration of feudal privileges and feudal jurisdictions, inimical alike to the Crown and to the growth of really popular liberties." Nor is its Bill of Rights of 1688 a bill of rights strictly so-called, both because it was concerned essentially to assert and secure, not the rights of the individual, but the supremacy of Parliament over the Crown and because the few individual rights protected — the right to bear arms, the prohibition of excessive bail, the right to jury trial and the prohibition of forfeiture before conviction — were not legally binding upon Parliament.

Constitutional protection in the form of a Bill of Rights as a legal restraint enforceable against not only the executive as in the past but also against the legislature was yet another product of the American Revolution of 1776-87. The initiative in the matter came from the thirteen colonies all of whom, in the course of the revolution, had adopted new revolutionary constitutions which, in every case, contained a list of inviolable individual rights, either as part of the constitution or as separate Bills of Rights.[19] The U.S. Constitution, as initially adopted in 1787, did not, to be sure, contain a Bill of Rights in any form, but the omission was not because protection was considered not essential to constitutionalism; on the contrary, it was simply out of fear that the inclusion

---

[17]   S. K. B. Asante "Nation Building and Human Rights in Emergent Africa," *Cornell International Law Journal 2, pp. 72-107 (1969).*

[18]   Dunstan M. Wai, "Human Rights in Sub-Saharan Africa," in A. Pollis and P. Schwab (eds.), *Human Rights: A Western Construct with Limited Applicability* (1980), pp. 115-45.

[19]   Roscoe Pound, *The Development of Constitutional Guarantee of Liberty* (1957).

of a Bill of Rights might be construed as limiting the civil rights of Americans to only those specified in the Constitution; and further that since the state constitutions contained elaborate Bills of Rights, it was unnecessary to duplicate them in the federal one.[20] It was also feared that "to postpone the adoption of the Constitution until a Bill of Rights was included might open the way to renewed discord and anarchy."[21] The omission was, however, made good four years later in 1791 when a Bill of Rights was then incorporated into the Constitution by way of an amendment.

There had, no doubt, been an earlier French Declaration of the Rights of Man of 1789, which is said to have been based in part on the Bill of Rights in the Constitution of Virginia. But the French Declaration was not really a constitutional Bill of Rights, being a purely political document, which did not then form part of the constitutional law of France; in any case, it soon fell by the wayside in the turmoil of the French Revolution and the emergence of the dictatorship of Napoleon, thus leaving the American Bills of Rights as the only enduring and credible precedent for the future.

It must not, however, be supposed that the American Bills of Rights were without intellectual roots in the past. They derived their inspiration and historical background from English common law principles and tradition of protection for individual rights. Nothing, as Gordon Wood says, was "more important for the development of American constitutionalism in 1787" than the influence of;

> the unique protections of the English common law. The colonists began the revolution in defence of their English liberties. Liberty was an English obsession before it was an American one ... Whatever Americans did to extend liberty and protect individual rights from the encroachments of governmental power, the English had done it first: trial by jury, writs of *habeas corpus*, concern for property rights, fear of standing armies, bills of rights — all were English before they were American. Without the influence of English constitutional and legal tradition, it is inconceivable that Americans in 1787 or later would have believed and acted as they did.[22]

---

20 Neal Reimer, *James Madison: Creating the American Constitution* (1980), p. 138.
21 Neal Reimer, *loc. cit.*
22 Gordon S. Wood, "The Intellectual Origins of the American Constitution," National Forum, *The Phi Kappa Phi Journal,* Fall 1984, No. 5 at pp. 8 and 13. For a detailed discussion of the roots of the American Bills of Rights in the English Common Law, C. H. McIlwain, *Constitutionalism and the Changing World* (1939), pp. 244-258.

The American Bill of Rights did not immediately win adherents in other countries, such was the deep-seated prejudice against the device because of its supposed ineffectiveness, especially in the absence of an enforcement machinery. Then followed the United Nations Universal Declaration of Human Rights in 1948, the next really significant development in the field of human rights protection. Its form is different from the American, yet it could not have failed to draw heavily, in terms of substance and guidance, from the earlier Bill and the court decisions in it. Today in 2002, the precedent has been adopted, in its full-blown form, in the constitutions of most countries of the world, some 130 countries at least, which indicates a growing universality.

Among the countries of the world in which the Bill of Rights, in its full-blown form, has been introduced are those in former British Africa (fifteen excluding Tanganyika), which, alike with North America, became the inheritors of the libertarian tradition of the English common law and its system of justice. The countries are: Botswana, The Gambia, Ghana, Kenya, Lesotho, Malawi, Mauritius, Nigeria, Seychelles, Sierra Leone, Sudan, Swaziland, Uganda, Zambia and Zimbabwe.

The limitation of the common law guarantee of individual rights is that it avails only against the executive, but not against the legislature. Courts in the common law jurisdiction have never countenanced the view of individual liberty as embodying eternal reason, unalterable by the legislature.[23] To them, the authority of the legislature to interfere with private rights is unquestioned and unfettered by any speculative theorising, seeking to erect them into immutable binding law. However, although the authority of the statute law to interfere with private rights is thus acknowledged, the courts look upon it as something of "an interloper upon the rounded majesty of the common law,"[24] and as such to be so interpreted as to avoid interference with private rights unless this should appear from the express words of the statute or from necessary intendment.

Yet, as self-government was being gradually conceded, the question had to be faced of how to preserve this libertarian heritage against not only the

---

[23] *Liyanage v. R.* [1967] I A.C. 259 (P.C.).
[24] R. T. E. Latham, "The Law and the Commonwealth," in *Survey of British Commonwealth Affairs*, Vol. 1 (1937), pp. 510-511.

executive but also against a legislature controlled by tribal majorities. It would have been wishful thinking to imagine that such a legislature, in an atmosphere dominated by tribal or racial sentiment, would have been tolerant towards the right to criticise and oppose the government. Self-restraint and respect for the rights of minorities are ingrained in British tradition, but they are qualities which it would have been imprudent to expect the new legislatures to have acquired in anything like a sufficient measure to counteract the blinding sentiment of tribal, racial or religious politics and so make meaningful a "presumption ... that the constitutional guarantee of principles of civil and political liberty is unnecessary."[25] It seems naive in such circumstances to put too much faith in the "sweet reasonableness of man." Clearly, therefore, there was a demonstrable need to grope for some constitutional means of extending to the legislature what the common law has achieved in relation to the executive. That constitutional guarantees are notoriously ineffective is no argument for not trying. In any case one cannot conceive of a carefully-constructed justiciable Bill of Rights that would be completely without any effect whatever.

> No knowledgeable person has ever suggested that constitutional safeguards provide in themselves complete and indefeasible security. But they do make the way of the transgressor, of the tyrant, more difficult. They are, so to speak, the outer bulwarks of defence.[26]

The Nigerian minorities commission has put it even more persuasively when it said:

> A government determined to abandon democratic courses will find ways of avoiding them, but they are of great value in preventing a steady deterioration in standards of freedom and the unobtrusive encroachment of a government on individual rights.[27]

Disparaging constitutional guarantees of rights, Sir Ivor Jennings has said that "in spite of the American Bill of Rights, that liberty is even better protected in Britain than in the United States."[28] This seems to miss the point. Against whom is individual liberty better protected in Britain than in America? Surely liberty is not **legally** protected against the British parliament, and this is precisely

---

[25] Jennings, *Approach to Self-Government* (1958), p. 100.
[26] Cowen, *The Foundation of Freedom* (1960), p 119.
[27] *Report Cmnd* 505 (1958), p. 97.
[28] Jennings, *op. cit.*, p. 20. See also K. C. Wheare, *Modern Constitutions* (1966), Ch. 11.

what a Bill of Rights seeks to do. That is why in common law jurisdiction a constitutional guarantee achieves little if it merely says that no one is to be deprived of his civil liberties save in accordance with law, for then it does no more than re-state an existing principle that the executive cannot interfere with private rights without legal authority. But it does add something to the existing law if the prohibition is extended to the legislature as well.

These were some of the considerations that led Britain to incorporate a justiciable Bill of Rights into the constitutions of all but one (Tanganyika) of its former African colonies either during the terminal stage of its rule, as in Nigeria, Lesotho, Swaziland and the Seychelles, or as part of the devices of the independence constitution.

It needs to be reiterated that the basis of these Bills of Rights is the common law, of which, it may be said, they are declaratory. The rights guaranteed are rights already possessed and enjoyed by the individual. The Bills of Rights created no rights *de novo* but declared and preserved already existing rights, which they extended against the legislature. This is borne out by the negative phraseology of some of the provisions. To say that "no person shall be deprived of his personal liberty"[29] clearly presupposes an existing right, for it would be an abuse of language to talk of "depriving" a person of a right which he does not have, unless we were to postulate the existence of the right by the so-called law of nature, a proposition whose untenability has already been demonstrated. It cannot be the fact, as Sir Ivor Jennings seems to imply, that when a common law jurisdiction adopts a formal bill of rights it thereby abolishes the common law on the matter completely.

The implication of this is important, and it lies in the fact that the abolition or suspension of the constitution or of the fundamental rights chapter will not operate to abolish or suppress these rights as against the executive, so long as the common law remains part of the law of the country; its effect will be to free the legislature from the fetters on its legislative competence imposed by the constitutional entrenchment of the rights while leaving them in full force against the executive. Indeed, the Bills of Rights in the constitutions of the countries of former British Africa are by no means exhaustive of the

---

[29] S. 21 (1), Nigerian Constitution 1963.

private rights protected by the common law, rights which, in spite of their non-inclusion, have continued to be enjoyed by the individual against the executive. There is no question here of *expressio unius est exclusio alterius*, though to avoid the possibility of such implication, the Americans have expressly had to declare that "the enumeration in the constitution of certain rights shall not be construed to deny or disparage others retained by the people."[30]

A characteristic of the Bills of Rights imported by Britain into its former colonies in Africa, and which deserves mention, is that, in addition to the jurisdiction conferred by the constitution on the courts to adjudicate all questions of constitutionality generally, when raised in litigation properly before them, the high court is specially empowered to hear and determine an application made to it by any person who alleges that any of the fundamental rights guaranteed by the constitution "has been, is being or is likely to be contravened in relation to him," and "may make such orders, issue such writs and give such direction as it may consider appropriate for the purpose of enforcing or securing the enforcement" of the rights in question. Additional powers "necessary or desirable for the purpose of enabling the court more effectively to exercise this special jurisdiction" may be conferred on it by the legislative assembly.

The Universality of the Concept of Human Rights Today

Whilst human rights originated as a Western concept, they have today attained universality or near universality as a result of several factors, viz: the introduction of European laws and ideas into Africa, America and Asia as a by-product of European colonialism, the inspiration of the U.N. Universal Declaration of Human Rights, the incorporation in the constitutions of most countries of the world of human rights protection in one form or another, the forces of modernisation, urbanisation, economic individualism, the general emancipation of the individual as an autonomous entity severed from the organic unity of the extended family system, the resultant disruptions and dislocations in the framework of the traditional society, etc.

But it is nonetheless contended that human rights, at any rate, as formulated in the United Nations Universal Declaration of Human Rights (1948), are not

---

[30] IXth Amendment.

universal. "Any system of ideas that claims to be universal," it is argued, "must contain critical elements in its fabric that are avowedly of African, Latin American or Asian derivation."[31] It is thus asserted that the U.N. Universal Declaration of Human Rights is only "universal in its intent but not in its derivation." As more elaborately stated, the argument asserts that the U.N. Universal Declaration is:

> a statement of values that derive directly from the liberal democracies of the Western world ... We have no difficulty identifying those ideas in the Universal Declaration of Human Rights that derive from the *Magna Carta*, the American and French revolutions, and the constitutions of the modern liberal democracies. Does anything in that document derive from Africa? If not, why should Africans see it as their charter, and not as an alien system of ideas that is, once again, imposed upon them from without?[32]

The argument seems to be effectively answered in the observations of Elaine Pagels. "In ancient times," she writes:

> the validity of ideas frequently was judged by their antiquity; today, this is no longer the case. Instead, we evaluate the validity of ideas, as in recent developments in biology, physics, psychology and political theory, on the basis of their applicability to experience. From this perspective, we may well argue for the universal validity of human rights. The question of **when** and **where** it originates may become an academic question as we see how people of various cultures now are laying claim to this idea.[33]

That should be the criterion of the universality of the concept of human rights, not whether all other approaches to the realisation of human dignity are incorporated in it. The concept of human rights is certainly applicable today to the experience of most, if not all, countries of the world, and is made so by changes in the conditions now prevailing in those countries brought about by the factors mentioned above. The point is well articulated by Jack Donnelly in an insightful passage that deserves quoting *in extenso*:

> Westernisation, modernisation, development and underdevelopment—the dominant contemporary social and economic forces — have in fact severed the individual from the small, supportive community. Economic,

---

[31] Asmarom Legesse, "Human Rights in African Political Culture," in K. W. Thompson (ed.), *The Moral Imperatives of Human Rights: A World Survey* (1980), p. 123.

[32] Asmarom Legesse, *op. cit.*, pp. 123-124.

[33] Elaine Pagels, *op. cit.*, pp. 6-7.

social, and cultural intrusions into, and disruptions of, the traditional community have removed the support and protection which would 'justify' or 'compensate for' the absence of individual human rights. These intrusions have created a largely isolated individual who is forced to go it alone against social, economic, and political forces that far too often appear to be aggressive and oppressive. Society, which once protected his dignity and provided him with an important place in the world, now appears, in the form of the modern state, the modern economy, and the modern city, an alien power that assaults his dignity and that of his family.[34]

"In such circumstances," he continues, "human rights appear as the natural response to changing conditions, a logical and necessary evolution of the means for realising human dignity. The individual needs the protection of individual rights, barring the implausible, and generally undesired, reemergence of the traditional order." There are scarcely any countries in the world today which have not experienced these changes, and which have not as a result embraced human rights as a logical and necessary response.

These counter-arguments seem to establish the case for the universality, or near universality, of the concept of human rights. It is a universal, not a "relativistic," concept. Countries or regions of the world may differ in their approaches to such issues as recognition of human rights, qualifications on them in favour of the state's interest in order, security, morality, health, economic development, etc., enforcement or promotion, but the concept, based as it is on the inherent attributes of the human person which are what is sought to be protected, must remain the same for all human societies. In the light of this, there can be nothing like a uniquely African concept of human rights. What has been called "the African conception of human rights" adumbrates no new concept of human rights. The African Charter on Human and Peoples Rights, which is said to embody an African conception of human rights, is, on the contrary, an adaptation, by and large, of the rights declared and enumerated in the U.N. Universal Declaration of Human Rights (1948) and the two International Covenants of 1976. The African Charter may be said to embody a distinctly African conception of human rights only in the sense that the protection it gives to these rights is counter-balanced by the duties of

---

[34] Jack Donnelly, "Human Rights and Human Dignity," *op. cit.*, p. 312.

support and solidarity it imposes on the individual towards his family, society, the state, Africa and the international community as well as its guarantee of certain collective rights designated as "peoples' rights." This represents only a difference in approach, whose implications and appropriateness are considered in later chapters of this volume.

But the drafters of the Charter are at pains to give it roots in African philosophy. According to them, "in traditional African societies, there is no opposition between rights and duties or between the individual and the community: they blend harmoniously." This, apparently, is the basis of the recital in the preamble that the provisions of the Charter took into "consideration the virtues of (African) historical tradition and the values of African civilisation." Whatever may be meant by this, there is nothing in the African Charter that can be called a uniquely African **concept** of human rights.

Human Rights and Liberty

The question raised here is whether human rights and liberty are co-terminous and interchangeable terms. Liberty, used either alone or with the qualifying adjective "individual," is a term of wide currency both in ordinary speech or writing and in the constitutions of most countries of the world either in the preamble or in the substantive provisions. Yet, in spite of its wide currency, its meaning is not free from disputation. Perhaps the most celebrated exposition of its meaning and scope is that by the famous English political philosopher, John Stuart Mill, in his essay, *On Liberty*, published in 1859. But we are not here concerned with the meaning and scope of liberty as conceived by classical liberalism represented by Mill, only with its meaning as protected or guaranteed in the constitutions of the countries of the world.

Liberty, as guaranteed in the Constitution of the United States — "no person shall be ... deprived of life, liberty, or property, without due process of law"[35] — is defined as follows by the country's supreme court in a 1897 case involving the validity of a statute that regulated marine insurance contracts:

The liberty mentioned in the amendment means not only the right of the

---

[35] Fifth Amendment; extended to the states by the Fourteenth Amendment.

citizen to be free from the mere physical restraint of his person as by incarceration, but the term is deemed to embrace the right of the citizen to be free in the enjoyment of all his faculties; to be free to use them in all lawful ways, to live and work where he will; to earn his livelihood by any lawful calling; to pursue any livelihood or a vocation, and for that purpose to enter into all contracts which may be proper, necessary or essential to his carrying out to a successful conclusion the purposes above mentioned.[36]

It is appropriate to point out here that, unlike in the United States, "liberty" or "individual liberty" as a general concept, is not guaranteed as such in the Constitutions of African countries, except in six cases, namely: Liberia (1847), Ethiopia (1955), Equatorial Guinea (1982), Burundi (1962), Congo (Leopoldville) (1964) and Sao Tome and Principe (1975). It should also be pointed out that liberty is not constitutionally guaranteed by a mere affirmation of it in a preamble as a fundamental ideal (Benin 1964, Chad 1962, Togo 1963, Senegal 1963, Congo (Brazzaville) 1963), as a fundamental objective or principle (Libya 1951, Algeria 1963 and Somalia 1960) or as part of the country's motto in the substantive part of the constitution (Rwanda 1962 and Togo 1963) or by its mere affirmation without reference to any object (like ideal or fundamental principle or motto), as in eleven other countries (Cote D'Ivoire 1960, Central African Republic 1959, Mauritania 1961, Madagascar 1959, Mali 1960, Niger 1960, Guinea 1958, Burkina Faso 1960, Tanzania 1962/65, the Comoros 1978 and Seychelles 1979).

So also no constitutional guarantee of liberty is imported by recital of it in preambulary form in the body of the Bills of Rights in the constitutions of nine countries of former British Africa (Botswana 1968, Sierra Leone 1978, Swaziland 1968, Zambia 1973, Uganda 1967 and Zimbabwe 1980). The recital reads: "Whereas every person ... is entitled to (or, in Uganda, shall enjoy) the fundamental rights and freedom of the individual, that is to say the right to (a) life, liberty, security of the person and the protection of the law".

By the U.S. supreme court's definition quoted above, liberty embraces all of a person's rights and interests in a free society,[37] including rights arising from contracts, property, inheritance, tort, shareholding in companies, etc.

---

36 *Allgever v. Louisiana*, 165 U.S. 578 (1897).
37 E. S. Corwin, *The Constitution and What It Means Today* (1958), p. 218 et seq., p. 248 et seq.

Defined as embracing all of a person's rights and interests in a free society, the concept of liberty is thus wider than that of human rights. As defined above, the latter are "rights attaching to man as man because of his humanity."[38] Human rights are not "the result of one's actions," they "arise from no special undertaking beyond membership in the human race."[39] Thus, not all rights held by human beings are human rights. Rights created by contract between two human beings, or by tort committed by one person against another, or through dealings in property or shares between two persons, arise otherwise than by virtue purely of their humanity, and are therefore not human rights; they are "rights of persons without being among the rights of man." The right acquired under a licence to carry on banking business, granted by the minister pursuant to the Banking Act, was held by the supreme court of Nigeria not to be "civil right" (i.e. human right) within the meaning of the guarantee of fundamental rights in the Nigerian Constitution (1960).[40] There is here involved a subtle and perhaps not entirely sensible distinction — between, on the one hand, the right to enter into a contract, to acquire property or to invest in shares of a company, which, because it pertains to a man's freedom of action, is indisputably a human right, and, on the other hand, rights arising from the contract so created or rights over property or shares acquired by virtue of the transaction, which are non-human rights.

But though subtle, the distinction has been consecrated and hallowed by long usage. Thus, the constitutions of the United States and many other countries of the world guarantee life, liberty and property as separate and distinct rights. Yet the distinction remains somewhat unreal because of the close, almost inseparable connection between liberty and property. Liberty of action is really nothing but the ability of the individual to acquire dominion over particular things, to appropriate estates or domains of which he can dispose; without this and its recognition and protection by the laws of the state, individual liberty is largely meaningless, for the purpose of all human economic activities is essentially the acquisition of ownership over particular things (land, chattels and intangible things), and the power to dispose of them

---

38   Per Oputa JSC in *Mustapha v. Governor of Lagos State* (1987) 2 NWLR 539 at p. 589.

39   Jack Donnelly, "Human Rights and Human Dignity," 76 *American Pol. Science Review* (1982) 305 at p. 305.

40   *Merchant Bank Ltd v. Fed. Minister of Finance* (1961) 1 All N.L.R. 589.

which is implied in ownership. Also justice between individuals in society rests on each being able to hold what he acquires by his efforts and initiative, subject to intervention by the state to protect the weaker members of society and to provide social amenities and services for all. Any arrangement of society that deprives the individual of the ownership of his acquisitions and appropriates them to the community at large is manifestly unjust. "Where there is no property there is no justice is," said John Locke, "a proposition as certain as any demonstration of Euclid."

The complete abolition of private property and its take-over by the state would therefore result in the total destruction of liberty and justice, as the experience in the socialist/communist states bears out. Nor is the development and growth of civilisation hardly possible without private property which is the motif force, the *raison d'etre* of the individual economic efforts and initiatives indispensable to social progress and prosperity. As Hayek tells us, private property is "the heart of the morals of any advanced civilisation," and "no advanced civilisation has yet developed without a government which saw its chief aim in the protection of private property."[41]

Personal liberty, not liberty simpliciter, as in the U.S. Bill of Rights, is what is guaranteed in the constitutions of many African countries, fifteen of which, including Nigeria, are in former British Africa. The meaning and ambit of the term is the subject of much conflict of opinion. According to Basu:

> Liberty is a very comprehensive term and let alone it would include not merely freedom to move about unrestricted but such liberty of conduct, choice and action as the law gives and protects. But by qualifying the word liberty by the word 'personal', the import of the word liberty in Art. 21 is narrowed down to the meaning given in English law to the expression 'liberty of the person' or 'personal freedom' i.e. the right not to be punished, imprisoned or coerced except according to the procedure established by law, or in the words of Dicey, 'the right not to be subjected to imprisonment, arrest or other physical coercion in any manner that does not admit of legal justification.' It is the antithesis of physical restraint or coercion. According to Blackstone, the right of personal liberty includes 'the power of locomotion, of changing situation, or removing one's person to whatsoever place one's inclination may direct, without imprisonment or restraint, unless by due course of law.[42]

---

[41] F. A. Hayek, *The Fatal Conceit* (1988), pp. 30 and 32.

[42] Basu, *Commentary on the Constitution of India*, Vol. 1 3rd edn. (1955), at p. 270.

The meaning of the term has, however, divided the Indian supreme court. A majority of the court in a 1950 case confined its meaning to freedom of the person against unlawful detention.[43] But in 1963 a different majority took the view that "personal liberty" as used in art. 21 of the Indian Constitution is a "compendious term" embracing within itself "all the varieties of rights which go to make up the 'personal liberties' of man."[44] Re-affirming this in 1978, again by a majority decision, the court held that "the expression 'personal liberty' in Art. 21 is of the widest amplitude and it covers a variety of rights which go to constitute the personal liberty of man."[45] It quoted with approval the observations of a lower court in a 1957 case:

> In our opinion, the language used in the Article (Art. 21) also indicates that the expression 'personal liberty' is not confined only to freedom from physical restraint, but includes a full range of conduct which an individual is free to pursue within law, for instance, eat and drink what he likes, mix with people whom he likes, read what he likes, travel wherever he likes, go wherever he likes, of course in the manner and to the extent permitted by law.[46]

Article 21 referred to in the quotations above provides that "no person shall be deprived of life or personal liberty except according to procedure established by law." We may also note article 19 which guarantees, *inter alia,* "freedom to practise any profession or to carry on any occupation or business."

The wider meaning of the term is also the view of Lord Denning. "By personal freedom," he wrote:

> I mean the freedom of every law-abiding citizen to think what he will, to say what he will, and to go where he will on his lawful occasions without let or hindrance from any other person. Despite all the great changes that have come about in the other freedoms, this freedom has in our country remained intact.[47]

Whatever "personal liberty" may mean in jurisprudential terms, its meaning for our present purposes can only be determined in the context in which it is

---

[43] *Gopalan v. State of Madras,* AIR 1950 SC 27.
[44] *Kharak Singh v. State of U.P.,* AIR 1963 SC 1295.
[45] *Maneka Gandhi v. Union of India,* AIR 1978 SC at p. 622.
[46] *A. G. Kari,* AIR 1957 Bom 235 at p. 240; quoted with approval in *Maneka Gandhi v. Union of India, ibid* at p. 654.
[47] A L. Denning, *Freedom Under the Law.* delivered on 6/7/89 (High Court, Ogun State, Nigeria).

guaranteed in the constitutions of the African countries concerned. The guarantee follows two forms in the constitutions of the countries of former British Africa. The terms of the guarantee in Nigeria (1960, 1963, 1979 and 1999), are as follows: "every person shall be entitled to his personal liberty and no person shall be deprived of **such liberty** save in the following cases and in accordance with a procedure permitted by law." (Emphasis supplied). The interpretative question arising from the terms of this guarantee is whether the two legs of the provision — the one giving to every person the right to "personal liberty" and the one setting out the circumstances and manner in which "such liberty" may be taken away — are to be read disjunctively as independent clauses.

A Nigerian high court has held that the two legs of the provision are independent of each other, and that the scope of personal liberty is not cut down by the fact that all the circumstances for deprivation specified in the second leg relate to freedom from physical restraint of the person only. In the view of the court, personal liberty guaranteed by the provision embraces all rights of a personal nature, including apparently freedom of contract, private enterprise and right of property.

This interpretation is clearly untenable. First, if "personal liberty" has the same meaning and scope as "liberty," then, the word "personal," which seems clearly intended to qualify "liberty," would have been made completely otiose. Second, the words "such liberty" in the second leg of the provision are conclusive that personal liberty has the same meaning under both legs of the provision, and that that meaning is the one delimited in the second leg. Third, if the first leg is construed independently of the second so as to guarantee freedom of choice and action, in particular freedom of contract, private enterprise and other personal rights, the result will be that, since the qualifications specified in the second leg all relate to freedom from physical restraint of the person by arrest or detention, freedom of choice and action is guaranteed free of any qualification in favour of the state's regulatory authority. This is especially so as the guarantee is not among those made subject to control by the state in normal times in the interest of defence, public morality or the protection of the rights and freedom of others. Freedom of choice and action (including freedom of contract, private enterprise and other personal rights) would then have been guaranteed free not only of the specific qualifications mentioned in the provision (because they are applicable only to freedom from physical restraint of the person) but also of the state's right to control it in the interest of defence, public safety, etc. It is inconceivable that a constitution should guarantee freedom of choice and action free of such qualifications.

The terms of the guarantee in the constitutions of 13 other countries of former British Africa omit the first leg of the Nigerian provision, i.e. that "every person shall be entitled to his personal liberty;" they go straight to provide that "no person shall be deprived of his personal liberty save as may be authorised by law in any of the following cases." The permitted cases of deprivation so specified all relate to deprivation of liberty of the person by arrest, detention or other physical restraint of the person, which again makes it clear that the term is used with a limited meaning.

The Constitution of Somalia (1960) leaves the matter in no doubt. The affirmation of liberty as a general concept is accompanied with two articles headed "personal liberty" and "Guarantee in case of restrictions of personal liberty", and which are devoted entirely to the prohibition of slavery or servitude, detention or other restriction of liberty of the person (except when it is ordered by a court or when a person is apprehended in the course of the commission of a criminal offence) and security measures.

CHAPTER 2

Respect for Human Rights:
Its Value and Importance

The importance of respect for human rights will here be considered from four perspectives as listed below:-

* the dignity, spirituality, and personality of the human person;
* respect for human rights and development;
* the value of popular participation in government;
* impact of conditions in Africa.

These will now be examined in turn.

Dignity, Spirituality and Personality of the Human Person

Human rights have a self-evident value because they are an expression of, an emanation from, the inherent dignity of the human being. This is so regardless of whether we define them in the narrow sense of rights stemming from the innate attributes of the human being (thought, emotions, conscience, belief, speech, movement and action) or in the broad sense as including not only rights inherent in man's humanity but also rights relating to material things necessary for the maintenance of a dignified existence as a human being (like food, shelter, health and medical care, clothing, education, etc.). All have their basis and source in the inherent dignity and worth of the human being.

The spiritual attributes of man are the very essence of his being and are therefore a condition of his existence in dignity, happiness and inner contentment. Deprived of them, the human being is reduced to a life of mere emptiness, a life without meaning, dreary and dismal. "Give me life

23

with liberty or give me death,"[1] so said Nnamdi Azikiwe, re-echoing the 18th century American revolutionary, Patrick Henry. Justice Louis Brandeis of the U.S. supreme court has put it in more eloquent words, thus: "The makers of our Constitution ... recognised the significance of man's spiritual nature, of his feelings and of his intellect. They knew that only part of the pain, pleasure and satisfaction of life are to be found in material things. They sought to protect Americans in their beliefs, their thoughts, their emotions and their sensations."[2]

Human rights, the supreme court of India has said,

> are calculated to protect the dignity of the individual and create conditions in which every human being can develop his personality to the fullest extent... Their purpose is to help the individual to find his own viability, to give expression to his creativity and to prevent governmental and other forces from 'alienating' the individual from his creative impulses.[3]

The good life, which is the common aspiration of all of us, is a product of both the spiritual and material; it can only be attained by a combination of the inner happiness that comes from freedom of thought, association, emotions, speech and movement with the material comforts implied by economic and social rights like food, shelter, health and medical care, education, clothing, etc. These material things are needed not solely for the material comforts they provide but also for their role in man's spiritual well-being. Man certainly needs education, knowledge and culture for the development of his mind. It is in this sense that development is intertwined with the spiritual nature of man. "The right to life," it has been rightly said, "implies conditions which ensure the security and dignity of man and which give content to his power to be free as well as his capacity for happiness."[4] Thus, civil and political rights and economic, social and cultural rights are inseparable components of one whole and integrated concept of human rights; the realization of the latter is a condition for the full enjoyment of the former.

Straddling the spiritual and the material, work is perhaps the greatest of

---

[1] Nnamdi Azikiwe, *Renascent Africa* (1937), p. 42.
[2] *Olmstead v United States,* 277 U.S. 438.
[3] Per Justice Bhagwati for the court in *Maneka Gandhi v Union of India* A.I.R. 1978 S.C. at p. 620.
[4] Quoted by Keba Mbaye, President of the International Commission of Jurists (ICJ), in his Opening Address at the ICJ's Conference on Development, Human Rights and the Rule of Law, held at The Hague, 27 April-1 May, 1981, Pergamon Press, p.8.

human rights. Because it stems from man's innate ability to act, work belongs in the same category as other innate human attributes—thought, conscience, belief, emotion, speech and movement, all of which are indeed involved in its material aspect as a vital factor in the production of the things needed for the comforts of life. Work is compounded by the fact that it can, and frequently does, take the form, not of self-employment, but of employment by others, the state or private employers, whereby an individual is employed to perform acts for such others in return for a remuneration. Even in this latter situation, work remains still the exercise of man's innate ability to act, involving the exercise of all of his innate human faculties, just as when a person is acting for himself in a self-employment situation. His will, conscience, thought, emotions, movement and speech are all engaged. But work presupposes freedom of action, freedom to choose, without compulsion by law or force, whether to work at all, and, if so, whether to be self-employed or to be employed to work for another for a remuneration and on terms and conditions mutually agreed.

Work is considered the greatest and most valuable of all human rights because, as proclaimed in the constitutions of four African countries, it is a means to development (Central African Republic), is essential to "the dignity of man and the prosperity of the country" (Madagascar), and because it is through work that "man develops his creative capacity to enrich the Nation for social well-being" (Equatorial Guinea). The rationale is more amply stated in the constitution of Tanzania of 1984. "Labour alone," it declares, "is the source of wealth or property in the community, is the foundation of prosperity for the people and the barometer for humanhood."

With work goes, of course, freedom of movement whose singular value in the whole concept of human rights requires also to be specially noticed. "Freedom of movement," says the U.S. Supreme Court speaking through Justice Douglas, "is important for jobs and business opportunities—for cultural, political and social activities—for all the commingling which gregarious man enjoys ... It is the very essence of our free society, setting us apart. Like the right of assembly and the right of association, it often makes all the other rights meaningful — knowing, studying, arguing, exploring, conversing, observing and even thinking."[5]

---

[5] *Aptheker v. Secretary of State.* 378 U.S. 500

The virtues of the concept of human rights thus incontestably establish the inherent superiority of constitutional democracy as a system of government founded on respect for, and protection of, human rights, without which government itself loses much of its *raison d'etre*.

Respect for Human Rights and Development

What is said above about the value of freedom of action, movement and work at once establishes the indispensability and imperative importance of civil and political rights in national, economic and social development. It shows that, just as the individual cannot fully realise and develop his personality without respect for, and protection of, his human rights by the government, so also the economic and social development of a country requires, for its full realisation, respect and protection by the state of the human rights of its individual members; full and meaningful development of a country is hardly attainable in an environment in which people are denied their freedom of action, movement and work. We may therefore agree with Mohammed Babu, a renowned African journalist, that

> in developing countries, where individual initiative on the part of hundreds of millions of individual peasants is the most essential pre-requisite for any economic activity to take place, the denial of human rights is an obstruction to development.[6]

Development does not come by itself, like manna from heaven. It is brought about by people applying all the hardwork, self-reliance, initiative, creativity, enthusiasm and entrepreneurship of which they are capable. The role of the leadership in economic and social development is to galvanise, mobilise and direct the people, to provide the necessary policy framework, incentives, infrastructures and other facilities. Far from galvanising the people and arousing in them the ardour for development, repression of civil and political rights by the rulers kills enthusiasm and the spirit of hardwork, self-reliance and of co-operation with the state to bring about development. The state and the people must co-operate and work together as free and voluntary partners in progress for development ever to take place. (See further below on the value of popular participation in government.)

---

[6] Mohammed Babu, "Africa and Human Rights," *New Africa*, March 1979, p. 84.

The link between human rights and development has witnessed a momentous transformation since 1972. From being two separate, if intertwined, concepts, they have become one integrated concept. Development has won recognition as a human right by the United Nations, the Organisation of African Unity (now African Union, AU) and the Conference of Heads of State and Governments of Non-aligned countries—what is called the human right to development. Its status as a human right is now firmly established in international law,[7] though not yet in municipal law. (Although not yet recognised in national constitutions, it now forms part of the municipal law of the African countries that have incorporated the African Charter on Human and Peoples' Rights into their municipal law.)

The difficulty is to define the nature and content of this newly admitted human right to development in terms clear and precise enough to make it meaningful. The nearest to a precise definition is that it is an aggregate of all human rights of the first and second generation categories. From the premise that all human rights derive from the inherent dignity of the human person, which entitles him to a dignified life, the right to development therefore aggregates all human rights, since a dignified life, implying a good standard of living for the individual, is, after all, what development is about. For "human rights can have no meaning unless they begin with the right to life itself at a tolerable level of existence,"[8] always bearing in mind that development embraces physical, economic, social as well as spiritual well-being.

Defined thus as a synthesis, or rather aggregate, of existing rights, the purpose of the right to development, viewed from the standpoint of the individual, is the realisation of all civil and political rights as well as economic, social and cultural rights, or at least so much of them as relate to "man's most basic material and non-material needs, without whose realization a dignified existence is not possible."[9] This basic minimum, Karel de Vey Mestdagh has suggested, should include the right to life and the closely associated right to

---

[7] See T. Akinola Aguda, "Human Rights and the Right to Development in Africa," NIIA Lecture Series No. 55 of 1987.

[8] Shridath Ramphal, Keynote Address, Report of ICJ Conference on Development, Human Rights and the Rule of Law (1981), Pergamon Press, p. 19.

[9] Karel de Vey Mestdagh, "The Right to Development: From Evolving Principles to 'legal' Right: In Search of its Substance," in Report of ICJ Conference, *op. cit.,* p. 169.

adequate food, clothing, housing and medical care; it should also include personal security, freedom of thought, conscience and religion as well as a minimum level of opportunities for individuals to participate in the development process.[10] But to be truly effective, the right of participation must include the right to education, freedom of expression, assembly and association, including the right to form free trade unions. "Only if the people as a whole can participate in decision-making, and be seen as partners in government rather than as recipients from it, can human resources be effectively mobilised for development."[11]

As Karel de Vey Mestdagh noted, the place and status of development as a human right may be more readily appreciated if it is viewed against

> the background of large-scale underdevelopment in the Third World and, in particular, the over 780 million people who according to estimates by the World Bank, live in absolute poverty. Absolute poverty means more than just extremely low income; it also means malnutrition, poor health, inadequate housing and illiteracy. In essence this situation, which is summarised rather euphemistically, and less forcefully, in the term 'underdevelopment', amounts to the fact that a whole host of elementary human rights are not being implemented. In view of the facts, the right to development cannot be concerned with anything other than the realisation of the most fundamental human[12]

needs of the individual in both the developing and developed countries of the world.

Amplifying the content or substance of the right to development, a U.N. Report of 1979 identifies its component elements as follows:

— the realization of the potentialities of the human person in harmony with the community should be seen as the central purpose of development;

— the human person should be regarded as the subject and not the object of the development process;

— development requires the satisfaction of both material and non-material basic needs;

— respect for human rights is fundamental to the development process;

---

[10] Karel de Vey Mestdagh, *op. cit,* pp. 169-171.

[11] Shridath Ramphal, *op. cit,* pp. 21-22.

[12] Karel de Vey Mestdagh, *op. cit.,* pp. 168-169.

— respect for the principles of equality and non-discrimination is essential; and

— the achievement of a degree of individual and collective self-reliance must be an integral part of the process.

In recognising the right to development as a human right, the U.N. Human Rights Commission and General Assembly stated that it is a right of states as of individuals. It should be emphasised, however, that the right belongs primarily to individuals and to the whole people in a state as a collectivity, and that the primary responsibility for its implementation is that of the state of which the individual and the people are members. "The state bears primary responsibility for the development of the community and thus for the realization of the most elementary rights of individuals."[13] The right to development is a right of states only in the sense that other states and the international community should assume a degree of responsibility to assist a state in its development effort. From the standpoint of the inter-state component of the right to development, the beneficiary of the right is the underdeveloped states while the corresponding obligation falls on states which are in a position to provide assistance. This coupling of the individual/group right against the state with the right of states against the international community, it has pertinently been observed, is "the most innovatory element of the right to development,"[14] but the right of a state to development is not itself and cannot be a human right.[15]

The definition of the right to development as an aggregate of civil and political rights as well as of economic, social and cultural rights raises the question whether it adds anything to the concept of human rights. The question touches thus on its usefulness. It has been argued that "what is required at the present time is not ... another set of rights, but the fullest possible realisation of the fundamental human rights and freedoms already anchored in the Universal Declaration and other relevant documents."[16] On the other hand, it is said that;

a synthesis of rights, such as the right to development, assumes dimensions

---

[13] Karel de Vey Mestdagh, *op. cit.*, p. 172.
[14] Karel de Vey Mestdagh, *op. cit.*, p. 174.
[15] Karel de Vey Mestdagh, *op. cit.*, pp. 166-169, 174.
[16] V. Kartashkin, "Human Rights and the Modern World," *International Affairs*, 1979, p. 54.

which are greater than the mere sum of its constituent parts. Through a
process of cross-fertilization the sum of the various component norms
forms a holistic entity.[17]

Just as the colonial and post-colonial society of the alien-created state in
Africa is different (not necessarily greater) from the sum of all the ethnic
groups comprised within it, characterised as it is by its own social dynamics,
so also may the right to development generate a different social force and
momentum from that resulting from the sum of the human rights it aggregates.
Standing on its own as an aggregate of all human rights, the right to
development may serve as a useful tool in exerting pressure on the international
community to give more urgent attention to the challenge of development
on a global level by drawing up and implementing a dynamic programme of
action.

The Value of Popular Participation in Government

Democratic government is simply a form of government in which popular
participation in governance is practised, a system in which political rights are
exercised by the people supposedly for their own benefit and welfare. So
defined, democratic government, being thus more or less synonymous with
human rights, has value that is also self-evident. To begin with, the
democratisation of government has, by tempering the arrogance of power,
had the effect, to some extent, of bringing rulers and the ruled closer together
in terms of equality. The degree of equality between the various members
of society which came in the wake of popular power, the liberation of the
masses of the people from subjugation to the hereditary power of the
aristocratic class, has brought greater fulfilment, contentment and harmony
by eliminating the injustice and tyranny associated with monarchical, aristocratic
and oligarchic rule and the envy and jealousy aroused by inequality in rank and
privileges between the classes. Being contrary to nature, all subjugation goes
against the grain, and almost invariably gives rise to resentment, and to resistance
by those who feel strongly enough about it.

Popular participation in government has in itself certain cardinal advantages.
When people participate freely in the government of their country, a sense of

---

[17] Philip Alston, in Report of ICJ Conference, *op. cit.*, p. 104.

involvement in, and identification with, its destiny and fortunes is created, thereby making them more public-spirited and more committed to its progress, for civic zeal flows from the exercise of political rights. Popular participation brings with it a certain identity of interests between the people and the government, a feeling that everyone has a stake in it, and that it is the property of all, and not the personal estate of any one individual or a few individuals, and accordingly an acceptance that whatever is harmful to its interests also harms the interests of all. In the words of Alexis de Tocqueville, "I maintain that the most powerful and perhaps the only means which we still possess of interesting men in the welfare of their country, is to make them partakers in the government."[18]

On the other hand, where government is by one or a few unelected persons,

> scarcely any sense is entertained that private persons ... owe any duties to society, except to obey the laws and submit to the government. There is no unselfish sentiment of identification with the public. Every thought or feeling, either of interest or duty, is absorbed in the individual and in the family. The man never thinks of any collective interest, of any objects to be pursued jointly with others, but only in competition with them, and in some measure at their expense.[19]

Participation creates for the individual citizen a sense of self-esteem, and a mechanism for obliging the government to take proper cognisance of his importance. With the authority bestowed by his vote, the individual is wooed and canvassed by a multitude of political office-seekers, and thereby acquires a certain degree of importance and respect. The notion of political rights is thus brought down to the level of the humblest citizen, making it the common property of all, rather than the exclusive prerogative of a privileged few.

Participation fosters in the people, or at any rate conduces to, an active and enquiring mind, the spirit of enterprise and self-reliance, of "the desire to keep moving, to be trying and accomplishing new things"[20]: the habits of perseverance against odds and of not giving up easily. It is, in short, an invaluable vehicle of education for the people, enabling them to be instructed

---

[18] *Democracy in America* (1835) ed. Richard Heffner (1956), p. 109.
[19] J. S. Mill, *Representative Government*, reprinted in *Utilitarianism, Liberty and Representative Government* (1910), Everyman's Library, p. 234.
[20] J. S. Mill, *op. cit.*, p. 228.

in the art of government, in civic virtues and in the responsibilities of citizenship. "In seeking to deceive him (the individual) in a thousand ways, they (the office-seekers) really enlighten him."[21]

Alexis de Tocqueville considers it perhaps the greatest advantage of democracy that, whilst it may not give the people the most skilful, competent or efficient government, or inspire men with a scorn of mere temporal advantage, whilst it may not bring about a refinement in manners, the cultivation of the arts or the promotion of the love of poetry, beauty and glory, and whilst it may neglect excellence and glorify the average, yet it "produces what the ablest governments are frequently unable to create; namely, an all-pervading and restless activity, a superabundant force, and an energy which is inseparable from it, and which may, however unfavourable the circumstances may be, produce wonders" in the way of promoting happiness, contentment and general well-being.[22]

From the standpoint of the government itself, the participation of the people in government, as for example in the making of a constitution or other law, enhances the legitimacy, authority and stability of the government and its laws. It secures acceptance of, and respect for, the government and the laws, and so assures the permanence and longevity of the laws. The will of the whole people expressed in their votes at an election or referendum has an overwhelming strength that carries everyone with it — the consenting majority, the abstainers and the dissenting minority — thereby removing all obstacles in the way of the government or a proposed measure.

In Africa where the state lacks legitimacy because it originated in colonisation by means of conquest or treaties of cession obtained through undue influence, the value of popular participation in government goes beyond what is stated above; it serves also as a means of trying to legitimise the state and the form of government. A referendum to adopt or approve a constitution bestows upon it the stamp of public recognition of its suitability for the government of the community, and therefore as worthy of respect and obedience. And, while popular elections are primarily a means to enable the people choose the persons to conduct public affairs on their behalf, they are also a circumstance from which, over a period of time, public acceptance of both the form of

---

[21] Alexis de Tocqueville, *op. cit.*, p. 110.
[22] *ibid*, pp. 110-111.

government and of the title of the state to govern may grow. So may it also grow from referenda to approve legislative measures or other specific matters submitted to the people for decision, from public discussions in the news media of matters of public interest and from public assemblies and processions.

Africa's state of underdevelopment is yet another circumstance that makes democratic government a necessity for the continent. The state of backwardness prevailing in Africa is such as can only be overcome by means of a social revolution which, by definition, requires that the people as a whole must be mobilised in a concerted effort to develop themselves and the country. Development in a backward country is an enterprise calling for the highest degree of self-reliance effort on the part of the people led by a ruler imbued with a fervour to transform the society from backwardness to modernity. No development programme can therefore achieve its purpose if the people are not fully involved as active participants. "Development is something that people do by themselves and for themselves, or it does not happen."[23] Now, meaningful participation by the people can only be ensured under a constitutional, democratic system in which freedom of individual action, private entrepreneurship, small and medium size business, competition, the accountability of rulers to the people, predictability of government actions in accordance with laid down rules, and the rule of law are given adequate scope and encouragement.

No doubt, the relationship between development and popular rule is a subject of much disputation among development scholars.[24] There are even some who assert that democracy is inimical to development. We, however, share the view that development can only be "driven by social will in the context of democracy," that "it is only in that context that the people can be the means ... of development," and that any development process which relies on coercion or authoritarian methods rather than on voluntary participation by the people cannot emancipate them from backwardness, and is indeed "a contradiction in terms."[25] As Claude Ake explains, the authoritarian regimes of the countries of East Asia have been able to achieve

---

[23] Claude Ake, *Democracy and Development* (1996), p. 123.
[24] See Alex Inkeles and Larry Sitowy, "The Effects of Democracy on Economic Growth and Inequality: A Review," in Alex Inkeles, ed. *On Measuring Democracy: Its Consequences and Concomitant* (1991), pp. 149-150.
[25] Claude Ake, *op. cit*, pp. 119, 126-127.

a considerable amount of economic growth because such democratic values as accountability, predictability, the rule of law and competition have been present there, albeit fortuitously, since their presence "depends on the character and the will of the dominant faction of the political class."[26] Therefore, he says:

> if these values are so necessary, their existence should not be merely fortuitous; it should be objective and guaranteed. But only in the context of a mature democracy can values such as the rule of law, accountability, transparency, and competitiveness be fully operational as well as guaranteed.[27]

Granted that democratic government has great merits, two caveats need to be entered. First, popular consent alone does not necessarily preclude or even insure against absolutism. As Professor Sir Kenneth Wheare pointedly observes:

> universal suffrage can create and support a tyranny of the majority or of a minority or of one man. The absolutisms of the twentieth century have usually been based upon universal suffrage — and a compulsory universal suffrage at that. Have not modern tyrannies been returned to power by majority of over 90 per cent?[28]

And Professor Charles McIlwain has said that

> the greatest delusion of the modern political world, is the delusion of 'popular sovereignty.' It is the fiction under which all the dictators have sprung up and now thrive. The people is not the sovereign; the government is. If the people sets up a sovereign government, they must in their own interest also set up or keep up all the necessary barriers against its despotic action, and the only effective barrier short of actual resistance is the barrier of law,[29]

i.e. the barrier of law that secures the liberty of the individual as a limitation enforceable against the government. In other words, a democratic government needs also to be a constitutional one. It is the combination of the twin notions of a democratic government and a constitutional government that is known as constitutional democracy, that is to say, a democratic government regulated and limited by law either in its executive capacity only, as in Britain, or, in both

---

[26] Claude Ake, *op. cit.*, p. 128.
[27] Claude Ake, *loc. cit.*
[28] K. C. Wheare, *Modern Constitutions* (1960), p. 157.
[29] C. H. McIlwain, *Constitutionalism and the Changing World* (1939), p. 264.

its executive and legislative capacities under the supreme law of a written constitution, as in most other countries of the world today.

The second caveat is that popular government does not necessarily assure the welfare of the people. No doubt, the expectation, indeed the rationale for it, is that when the people govern, they do so for the benefit of all. Government **by** the people is expected to be government **for** the people because the people embody all of the community's wisdom, goodness, honesty, justice, its sense of right and wrong, in short, all the civic virtues available in it, which should outweigh all its vices. Animated by a concern for their own good, i.e. their own safety, liberty, prosperity, well-being and happiness, which is the same as the public good or the welfare of the community, government by the people cannot but be government for the people. The people, it is said, "cannot have an interest opposed to their own advantage."[30] "Representation, as 'a substitute for a meeting of the citizens in person,'[31] is intended to replicate the people's concern with their own good"[32] as elected representatives are supposed to have "a communion of interests and sympathy of sentiments with the ruled."[33]

But the actual working of popular government has proved all this to be largely an idealistic picture, quite removed from reality. To begin with, "the 'self-government' spoken of is not the government of each by himself, but of each by all the rest."[34] An assemblage of the whole citizenry in a direct democracy would often be swayed by passion rather than by reason, and even when it is not, the governing interest would usually be not that of the whole people, but of the majority which may trample on the interest of the minority. In a representative democracy, the premise that representation replicates the people's concern for their own good, and that representatives have a communion of interests and sentiments with the people presupposes the capacity of the people to choose representatives animated by a spirit for the public good, which is often not the case. In reality, elected representatives are not, for the most part, persons so animated, their actions being motivated

---

[30] Alexis de Tocqueville, *Democracy in America* (1835), ed. Richard Heffner (1956), p. 101.

[31] James Madison, *The Federalist*, No. 52, ed. Clinton Rossiter (1961), p. 327.

[32] David Epstein, *The Political Theory of the Federalist* (1984), p. 148.

[33] James Madison, *The Federalist, No. 57, op. cit*, p. 352.

[34] J. S. Mill, *Representative Government*, reprinted in *Utilitarianism, Liberty and Representative Government* (1910), Everyman's Library, p. 72.

more by selfish or other private interests than by the public good.

Despite this, government for the people is and must remain an important objective even if not an essential requirement, of democratic rule. In this connection, it is of interest to note that "government of the people by the people for the people" is expressly affirmed in the constitutions of most African countries outside former British Africa as a fundamental objective of governance while the welfare of the people is also expressly proclaimed in the constitutions of Nigeria of 1979 and 1999 as the object of government.

By its own inherent logic, democratic government ought really to conduce more to the welfare of the people than any other form of government. For whilst the self-government implied by democracy is not government of each by himself, democracy is nevertheless man-based, characterised by a humanist or individualist concern for the good life of each man in society. And although a representative government is not in every case dedicated to the welfare of the people, yet the fact that it is answerable to the people, and is dismissable by them should it completely neglect their wishes and needs, obliges it to be more responsive to the people's wishes and needs than one not chosen and not removable by them. There can be no question but that a representative government would have a greater appreciation of, and concern for, the public good, and would conduce more to justice and happiness among the population, than an unelected one.

For Bratton and Walle, however, "the distinctive feature of democracy is ..., rule **by** the people," they "dissociate it from rule **for** the people, which implies, substantively, a distributive socio-economic order."[35] Rule for the people, as an objective of democracy, connotes simply a welfare state or the good life for all (social democracy), not a distributive socio-economic order if by this is meant a thorough-going socialist socio-economic order. Democracy, dissociated from the welfare of the people as part of its objective, is not worthy of being so-called.

Finally, according to Karl Marx, democratic government is but "a pretence and a sham," "a facade behind which the real rule is exercised by some oligarchy." Vilfredo Pareto is equally strong and emphatic upon the point.

---

[35] Michael Bratton and Nicolas van de Walle, *Democratic Experiment in Africa* (1997), pp. 10 and 12.

"Whether universal suffrage prevails or not," he maintains, "it is always an oligarchy that governs."[36] Popular consent in government expressed by the vote of the majority at an election based on universal adult suffrage is "an unmitigated lie"[37] and "a fiction," because it is frequently secured by chicanery, fraud, corruption and "manipulation of political followings."[38] In any case, the elitist school says, democratic government is impossible of attainment in actual practice.

These views seem rather overblown. The faults in the democratic system, upon which they focus, are essentially not structural or conceptual, but rather the result of human failings and weaknesses; such is the incidence of chicanery, fraud, corruption and manipulation at elections. In the hundred years or so that lie between the writings of those critics and our time, vast improvements have taken place in the practice of the principles of democratic government that make the criticisms seem somewhat out-dated today, except in backward societies where conditions, especially mass illiteracy (with its resultant ignorance), poverty, the absence of a middle class comprising a majority of the population and wholesale election rigging, are unfavourable to a faithful observance of democratic principles. With all its shortcomings, democratic government has merits which place it far above any other form of government so far devised by the genius of man.

Impact of Conditions in Africa

Self-evident as the value of human rights appears to be, the late Professor Claude Ake, radical as always, questions it as regards the rural peasants in Africa. He argues with his characteristic pungency that human rights in the western conception of them have and can have no "interest and value" in most of Africa which is still rural and shackled by illiteracy, ignorance, poverty and disease. For an illiterate, ignorant and poverty-stricken peasant eternally oppressed by the harsh conditions of life in rural Africa, Ake maintains, the western conception of human rights is but a hollow, abstract concept devoid of any concrete meaning and value. Echoing much the same view, Professor Osita Eze, another African writer of the radical persuasion, also says that

---

[36] Vilfredo Pareto, *The Mind and Society* (1935), p. 273.
[37] Mosca, *The Ruling Class* (1935).
[38] Pareto, *The Mind and Society* (1935), *op. cit.*, pp. 273-274.

human rights, insofar as they relate to civil and political rights, "meant little to the impoverished and alienated majority of African people."[39] As elaborated by Claude Ake, the western notion of human rights addresses itself to:

> people with a full stomach who can now afford to pursue the more esoteric aspects of self-fulfilment. The vast majority of our people are not in this position. They are facing the struggle for existence in its brutal immediacy ... They have little interest in choice for there is no choice in ignorance. There is no freedom for hungry people or those eternally oppressed by disease ... There is not enough concern for the historical conditions in which human rights can actually be realised. As it turns out, only a few people are in a position to exercise the rights which society allows. The few who have the resources to exercise these rights do not need a bill of rights. Their power secures them. The many who do not have the resources to exercise their rights are not helped by the existence of these rights. Their powerlessness dooms them.[40]

The argument is seemingly, but only superficially, appealing. It suffers from the very flaw with which it charges the western notion of human rights — it focuses too much on political rights, particularly freedom of speech on political affairs, freedom of assembly and elections. Whilst undeniably the widespread illiteracy, ignorance and poverty prevailing in Africa seriously undermines the enjoyment of political rights by the vast majority of Africans, yet the phenomenon is one that is gradually changing. Besides, political rights are essentially collective rights which bear more on the life of people as a collectivity than on the life of the individual. The human rights that have a more direct bearing on the life of the individual are: the right to breathe the open air freely, to think, to believe or misbelieve, to feel, to move about, to speak (on other than political matters), to work and to act generally. These have supreme value for the illiterate, poverty-stricken rural African by reason simply of his being human, with a mind, a soul, emotions, sensations, feelings and other human faculties, and the same inherent human dignity and worth, just like the educated urban elite.

The rural African peasant of today cherishes his freedom of action and abhors servitude and forced labour just as the educated urban elite does. If

---

[39] Osita Eze, "The Organisation of African Unity and Human Rights: Twenty-five Years After," *Nig. Journal of International Affairs* (1988/89) Vols 14-15, p. 154 at p. 154.

[40] Claude Ake, "The African Context of Human Rights," *Africa Today* (1987), pp. 5-6; T. Akinola Aguda agreed with him, see his "Human Rights and the Right to Development in Africa," NIIA Lecture Series No. 55, 1989, p. 26.

detained in prison without trial for slighting a minister on tour of the village by not coming out to the village square to welcome him or for a criminal offence trumped up against him, he would be depressed and agonised by a sense of mental, emotional and psychological injury as would an educated urban elite in a similar situation, and in Africa today both face this danger to a greater or less extent. The conditions in an African prison are soul-destroying for both alike. The illiterate, rural African peasant values his creed, his belief in the spirit of ancestors and other pagan divinities, just as the educated urban elite values his Christian or Moslem faith, and would be as spiritually outraged as the latter by any desecration of them by agents of government. He is affronted by any encroachment on his land whether owned individually by himself alone or in common with other members of his family, and is ready to defend it to the limit of his power; his personal property may be few, but he values it all the same.

In affirming the "inviolability of the human being" — perhaps the only international Bill of Rights to do so in such explicit terms — the African Charter on Human and Peoples' Rights (art. 4) truly reflects the supreme value and worth which Africans place on the human being, both the illiterate, rural peasant and the educated urban elite. The Charter reinforces this affirmation of the inviolability of the human being with a further affirmation of "the dignity inherent in a human being" and "the integrity of his person," which it protects by prohibiting, without qualification, the "degradation of man" by slavery, torture, cruel or other inhuman treatment or by arbitrary arrest and detention (articles 4, 5 and 6). These rights are inherent in all men and women by virtue of the dignity and worth inherent in all human beings, the educated urban elite no less than the illiterate rural African peasant. We must avoid the impression, which Claude Ake's argument seems apt to create, that the latter is less than human, which was the view of the African on which the pernicious apartheid policy in South Africa was based — a view now happily rejected in the preamble to the U.N. Universal Declaration of Human Rights (1948) wherein it is solemnly affirmed that "recognition ... of the equal ... rights of **all members** of the human family is the foundation of freedom, justice and peace in the world" (emphasis supplied). The recognition of the blackman as a full member of the human family, endowed with equal dignity, equal worth and equal rights as other human beings, and the consequent rejection of the monstrous view of him as "half child, half devil," in Kipling's deprecatory words, is perhaps one of the revolutionary changes of the 20th century. It should not be for us Africans, however unwittingly, to repudiate that recognition.

Professor Claude Ake's argument is also questionable even as regards political rights on which it focuses so much. It is a distortion to say that political rights have no value for the rural majority in Africa merely because of their illiteracy, ignorance and poverty. These, as earlier stated, are essentially collective rights, the right of a people to govern itself through its own chosen representatives.[41] "The self-government spoken of," writes John Stuart Mill, "is not the government of each by himself, but of each by all the rest."[42] Those whose education and resources enable them to exercise political rights do so on behalf of themselves and the silent majority in the rural areas. And the fact that the latter are presently not in a position to exercise political rights does not detract from the value of these rights for the entire society or community as a collectivity.

There is a basic fallacy in the argument that the value and importance of political rights for the masses of the people consists only in the performance of government in catering for their happiness and welfare. For the society or community as a collectivity, the basis and source of the authority exercised by government raises an issue of a deeper, more transcendental interest than its form or the performance of a particular government in securing the welfare of the people. Human nature is not disposed to accept that any group of persons should impose themselves on an entire people as the government, however benevolent and efficient such a government may be, and the imposition has no more justification and is no less obnoxious, because the majority of the people, being illiterate, ignorant and poverty-stricken, are not in a position to exercise political rights. A people so imposed upon is not a self-governing people; they are rather like a colonised people. No doubt, it is necessary to devise a method to enable the illiterate rural dwellers to participate effectively in the processes of decision-taking, particularly the development

---

[41] F. A. Hayek, *The Constitution of Liberty* (1960), pp. 13-14.
[42] J. S. Mill, *Representative Government*, reprinted in *Utilitarianism, Liberty and Representative Government* (1910) Everyman's Library edn., p. 72.

process, so as to enhance the value of political rights for them. Still, the point being emphasised is that the exercise of political rights by an urban minority on behalf of themselves and the rural majority has value for them both, considered as one indivisible sovereign community.

It is necessary to refer briefly to another aspect of Claude Ake's thesis. He argues that human rights, being rights which are specifically ascribed to the individual, do not have much meaning in Africa because, in most of the continent, the society has not become atomised to an extent presupposed by the western notion of human rights. According to him, this is because of "the limited penetration of capitalism and commodity relations." He maintains that:

> many people are still locked into natural economies and have a sense of belonging to an organic whole, be it a family, a clan, a lineage or an ethnic group. The phenomenon of the legal subject, the autonomous individual conceived as a bundle of rights which are asserted against all comers, has not really developed much, especially outside the urban areas.[43]

The issue raised by this aspect of his argument is one on which there is a considerable conflict of opinion, namely, whether pre-colonial African societies recognised the notion of "human rights" as a legal claim which the individual could assert against his community and private persons.[44] All that we need say here on the issue is that, whatever might have been the position in pre-colonial days, and whilst economic individualism is still today in an embryonic stage of development in most of rural Africa, the notion of human rights as a legal claim by the individual against the type of state created in Africa by European colonialism is recognised and applicable in both the urban and rural areas of the continent. The western notion of a "right" as a legal claim for the preservation of the inherent dignity of the human being and in other social

---

[43] Claude Ake, *op. cit.,* p. 9; the same argument is advanced by Asmarom Legesse, "Human Rights in African Political Culture," in K. W. Thompson (ed.), *The Moral Imperative of Human Rights: A World Survey* (1980), p. 123 at pp. 124 ff.

[44] Claude Ake's view on the issue is further supported by Jack Donnelly, "Human Rights and Human Dignity: An Analytic Critique of Non-Western Human Rights Conceptions," *American Political Science Review,* 76 (1982), pp. 303-16; and "The Right to Development: How not to link Human Rights and Development," in Claude Welch and Ronald Meltzer (eds.), *Human Rights and Development in Africa* (1984) p. 261 at pp. 268-270. For the contrary view, see S. K. B. Asante, "Nation Building and Human Rights in Emergent African Nations," *Cornell International Law Journal* 2 (1969), p. 74; and Dustan M. Wai, "Human Rights in Sub-Saharan Africa," in Adamantia Pollis and Peter Schwab (eds.) *Human Rights: Cultural and Ideological Perspectives* (1980), p. 116.

relations is certainly part of Africa's inheritance from European colonialism. If it be true, as the drafters of the African Charter on Human and People's Rights assert, that there was no opposition between the individual and his community in pre-colonial times, no such total harmony exists today between him and the alien-created state; that is precisely why human rights violations by the state have become such a major and worrying problem in Africa today.

Yet, although civil and political rights have no less value in the rural than in the urban areas of Africa, the illiteracy, ignorance and poverty prevailing in the continent, particularly in the rural areas, do demand that more (but not preferential) attention should be given to rights of a social and economic type than is presently being given to them. (According to Mathews, it is "morally, politically and otherwise untenable" for the state to give preferential treatment to one group of rights.[45]) We should applaud Claude Ake for making the point in his telling manner that Africa needs to focus more emphasis on rights which, as he puts it, "can mean something for people fighting to survive ... rights which can mean something for women who are cruelly used. Rights which can mean something for the young whose future we render more improbable every day."[46]

The protection needed is, of course, not for these categories of persons alone. All Africans are sufferers from the deprivation and neglect of successive regimes of African rulers. The economic development which is the material condition for the realization of the economic and social rights we all clamour for has continued to elude us. The prevailing condition is well described by Pius Okigbo. "There is no doubt," he writes:

> that the level of aggregate consumption and the potentials for increased welfare had been generated by the rapid economic growth. But can we assert that the level of consumption is what the society desires, or that it has added as much as it could have, to the welfare of the citizens? We see today new artifacts of modern living: television, cars, electricity, radios, telephones, college degrees, etc. These were not within the reach of the average citizen some thirty years ago. In the midst of all these, we see

---

[45] K. Mathews, "The OAU and Political Economy of Human Rights in Africa: An analysis of African Charter on Human and Peoples' Rights 1982," 1987 1st/2nd Quarters, *Africa Today*, p. 96.

[46] Claude Ake, *op. cit.*, p. 10.

signs of frustration on the faces of the youth of today that were not so visible some thirty years ago. The television does not function, the electricity is not continuous, the phones do not work, the cars clog the inadequate roads, and the colleges repudiate their own degrees.[47]

Need we mention the utter inadequacy of all the basic necessities of life, rising inflation and the increasing threat of hunger and disease?

Apart from illiteracy, ignorance, poverty and disease, there are evidently other factors militating against the effective application of liberty and democracy in African countries, notably the virtual nonexistence or weakness of civil society and the fact that societies of these countries are yet to be permeated by a libertarian, democratic ethic and ethos. These other factors form the subject of the discussion in Part V of Volume 3.

Concluding Remarks

Freedom in the sense of the concept of human rights as legal claims enforceable by the individual against the state, on which the foregoing discussion is based, is a somewhat limited conception of the term *freedom*. The discussion needs therefore to be supplemented, for completeness, by viewing the term from the wider perspective of a free society: i.e. a society in which the individual is free to live his or her life as he or she chooses without control or coercion by not only the state (which is the only concern of the concept of human rights), but also by private organisations or other individuals, subject of course to generally accepted legitimate qualifications. A discussion of the importance of freedom from this wider perspective of a free society belongs more appropriately to Volume 3 (see chapter 14).

---

[47] P. N. C. Okigbo, *Essays in the Public Philosophy of Development* (1987), p. 182.

CHAPTER 3

Promoting Respect for Human Rights: The Role and Purpose of a Bill of Rights

Rationale for Legal Protection of Human Rights

Before examining the four purposes which a Bill of Rights seeks to fulfill, it is appropriate first to note the rationale or justifications for it as declared in the preambles to various Bills of Rights, both national and international, as such preambulary declarations provide a good mirror of the purposes the makers of these instruments intended them to serve.

The preamble to the U.N. Universal Declaration of Human Rights (1948), taken in conjunction with the preambles to the two International Covenants of 1976, is perhaps the most expressive and noteworthy on this point. It proclaims "recognition of the ... inalienable rights of all members of the human family (as) the foundation of freedom, justice and peace in the world," and the "disregard and contempt for human rights" as the cause of the "barbarous acts which have outraged the conscience of mankind;" accordingly, their protection under the rule of law is affirmed as an essential guarantee against tyranny and oppression, and against a consequent uprising by the people in revolt to rid themselves of such tyranny. The importance of respect for human rights in the promotion of social progress and better standards of life is likewise affirmed as is its indispensability to the attainment of "the ideal of free human beings enjoying freedom from fear and want."

The European Convention on Human Rights and Fundamental Freedoms may be said to incorporate, by implication, into its preamble the rationale or justifications stated in the U.N. Universal Declaration, in particular the affirmation of respect for human rights as the foundation of justice and peace in the world which it proclaims in explicit terms itself. Additionally, the

Convention also affirms, as does the European Social Charter, the belief that "the maintenance and further realisation of Human Rights and Fundamental Freedoms" is one of the methods by which to try to achieve the aim of greater unity between the member states of the Council of Europe for the purpose of facilitating their economic and social progress. Significantly, the preamble concludes by proclaiming the resolve of

> the Governments of European countries which are like-minded and have a common heritage of political traditions, ideals, freedom and the rule of law, to take the first steps for the collective enforcement of human rights as a way of safeguarding and further facilitating the realisation of these ideals and principles.

The rationale or justification for its guarantee of human rights is not as clearly articulated in the African Charter on Human and Peoples' Rights. It rather begs the question to say that human rights have an inherent value that "justifies their international protection." The justification needed, if it is to be really meaningful, must not be one derived solely from the inherent value of human rights. However, the African Charter reaffirms the declaration, contained in the OAU Charter, that "freedom, equality, justice and dignity are essential objectives for the achievement of the legitimate aspirations of the African people," which must be taken to include peace, development (or "a better life for the people"), international co-operation, the elimination of all forms of colonialism, neo-colonialism, apartheid and discrimination.

Nineteen African countries, all of whom are countries in former French Africa (with the exception of four: Congo (Leopoldville), Rwanda, Somalia and Burundi), affirm, in the preamble to their constitutions, adherence to the U.N. Universal Declaration of Human Rights. It is not unreasonable to infer from this, acceptance by these countries of the rationale or justifications proclaimed in the Universal Declaration for the legal protection of human rights. But apart from this, no explicit justification is stated in any of the constitutions of the countries of Africa containing provision for the protection of human rights by means of a Bill of Rights. This is understandable considering that a national constitution deals with a host of subjects, the protection of human rights being just one such subject. We may note in parenthesis, as an exception, the affirmation of human rights in the Constitution of Senegal (1963) as "the basis of human community, of peace and justice in the world" as well as the provision in the Algerian Constitution of 1963 to the effect that the recognition of human rights is in order to permit the individual to participate fully and effectively in the task of nation building and of developing and fulfilling himself "harmoniously within the community."

The Role and Purpose of a Bill of Rights

A Bill of Rights is intended to serve four purposes, viz:

— to bestow state recognition upon human rights;

— to set out, in as precise a manner as can be attained by legal formulation, the basic rights of the individual, their extent and limits *vis-a-vis* the state;

— to establish appropriate mechanisms by which the rights may be realized or implemented in practice, preferably by means of an enforcement machinery; and

— to institute appropriate measures for the promotion of respect for human rights.

The four purposes stated above will now be examined.

Bestowal of State Recognition on Human Rights

The first step in any system of legal protection of human rights is to secure for them, the recognition of the law, since nothing is or becomes a "right" in the strict legal sense unless and until it is recognised as such by the law, whether customary law, the common law, the statute law, the law of the constitution or international law. Human rights cannot be asserted as legal claims against the state or private persons purely by virtue of the law of nature. Natural law can have no more than a moral force, providing merely "a basis of comparison ... an intellectual standard."[1] It has been laid down on high judicial authority that a legislature is not limited in its law-making power by the law of nature.[2]

Setting a Standard of Behaviour

The central purpose of a Bill of Rights is to serve as a standard of behaviour towards the individual in the conduct of public affairs by the organs and

---

[1]   C. H. McIlwain, *Constitutionalism: Ancient and Modern* (1947), p. 152.

[2]   *Liyanage v. R* [1967] 1 A.C. 259 (Privy Council).

functionaries of government, with a view to minimising the arbitrariness and tyranny attendant upon state power. Like law generally, its provisions are designed to regulate and control human behaviour, but, unlike ordinary law, the standard so set does not apply to persons generally; it is limited in its application to conduct or acts done in the administration of the state. In general, acts of private persons having no connection with the administration of the state are not within the regulatory control of a Bill of Rights.

Mill's conception of liberty as availing against the actions of both the government and society (in its informal character as a collection of individuals) as well as against the actions of individual persons is inapplicable to the protection of liberty provided by a Bill of Rights. A national constitution enshrining a Bill of Rights is necessarily limited by the nature of a constitution, its purpose and function. A constitution is a charter of government. It is a body of fundamental principles by which a society organises a government for itself, defines and limits its powers, and regulates the relations of its organs *inter se* and with the citizens. It is not its purpose or concern to regulate relations between private persons; it is not concerned with rights between man and man, such as rights arising from contract, tort, property, family or domestic relations, succession, etc., that being the function of the ordinary law. Only a person's relations with the state, his rights against it, are properly the concern of a constitution, and such rights may be enshrined in it in order to protect and secure them against the enormous powers granted to the state by the constitution. As the constitution grants no power to private persons, the necessity does not arise of using it to protect an individual from the actions of other private persons.

The U.S. supreme court in the *Civil Rights Cases* decided in 1883 has stated another reason why liberty protected in the constitution is unavailing against the actions of private persons. The wrongful act of an individual by itself alone cannot abrogate or destroy a person's right or deprive him of it; on the contrary, the right infringed remains in full force, and the infringement may be redressed by recourse to the laws of the state, as, for instance, laws making certain conduct a crime, a tort or breach of contract. Only the action of the state can have the effect of abrogating or denying a right, and thereby creating the need for constitutional protection. "The abrogation and denial of rights, for which the States alone were or could be responsible, was the great seminal and fundamental wrong which was intended to be remedied."[3] The exceptions to this must, however, be noted. A wrongful act by a private person constitutes a violation of constitutional protection of liberty if it is supported by state authority in the shape of laws, customs or judicial or executive action. Thus, judicial enforcement of a covenant in a private letting agreement which forbade subletting to a negro was held to give to the discrimination the character of a state-backed discrimination so as to bring it within the ambit of the constitutional prohibition.[4] It has been said that:

> Between the *Civil Rights Cases* and *Shelley v. Kraemer*, the concept of state action underwent considerable expansion. State action was found in acts of legislature, judiciary, executive, administrative agencies and political subdivisions of the state; in the action of government officials clothed with state power, even though their action may not have been sanctioned by the state; in the refusal of a state to act where a duty required it to do so; in attempts to effect discrimination by delegation of what is normally a state function to private agencies; in the discriminatory acts of a labour union granted sole bargaining rights under congressional mandate, and in the action of a private company maintaining a company-owned town.[5]

The other exception is where, from the wording and the context, it is clear that acts done by private persons are within the ambit of the prohibition in a Bill of Rights. The wording of the Thirteenth Amendment in the U.S. Constitution to the effect that "neither slavery nor involuntary servitude ... shall exist within the United States" has been held to be a protection against both state action and the actions of private persons.[6] The Court of Appeal (Nigeria) also thinks that the equivalent provision in the Nigerian constitution has the same scope.[7]

As an international Bill of Rights derives its binding force in international law from treaty between sovereign states, the states–parties to the treaty are

---

[3] *The Civil Rights Cases, United States v. Murray Stanley* 27 L.Ed. 835, at p. 841, per Justice Bradley (1883); *Butchers Union v. Crescent City Co.*, 28 L.Ed. 585 (1883); see the decision of the Supreme Court of India in *Shamdasani v. The Central Bank of India Ltd* (1952) A.I.R. (S.C.) 59; also *Citizens' Savings and Loan Association v. Topeka*, 20 Wall 655 (1874); *Board of Education v. Barnette* 319 U.S. 624 (1943); *Inspector Henry Ale v. General Olusegun Obasanjo*, Suit No. M/T/1/89 delivered on 6/7/89 (High Court, Ogun State, Nigeria).
[4] *Shelley v. Kraemer*, 334 U.S. 1 (1948).
[5] Thurgood Marshall in an article reproduced in *The Freedom Reader* by Edwin S. Newman, 2nd ed. (1963), p. 190.
[6] *Bailey v. Alabama*, 219 U.S. 207 (1913).
[7] *Nwosu & Ors v. Igwe of Atani & Ors*, CA/E/132/90 delivered on 22 July, 1991; s. 31 (1) (b).

the entities obligated under it to recognise the guaranteed rights in their municipal law, to take appropriate measures to secure their protection, and not to violate them by their legislative, executive and administrative actions. These obligations are not proper to a private person, and cannot in any case be laid on him by treaty, he not being a proper party to an international treaty.

There is considerable scepticism about the usefulness of a bill of rights owing to its alleged ineffectiveness as a regulatory device for controlling the behaviour of government agencies and functionaries towards the individual. It is an indisputable fact that, in spite of the existence of various bills of rights, national and international, gross human rights violations, often on a massive scale, do occur in many parts of the world, Africa in particular. But, surely, this fact alone is not conclusive on the issue of the usefulness or otherwise of a Bill of Rights as a means of regulating and controlling the exercise and use of state power. Complete effectiveness of a bill of rights in stopping human rights violations cannot justifiably be insisted upon as the sole measure of its usefulness any more than we can insist on complete effectiveness of the criminal law in wiping out crimes as the test of its value. It seems too cynical to endorse as a "sobering realism" the view that the rampant and incessant human rights violations in many countries of the world makes international legal protection an exercise in futility.[8] With regard to the African Charter on Human and Peoples' Rights, it is said that the procedures for complaints to the African Commission and the corrective action, if any, that might be taken on such complaints can be considered effective only to the extent that they "produce satisfactory results,"[9] and by satisfactory results is apparently meant the stoppage or minimisation of violations. The commentator then continues somewhat more cynically:

> The adoption of human rights instruments does not by and of itself ensure respect for or protection of human rights. In the kind of situation, both socio-political and economic, prevailing in Africa, one can well visualise the chances of the African system making any dent on the problem of mass violations. ... All independent African states, as members

---

[8]   Adamantia Pollis, *Liberal, Socialist and Third World Perspective on Human Rights* (1982), p. 22.

[9]   K. Mathews, "The OAU and Political Economy of Human Rights in Africa: An Analysis of the African Charter on Human and Peoples' Rights," (1987) 1st/2nd Quarters, *Africa Today*, pp. 97-98.

of the U.N., have been parties to many international conventions or other instruments on human rights, including the U.N. Covenant on Civil and Political Rights and that on Economic, Social and Cultural Rights. Yet, with few, if any, exceptions, little change has occurred in the pattern of increasing numbers of oppressive, increasingly centralised ... regimes in Africa. Moreover, there is no reasonable basis to conclude that the present ruling class in Africa or those that are likely to succeed them will suddenly modify past behaviours.[10]

Such an unduly cynical view on the value of legal protection by means of a Bill of Rights misses the point about the fundamental purpose of human rights protection by the instrumentality of the law. It is a truism that law — laying down rules of conduct — in society has value in the establishment of standards of social behaviour. No society is known to have attained ordered and civilised life without rules of conduct prescribed by law; the idea of such society existing without law, of an ordered and civilised society in which law completely "withers away," is sheer fantasy. Rules of conduct prescribed by law are indispensable in the establishment of standards of behaviour in society, and in the gradual evolution of habits or traditions of observance of such standards. Before such standards can get established and be observed in society, there must be rules laying them down, rules that embody the ethical values of the society, and which, if regularly applied, may give rise to habits of respect over a period of time.

Respect for standards comes, not out of the blues, but initially from law prescribing such standards, which may later grow into conventions, habits or traditions. Here lies the primary value of a Bill of Rights, national as well as international. By laying down, in as precise a manner as legal formulation can achieve, the basic rights of the individual, a Bill of Rights establishes them as the standard of behaviour required of the state in its dealings with the individual. It fulfils the same role as law does in the regulation and control of social behaviour generally.

A Bill of Rights, not only sets standards, it serves as a rallying and reference point as well as a source of inspiration in the struggle for human rights. The need for a focal point from which the struggle is to be waged cannot be over-emphasised.

We do not condemn all criminal laws as valueless because crimes still

---

[10] K. Mathews, *op. cit.*

occur in spite of them. No system of social control is ever completely effective.

> No knowledgeable person has ever suggested that constitutional safeguards provide in themselves complete and indefeasible security. But they do make the way of the transgressor, of the tyrant, more difficult. They are, so to speak, the outer bulwarks of defence.[11]

The Nigerian Minorities Commission (1958) has put it even more persuasively when it said:

> A government determined to abandon democratic course will find ways of avoiding them, but they are of great value in preventing a steady deterioration in standards of freedom and the unobtrusive encroachment of a government on individual rights.[12]

The standards of behaviour prescribed in a Bill of Rights cannot by themselves alone eliminate the factors responsible for the lack of respect for human rights in Africa any more than the prohibitions and penalties embodied in the criminal law can eliminate the causes of aberrant behaviour in the wider society. These causative factors must be identified and efforts made to remedy them. Whilst efforts to identify and remedy the causes are being made, the standards prescribed in the Bills of Rights must be maintained and, where necessary, improved for greater utility.

Enforcement and Its Significance

The point about the ineffectiveness of a Bill of Rights seems certainly exaggerated insofar, at any rate, as it relates to a Bill of Rights that guarantees a full range of basic human rights, is backed by effective enforcement machinery, and is free of stultifying qualifications, as where it is made subject to law or to any law enacted to secure public order, public security, etc. It is simply inconceivable that such a Bill of Rights will be totally ineffective in checking gross human rights violations. No repressive regime of tyranny is known to have arisen or existed in Africa with such a Bill of Rights; the two simply cannot exist together. In all African countries in which the constitution enshrined such a Bill of Rights, the establishment of an authoritarian regime, e.g. a one-party regime or a military dictatorship, had been preceded by an amendment of the

---

[11] Cowen, *The Foundation of Freedom* (1960), p. 119.
[12] Report Cmnd 505 (1958), p. 97.

constitution to attenuate or abolish the Bill of Rights and to remove other constitutional restrictions on power, which therefore paved the way for the enthronement of the authoritarian regime. In the period between independence and 1973, the constitution had been amended 17 times in Zambia, 13 times in Malawi, 11 in Kenya, 10 in Tanzania, 6 in Uganda, 5 in Ghana and 4 in Botswana for precisely this purpose.

Certainly, if the Bill of Rights or other constitutional restrictions on power did not constitute an effective obstacle in the way of the assumption of authoritarian power by government, there would have been no need to amend the constitution to abolish, suspend or attenuate them. There seems to be a tendency in discussions upon this point to mistake the lack of respect for human rights for the ineffectiveness of a legal guarantee of them. These are two separate things. It is the absence of respect for human rights on the part of the governments in these African countries that led them to resort to the amendment of the constitution in order to achieve their ambition for authoritarian power. At any rate, their love of power was so much more than their respect for human rights, which therefore predisposed them to succumb readily to the temptation to pervert the constitution and its Bill of Rights into an instrument in aid of their drive for authoritarian power. This clearly proves the usefulness, if not the effectiveness, but not the ineffectiveness, of a Bill of Rights.

Enforcement action through the courts affords a further proof of the value of a Bill of Rights that guarantees a full range of basic rights, is backed by effective enforcement machinery, and is free of stultifying qualifications, but a discussion of this belongs more appropriately to chapter 3, vol. 3.

Yet, whilst, as earlier indicated, a well-drafted Bill of Rights is a factor that may, over time, induce respect for human rights among the rulers and the ruled alike, it does not guarantee it. Essentially, respect for human rights comes more from promotional measures; it has to be actively promoted through appropriate measures instituted by law and complemented by measures originated by non-governmental organisations.

Promotion of Respect for Human Rights

A significant weakness in the system of human rights protection in African countries is the lack of recognition of the important truth, namely, that respect for human rights is something to be actively promoted. Thus, until the recent transitions to constitutional democracy from 1990, in none of the African constitutions is anything said or any measure instituted for this purpose. And so we find that, without a directive in the constitution to that effect, no national effort is mounted to generate public awareness of the need for respect for human rights, much less to instill it in the moral consciousness of the people, with a view to its eventual evolution into a habit for individuals and a tradition for the nation. The departure from the past in the transition constitutions of at least four African countries is therefore a welcome development. They (i.e. the transition constitutions of South Africa 1996, Zambia 1991, Benin 1990 and Niger 1996) lay on the state the duty to promote respect for human rights. Three of these constitutions (South Africa, Zambia and Niger) go further to establish a human rights commission, charged with the promotional function through such means as education, research, investigation of cases of human rights violations and taking steps to secure appropriate redress in cases of human rights violations. Though it does not directly establish a human rights commission, the provision in Benin's transition Constitution is the widest in the duty of promotion laid on the state. It says (art. 40):

> The state has the duty to assure the diffusion and teaching of the Constitution, of the Universal Declaration of Human Rights of 1948, of the African Charter on Human and Peoples' Rights of 1981 as well as all of the international instruments duly ratified and relative to Human Rights.
>
> The state must integrate the rights of the individual into the programs of literacy and of teaching in the various scholastic and university academic cycles and into all the educational programs of the Armed Forces, of the Public Security Forces and of comparable categories.
>
> The State must equally assure the diffusion and teaching of these same rights in the national languages by all the means of mass communication, and in particular by radio and television.

This weakness in the national system of protection is somewhat offset, though not to an extent that might be wished, by the refreshing concern with the promotion of respect for human rights exhibited in the international Bills of Rights. It is noteworthy that the U.N. Universal Declaration of Human Rights (1948), after reciting in a preamble the justification for the legal protection of human rights, opens with a directive to "every individual and every organ of society" to "strive by teaching and education to promote respect for these rights and freedoms and by progressive measures, national and international, to secure their universal and effective recognition and observance." Thus, the promotional responsibility is not only that of society in its formal character as a state; it belongs also to individuals and private organisations.

In their respective preambles, the two International Covenants (1976), which implement the Universal Declaration, not only recite "the obligation of States under the Charter of the United Nations to promote universal respect for, and observance of, human rights and freedoms," but also proclaim it the responsibility of every individual to "strive for the promotion and observance of the rights recognised" in the Covenants, in furtherance of his duties to other individuals and to the community at large.

Respect for human rights is promoted mainly by making people aware, through teaching and education and through publicity generally, of their rights under the law, by gathering information about, and focusing pubic attention on, violations of them, by enabling victims, by means of advice and other assistance, to seek appropriate redress, and by continual public debate of the value of respect for human rights in the development of the individual, society and the state. The contributions of the United Nations in this regard have not stopped with merely declaring the rights and proclaiming the need to promote respect for them; it lies even more in the concrete efforts it had made in actively promoting respect for human rights, using the 1948 Universal Declaration, in the words of the preamble, as "a common standard of achievement for all peoples and all nations." Through public debate in the General Assembly, seminars or conferences organised or sponsored by subsidiary agencies of the U.N., various publications on human rights, and through publicity throughout the world, the Declaration "has worked as a formation of an international conscience."[13] The U.N. system of supervising the implementation of protection through both the reporting and complaints procedures is characterised by the importance placed on publicity as a way to engage the conscience of states to refrain from human rights violations.

---

[13] See J. E. S. Fawcett, "The Protection of Human Rights on a Universal Basis: Recent Experience and Proposals," in A. H. Robertson (ed.), *Human Rights in National and International Law* (1968), p. 29.

The African Charter on Human and Peoples' Rights also manifests a commendable concern for the promotion of respect for human rights, as is borne out by the fact that promotion of human and peoples' rights constitutes a major part of the functions of the Commission set up under its provisions. The Commission is directed and mandated in particular:

(i)   to collect documents, undertake studies and researches on African problems in the field of human and peoples' rights; organise seminars, symposia and conferences, disseminate information, and encourage national and local institutions concerned with human and peoples' rights;

(ii)   to co-operate with other African and other international institutions concerned with promotion and protection of human and peoples' rights (art. 45 (1)).

A duty is laid on a ratifying state not only to promote and ensure, through teaching, education and publication, respect for the guaranteed rights, and "to see to it" that they are understood (art. 25), but also to allow the establishment and improvement of appropriate national institutions for the promotion and protection of the guaranteed rights and freedoms (art. 26). In implementation of its obligation under articles 25 and 26 above, Nigeria has set up a National Human Rights Commission by a 1995 Decree of the Federal Military Government, with promotional functions similar to those of the African Commission. A Human Rights Violations Investigation Panel was set up in 2000.

The work of the non-governmental organisations (NGOs), especially the International Commission of Jurists (ICJ), Amnesty International, and the Civil Liberties Union, also deserves mention. Now numbered in hundreds, an increase described as a "veritable explosion" in numbers, they have rendered and still render very useful services in the promotion of respect for human rights. Regrettably, Africa again lags behind in this respect, as the vast majority of human rights NGOs operating in the continent are foreign organisations based outside Africa.

The work of these human rights NGOs includes: focusing attention on specific cases of human rights violations, often turning them into issues of international concern, with possible international consequences for the state concerned in the violation; taking up the case of those whose rights are violated but who are unable or are prevented to seek redress within their own political system, including intervention with the governments concerned, provision of humanitarian relief and legal assistance; identifying with the oppressed to create in them a sense of strength that comes from the knowledge that they are not alone and that their struggle has the backing of powerful allies, what has been described as "solidarity building;" exerting their moral authority by publicly expressing condemnation of human rights violations by repressive regimes, which may be said to constitute the main power of human rights NGOs; lobbying other governments and their functionaries to support actions against repressive regimes; and, most important of all, gathering, evaluating and disseminating information about human rights violations, particularly through the mass media and through publication of reports.[14] It has been truly said that "without information on the status of human rights observance, and the particular nature and context of human rights violations, there is little hope for the protection of human rights."[15]

---

[14]   Harry M. Scoble, "Human Rights Non-Governmental Organisations in Black Africa: Their Problems and Prospects in the Wake of the Banjul Charter," in Claude E. Welch and Ronald I. Meltzer (eds.), *Human Rights and Development in Africa* (1984), pp. 177-203.

[15]   Harry M. Scoble, *op. cit.*, pp. 177-178.

CHAPTER 4

The African Charter on Human and Peoples' Rights: Its Role in Human Rights Protection

Significance of the Charter

The African Charter on Human and Peoples' Rights, adopted by the Organisation of African Unity (OAU) on 19 January, 1981 (it entered into force on 21 October, 1986), is a law-creating instrument of considerable significance. It is so because it carries the protection of the fundamental rights of the individual beyond the confines of the domestic laws of the individual African countries into the arena of the comity of all African states, thereby engaging the collective conscience and the common concern of the entire continent in the matter. Constitutional protection is a domestic process by which a state binds itself to its citizens by the supreme law of the land to respect and secure their fundamental rights. Protection by the binding force of domestic law, even the supreme law of the constitution, is considered not enough in a world, particularly the African world, driven by internal strife and conflicts.

The machinery of international law has had to be called into use to reinforce that of domestic law. By involving the machinery of international law for this purpose and thus carrying the process beyond the domestic frontiers, the state binds itself to other states by means of a treaty to respect and secure the fundamental rights of its citizens, a treaty being a contractual engagement based on the mutual consent of the contracting states and deriving its obligatory force from the good faith due to agreements in international law by the inviolable principle of *pacta sunt servanda*. A state-party to such a treaty is thereby enabled to complain, using the procedure provided in the treaty, about fundamental rights violation by another state-party without rendering

57

itself open to accusation of breaching the principle of non-interference in the internal affairs of other states. But the matter does not stop with merely binding the state to other states in contract. International protection of human rights has brought about a remarkable expansion in the traditional frontiers of international law itself through the use of a treaty not only to bind a state to other contracting states but also to confer upon the citizens of the state a right to redress against it at both the domestic and international levels for violations of their rights in contravention of the treaty stipulations. The individual citizen too has thus gained recognition, albeit a limited one, as a subject of international law.[1]

The title of the treaty in this case underlines its significance. It is significant indeed that it is styled a **Charter on Human and Peoples' Rights**, instead of a "Convention," like the European Convention on Human Rights or the American Convention on Human Rights. A Charter connotes something done in due form and solemnity, and is therefore to be accorded great respect and binding force, almost as an article of faith; it implies, further, the idea that the rights guaranteed are to have a real existence in the practice of government in the ratifying states. If the treaty is to be truly a charter of freedom for Africans then, the states-parties to it must be taken to have assumed a greater or higher obligation to respect and implement its stipulations than is normally assumed by a state under an ordinary treaty.

The significance of the Charter must also be viewed against the background of a continent comprising a great diversity of governmental regimes, with different constitutional systems and traditions in the matter of fundamental rights protection, a continent in which human rights violations are rampant and widespread. Viewed against that background, it is remarkable that agreement was reached at all on the Charter, and more remarkable still that it was able, within a matter of five years (1981-1986), to secure the ratification of a majority of the then 50 members of the OAU necessary for it to enter into force. (By 1988, 35 states had ratified the Charter; as at the end of 1995, all except three (Ethiopia, Eritrea and South Africa) of the present 53 states in Africa have ratified it.) This is no mean achievement, judged by the records at the global sphere. After the adoption of the Universal Declaration of Human

---

[1] See A.H. Robertson and J.G. Merrills, *Human Rights in the World* (1992), p.2

Rights in 1948, it took 18 years (1948-1966) to agree and adopt the two instruments that translated the Declaration into a form capable of ratification as legally binding treaties — the International Covenant on Civil and Political Rights, and the International Covenant on Economic, Social and Cultural Rights — and another 10 years (1966-1976) for the two Covenants to secure the 35 ratifications required for them to enter into force. Upon its entry into force, the African Charter on Human and Peoples' Rights takes a respectable place among regional Bills of Rights; the European Convention on Human Rights (adopted 1950, entered into force 1953); the American Convention on Human Rights (adopted 1969, entered into force, 1978).[2]

The adoption and entry into force of the African Charter demonstrates an appreciation and conviction on the part of the African leaders that the securing and maintenance of fundamental rights at the continental level is necessary not only for the well-being and happiness of the individual citizen but also as an instrument for fostering the objective of African unity. The Charter's rather lengthy and grandiose preamble amply manifests that appreciation and conviction. Proclaiming adherence to the U.N. Universal Declaration of Human Rights of 1948, it affirms the nature of human rights as stemming from attributes of the human being as well as their indispensability, together with justice, to the attainment of the legitimate aspirations of the African peoples. It also affirms the inexorable linkage between human rights on one hand and economic, social and cultural rights on the other, proclaiming the provision of the latter as a necessary foundation for the enjoyment of the former. The elimination of all forms of discrimination, particularly discrimination based on race, ethnicity, colour, sex, language, religion or political opinion, is likewise affirmed.

The verdict of Robertson and Merrills is that:

> despite certain limitations, the African Charter on Human and People's Rights, is a very significant step in international human rights law. Not only does the Charter itself contain many innovative provisions, but when the system as a whole comes into full operation it will be the largest regional human rights system in terms of the number of States concerned, as well as the only functioning arrangement in the Afro-Asian world.[3]

---

[2]   See Paul Sieghart, *The International Law of Human Rights* (1983), where the provisions of the three regional Bills of Rights and the International Covenants are set out side by side for purposes of comparison.

[3]   A.H. Robertson & J.G. Merrills, *Human Rights in the World* (1992 edn), p. 221.

And Richard Gittleman has described it as "a milestone in the promotion and protection of human rights in Africa."[4] Professor Umozurike also applauds it for combining "an impressive array of individual rights and duties, group rights, and state rights and duties;" according to him, "some of these, like the right to development and the right to national and international peace and security, appear to be new additions to the list of internationally recognised rights."[5]

When all this has been said, however, the real significance of the Charter, its impact on human rights protection, is determined less by its mere binding force as a treaty in international law than by the:

(1) range and amplitude of the rights it guarantees;

(2) nature and extent of a ratifying state's obligations in international law to give effect to the guaranteed rights within its territory;

(3) remedies provided by the Charter in international law for violations of the guaranteed rights;

(4) juridical status of the Charter in domestic law; and, above all,

(5) remedies available in domestic law for violations of the guaranteed rights if and when the Charter is applicable in domestic law.

These are the things that determine the real significance of the Charter as a device for the protection of the individual's fundamental rights. They will now be examined but, before doing that, we should first consider the African Charter's definition and classification of human rights.

Definition and Classification of Human Rights in the African Charter

The terminology of "human rights" has gained universal currency and acceptation, especially since it was popularised by the United Nations Declaration of Human Rights of 1948, but its exact scope remains still far from being clear. Does the term "human rights" mean rights inherent in the individual as

---

[4]   R. Gittleman, "The African Commission on Human and Peoples' Rights", in H. Hannum (ed.), *Guide to International Human Rights Practice* (1984), 153 at pp. 160-161.

[5]   U.O. Umozurike, "The African Charter on Human and Peoples' Rights", 1983, 77 *The American Journal of International Law*, p. 902, at p. 911.

an innate attribute of his humanity, like thought, conscience, emotions, belief, speech, movement and action, or does it include as well rights necessary to maintain or sustain the human person in dignity, by which are implied rights relating to material things necessary for the maintenance of a dignified existence as a human being, like food, water, health and medical care, shelter, clothing?

In proclaiming in their respective preambles that human rights "derive from the inherent dignity of the human person," the two International Covenants of 1976 (the International Covenant on Civil and Political Rights and the International Covenant on Economic, Social and Cultural Rights) appear to adopt the latter, wider meaning of the term. For clearly, the inherent dignity of the human person requires these material things to maintain a dignified existence. But the wider meaning cannot easily be rested on the definition of human rights in the African Charter on Human and Peoples' Rights (1986) as rights "stemming from the attributes of human beings." Whilst economic, social and cultural rights may be said to "derive from the inherent dignity of the human person" in the sense of being necessary to maintain the human person in dignity, it is difficult to see in what sense food, shelter, clothing etc. are **attributes** of human beings. The European instruments on the matter contain no explicit definition of the term. However, the fact that the Convention on Human Rights (1953) deals only with civil and political rights may be construed as restricting the scope of "human rights" to civil and political rights; yet the reference in the other instrument, the Social Charter (1965), to human rights would seem to imply that economic, social and cultural rights (with which it deals) are also comprehended in the term.

Be that as it may, in accepted current usage, human rights embrace civil and political rights as well as economic, social and cultural rights. And, there is perhaps justification for the preamble to the African Charter proclaiming that "civil and political rights cannot be dissociated from economic, social and cultural rights in their conception as well as universality" and that "the satisfaction of economic, social and cultural rights is a guarantee for the enjoyment of civil and political rights." Both are best regarded as complementary aspects of the concept of human rights, with the caveat that the economic, social and cultural rights are called "rights" only in the loosest sense of the term.

Defined as rights stemming from a person's existence in dignity as a human being, it is clear that human rights embrace two types of rights–individual and collective. The individual rights are distinguished by the use of the word "everyone" to designate the repository of the rights in the two International Covenants and the European Convention and "every individual" or "every citizen" in the African Charter. The individual as the repository of the rights guaranteed in the U.S. Bill of Rights is also affirmed in the decision by the trial court and a majority of the California supreme court and the U.S. supreme court in the celebrated **Bakke Case**, *Regents of the University of California v. Bakke*,[6] to the effect that the Fourteenth Amendment predicates "individual not group-based attributes as the only permissible factors to be counted."

But this by no means implies that the individual is the only repository of human rights or, to put it in a different way, that only individual rights qualify as human rights, on the ground, as it is argued, that the word "human" refers to a human being in his individual capacity.[7] For this purpose, no sensible distinction can be drawn between a human being in his individual capacity and a human being in his capacity as a member of a group or collectivity. The individual remains the ultimate repository of human rights whether he is to possess and enjoy them alone or jointly and collectively with others, and the term "human rights" does not become inappropriate simply because the rights belong to a group of individual human beings as a collectivity. It is an appropriate compendious term to embrace both individual and collective rights, so long as the right in question can be said to be necessary to the inherent dignity of the human person. Genocide, the trans-Atlantic slave trade, the repression of ethnic or racial minorities, and the brutalities of apartheid in South Africa were no less violations of human rights because they were directed against groups rather than individuals. Political liberty too implies, essentially, a collective liberty, i.e. the freedom of a people as a community to govern itself (self-government), a community whose members collectively possess and enjoy full political rights or freedom to govern themselves and to determine their destiny as a group.[8] "Self-government ... is not the government

---

[6]   438 U.S. 265 (1978).
[7]   See A.H. Robertson & J.G. Merrills, *Human Rights in the World* (1992 edn.), p. 258.
[8]   See F.A. Hayek, *The Constitution of Liberty* (1960), pp. 13-14.

of each by himself, but of each by all the rest."[9] Economic, social and cultural rights are also largely collective rights of the entire people. But it has never been suggested that political rights or economic, social and cultural rights are not human rights because of their nature as collective rights.

However, rights of society, viewed not as a collection of individuals but in its formal character as a state, are not collective human rights; the state is in the nature of a corporation which in law is an entity separate from the individuals that compose it, with independent existence and rights of its own. The rights of a corporate body are not human rights.

The distinction which the African Charter draws between, on the one hand, "human rights" and, on the other, "peoples' rights" (meaning collective rights) is thus unreal and confusing. "Peoples" are humans, not a different specie of creatures, so the only sensible distinction that can be drawn, is not between human rights and peoples' rights, but between individual and collective rights, both being separate types of human rights; the one belongs no less to the category of human rights than the other.

Seven rights are guaranteed by the African Charter under the designation of "peoples' rights," namely: the right of all peoples to equal rights and equal respect, without domination of one people by another (art. 19); the right to self-determination, with freedom to determine their political status and to pursue their economic and social development according to a policy chosen by themselves (art. 20(1)); the right of colonised people to free themselves from the bonds of domination, using any means recognised by the international community, and to assistance from the states-parties in their liberation struggle (art. 20(2) and (3)); the right freely to dispose of their wealth and natural resources as the interest of the people may require (art. 21); the right to economic, social and cultural development (art. 22); the right to peace and security as the blessings flowing from solidarity and friendship as the principles governing relations among nations (art. 23); and the right to general satisfactory environment favourable to development (art. 24).

But it is objected that the rights so guaranteed as "peoples' rights" are not rights in any meaningful sense of the term, and that it distorts language to call

---

[9] J.S. Mill, *Representative Government*, reprinted in *Utilitarianism, Liberty and Representative Government* (1910), Everyman's Library, p. 72.

them so.[10] True, but the same can be said of economic, social and cultural rights. Once the word "rights" is applied to economic, social and cultural rights, then, it cannot justifiably be denied to the right to a satisfactory environment, peace, self-determination, to free disposal of national wealth and natural resources and to development. Development is, after all, what economic and social rights are about, and self-determination means not much else than self-government. A healthy environment, peace and freedom to dispose of wealth and natural resources are as much necessary to the maintenance of the inherent dignity of the human person as food, health and medical care, shelter and clothing; any difference there may be is one of degree only. The rights designated as "peoples' rights" in the African Charter and economic, social and cultural rights both belong to same category of distorted application of the word "rights," and there seems to be no good reason for admitting one and excluding the other from this loose, distorted usage. Usage, as Robertson and Merrills themselves say, is, after all, "a matter of convention."[11]

Range, Scope and Amplitude of Rights Guaranteed

The list of civil and political rights guaranteed by the African Charter covers all the rights and freedoms usually found in a full-blown Bill of Rights, and is, at any rate, as extensive as that in the International Covenant on Civil and Political Rights or the Bills of Rights in the constitutions of the countries of former British Africa. In terms of wording, the provisions in which many of the rights are set out are modelled closely on the International Covenant.

The list embraces: equality before the law; the right to life and the integrity of the human person; right to the inherent dignity of the human being and freedom from cruel, degrading or inhuman treatment, including slavery and torture; right to liberty and the security of the person; freedom from arbitrary arrest and detention; the right to have one's cause in civil cases heard and in criminal cases the right to be tried within a reasonable time by an impartial and independent court or tribunal; freedom of conscience, religion, expression, association, assembly and movement; right of private property; and the right

---

[10] Robertson and Merrills, *op. cit.*, pp. 258-259.
[11] *ibid,* p. 258.

of participation in government, of equal access to government service and to public property and services (arts. 3-14).

Yet, the amplitude (that is to say the sufficiency or adequacy) of rights guaranteed in a Bill of Rights cannot be judged by simply listing them as we have done above; their scope is determined also by the terms in which they are defined and delimited. There are at least six main respects in which the rights guaranteed in the African Charter differ substantially in scope from the same rights in the International Covenant or the Bills of Rights in the constitutions of the countries of former British Africa.

First, article 6 of the African Charter, by guaranteeing to every individual "the right to liberty and to the security of his person"– the words are exactly the same as in article 9 of the International Covenant – makes it clear that what is guaranteed is not just personal liberty (liberty or security of the person), as is the case in the Bills of Rights in the constitutions of the countries of former British Africa, but covers liberty as a generalised concept in the sense of the U.S. Bill of Rights. Indeed, the words, "in particular" in the accompanying sentence in article 6 of the Charter (viz "in particular, no one may be arbitrarily arrested or detained"– the identical sentence in article 9 of the International Covenant does not contain the two words) show that freedom from arbitrary arrest or detention is just one particular aspect of the general right of liberty guaranteed in article 6. But the guarantee is severely qualified by making the right subject to deprivation for "reasons and conditions previously laid down by law."

Secondly, the prohibition of arbitrary arrest or detention in article 6 of the African Charter and in article 9 of the International Covenant gives no indication as to what exactly is meant or when arrest or detention is arbitrary. It seems reasonably inferable from the context of the two articles that arbitrary arrest or detention is arrest or detention not authorised by law. Clearly, protection that avails against arrest or detention by the executive without authorisation by a law but which in no way limits the power of the legislative organ of the state to make law conferring the necessary legal authorisation on the executive is inadequate. In the Bills of Rights in the constitutions of the countries of former British Africa, the legislature can only authorise by law the arrest or detention of a person "upon reasonable suspicion of his having committed, or being about to commit, a criminal offence;" its power is further circumscribed by safeguards designed to reinforce the protection of the guarantee of the individual's personal liberty. These safeguards – the person concerned must be brought promptly before a court and must be tried within a reasonable time or else be released either unconditionally or subject to conditions – are provided for in the International Covenant (art. 9(3)), but not in the African Charter. Nor does the Charter guarantee, as does the Covenant (art. 9(2), (3) and (4)), the right of a person arrested or detained to be informed, at the time of arrest, of the reasons for his arrest, the right to take proceedings before a court to determine the lawfulness of his detention and to secure his release where the detention is not lawful, and his right to compensation for unlawful detention.

Thirdly, whereas the International Covenant (art. 14) and the Bills of Rights in the constitutions of the countries of former British Africa guarantee to everyone, in civil and criminal cases alike, the right to a fair hearing by an independent and impartial court or tribunal established by law, the African Charter only guarantees in civil cases the right "to have his case heard" (art. 7(1)) without any indication as to who — a court, a tribunal or some other body — is to conduct the hearing. (The point is further considered later.) Only in criminal cases does the Charter guarantee "the right to be tried within a reasonable time by an impartial court or tribunal," and even here, only three safeguards for a fair trial are guaranteed (the presumption of innocence, the right to defence and the prohibition of trial for a retroactive offence and the infliction of retroactive penalties) as against ten safeguards guaranteed by both the International Covenant and the Bills of Rights in the constitutions of the countries of the former British Africa.

Fourthly, the Charter's guarantee of the right to property, subject only to "the interest of public need or in the general interest of the community and in accordance with the provisions of appropriate laws" (art. 14), is inadequate for not guaranteeing to the individual the right to compensation for his property compulsorily acquired by the state, however the compensation may be arrived at, whether on the basis of a fair market price or otherwise, and whether the payment is to be made promptly or not. Thus, under the Charter, no obligation is laid on the state to compensate the owner of property compulsorily acquired.

Whilst a young, developing African state should not be crippled by an obligation to pay "adequate and prompt compensation" and thereby disabled from pursuing desirable programmes of economic development based on public ownership of certain economic enterprises, it is wrong that it should be freed from such obligation altogether.

Fifthly, under the African Charter, freedom of conscience and religion is guaranteed "subject to law" (art. 8); freedom of expression is guaranteed "within the law" (art. 9); freedom of association is guaranteed provided the individual "abides by the law" (art. 10); while the right to assemble freely with others is guaranteed subject to necessary restriction by law "in particular" laws enacted in the interest of national security, the safety, health, ethics and rights and freedoms of others (art. 11); and "the right to liberty and to the security of the person" including, in particular, freedom from arrest or detention, guaranteed by articles 6 may be taken away for "reasons and conditions previously laid down by law." (The influence of the approach in most of the Bills of Rights in the constitutions of countries outside former British Africa is easily discernible here.) Thus, these rights have only such scope as is allowed by law, which means in effect that they are not protected against the legislative power of the state, which is the state power against which individual liberty stands in most need of protection.

This contrasts strikingly with the scope of these rights under the guarantee in the International Covenant and the Bills of Rights in the constitutions of the countries of former British Africa, which permit only "such limitations as are prescribed by law and are necessary to protect public safety, order, health or morals or the fundamental rights and freedoms of others" (arts. 18, 19, 21 and 22); the guarantee of the security of the person is not even so limited. The limiting effect of guaranteeing a right "subject to law" may be mitigated by an activist interpretation such as was displayed by the European Court on Human Rights when it ruled that such laws are acceptable only in so far as they do not interfere with the "substance" of the guaranteed right.[12] The ruling of the European Court may well be within the scope of legitimate interpretation, but that can hardly be said for the suggestion that the African

---

[12]   A.H. Robertson and J.G. Merrills, *Human Rights in the World* (1992 edn), pp. 216-217.

Commission should, in the exercise of the interpretative discretion vested in it, read into the African Charter, the provisions of the International Covenant on Civil and Political Rights limiting the powers of the state to take away by law the right to the security of the person (i.e. freedom from arrest or detention) guaranteed therein or the other guaranteed rights mentioned above — freedom of conscience and religion, expression, association and assembly.[13]

It is probably because all the above-mentioned rights are guaranteed subject to the law that "derogation" during an emergency is not specifically provided for in the African Charter. A power in the state to take away or curtail guaranteed rights by law when times are normal and peace and order reigns in society gives it all the power it needs to deal with a situation of emergency, thus making it unnecessary to provide specifically for derogation from guaranteed rights during such emergency periods.

Sixthly, the scope of the guaranteed rights and freedoms is bound to be affected when taken together with the duties the Charter lays on the individual. Eight duties are set out in article 29, of which only six need be mentioned here, viz: the duty to use one's physical and intellectual abilities for the benefit of the state; not to compromise the security of the state; to preserve and strengthen social and national solidarity, national independence and the territorial integrity of the country; to contribute to its defence; to work to the best of one's abilities and competence and to pay taxes; and to preserve and strengthen "positive African cultural values" and to promote the moral well-being of society.

As has been pertinently remarked, a conscientious objection to military service based on the guarantee of freedom of conscience can be met by setting up the individual's duty to contribute to national defence. Similarly, the duty to preserve and strengthen social and national solidarity as well as the stipulation in article 27(2) that the rights and freedoms "shall be exercised with due regard to ... common interest" can be invoked to defeat many of the guaranteed rights and freedoms. There is thus validity in the criticism that "in a treaty which places so much weight on duties, provisions dealing with rights cannot be interpreted as if they stood alone," and that the duties are

---

[13] Richard Gittleman, "The Banjul Charter on Human and Peoples' Rights: A Legal Analysis", in Claude Welch & Ronald Meltzer (eds), *Human Rights and Development in Africa* (1994), p. 161.

incorporated into the Charter because the African rulers responsible for it "wished to put forward a distinctive conception of human rights in which civil and political rights were seen to be counter-balanced by duties of social solidarity," the end result of which may be to neutralise the rights, depending on how they are interpreted by the Commission.

We need not consider here less substantial respects in which the civil and political rights guaranteed in the African Charter differ from those in other Bills of Rights — international, regional and national.

The African Charter guarantees only seven economic, social and cultural rights and is therefore much less extensive in the range of rights covered than the International Covenant on Economic, Social and Cultural Rights, and still far less so than the European Social Charter. It guarantees only the right to work, to education and health care; the protection of women against discrimination; the right of the aged and disabled to special measures of protection; the promotion and protection of morals and traditional values by the state; and state assistance to the family as the custodian of morals and traditional values. The question whether, having regard to the nature of these rights, the guarantee of them in the Charter is amenable to enforcement is considered later.

Nature and Extent of a Ratifying State's Obligation with Regard to Rights Guaranteed by the Charter

Two types of obligation need to be distinguished, viz the negative obligation not to violate the guaranteed rights and the positive obligation to take some action, e.g. to adopt legislation, to provide medical care by building hospitals and medical centres or to adopt other measures to give effect to them. The distinction has important implications in regard to the applicability of the Charter as a treaty in municipal law, as will be explained later.

With this distinction in mind, the obligation cast on a ratifying state is to "recognise the rights, duties and freedoms enshrined in this Charter and (to) undertake to adopt legislative or other measures to give effect to them" (art. 1). By article 26 the "States Parties to the present Charter shall have the duty to guarantee the independence of the Courts and shall allow the establishment and improvement of appropriate national institutions entrusted with the promotion and protection of the rights and freedoms guaranteed by the present Charter." The point for consideration here is to determine exactly what articles 1 and 26 of the Charter obligate a ratifying state to do. Is a ratifying state obligated to make the rights and freedoms enforceable through the process of the courts of law? Does giving effect to the rights and freedoms obligate a ratifying state not only to give them the force of law (i.e. by legislation) but also to secure their enforcement as well as provide the economic, social and cultural rights in actual practice?

According to the Nigerian Court of Appeal in a case shortly to be reviewed, article 1 of the Charter "enjoins all member states to put up a suitable procedure for the **enforcement**" of the guaranteed rights.[14] This decision is questionable; it suffers from lack of analysis of the relevant provisions to determine the precise nature and extent of a ratifying state's obligations under the Charter. For the purpose of such an analysis, articles 1 and 26 must be read together with article 7(1), which provides as follows: "Every individual shall have the right to have his cause heard. This comprises:

(a) the right to an appeal to competent national organs against acts of violating his fundamental rights as recognised and guaranteed by conventions, laws, regulations and customs in force;

(b) the right to be presumed innocent until proved guilty by a competent court or tribunal;

(c) the right to defence, including the right to be defended by counsel of his choice;

(d) the right to be tried within a reasonable time by an impartial court or tribunal."

One is immediately struck by the vagueness of the first sentence and clause (a) of article 7(1) above, a vagueness that is, apparently, motivated by an intention to limit the extent of a ratifying state's obligations in civil causes, especially civil causes involving questions of constitutionality. For, whilst

---

[14] *General Sani Abacha & Others v. Chief Gani Fawehinmi* Suit No. CA/L/141/96; Judgment delivered on 12/12/96 (emphasis supplied).

guaranteeing to every individual "the right to have his cause heard," the first sentence refrains, advisedly it seems, from specifying by whom — a court, tribunal or other body – one's cause is to be heard. As far as civil causes are concerned, this lack of specificity is hardly made good by the provision in clause (a) that the right to have one's cause heard **comprises** "the right to an appeal to competent national organs against acts of violating his fundamental rights as recognised and guaranteed by conventions, laws, regulations and customs in force." The vagueness here lies in the use of the term "an appeal to competent national organs" instead of a hearing by a "court or tribunal" used in clause (d), which clearly applies only to criminal trials, as do clauses (b) and (c) and article 7(2). The intention for the vagueness seems to be to avoid putting on a ratifying state an obligation to set up an enforcement procedure in civil causes, particularly those involving questions of constitutionality, which is staunchly rejected by the inherited constitutional tradition in those African countries that are governed by European principles and tradition (as opposed to British principles and tradition) in questions of constitutionality.

It seems therefore that article 1, together with article 7(1), hardly contemplates enforcement by a court or tribunal as the means of giving effect to the guaranteed rights in civil causes. A ratifying state would have discharged its obligations to give effect to the guaranteed rights in civil causes by enacting a law that declares or affirms the rights and establishes a machinery for securing them against the state but which falls short of being an enforcement procedure. That, after all, is all what the Charter itself does. The African Commission on Human Rights, which it establishes, is not an enforcement machinery at all, but only a fact-finding one. It is in the light of the machinery provided by the Charter for securing the guaranteed rights against a ratifying state that the nature or extent of the obligation cast on it by articles 1 and 7(1) in civil cases is to be determined. The Charter cannot have imposed upon a ratifying state an obligation to establish a machinery of human rights protection in civil cases that is more onerous than that established by itself. The most that can be said of the obligation put on a ratifying state by the two articles is that it requires the state to give effect to the guaranteed rights through a body similar in membership, functions, procedure and governing principles to the African Commission on Human Rights, but not anything higher than that.

The National Human Rights Commission established by Nigeria in 1995 is such a body. The Nigerian Commission is not a court by its membership, functions or process in all of which respects it resembles the African Commission. A National Human Rights Commission with similar status, functions and process, not a judicial tribunal with enforcement powers, is also the machinery established by Togo in 1987 to give effect to the Charter.

Article 26, quoted above, adds nothing to the obligation cast on a state party by articles 1 and 7(1) in civil cases. Guaranteeing the independence of the courts imports no obligation to make them the medium for enforcing the rights and freedoms. Conversely, the courts do not necessarily cease to be independent because they are not given jurisdiction to apply and enforce the rights and freedoms or because the jurisdiction is taken away from them. Even the latter part of the provision in article 26 stops short of enjoining a state party to establish or improve such institutions, it only requires it to "allow" their establishment and improvement. The clear meaning is that the state party shall not impede or forbid their establishment or improvement by individual and/ or private organisations. Most human rights organisations are in fact established, not by the state, but by private persons. A direct duty is, however, laid on a ratifying state under article 25 to "promote and ensure through teaching, education and publication" respect for the guaranteed rights and freedoms.

The states-parties' obligations under article 1, 7(1) and 26 have been made minimally burdensome because, as Edward Kannyo says, "the preponderance of arbitrary regimes within the OAU" created a need to design a "human rights system that would win the support of the majority of African states. It is difficult to read the African Charter without sensing the influence of authoritarian regimes that had to be accommodated."[15] A member of the African Commission on Human and Peoples' Rights has observed that "the Charter was a compromise between the few states that genuinely wanted to promote human rights and the many that were merely concerned with entrenching non-interference with what they considered to be matters of internal affairs or indeed the enlargement of exclusive state jurisdiction."[16]

---

[15] Edward Kannyo, "The OAU and Human Rights," in Yassim El-Ayouty and William Zartman, (eds.) *The OAU After Twenty Years* (1984), p. 155, at pp. 168-169.

[16] U.O. Umozurike, *The African Charter on Human and Peoples' Rights* (1997), p. 82.

He goes on to say that "efforts to promote the Charter are stultified or impeded" by the prevalence in the continent of so many authoritarian regimes who are inclined to view such efforts as confrontation or opposition, and that the personnel of the media in those countries, which are mostly, if not wholly, state-owned, "are under close surveillance and therefore hesitant to publish materials that might offend their employers."[17] The Charter would most certainly have failed to get the ratification of a majority of the member states required for it to enter into force (i.e. 26 members at that time), had it contained a provision obligating a state party to make the rights enforceable in civil cases through the process of a court of law.

It follows from all what is said above that, since articles 1, 7(1) and 26 do not obligate a ratifying state to make the rights enforceable in civil cases through the process of a court of law, a ratifying state is not in breach of its obligation under the Charter if, in a legislation giving effect to the guaranteed rights, or in any other legislation, the courts are not given or are deprived of jurisdiction to enforce them in civil matters.

With respect to criminal matters, however, the Charter seems to obligate a ratifying state to have them tried by a court or tribunal. That is the only way to give effect to the right, guaranteed by article 7(1)(d), "to be tried within a reasonable time by an impartial court or tribunal."

The decision of the Nigerian Court of Appeal that article 1 "enjoins all members to put up a suitable procedure for enforcement" is, with great respect, more questionable in regard to the economic, social and cultural rights guaranteed by the Charter. To begin with, the Charter imposes no obligation on a ratifying state to **provide** in actual practice, the benefits implied by these rights, which pre-supposes that the state has the resources needed for the purposes. The Charter has no such provision as is contained in the International Covenant on Economic, Social and Cultural Rights (1976) requiring a ratifying state to "take steps ... with a view to achieving **progressively** the full **realization** of the rights recognised in the present Covenant by all appropriate means" (art. 2(1) emphasis supplied). The comments of Robertson and Merrills on this provision are quite pertinent:

> It is quite clear, that this is what is known as a promotional convention,

---

[17] *ibid,* p. 72.

> that is to say it does not set out rights which the parties are required to implement immediately, but rather lists standards which they undertake to promote and which they pledge themselves to secure progressively, to the greatest extent possible, having regard to their resources. As already indicated, this difference in the obligation results from the very nature of the rights recognised in this Covenant. ... When it is recalled that the undertaking of the contracting parties in Article 2 of the Covenant is ... to take steps ... with a view to achieving progressively the full realisation of the rights recognised in the present Covenant, the promotional character of the instrument is unmistakable.[18]

There is thus a recognition that, with the best will in the world, a state may still not be able to provide the benefits and services implied by the rights, owing to lack of resources needed for the purpose.

As regards enforcement, economic, social and cultural rights are not amenable to judicial enforcement because of the nature of the subject-matter to which they relate and the terms in which the obligation in respect of them is cast on a ratifying state. With respect to health and medical care, the political nature of the obligation laid on a ratifying state is clear from the wording and context of the relevant provision. Article 16(1), which says that "every individual shall have the right to enjoy the best attainable state of physical and mental health" has no intelligible meaning which a court of law might enforce; it may well be meaningful as a political manifesto; indeed, it reads like one. Likewise, the duty put on ratifying states by article 16(2) to "take the necessary measures to protect the health of their people and to ensure that they receive medical attention when they are sick" is political, in part because it is owed to the people as a whole, not to an individual. Similarly unamenable to judicial enforcement is the duty laid on a ratifying state to promote and protect the "morals and traditional values recognised by the community" (art. 17(3)); to assist the family as the custodian of morals and traditional values (art. 18(2)); to "eliminate all forms of foreign economic exploitation particularly that practised by international monopolies so as to enable their peoples to fully benefit from the advantage derived from their national resources" (art. 21(5)); to ensure "individually or collectively, the exercise of the right to development" (art. 22(2)). The right of every individual to education (art. 17(1)) and to

---

[18]   A.H. Robertson and J.G. Merrills, *Human Rights in the World* (1992 edn), pp. 230 & 232.

"freely take part in the cultural life of his community" (art. 17(2)) partakes of the same non-justiciable nature.

Although it has become fashionable to speak of the individual as having a "right" to the social and economic benefits provided by the modern welfare state, the so-called right is not really a right in the same sense of the freedom of the individual to think, believe or disbelieve, speak, move about or act without undue coercion or restraint by the state or other persons; it is not a legal right but only a social, economic or cultural right, as it is rightly called. The duty cast on the state to provide the benefits implied by the rights is also a social or moral duty, not a legal one.

It is for reasons connected with the nature of the subject-matter that the Fundamental Objectives and Directive Principles of State Policy in Chapter II of the 1979/1999 Constitutions of Nigeria is made non-justiciable. And the European Social Charter too (adopted 1961 and entered into force in 1965). The nature of economic, social and cultural rights and the kind of protection appropriate to them had provoked the hottest debates in the course of the preparation and adoption of the European Social Charter, a debate that spanned over a period of more than seven years (1953-1961), involving representatives of governments, employers, employees, experts of various kinds and the I.L.O. The difficulty about the question is well stated by Dr A.H. Robertson, one of the foremost authorities on international protection of fundamental rights:

> The civil and political rights of the citizen can be enforced by a court of law: if a man is wrongfully imprisoned, he can apply for a writ of *habeas corpus*; if he is not given a fair trial, he can appeal to a superior court; and so on. With economic and social rights, however, it is different. The realization of the right to work depends on economic circumstances, and if the labour exchange is unable to find a man employment the writ of a court of law will be of no avail. A reasonable standard of living for everyone is an objective of social policy, but it depends much more on a flourishing export trade than on legislation. Consequently, the approach to the protection of economic and social rights had to be different from that of the European Convention dealing with civil and political rights...[19]

> The problem, he further explains, is that if the rights are treated merely

---

[19] A.H. Robertson, *Human Rights in Europe* (1963), pp. 140-141; reproduced in Robertson and Merrills, *Human Rights in the World* (1992 edn), p. 246.

as "objects of social policy," which is what they really are, "the Charter would have little value as an effective guarantee of economic and social standards. The solution adopted was to divide the Charter (i.e. the European Social Charter) into several distinct parts. In the first part are set out nineteen separate rights, the realisation of which the Contracting Parties accept as the aim of their policy; this permits general affirmation of a far-reaching character, as statements of policy without precise legal commitments."[20]

For purposes of illustration, three of the nineteen rights may be mentioned: "all workers have the right to safe and healthy working conditions;" "all workers have the right to a fair remuneration sufficient for a decent standard of living for themselves and their families;" "everyone has the right to benefit from any measures enabling him to enjoy the highest possible standard of health attainable." It can be seen that the provision in article 16(1) of the African Charter, quoted above, is an adaptation of the last-mentioned right. (The wording is taken verbatim from article 12(1) of the International Covenant.)

In Part II of the European Social Charter, each of the nineteen generalised rights in Part I is broken into various specific rights; the realization of which a state-party can meaningfully undertake to "ensure." For example, the right to "enjoy the highest possible standard of health attainable" in Part I is dealt with as follows in Part II: "With a view to ensuring the effective exercise of the right to protection of health, the Contracting Parties undertake, either directly or in cooperation with public or private organisations, to take appropriate measures designed *inter alia*: 1. to remove as far as possible the causes of ill-health; 2. to provide advisory and educational facilities for the promotion of health and the encouragement of individual responsibility in matters of health; 3. to prevent as far as possible epidemic, endemic and other diseases." (art. 11). But the specific rights in Part II are not thereby elevated into legal rights enforceable by a court of law. For their implementation, therefore, as Robertson explains, "the Commission and Court of Human Rights were not suitable for this purpose, since the rights to be guaranteed did not have the same legal character."[21] The machinery agreed and instituted consists of "an elaborate system of control based on the sending

---

20   *ibid*, at p. 145.
21   *ibid*, p. 146.

of reports by Governments on the way in which they are implementing the Charter and the examination of these reports by the various committees and organs of the Council of Europe."[22] (arts. 24-29). This is also the system of control instituted by the International Covenant on Economic, Social and Cultural Rights to ensure the implementation of the rights it guarantees (arts. 16-25). It certainly does not seem to make sense to speak of enforcement in relation to the right of everyone, under article II of the International Covenant, to "an adequate standard of living for himself and his family, including adequate food, clothing and housing," or "to be free from hunger."

Thus, even in Western Europe, developed as it is, social and economic rights are recognised as being by their nature, unamenable to enforcement by a court. It follows that their enforcement could not have been contemplated by the African Charter, either at the international or national levels.

The view of economic and social rights as not partaking of the nature of rights enforceable by a court of law finds ample support in the doctrine of the Political Question enunciated and developed by the U.S. Supreme Court in a long line of decisions. As Justice Felix Frankfurter of that court has said, "the explicit provision requiring one state to surrender to another a fugitive from justice[23] is 'merely declaratory of a moral duty' and is not, because of the subject-matter, enforceable in the courts. Likewise, the 'guarantee to every state' of 'a Republican form of Government'[24] must, because of the subject-matter, look elsewhere than to the courts for observance."[25]

The guarantee of a republican form of government is, by the nature of its subject-matter, non-justiciable, because it envisages the possible use of military force – an exclusively political action. The provision about the surrender of a fugitive offender, it has been held, implies no power in the demanding state or even in the national government to coerce the state of refuge to surrender the fugitive. In the absence of a power of coercion based in the Constitution, "the performance of this duty ... is left to depend on the fidelity

---

[22] *ibid*, p. 146.

[23] Art. iv, sec. 2, U.S. Constitution.

[24] Art. v, sec. 4.

[25] Frankfurter, "John Marshall and the Judicial Function", Harv. L. Rev. 69, pp. 317-327, citing *Kentucky v. Dennison*, 24 Harv. 66 (1861) and *Pacific Telephone and Teleg. Co. v. Oregon* 225 U.S. 118 (1912) for the first and second examples respectively; see also per Frankfurter J. in *Colegrove v. Miller* 307 U.S. 433, at p. 556.

of the state executive,"[26] which should be imbued with the sense of comity and of mutual support and cooperation so essential to the effective and orderly working of a federal system.

The characterisation of such questions as "political" is not because judicial involvement in them might have political repercussions. For every constitutional issue of importance has in a sense political overtones. "It is not a question whether the considerations are political, for nearly every consideration arising from the constitution can be so described."[27]

Finally, in so far as the economic, social and cultural rights guaranteed by the African Charter require a ratifying state to perform some act or to take some positive measures, like building hospitals or providing doctors and drugs, the duty is, under the rule in *Foster and Elain v. Neilson* noted below, owed to the other ratifying states as parties to the contract embodied in the treaty, and remains so even when the treaty is incorporated into domestic law by any of the methods considered below; accordingly, no individual can sue on it in a municipal court.

From what is said above, the African Charter is manifestly inadequate, for not laying sufficient obligation on a ratifying state, to provide effective domestic remedies for the redress of fundamental rights violations. It is a mark of its inadequacy that it has no provision, such as that in article 8 of the UN Universal Declaration, guaranteeing to everyone "the right to an effective remedy by the competent national tribunals for acts violating the fundamental rights granted him by the constitution or by law." The obligation cast on the state by this guarantee is set out in a fuller form in article 2(3) of the Covenant on Civil and Political Rights, as follows:

Each State Party to the present Covenant undertakes:

(a) To ensure that any person whose rights or freedoms as herein recognised are violated shall have an effective remedy, notwithstanding that the violation has been committed by persons acting in an official capacity;

---

[26] *Kentucky v. Dennison, ibid.,* at p. 109; on the Political Question doctrine generally, see B.O. Nwabueze, *Judicialism* (1977), pp. 20-43.

[27] Per Dixon J. in *Melbourne v. Commonwealth of Australia* (1947) C.L.R. 31, 32.

(b) To ensure that any person claiming such a remedy shall have his right thereto determined by competent judicial, administrative or legislative authorities, and to develop the possibilities of judicial remedy;

(c) To ensure that the competent authorities shall enforce such remedies when granted.

The European Convention on Human Rights and Fundamental Freedoms has an identical provision to that in article 2(3)(a) of the Covenant quoted above. These provisions are additional to the guarantee of "a fair and public hearing by an independent and impartial tribunal in the determination of (a person's) rights and obligations and of any criminal charge against him" (art. 10, Universal Declaration; art. 14 Covenant on Civil and Political Rights.)

The Machinery Provided in the Charter for Implementing and Securing the Rights Against a Ratifying State in International Law

Like the International Covenant on Civil and Political Rights, the African Charter has no provision for the **enforcement**, properly so-called, of the guaranteed rights by a court or other tribunal. The machinery provided for securing the rights against a ratifying state, which is again patterned on that under the International Covenant, is not at all comparable to a court for the following reasons.

First, the machinery provided for the purpose is only a Commission, called the African Commission on Human and Peoples' Rights. It consists of eleven members elected for a renewable term of six years by the Assembly of Heads of State and Government of the OAU from a list of persons nominated by the states parties to the Charter. The members need not necessarily be lawyers. The Charter only requires that they shall be persons of "the highest reputation, known for their high morality, integrity, impartiality and competence in matters of human and peoples' rights, particular consideration being given to persons having legal experience" (art. 31(1)).

In the second place, the function of the Commission is not, in its essential character, judicial; it is to "promote human and peoples' rights and ensure their protection in Africa." (art. 30). The promotional function, as spelt out more particularly in article 45(1), is (a) to "collect documents, undertake studies and researches on African problems in the field of human and peoples' rights, organise seminars, symposia and conferences, disseminate information, encourage national and local institutions concerned with human and peoples' rights" (b) to formulate and lay down principles and rules aimed at solving legal problems relating to human and peoples' rights and fundamental freedoms upon which African Governments may base their legislation; (c) cooperate with other African and International institutions concerned with promotion and protection of human and peoples' rights." These are clearly not judicial functions.

Article 45(3) requires the Commission to "interpret all provisions of the present Charter at the request of a State Party, an institution of the OAU or an African organisation recognised by the OAU." This imports simply the rendering of an advisory opinion, which is not a judicial function. The only function which may involve adjudication is that of ensuring "the protection of human and people's rights under conditions laid down by the present Charter." (art. 45(2)).

In the third place, the process of the Commission is not that of a court. The main thrust of the process is amicable settlement. While its process may be invoked by a state party as well as by individuals and organisations (arts. 47, 49, 55 and 56), the Commission does not give binding decision or judgment; it can only render "a report stating the facts and its findings," with or without "such recommendations as it deems useful" (arts 52 and 53). It is not required in its work to be governed or even guided by international law on human rights but only to "draw inspiration" from it (arts 60 and 61). Admittedly, a process involving only the finding of facts and the rendering of a report based on facts so found, with recommendations, does not necessarily preclude a body from being a court or a judicial tribunal, as the case of the Judicial Committee of the Privy Council in London shows. Yet the latter differs markedly from the African Commission. The report or recommendation of the Judicial Committee is "in everything but form the equivalent of a legal judgment," which disposes of the matter in controversy, and which binds the Sovereign to give effect to it by means of an implementing order-in-council.[28]

---

[28] *Ibralebbe v. the Queen* [1964] 2 W.L.R. 76.

The report or recommendation of the Commission on Human and Peoples' Rights is not a judgment, does not bind the Assembly of Heads of State and Government to accept or give effect to it, and does not dispose of a complaint in a manner binding on the parties. Thus, the relevant provisions of the Charter establish, not an enforcement machinery or process, but only a fact-finding one. The process is primarily at the instance of a state that has ratified the Charter. A state party, which considers that a violation of the provisions of the Charter has been committed by another state party, may either refer the matter directly to the Commission and notify the other state or draw the attention of that other state to it and notify the Secretary-General of the OAU and the Commission. The state complained against must then, within three months of the receipt of the notification or communication, furnish the enquiring state a written statement containing an explanation of the matter, with as much relevant information as possible on the law applicable, and the redress already given or course of action available. The two states will then try to settle the matter through bilateral negotiation or other peaceful procedure, but in default of an amicable settlement within three months of the complaint, either state may submit the matter to the Commission and notify the other state of such submission.

The Commission is not to deal with a matter referred or submitted to it unless and until it has satisfied itself that all local remedies, if any exists, have been exhausted, except where it is obvious to it that the process of accomplishing such local remedies would be unduly prolonged. In considering the complaint, the Commission may employ any appropriate method of investigation; it may take testimony from the Secretary-General of the OAU or any other person capable of enlightening it. The states-parties concerned may be represented before it, and submit written or oral representations.

Having carried out investigation into the matter, the Commission will try by all appropriate means to resolve it amicably on the basis of respect for human and peoples' rights. In default of amicable settlement, it shall, within a reasonable time, prepare a report stating the facts and its findings, and send it to the states concerned and to the Assembly of Heads of State and Government, accompanying its report to the latter with such recommendations as it deems useful.

Interestingly, as an exception to the principle that states, but not individuals or private organisations, are the only subjects of international law, individuals and private organisations are enabled, to a limited extent, to invoke the process of the African Commission on Human and Peoples' Rights, in regard to human and peoples' rights violation by a ratifying state. The relevant provisions are, however, far from clear. It is left to the members of the Commission to decide, by a simple majority of its members, which, if any, of the complaints or communications sent in by individuals or organisations other than states parties "should be considered by the Commission." (art. 55) Consideration by the Commission of complaints from individuals or organisations other than states parties is therefore not a right. This differs from the position under the European Convention where petition by private persons, non-governmental organisations or groups of individuals is allowed as of right but the Commission cannot entertain it unless its competence to do so is accepted by the state complained against (art. 26); under the African Charter, the Commission has a mandatory competence which is not dependent on its acceptance by the state complained against, but it has a discretion whether or not to entertain a private complaint. Secondly, recourse to the Commission by an individual or private organisation may be had only for complaints "relating to human and peoples' rights" (art. 56), but not for breaches of a state party's positive obligations under the Charter, which are not related to violations of the guaranteed rights. Thirdly, recourse is restricted by certain specified conditions one of which is that local remedies must first be exhausted, unless the process of doing so would be unduly prolonged.

The function of the Commission in respect of complaints from individuals and private organisations is not altogether clear, but it appears that the Commission can investigate, deliberate and report on them just as in the case of complaints by states.

Complaints by individuals, groups of individuals and NGOs have in practice proved to be the effective way of invoking the protective function of the Commission, as is borne out by the large number of such complaints; in contrast, only one complaint by a state-party, Libya, had been lodged with the Commission as at April 1995, and even that one complaint was declared inadmissible because the state complained against, U.S.A., is not a party to the Charter.

The effectiveness of human rights protection under the Charter is further limited by the provision making "all measures" taken by the Commission confidential "until such time as the Assembly of Heads of State and Government shall otherwise decide" (art. 59(1)); this is, however, without prejudice to the authorisation given to the chairman of the Commission to publish an annual report of its activities "after it has been considered by the Assembly" (art. 59(3)). Information contained in the Commission's annual report concerning complaints lodged with it, the names of the states complained against, a summary of the facts and of its recommendations is thus an exception to the requirement of confidentiality or non-disclosure except as otherwise specifically authorised by the Assembly. The confidentiality requirement undermines the Charter's effectiveness, since publicity is "a potent weapon against abuses of human rights," while information in the annual report published at an interval of one year does not meet the need for the public to be kept informed from time to time as the measures are taken.[29]

It is remarkable that the Assembly of Heads of State and Government is only required to consider the Commission's report, and that nothing is said on what action it is to take on it, whether it can or should, by resolution, accept or reject it. Presumably, it is precluded from doing more than just note the report, because of the principle of non-interference in the internal affairs of member states enshrined in article 111 of the OAU Charter.

The silence of the Charter on the role of the Assembly of Heads of State and Government is considered an impediment to the effectiveness of the system of protection instituted by the Charter. In cases of serious or massive human rights violation so found and reported on by the Commission, a resolution by the Assembly accepting the report and condemning the state concerned would, it has been said, serve as a deterrent to other states, since no country would want to be so disgraced and turned into a pariah state among the nations of the world.[30] This lack of explicit provision on the action the Assembly is to take on a report submitted to it by the Commission is in striking contrast to the role explicitly given by the European Convention

---

[29] See U.O. Umozurike, *The African Charter on Human and Peoples' Rights* (1997), pp. 78-79.

[30] J.A. Oni, *OAU and Human Rights: A Critical Review of the African Charter on Human and Peoples' Rights* - an unpublished Dissertation for a Masters Degree of the University of Lagos (1989), p. 52.

to the Committee of Ministers to which also the Commission's report has to be sent. Where, on the basis of the report (unless the matter has been referred to the Court on Human Rights by the Commission or a state-party) the Committee decides that a violation had been committed, then, it is empowered to call on the state concerned to take specified remedial measures within a prescribed time, failing which the Committee shall decide "what effect shall be given to its original decision and shall publish the Report." (art. 32). And by article 32(4) of the Convention, the states-parties "undertake to regard as binding on them any decision which the Committee of Ministers may take in application of the preceding paragraphs" of article 32.

A fact-finding Commission is useful, but it needs to be reinforced by a machinery with compulsory jurisdiction to interpret and enforce, by the rendering of binding decisions, the provisions of the Charter when efforts at amicable settlement fail. Such is the position in the European Convention on Human Rights under which both a European Commission of Human Rights and a European Court of Human Rights are established (arts 19-56),[31] although allowance is made for difference in governmental systems and constitutional traditions by making the jurisdiction of the Court compulsory only for states-parties who, by a declaration deposited with the Secretary-General of the Council of Europe, have accepted the Court's jurisdiction either unconditionally or upon condition of reciprocity on the part of several or certain other states-parties (art. 46). A proposal to include an enforcement machinery of this kind in the African Charter was rejected as premature by the OAU ministerial meeting that deliberated on the draft Charter at Banjul, Gambia, in 1982.[32]

Given thus the lack, at the regional level, of effective remedies, particularly an enforcement machinery, and the absence of an obligation on a ratifying state to establish one at the municipal level, the real significance of the guarantees enshrined in the Charter depends on the availability of effective domestic remedies in actual practice; this will be considered later. The absence of enforcement procedures at the international level has been rationalised on the unsatisfactory basis of African customs and traditions which are said to

---

[31] See A.H. Robertson (ed) *Human Rights in National and International Law* (1968); A.H. Robertson, *Human Rights in Europe* (1963), pp. 43-100.

[32] See O. Aluko, "The OAU and Human Rights" (1981) 71 *Round Table* 234, at p. 241, J.A. Oni, *op. cit.*

"emphasise conciliation rather than judicial settlement of disputes".[33] The relations of the individual to an alien state system brought to Africa by European colonialism cannot adequately be based on African custom and tradition; such would be a sheer contradiction in ideas. Besides, human rights protection "has been clearly internationalised and is not restricted to African procedure."[34] The point is not whether amicable settlement by traditional reconciliatory or diplomatic procedures conduces more to harmonious relations between disputants or is more likely to achieve faster results than enforcement by judicial process, but rather whether there is justification for the African Charter instituting the former procedure to the complete exclusion of the latter. In our view, both should be combined together with a view to a more effective implementation of the Charter.

Application of the Charter in Municipal Law
Nature of a Treaty: Its Force and Effect

A treaty between two or more sovereign states is a contract, and is exactly of the same nature as a contract between two or more individuals; they differ only in the respect that a treaty derives its binding force and effect from international law, and a contract between individuals, from municipal law. The basis of the binding force of a treaty as a contract is agreement and the recognition given to agreements between states in international law as a law-creating fact – *pacta sunt servanda*. Similarly, the basis of the binding force of a contract between individuals is agreement and the recognition given to agreements by municipal law as a law-creating fact. As a contract, a treaty binds only the states-parties to it, just as a contract between individuals binds only the individuals who are parties to it. Thus, a treaty, not being a statute, and not having the force and effect of a statute, does not bind those, whether individuals or other states, who are not parties to it. The important point which must be re-emphasised is that a treaty, **by its own inherent force as a treaty**, is binding and applicable ONLY in international law but NOT in municipal law.

---

[33] U.O. Umozurike, *op. cit.*, p. 909; but see his *The African Charter on Human and Peoples' Rights* (1997), pp. 92-93.
[34] U.O. Umozurike, *The African Charter on Human and Peoples' Rights* (1997), p. 93.

The nature of a treaty is firmly established by both academic opinion and judicial decisions with reference to an "act of state," an international treaty being the most typical example of an act of state.[35] An act of state, writes Sir William More, is a "matter between states, which, whether it be regulated by international law or not, and whether the acts in question are or are not in accord with international law, is not a subject of municipal jurisdiction."[36] And, said E.C.S. Wade, although "the Crown is bound to act in accordance with international law, no means exist in municipal law of enforcing the obligations." The only sanction, he says, is in international law.[37]

The classic judicial statement of the law on the point is that by Fletcher Moulton L.J. (later Lord Moulton) in *Salaman v. Secretary of State for India*,[38] a case involving an international agreement. "An act of State," he said, "is essentially an exercise of sovereign power, and hence cannot be challenged, controlled or interfered with by municipal Courts. **Its sanction is not that of law but that of sovereign power**." The stipulations in a treaty between two states, he continues, "**are entirely beyond the cognisance of municipal Courts, because they do not administer treaty obligations between independent states**." Only for the limited purpose of construing it to ascertain its true meaning or purport (but without otherwise applying or enforcing it) may a municipal court take cognisance of an international treaty.[39] Lord Justice Fletcher Moulton's statement of the law has been approved and applied by both the House of Lords and the Privy Council in a number of cases,[40] and was adopted *verbatim* in Halbury, **Laws of England.**[41]

Even when a treaty is incorporated into municipal law in any of the ways shortly to be noted, such obligations as are created by article 1 of the African Charter, being an obligation cast on a state in relation to other states to perform some act, remain still outside the competence of municipal courts. As Chief Justice John Marshall held concerning an obligation in a treaty incorporated

---

[35]   See Halsbury, *Laws of England*, Vol. 18, 4th edn (1977), para. 1413.
[36]   William More, *Acts of State in English Law* (1906).
[37]   E.C.S. Wade, "Act of State in English Law: Its Relations with International Law," *British Yearbook of International Law* (1934), p. 98 at p. 101.
[38]   [1906] 1 K.B. 603 at p. 639 - emphasis supplied.
[39]   See *Walker v. Baird* [1892] A.C. 491 at p. 497.
[40]   See, e.g. *Sobhuza II v. Miller* [1926], A.C. 518, 522-524.
[41]   *Op. cit.*, p. 1414.

into the domestic law of the United States by virtue of the country's Constitution:

> Our constitution declares a treaty to be the law of the land. It is, consequently, to be regarded in courts of justice as equivalent to an act of the legislature ... But when the terms of the stipulation import a contract, when either of the parties engages to perform a particular act, the treaty addresses itself to the political, not to the judicial department, and the legislature must execute the contract before it can become a rule for the Court.[42]

Accordingly, in such a situation where a treaty is incorporated into municipal law, a municipal court cannot enforce by judicial process the obligation laid on the legislature to enact legislation or to take any other measures to give effect to the stipulations of the treaty. As Max Sorensen puts it, relying on *Foster and Elain v. Neilson,* if "a provision in a treaty which is incorporated into municipal law is so worded that it addresses itself to the contracting states as subjects of international law and requires them to introduce laws and regulations to give it effect in municipal law, then the courts cannot make use of it in determining an individual's rights and obligations."[43]

The statement by the Nigerian Court of Appeal to the effect that "no Government will be allowed to contract out by local legislation its international obligation", expresses, indisputably, a well-recognised principle of international law; equally indisputably, it is not a principle of municipal law, since a treaty, **of its own**, has no force or effect in municipal law. As stated by the International Court of Justice in a series of cases, the principle is only applicable in "the relations between Powers who are contracting Parties to a treaty,"[44] certainly not in relations under the municipal law of the contracting states so as to enable a municipal court to enforce against its own state, the principle not to legislate itself out of its treaty obligations. All what is meant by the principle is that, **as against a state-party to a treaty in its relations to another state-party under international law,** the state cannot escape from its treaty obligations by pleading a contrary provision in its existing municipal

---

[42] *Foster and Elain v. Neilson* (1892) 2 Pet. 253 at p. 314.

[43] Max Sorensen, "Obligations of a State-Party to a Treaty as regards its Municipal Law," in A.H. Robertson (ed), *Human Rights in National and International Law* (1968), p. 24.

[44] P.C.I.J. Series B. No. 10, pp. 20-21 (Exchange of Greek and Turkish populations); P.C.I.J. Series B. No. 17, p. 32 (The Greco-Bulgarian Communities); P.C.I.J. Series A/B No. 44, p. 24 (Treatment of Polish Nationals in the Danzing territory).

law or by adopting a new legislation inconsistent with those obligations. The state is perfectly competent and at liberty to enact laws inconsistent with its treaty obligations, but this is without prejudice to any remedies available against it in international law at the instance of the other state-party to the treaty.

Put differently, subject to limitations, if any, in the national constitution, a state does not, by entering into a treaty, lose any part of its sovereign power over its own domestic affairs, in particular, its power to make law, even when such law is inconsistent with or derogates from the treaty, but this is without prejudice to any remedies available in international law to the other state-party (or parties) to the treaty for any violation or breach of its terms resulting from the inconsistent municipal legislation; as against other state-parties to a treaty, a state cannot plead its own domestic law to escape from the consequences of such violation or breach in international law.[45] But municipal law recognises nothing like the inherent superiority of the provisions of a treaty or of the rules of customary international law over those of municipal law.[46] Such a view would be subversive of the concept of the sovereignty of each state, which is a pre-supposition of international law itself.

When, therefore, the Nigerian Court of Appeal held that a state will not be allowed by the municipal courts to legislate itself out of its treaty obligations, and when it then proceeded on the basis of that to hold the ouster provisions in Decrees of the FMG ineffective to free Nigeria **in municipal law** from its supposed obligation under the African Charter to establish a machinery for the enforcement of the rights and freedoms guaranteed by that Charter, its decision clearly runs contrary to the nature and effect of a treaty, as firmly established by decisions of the International Court of Justice, the Supreme Court of the United States, the House of Lords, the Privy Council and the Court of Appeal (England). I say supposed obligation, because, as shown earlier, no such obligation as is affirmed by the Nigerian Court of Appeal is in fact laid on a ratifying state, including Nigeria, by the African Charter.

---

[45] See A.H. Robertson (ed), *Human Rights in National and International Law* (1968), p. 12.
[46] Ignaz Seidi-Hohenveldern, "Transformation or Adoption of International Law into Municipal Law" (1963) 12 Inter and Comp. L.Q. 88 at p. 90.

Methods by Which a Treaty May Be Made Applicable in Municipal Law

As earlier stated, a treaty, by its own inherent force, is applicable **only** in international law. However, a treaty may become applicable in the municipal law of a state in either of two main ways, viz: (a) by direct incorporation into municipal law by an express provision to that effect in the constitution of the state; and (b) by adoption or transformation by statute enacted by the legislature of the state to give effect to it in its municipal law.

The first method is exemplified by the Constitution of the United States, art. III sec.2 of which provides that "the judicial power shall extend to all cases in law and equity, arising under the Constitution and the laws of the United States and treaties made, or which shall be made, under their authority." As further examples, art. 5(4) of the Constitution of Bulgaria 1991 provides that "any international instruments which have been ratified by the constitutionally established procedure, promulgated and come into force with respect to the Republic of Bulgaria, shall be considered part of the domestic legislation of the country." A provision in the Bill of Basic Rights and Freedoms of the Czech and Slovak Federal Republic, adopted on 9 January, 1991 as part of the country's Constitution, declares that "international agreements on human rights and basic freedoms, ratified and promulgated by the Czech and Slovak Federal Republic are generally binding within its territory" (art. 2). Treaties are also incorporated into domestic law by the constitutions of 13 African countries: Egypt (1964), Congo (Leopoldville) (1964), Togo (1963), Cote d'Ivoire (1960), Gabon (1961), Chad (1962), Central African Republic (1959), Burkina Faso (1960), Senegal (1963), Mauritania (1961), Niger (1960), Congo (Brazzaville) (1963), and Somalia (1960). The provision in all 13 countries is identical with each other and with that in the 1958 Constitution of France from where, apparently, it is copied into the constitutions of the 13 African countries.

In the absence of direct incorporation by the express provision of the constitution, as is the case in Britain (which has no written constitution anyway) and in the countries of former British Africa, a treaty is not applicable in domestic law unless it is adopted or transformed into it by statute enacted by the legislature of the state. The principle is embodied in the Constitution of

Nigeria 1979/1999 section 12 of which provides that "no treaty between the Federation and any other country shall have the force of law except to the extent to which any such treaty has been enacted."

Without direct incorporation by the constitution, the question, frequently agitated, is whether the application of a treaty in domestic law through the intermediary of the legislative organ of the state is to be brought about by way of the adoption of the treaty *qua* treaty into domestic law, just as in the case of direct incorporation by the constitution, or by way of transformation, with the consequence that its provisions lose their character as treaty stipulations and become transformed into domestic statutory or legislative provisions. The method to be used depends on whether the treaty itself makes it mandatory on a ratifying state to use the adoption method rather than transformation. If the adoption method is not made obligatory by the treaty, then, either method is open to a ratifying state, and would seem to be equally acceptable, so long as effect is adequately given to the treaty stipulations by the transformation method. Thus, "there is freedom of choice between the various methods. States which transform treaties into internal laws worded differently from the treaties are fulfilling their international obligations just as much as those which incorporate the text of the treaty into their municipal law."[47] In any case, unlike transformation, the incorporation or adoption method is not an "obligation which normally derives from international law."[48] It is unnecessary to examine here the differences between the two methods, although "the general results of both ... appear identical."[49]

The African Charter of Human and Peoples' Rights does not appear to make it obligatory on a ratifying state to use the adoption method. Certainly, giving effect to the guaranteed rights by legislative or other measures does not obligate a ratifying state to adopt the Charter, in its character as a treaty, into domestic law, with all its provisions precisely as they are. Nor does the obligation to report every two years on the legislative or other measures taken with a view to giving effect to the guaranteed rights (art. 62) imply an obligation to adopt the method of incorporation rather than transformation. Whilst adoption

---

[47]   Max Sorensen, *op. cit.*, p. 18.
[48]   Max Sorensen, *op. cit.*, p. 20.
[49]   See Ignaz Seidl-Hohenveldern, "Transformation or Adoption of International Law into Municipal Law" (1963) 12 Inter. and Comp. L.Q. 88 at p. 115.

of the Charter into domestic law in the totality of its provisions is a permissible approach, what article 1 seems to require of a ratifying state is to enact legislation to give effect to the substance, the tenor and the spirit of the provisions of the Charter, using its own formulation or wording, and omitting all such stipulations as are irrelevant or inapplicable in the domestic context, e.g. the provisions relating to the constitution of the African Commission on Human Rights, nomination and election of its members, ratification of the Charter, the submission of report every two years by a ratifying state, etc.

On the other hand, the European Convention on Human Rights is said to require implementation by the method of adoption.[50] The argument in support of this view of the Convention is predicated mainly on its article 1; whereas article 1 of the African Charter only requires states–parties to "adopt legislative or other measures to give effect" to "the rights, duties and freedoms enshrined in this Charter," article 1 of the European Convention provides that "the High Contracting Parties shall secure to everyone within their jurisdiction, the rights and freedoms defined in SECTION 1 of this Convention." SECTION 1 consists of 17 articles in which the rights and freedoms are set out and defined. There is certainly a significant difference between the duty to adopt legislative or other measures to give effect to the guaranteed rights and the duty to secure them to everyone. The duty to secure requires that the rights and freedoms to be secured shall be incorporated in municipal law in the precise terms in which they are set out and defined in the 17 articles of the Convention. The argument seems persuasive enough; in fact, however, six of the states-parties gave effect to it by the transformation method without objection from the others.

The method followed by Nigeria in giving effect in its municipal law to the African Charter on Human and Peoples' Rights may perhaps be described as that of adoption. By the African Charter on Human and People's Rights (Ratification and Enforcement) Act 1983, cap. 10 Laws of the Federation 1990 edition, it is provided that "the provisions of the African Charter on Human and Peoples' Rights which are set out in the Schedule to this Act shall, subject as thereunder provided, have force of law in Nigeria and shall be

---

[50]   Max Sorensen, *op. cit.*, pp. 18-22.

given full recognition and effect and be applied by all authorities and persons exercising legislative, executive or judicial powers in Nigeria."

Ranking of the Charter on Incorporation into Municipal Law

It may be noted that the question to be considered under this head does not arise where the method of transformation is used, since when a treaty is transformed, its stipulations lose their character as treaty stipulations and become transformed into ordinary statutory or legislative provisions. The transforming statute is entirely at par with other statutes enacted by the same legislature.

In the case of incorporation or adoption, the ranking of the treaty among other municipal laws depends on what provisions are contained in that behalf in the national constitution. A constitution which incorporates treaties directly into municipal law may provide that treaties shall rank at par with ordinary laws, or it may rank them above ordinary laws, as do the constitutions of Bulgaria (1991), the Czech and Slovak Republic (1991), France (1958) and the 13 African countries mentioned above. By the provision in France and the 13 African countries, "treaties or international agreements duly ratified or approved shall have, upon their publication, an authority superior to that of the laws, subject in each case to their application by the other party." In the U.S., treaties are, by the Constitution, ranked with federal laws, but above the constitutions and laws of the states. Exceptionally, the constitution may rank treaties with itself, as in Austria in cases where a treaty is specially approved by a two-thirds majority of members of parliament. Where, however, a constitution, which incorporates treaties directly into domestic law, is silent on their status *vis-a-vis* the ordinary laws, the rule is that they rank at par with the latter and may, in their application as part of domestic law, be modified or abrogated by later domestic enactment, without prejudice of course to their continued application in international law. The rule is stated thus by Professor Ignaz Seidl-Hohenveldern, a leading authority on the subject: "treaties ranking as ordinary or constitutional laws may be set aside (as far as the municipal sphere is concerned) by subsequent laws of equal rank."[51] A treaty adopted or incorporated into domestic law by statute cannot rank above the adopting

---

[51]   Ignaz Seidl-Hohenveldern, *op. at.*, at pp. 111-112.

or incorporating legislation. That would be a manifest illogicality and contradiction.

The decision of the Nigerian Court of Appeal in the case referred to earlier runs totally contrary to these principles which are implemented in the constitutions of many countries and accepted by all the leading authorities on the subject, and which are firmly anchored in reason and logic. The *ratio decidendi* is stated as follows in the lead judgment delivered on behalf of the Court of Appeal by Musdapher J.C.A.:

> The provisions of the Charter are in a class of their own and do not fall within the classification of the hierarchy of laws in Nigeria in order of superiority as enunciated in *Labiyi v. Anretiola*,[52] ... It seems to me that the learned trial Judge acted erroneously when he held that the African Charter contained in Cap.10 of the Laws of the Federation of Nigeria 1990 is inferior to Decrees of the Federal Military Government. It is common place, that no Government will be **allowed** to contract out by local legislation, its international obligations. It is my view, that notwithstanding the fact that Cap.10 was promulgated by the National Assembly in 1983, it is a legislation with international flavour and the ouster clauses contained in Decree No.107 of the 1993 or No.12 of 1994 cannot affect its operation in Nigeria ... While the Decrees of the Federal Military Government may override other municipal laws, they cannot oust the jurisdiction of the Court whenever properly called upon to do so in relation to matter pertaining to human rights under the African Charter. They are protected by the International Law and the Federal Military Government is not legally permitted to legislate out of its obligations (emphasis supplied).

In a separate concurring judgment, Pats-Acholonu J.C.A. said that "by not merely adopting the African Charter but enacting it into our organic law, the tenor and intendment of the preamble and section seem to vest that Act with a greater vigour and strength than mere decree for it has been elevated to a high pedestal." Also concurring, Mohammed J.C.A., the other member of the Court, said that "ordinarily, a state, which is a party to a treaty, will not be **permitted** to legislate locally out of its obligations" (emphasis supplied). The context suggests that it is the municipal courts which will not "allow" or "permit" a state-party, by local legislation, to contract out of its treaty obligations.

The untenability of the decision and the reasoning behind it seem so palpable. First, the implementing statute was enacted by the National Assembly by virtue

---

[52]   (1992) 8 NWLR (Part 258) 139.

of its power under the Constitution to make laws for the purpose of implementing treaties (s.4). The same Constitution that empowers the National Assembly to implement treaties by means of legislation also declares itself the "supreme" law of the land, and that "any other law" inconsistent with its provisions "shall to the extent of the inconsistency by void" (s.1). Section 1 does not except from the coercive sanction laws enacted by the National Assembly for the purpose of implementing treaties. All laws in Nigeria inconsistent with the Constitution, including laws enacted for the purpose of implementing treaties, are void to the extent of their inconsistency with the Constitution. (Their voidness in municipal law does not, as earlier explained, absolve the state from its treaty obligation in international law, as a state cannot plead municipal law in order to escape from its international obligations, but that in no way affects the validity of the legislation in domestic law). It cannot be suggested that all laws enacted to give effect to treaties stand on "a higher pedestral" above all other laws.

But the effect of the Nigerian Court of Appeal's decision would be to elevate above the Constitution, the Charter and the statute that incorporated it into Nigeria's municipal law. For, if, as affirmed in a series of decisions of the Supreme Court, Decrees of the FMG can effectively oust the jurisdiction vested in the courts by the Constitution to enforce its supremacy and, in particular, to enforce the fundamental rights it guarantees, but cannot oust their jurisdiction to enforce the rights guaranteed by the African Charter, then, the Charter and the statute incorporating it into Nigerian municipal law would have been elevated to a status above the Constitution. That would seem to me a monstrous result to inflict upon a country by judicial decision. With the greatest respect, the decision seems like judicial activism run riot.

It is also settled beyond dispute by a series of decisions of the supreme court that Decrees of the Federal Military Government are superior to the Constitution, and override it to the extent of any inconsistency between them. If a Decree is superior to and overrides the Constitution in the event of inconsistency between them, and the Constitution is superior to and overrides all other laws, then, Pats-Acholonu J.C.A. cannot, with respect, have been more inconsistent than to say, as he did, that the Charter and the statute incorporating it into Nigeria's municipal law have "a greater vigour and strength than mere decree," and is "elevated to a high pedestal." The contradiction is further compounded by the learned Judge's statement that the incorporating statute is clothed with "sacrosanctity" and "inviolability" "except where a decree specifically repeals it." If the statute (cap 10) is superior to, or has "greater vigour and strength" than a Decree, then, surely, it cannot be repealed by a Decree.

In the second place, the learned Justices of the Court of Appeal seem not to have addressed their minds to the implications of their decision in the context of an absolute military government invested with the entire sovereign power of the Nigerian state, and whose supremacy is the *grundnorm* of the Nigerian legal order during the duration of military rule. If the Charter, as incorporated into Nigeria's municipal law by an act of the national assembly, is superior to Decrees of the FMG, or, in the words of Pats-Acholonu J.C.A., possesses "a greater vigour and strength," and is "elevated to a higher pedestal," than Decrees of the FMG, then, it follows that the Charter and the incorporating statute are outside the sovereign power of the Nigerian state, and that no authority in the country, not excepting the people as a body, can abrogate or legislate inconsistently with it. The monstrosity of such a view affronts all reason. The idea of an "inviolable" and "sacrosanct" law (these terms are used in the judgment of Pats-Acholonu J.C.A.), a law unalterable by the sovereign power in a state, is altogether subversive of the concept of sovereignty. The state would have ceased to have complete mastery over its affairs.

In the third place, the decision of the Nigerian Court of Appeal in this case can only be rationalised and harmonised with the hierarchical order of norms in the Nigerian legal order, and with the supremacy of the FMG, which is the *grundnorm* of the legal order, if the Charter and the implementing statute are treated as an abdication, a surrender or cession, of part of Nigeria's sovereignty. This may probably be what Musdapher J.C.A. had in mind when he said:

> In England, where there is no written Constitution and the Parliament is supreme, it could legislate on any issue. But the sovereignty is now somewhat **limited** through the impact of European Community Act of 1972. Although the British Parliament passed the E.C. Law, and can in theory, repeal it, but there are constraints and limitations and thus the Parliament in Britain is no longer supreme. **The Parliamentary supremacy has been surrendered, by implication, by the signing of the Union Law** (emphasis supplied).

It is not intended to consider here the concept of the surrender or abdication of sovereignty in the strict and proper sense in which it is understood in constitutional law,[53] (the term is sometimes used in a loose sense in international law,[54]) but it is certainly inapplicable here, because, among other reasons, the 1979/1999 Nigerian Constitution could not have contemplated that the power it gives the national assembly to make laws for the purpose of implementing treaties would enable it to abdicate or surrender the whole or part of the country's sovereignty. Nor, in enacting the implementing statute, did the national assembly intend it as a surrender of any part of Nigeria's sovereignty.

Importance of the Availability of Domestic Remedies for Violations of the Rights and Freedoms Guaranteed by the Charter When It Is Applicable in Municipal Law

The role of the African Charter on Human and Peoples' Rights is determined more essentially by the availability of domestic remedies for violations of the guaranteed rights and freedoms when the Charter is applicable in municipal law. In this respect, the Charter is distinctly inferior to the European Convention on Human Rights, which not only obligates the states-parties to "secure to **everyone** within their jurisdiction the rights and freedoms" it guarantees (art. 1), but also provides that "everyone whose rights and freedoms as set forth in this Convention are violated shall have an effective remedy before a national authority notwithstanding that the violation has been committed by persons acting in an official capacity" (art. 13).

Once the Convention becomes applicable in municipal law by whatever method, article 1 gives to "everyone," as against a state-party, the right to have secured to him the guaranteed rights and freedoms. The duty, it is argued, is not in the nature of an obligation to perform some act which, under the rule in *Foster and Elain v. Neilson,* is owed by a state-party only to other states-parties even when a treaty has become applicable in municipal law; rather, it is one which, in the context of the Convention and the treaties

---

[53]   As to which, see A.V. Dicey, *England's Case Against Home Rule* (1886), p. 244; also his *Law of the Constitution,* 10th edition, pp. 68-69; William Anson, *Law and Custom of the Constitution,* 5th edition, p. 8; B.O. Nwabueze, *Constitutionalism* (1973), pp. 196-202.

[54]   See Lauterpacht, *International Law and Human Rights.*

establishing the European Community, is owed also to individuals. While the controversy on this point remains still unresolved, article 13 of the Convention admits of no dispute or doubt; it unequivocally confers on everyone whose guaranteed right is violated, a right to an effective remedy before a national authority.

The failure of the African Charter to guarantee a similar right, with a correlative obligation on the state to secure it, means that domestic remedies for the redress of violations are a matter entirely for a ratifying state and the national constitution, except in criminal cases where, under article 7(1)(d), the individual is guaranteed the right to be "tried within a reasonable time by an impartial court or tribunal." Thus, the value of the Charter as a guarantee of fundamental rights is made to depend on the character of the governmental system and the constitutional tradition prevailing in the various African states.

In the socialist states (or former socialist states) in Africa, where the control of governmental acts by the courts to ensure their conformance with the constitution is unknown and where "socialist legality" is the governing principle, the "guarantees" of the Charter have little or no effect. Eleven African countries have been proclaimed socialist states in their constitutions, and have existed and functioned as such for varying periods of time, viz Algeria (1963 and 1976 Constitutions), Angola (1975), Benin (1979), Congo (Brazzaville) (1979), Egypt (1964 and 1980), Ethiopia (1987), Libya (1977), Madagascar (1975), Mozambique (1975), Somalia (1979) and Tanzania (1984).

Then there are 16 other countries in which, based on tradition inherited from European countries, mainly France, Switzerland and the Netherlands, the notions of constitutionality and of a constitutional Bill of Rights enforceable at the instance of an aggrieved individual by courts of law established and invested with jurisdiction in that behalf by the constitution, are unrecognised — Cote d'Ivoire (1960), Central African Republic (1959), Mauritania (1961), Madagascar (1959), Mali (1960), Niger (1961), Guinea (1958), Burkina Faso (1961), Comoros (1978), Libya (1951), Burundi (1962), Ethiopia (1955), Cape Verde (1975), Guinea Bissau (1975), Sao Tome and Principe (1975) and Seychelles (1985).

However, the two notions mentioned above are practised, maintained and form the cornerstone of the constitutional system in the 15 countries of former British Africa (Botswana, The Gambia, Ghana, Kenya, Lesotho, Malawi, Mauritius, Nigeria, Sierra Leone, Seychelles (until 1985), Sudan, Swaziland, Uganda, Zambia and Zimbabwe) as well as in 12 other countries outside former British Africa (Liberia 1847, Congo (Leopoldville) 1964, Rwanda 1962, Togo 1963, Benin 1964, Gabon 1961, Chad 1962, Cameroon 1961, Senegal 1963, Congo (Brazzaville) 1963, Morocco 1961 and Somalia 1960). As the supreme court of Nigeria has held, with the incorporation of the Charter into the country's municipal law by the African Charter on Human and Peoples' Rights (Ratification and Enforcement) Act 1983, the rights and freedoms guaranteed by the Charter "are enforceable by the several High Courts depending on the circumstances of each case and in accordance with the rules, practice and procedure of each court"[55] subject of course to the limitations noted earlier in this chapter.

It is something of an irony that the Charter has little or no effect in countries where its application would have made a desirable impact as an instrument for change in the prevailing system, but is lamentably prevented from playing that role because it does not, save in criminal cases, guarantee to the individual the right to "an effective remedy before a national authority" in terms of article 13 of the European Convention on Human Rights, with a correlative obligation on a ratifying state to secure the right. The other side of the irony is that the Charter is able to operate as a full-blown Bill of Rights backed by effective enforcement machinery only in countries where the need for it is far less, because the field of fundamental rights protection is more or less adequately covered already by an existing justiciable Bill of Rights enshrined in the national constitution.

The consequences of this irony are reflected in what Justice Pats-Acholonu of the Nigerian Court of Appeal said in the Nigerian case of *Gen. Sani Abacha and others v. Chief Gani Fawehinmi,*[56]

"The Nigerian government," he said,

> could have left the matter there as adequate provision has been made for remedy where there has been violation of the provision of the fundamental rights of a citizen. There would have been no need to re-enact the convention

---

[55]   *Ogugu v. State* (1994) 9 NWLR (Part 366) 1 at p. 27.
[56]   Suit No. CA/L/141/96; judgment delivered on 12/12/96.

to give it further force. The impression seemed to be given is that ... the government sends a message across that either the contents of Chap. 4 (i.e. the chapter of the Constitution containing the Bill of Rights) are not adequate enough or that Cap. 10 (i.e. the implementing statute) is an alternative remedy ... The government could have avoided being irretrievably immersed into the nuances of this Charter by not incorporating it into the law of the land.

Yet the incorporation of the Charter into the municipal law of this latter group of countries, especially those in former British Africa, is not without some value. It may be useful in filling any gap or making good any shortcoming in the amplitude of the rights guaranteed in the Bills of Rights in the national constitutions.

CHAPTER 5

Alleged Irreconcilability of Democracy with Human Rights

Introduction

In his oft-quoted remarks about the connection between liberty and democratic rule, Professor Sir Isaiah Berlin O.M. has said that they are "two profoundly divergent and irreconcilable attitudes to the ends of life", and that "there is no necessary connection" between them, describing the connection as "a good deal more tenuous than it seemed to many advocates of both."[1]

The issue raised by Isaiah Berlin's remarks is whether democracy, defined as rule by the people for the people, is incompatible with liberty and constitutional limitation for its protection; in other words, whether constitutional democracy is not really a self-contradictory concept. The issue may be examined from three perspectives, viz: (i) the illimitability of the sovereignty of the people; (ii) limitations inherent in representative democracy; and (iii) social democracy (or rule for the people) as involving inherent derogation from liberty.

Illimitability of the Sovereignty of the People

In concession, Isaiah Berlin is right but only in so far as democratic rule is taken as resting on the sovereignty of the people. A sovereign people cannot be subject to any legal limitation on its sovereign power beyond its capacity to overcome; it cannot be subject to a power outside of or above itself. That would be a palpable contradiction in terms. To put it differently, a people as an independent political community which is subject to a power outside of

---

[1] *Four Essays on Liberty* (1969) pp. 139-140

or above itself is not a sovereign but a subject people – a dependency. In his influential book, *Constitutionalism and the Changing World* (1939), Professor Charles McIlwain has affirmed that "sovereign power as distinct from any other power is the highest legal power in the state, **itself subject to no law**" adding that "the power of the people can have no limit"[2] (emphasis supplied). It is in this sense that sovereignty is said to be unlimited and illimitable.

A constitution, as a device for limiting power, may be notionally supreme, but it cannot, logically or in point of actual physical power relations, be superior to or above the people who make it and bestow on it the force of law. By the famous definition of it by Thomas Paine in his *Rights of Man* (1789), which is generally acknowledged as valid, "a constitution is not an act of government but of a people constituting a government." If a constitution is the source from which government derives its existence and power, it cannot, logically, be an act of the government; government cannot create itself. As the act by which a frame of government is constituted for a people, a constitution has to be an original act of the people.

The notion of the people as a constituent power and law-maker, with authority not only to make a constitution but, what is more important, to bestow force of law on it, is only an integral part of the wider concept of the people as the repository of the totality of a country's sovereignty, constituent power being the crowning point of sovereignty. Therefore, it would be a logical absurdity that a constitution should be superior to or above the people that created it.

Ever since the U.S. Constitution of 1787, the people are now generally accepted as the repository of a country's sovereignty, not just as a mere matter of political theory. "We the people ... do ordain and establish this Constitution for the United States of America" — the opening words of the U.S. Constitution of 1787 – writes David Mathews, "does not merely echo a revolutionary sentiment, it reflects a common practice." In the words of a leading authority, Edward Corwin, "the U.S. Constitution obtains its entire force and efficacy, not from the fact that it was ratified by a pre-existent political community or communities – for it was not – but from the fact that it was established by the people to be governed by it."

---

[2] *op. cit.*, pp. 29 and 32

The great French philosopher and jurist, Alexis de Tocqueville, in his great classic, *Democracy in America* (1835), has, in characteristically trenchant language, described for us the emergence of the people as a constituent power and law-maker, not as a matter of political theory but in the real practice of government. "The doctrine of the sovereignty of the people," he wrote, "took possession of the state. Every class was enlisted in its cause; battles were fought and victories obtained for it; it became the law of laws ... The people reign in the American political world as the Deity does in the universe. They are the cause and the aim of all things; everything comes from them, and everything is absorbed in them."

The characterisation of the people as "the law of laws" underlines the point about the illimitability of the sovereign power inherent in a sovereign people. The logic that a thing, like the constitution of a country, cannot be superior to or above its maker or creator also means, by the same logic, that the people, as the repository of a country's sovereignty and the maker of its constitution, is not only superior to and above the constitution, but also has the power to unmake or change it. If a constitution is the creation of the people, not by virtue of any law enabling it in that behalf, but by virtue of the sovereign power inherent in it, then, it must have power, equally unlimited and illimitable by law, to unmake or undo what it created (i.e. the constitution); the power derives from, and can be predicated on, the same source, namely sovereignty inherent in the people as an independent political community. That is what is usually referred to as the people's right of revolution, its right to **jettison** or do away with the constitution — to be distinguished from a rebellion or *coup d'etat* by a minority of the people or a minority group, like the military.

It is generally agreed among both political theorists and constitutional lawyers that in a situation of tyranny, arbitrariness, abuse of power, violation or denial of its right to govern itself, etc., a people can, in exercise of its sovereign power, overturn the constitution — law does not come into the matter, since the power being so exercised, like the power to make a constitution in the first place, lies outside the realm of law in the narrow positivist sense. Thus, Professor Sir Karl Popper in his great work, *The Open Society and its Enemies* (1966), affirms the right of a people to jettison the constitution "under a tyranny which makes reforms without violence impossible." "The working of democracy," he continues, "rests largely upon the understanding that a government which attempts to misuse its powers and to establish itself as a tyranny (or which tolerates the establishment of tyranny by anybody else) outlaws itself, and the citizens have not only the right but also a duty to consider the action of such a government as a crime, and its members as a dangerous gang of criminals."

A people's revolution need not be directed against the government. Changes in the conditions of society or in its fundamental conceptions may give rise to a popular demand for a change in the constitution, which may be shared by the rulers and the ruled alike. It is the essential purpose for inserting an amending procedure in the constitution to prevent such a demand from being canalised into revolutionary action. But the constitution may have been made unalterable or the procedure for amending it cannot yield to the sort of change desired. In that event, recourse may be had to the residuary constituent power inherent in the community in order to overturn the existing constitution. A change brought about in this manner is a revolution because it is not effected in accordance with the constitution but it is not a rebellion or a *coup d'etat* since the hypothesis is that it is concurred in by both the rulers and the governed or a majority of them. It does not seek to subvert the authority of the government, but rather to create a new order better suited to the present needs and circumstances of the society.

Limitations Inherent in Representative Democracy

Direct democracy, as practised in the ancient Greek city-states, is impracticable today and is scarcely practised anywhere in the modern world (referenda on specific aspects of the constitution and other issues apart), largely because of the great size of the modern state spread over a large territory and embracing millions of people who cannot be assembled together in one place to take part in the discussion and deciding of the common affairs of the community. This has called forth a modified form of democratic rule known as representative democracy whereby the people, instead of ruling directly by themselves as a body, delegate powers of government to agents chosen and removable by them by means of popular elections in a free and fair competition sponsored for the most part by different political parties.

Thus, far from being irreconcilable with limited government, representative democracy is itself a device for limiting power. It necessarily implies, in its essential elements and purpose, the limitation of government. To begin with, competition for popular support amongst contenders for political office sponsored by different political parties has an intrinsic limiting effect. It subjects the contenders to institutionalised and regularised processes, procedures and rules of the political game accepted and respected as binding by all players: elections at periodic intervals of time (say four or five years), multi-partyism, freedom to form or join political parties or other political associations, public discussions in the news media, public assembly and procession, etc.

By subjecting all political groups to competition, representative democracy deprives them of the ability to dictate *ex ante* or to reverse *ex post* outcomes of the political process adverse to their interests, and so leaves uncertain and indeterminate the group whose interests will triumph in the struggle for power. This, as Adam Przeworski pertinently observes, is what constitutes the decisive element of democratic rule, and which distinguishes it from an authoritarian one. The latter, he says, "has an effective capacity to prevent political outcomes that would be highly adverse to its interests." On the other hand in a democracy, competition ensures that "no one can be certain that their interests will ultimately triumph ... One's current position within the political system does not guarantee future victories: incumbency may be an advantage, but incumbents do lose. In a democracy, all forces must struggle repeatedly for the realisation of their interests since no one is protected by virtue of their position."[3] He accordingly defines democratisation as "a process of subjecting all interests to competition, of institutionalising uncertainty," of devolving power from "a group of people to a set of rules" (at p. 63), with all the limitations which that implies.

In the second place, the principle of the accountability and the responsibility of rulers to the people, which underlies representative democracy, necessarily implies limitation on power. This principle, whose object is to make government responsive to the needs and aspirations of the people, is reinforced and sanctioned by the removability of a government for failure to live up to its responsibilities to the people. (See chap. 2 for an examination of the concept

---

[3]   "Democracy as a contingent outcome of conflict," in Elster and Slagstad (eds), *Constitutionalism and Democracy* (1993), p. 62.

of accountability) And, in the view of Charles McIlwain, constitutionalism consists, in its essential elements, of "the ancient legal restraint of a guarantee of civil liberties enforceable by an independent court and the modern concept of the full responsibility of government to the whole mass of the governed"– see his *Constitutionalism: Ancient and Modern* (1947) at pp. 141-6.

Professor Stanley de Smith, the renowned English constitutional lawyer, has expressed substantially the same view in his book.[4]

> A contemporary liberal democrat, if asked to lay down a set of minimum standards, may be very willing to concede that constitutionalism is practised in a country where the government is genuinely accountable to an entity or organ distinct from itself, where elections are freely held on a wide franchise at frequent intervals, where political groups are free to organise in opposition to the government in office and where there are effective legal guarantees of fundamental civil liberties enforced by an independent judiciary; and he may not easily be persuaded to identify constitutionalism in a country where any of these conditions is lacking.

Today, therefore, the democratic control mechanisms of popular election of representatives and the responsibility of the government to the governed together with an effective legal guarantee of individual liberty are generally accepted as constituting the core and the mainstay of constitutionalism. Indeed, an extreme view of political responsibility postulates public opinion as the determinant of policy, since, as it is said, a responsible person is one whose "conduct responds to an outside determinant."[5]

In the third place, the fact that power exercised by government is a delegated, not original power also necessarily implies a limitation. The people, to whom the original sovereign power belongs, cannot have delegated and thereby abdicated the entirety of it to the government. On the contrary, the delegation is made subject to terms and conditions set out in the constitution, which, as the instrument of the delegation, binds the rulers, as agents, to keep within the limits so set out. Any representative government not limited and bound by rules embodying the terms and conditions on which power is delegated to it by the people is not a democratic government but an autocratic and arbitrary one.

---

4   *The New Commonwealth and Its Constitutions* (1964) at p. 106.
5   Carl J. Friedrich, *Man and His Government* (1963) at p. 310.

An important term of the delegation found in the constitutions of most countries of the world today is that which protects individual liberty from interference by government, otherwise known as a bill of rights. Such a guarantee of rights becomes an essential feature of the constitution of a modern democratic government. A government of the people by the people for the people is not fully democratic unless the instrument constituting it also guarantees and protects the basic rights of the individual. A constitution, which grants powers of government without limitations designed to safeguard the liberty of the individual is not worthy to be so called. To merit being so called, a constitution, says the Nobel Laureate, Friedrich Hayek, in his seminal work, *The Constitution of Liberty* (1960), has to be "a constitution of liberty, a constitution that would protect the individual against all arbitrary coercion"[6]

Yet, the safeguard of a constitutional bill of rights would be rendered largely nugatory if an individual who alleges that his guaranteed rights are being violated by the legislature or executive is not able to appeal to a body independent of these organs, whether the ordinary courts or some other kind of tribunal. Review of governmental acts by an independent body in the interest of maintaining the efficacy of the constitutional guarantee of individual rights is thus also an essential and important mechanism of democratic government. Being at the instance of an aggrieved individual, the democratic virtue of such a review is that it assures the individual's personal participation in government, thus imparting greater reality to the concept of self-government. The "self" in the concept refers not only to the people as a free and independent community but also to the attribute of personal participation by the several individuals comprising the community. Democracy is thus a form of government in which the highest premium is placed on the participation of the individual in government. "The primary meaning of democracy," writes Professor Sir Arthur Lewis, "is that all those affected by a decision should participate in making it."[7] It connotes, essentially, a government conducted by the people both as individuals and as a collectivity.

Being a practical incident of the terms and conditions upon which the elected majority in the legislature and executive holds its power, review of

---

[6]   *The Constitution of Liberty* (1960), at p.182.
[7]   *Politics in West Africa* (1965), p. 75

governmental acts in terms of their conformance with constitutional limitations on power is indeed a constituent element of rule by the people's elected representatives; to regard it as antithetical to democratic rule merely because the court or other reviewing tribunal is unelected is to mis-conceive the true basis of rule by elected representatives exercising power delegated to them by the people.

We may therefore say that the virtual obsolescence of direct democracy in the modern states of today and its replacement by representative democracy has rendered largely untenable and irrelevant the argument about the irreconcilability of democratic rule with civil liberty. The argument about the irreconcilability of individual liberty and social democracy is considered later.

Constitutional Democracy: Not a Contradiction in Terms

If government limited by law (i.e. the rule of law) and democracy are in Isaiah Berlin's words, "two profoundly divergent and irreconcilable" objects, then, it must follow that it is a contradiction in terms to speak of constitutional democracy as a synthesis of the two. Two divergent and irreconcilable governmental concepts cannot be synthesised into a consistent, viable and credible form of government. But, not only does representative democracy necessarily imply limitation on government by law, but the two are complementary concepts which in combination serve, more adequately than any other known form of government, "the ends of life."

The supposed divergence and irreconcilability of democracy with constitutional limitation for the protection of civil liberty enforceable by the courts arises from a rather narrow conception of democracy as being concerned simply and solely with the exercise of power over the affairs of men and women in society. But democracy is more than a form of government; it is also a way of life. It describes a polity in which rule by the people through their elected agents is conducted within, or which presupposes, a given social, political and ethical milieu and conditions. It presupposes a social, political, legal and ethical order characterised by democratic ethos, ethic, values, norms and habits; that is to say, a society in which, within the limits dictated by the necessity to maintain public order, public morality and state security, and to promote development, people actually live their lives freely as they like; a society in which conditions of life are in fact equal (or nearly equal) among the citizenry; relations between individuals and groups are just; a society characterised by autonomy *vis-a-vis* the government; a society in which there is order, and, lastly, a society governed by law. In short, democracy, as defined above, presupposes a free society, a democratic society, a just society, a vigilant, virile civil society, and an ordered, law-governed society. It requires as an essential, indispensable requirement thereof the rule of law, with its various elements the protection of individual rights, the guarantee of fair trial and due process of law, the subjection of the state and its officials to the law, the institutions and devices necessary for the operation of the rule of law (like the separation of powers between a legislative assembly, executive and judiciary). And torn from justice, individual liberty loses much of its meaning.

Not only must the state, conceived as a legal order, and the institutions of government be based on democratic principles and norms, the society itself and relations within it, and "the minutiae of daily life" must be permeated by democratic ethos, ethic, values and habits, reinforced by a vigilant, virile civil society, with its variegated institutions. There must not be a gulf in democratic norms between, on the one hand, the law as embodied in the constitution and other legal instruments that establish the institutions of government and define their relations to the individual, and, on the other hand, life and social relations as they actually obtain in practice. Both must conform to, and be permeated by, democratic principles and norms.

Whilst happiness, the good life and public welfare generally are not, unlike the rule of law, equality and justice, essential requirements of democracy, they do form part of its objectives, part of the ends of life which both democracy and individual civil liberty under the rule of law alike seek to secure and promote. "Democracy," writes Professor Lord James Bryce, "is supposed to be the product and the guardian both of Equality and of Liberty, being so consecrated by its relationship to both these precious possessions as to be almost above criticism."[8] Democracy, as a form of government, is man-based; it is a humanist, individualist and moralist institution, "created for the sake of what the ancient philosophers called the Good Life" of society (James

---

[8] *Modern Democracies*, vol. 2 (1920), p. 654.

Bryce, *loc. cit.*). Herein lies one of the essential differences between democracy and socialism. Alexis de Tocqueville again tells us: "Democracy attaches all possible values to each man; socialism makes each man a mere agent, a mere number ... While democracy seeks equality in liberty, socialism seeks equality in restraint and servitude."[9]

"It is our common creed", writes Lord Devlin, "that no society can be perfect unless it is a free society"[10] in the true sense of the term. Some of the benefits of a free society have been described for us by that great political philosopher and champion of liberty, John Stuart Mill, in his celebrated treatise, *On Liberty* (1859). According to him, "unless men are left to live as they wish `in the path which merely concern themselves', civilisation cannot advance ... there will be no scope for spontaneity, originality, genius, for mental energy, for moral courage. Society will be crushed by the weight of `collective mediocrity'. Whatever is rich and diversified will be crushed by the weight of custom, by men's constant tendency to conformity, which breeds only `withered capacities', `pinched and hidebound', `cramped and warped' human beings" (The passage quoted is Isaiah Berlin's rendering of Mill — see his *Four Essays on Liberty, loc. cit.*).

Thus constitutional democracy, as a synthesis of constitutional limitation for the protection of liberty and representative democracy, is not a contradiction in terms, but rather a consistent, viable and credible form of government that assures to humankind the desired ends of life. (The ideas adumbrated in brief outline in this section are the subject matter of volume 3 wherein they are extensively discussed.)

It is not intended to suggest that, because happiness, the good life and public welfare generally are part of its objectives, democracy necessarily assures them. No doubt, the expectation indeed the rationale for it, is that when the people govern, they do so for the benefit of all. Government by the people is expected to be government for the people because the people embody all of the community's wisdom, goodness, honesty, justice, its sense of right and wrong, in short all the civic virtues available in it, which should outweigh all its vices. Animated by a concern for their own good, i.e. their own safety, liberty,

---

9   *Democracy in America* (1835).
10   *The Enforcement of Morals* (1963), p. 104.

prosperity, well-being and happiness, which is the same as the public good or the welfare of the community, government by the people cannot but be government for the people. The people, said de Tocqueville, "cannot have an interest opposed to their own advantage." "Representation, as a substitute for a meeting of the citizens in person," is intended to replicate the people's concern with their own good, as elected representatives are supposed to have "a communion of interests and sympathy of sentiments with the ruled."[11]

But the actual working of popular government has proved all this to be largely an idealistic picture, quite removed from reality. To begin with, "the self-government spoken of is not the government of each by himself but of each by all the rest."[12] An assemblage of the whole citizenry in a direct democracy would often be swayed by passion rather than by reason, and even when it is not, the governing interest would usually be not that of the whole people but of the majority which may trample on the interest of the minority. In a representative democracy, the premise that representation replicates the people's concern for their own good and that representatives have a communion of interests and sentiments with the people presupposes the capacity of the people to choose representatives animated by a spirit of the public good, which is often not the case. In reality, elected representatives are not, for the most part, persons so animated, their actions being motivated more by selfish or other private interests than by the public good.

The Supposed Irreconcilability of Social Democracy (or Rule for the People) with Individual Liberty

Indisputably, individual liberty is inevitably restricted when the state intervenes in social and economic life in order to redress social imbalances and injustices, as by regulative legislation which fixes minimum wages or maximum working hours, prescribes compulsory methods of settling labour disputes or which controls prices and rents. There is thus a certain conflict between the demands of individual liberty and those of social justice, of which it is necessary to take due cognisance and account. But the question is whether these inevitable restrictions are really such as to make the pursuit of social justice by the state

---

11.   James Madison, *The Federalist No.25*
12.   J. S. Mill, *Representative Government, p.72*

altogether incompatible or irreconcilable with individual liberty and the Rule of Law; in other words, whether the two are mutually exclusive objects which cannot co-exist or be pursued together. Will the pursuit of social justice in the full blown form it has taken under the modern welfare state inevitably result in the complete relegation of individual liberty? Will it lead to a state of affairs in which "the liberty of the individual gradually recedes into the background and the liberty of the social collective occupies the front of the stage?"[13]

In the view of a renowned modern advocate of liberalism following in the tradition of Adam Smith and John Stuart Mill, the relegation, indeed the complete destruction, of individual liberty is an inevitable consequence of the social justice objectives of the modern welfare state, from which it therefore follows that those objectives are incompatible and irreconcilable with a free society.[14] "Redistribution of income or distributive justice," he asserts, "can never be achieved within the limits of the rule of law."[15] He rests this incompatibility on various grounds. First, measures designed to redistribute incomes, by their nature, necessarily involve the exercise of arbitrary power, since they inevitably confer wide discretion upon the authorities. "The restrictions which the rule of law imposes upon government," he maintains, "preclude all those measures which would be necessary to insure that individuals be rewarded according to another's conception of merit or desert ... Distributive justice requires that people be told what to do and what ends to serve. Where distributive justice is the goal, the decisions as to what the different individuals must be made to do cannot be derived from general rules but must be made in the light of the particular aims and knowledge of the planning authority ... Thus the welfare state becomes a household state in which a paternalistic power controls most of the income of the community and allocates it to individuals in the forms and quantities which it thinks they need or deserve."[16]

Price control, for example, is said necessarily to involve *ad hoc* decisions that discriminate between persons on essentially arbitrary grounds. This is so because it "can be made effective only by quantitative controls, by decisions

---

[13] Hans Kelsen, quoted in Hayek, *The Constitution of Liberty*, p. 216.
[14] Hayek, *ibid*, pp. 259-260.
[15] *ibid*, p. 260.
[16] *ibid*, pp. 260-1

on the part of authority as to how much particular persons or firms are to be allowed to buy or sell. And the exercise of all controls of quantities must, of necessity, be discriminatory, determined not by rule but by the judgment of authority concerning the relative importance of particular ends ... To grant such powers to authority means in effect to give it power to arbitrarily determine what is to be produced, by whom, and for whom."[17]

Rent control is equally characterised by the exercise of arbitrary power on the part of the authority. For, "whether an owner, with an invalid wife and three young children, who wishes to obtain occupation of his house (would) suffer more hardship if his request were refused than the tenant, with only one child, but a bed-ridden mother-in-law, would suffer if it were granted is a problem that cannot be settled by appeal to any recognized principles of justice but only by the arbitrary intervention of authority."[18]

Progressive taxation, which is the chief instrument of income redistribution, is represented as "simply hateful arbitrariness," resting on no principle whatever, unlike proportional taxation. Furthermore it amounts to singling out a group, a minority group, (that is those in the highest income bracket), for discriminatory and oppressive treatment by legislation enacted by an elected majority; it thus infringes "a principle much more fundamental than democracy itself."[19]

In the second place, state intervention in furtherance of social justice has resulted not only in the state arrogating to itself exclusive rights in fields in which it ought not legitimately to have a monopoly, as, for example, the nationalisation of education, health services and the running of certain social security schemes, but also in the use of coercion to force individuals to take certain actions either in their own interest or for the protection of others or the public at large. State monopoly in such matters as mentioned above deprives individuals of a choice in what obviously affects vital aspects of their lives, and what they get is thus made to depend entirely upon the evaluation of their needs or desert by some state official. As regards social security systems, it is said that, while some of their objectives are not incompatible with individual liberty, their pursuit by means of compulsory schemes run by unitary

---

[17] p.228
[18] *ibid*, p. 344
[19] *ibid*, p. 314

monopolistic state machinery and the consequent exclusion of private enterprise are. It deprives the community of the opportunity of experimenting on alternative methods from which better solutions might well emerge.

In the third place, by reducing rents to a fraction of what they would be in a free market, rent control is said to amount, in effect, to expropriation of house property, and generally undermines respect for private property.

Finally, the attempt by the welfare state to eradicate want, disease, ignorance, squalor and idleness (the "five giants," as they are called) has created the far greater problem of an ever-increasing dominance of government in education, a social service bureaucracy with far-reaching arbitrary powers and of a paralysing taxation. The evil of social service bureaucracy is accentuated by the fact that it does not lend itself to effective democratic control by the elected majority in the legislature. "It is inevitable that this sort of administration of the welfare of the people should become a self-willed and uncontrollable apparatus before which the individual is helpless."[20]

Thus, while renouncing the old liberal stand that the maintenance of law and order is the sole legitimate concern of government, this brand of liberalism maintains that state intervention in social and economic life in a free society should be limited to:

(a)   the provision of a framework of general rules of law and of infrastructural services like roads, electricity, water, education, health care, telecommunications, a monetary system, weights and measure, statistics and other similar services designed to assist people to achieve prosperity through their own efforts provided they involve no coercion of the individual or involve it only incidentally (as with the compulsory acquisition of land needed for road construction or proportional taxation to raise money to provide such services);

(b)   the provision of other assistance and incentives to private enterprise, e.g. subsidies to agriculture, education and housing; and

(c)   the relief of poverty, want and destitution among the disabled, elderly and young persons with no or inadequate means of support, the poor and other needy persons, and even the provision of an equal minimum

---

[20]   *ibid*, p. 262

income for all but not the guarantee to particular individuals of the standards of living to which they have been accustomed, which is objected to, because it is not based on proof of need as does the provision of a uniform minimum income for all.

In addition, state participation in economic activities is also conceded as not involving coercion or interference with individual liberty so long as it is on the same terms as economic activities carried on by private persons and does not entail state monopoly of any particular activity except where a state monopoly relates to services that can only be provided by collective action or which cannot, for economic reasons, be provided by competitive enterprise. In the main, therefore, these extensions in the functions of the state beyond the maintenance of law and order, to which the liberals are prepared to subscribe, merely conceive of the state as a purely service agency, but insofar as a service activity will involve coercion of the individual, their position that the state should not encroach upon the private domain of the individual remains substantially unchanged.

On the other hand, an ardent liberal and constitutionalist, Professor Charles McIlwain, maintains that, far from being affronted by the welfare state, true liberalism must combine the guarantee of individual liberty with the securing of the good of the whole people, the security of the common weal, the elimination or amelioration of wretchedness and misery among the people. A state, he says, is "not any chance aggregation of men but a multitude united in the common purpose of securing this common good, and that can mean nothing less than the individual good of all, not just some, of its members." "In a word," he asserts, "liberalism means a common welfare with constitutional guarantee. I maintain that not one part, but both parts of this definition must be translated into working fact if we mean to live in a true commonwealth and hope to keep it in being. So-called liberals have ignored the first part of the definition and have fouled the nest by invoking the guarantee for privileges of their own, conducive only to the destruction of any true common weal,"[21] castigating them (i.e. the so-called liberals) as "reactionaries" and as "traitors within the gates who have probably done more than all others to betray

---

[21] *Constitutionalism and the Changing World,* (1939) p. 285.

liberalism to its enemies and put it to its defence."[22] To him, the extreme doctrine of *laissez-faire*, with its "unhistorical definition of contract under which the sanction of the law could be obtained for almost any enormity to which men could be induced to agree," is "one of the strangest fantasies that ever discredited human reason, a caricature of liberalism."[23]

Between the position of the brand of liberalism represented by Hayek and the extreme form of social justice based on the nationalisation of all means of production (socialism/communism), there is quite ample room for the pursuit of the aims and goals of social justice within the overall framework of individual liberty and the Rule of Law. No doubt, individual liberty and the rule of law will suffer considerable incursions and inroads as a result but so long as they remain the general principles governing the social order, the conflict posed by the pursuit of social justice can be accommodated. It seems rather an extreme position to maintain, as does Hayek, that the conception of social justice would necessarily "lead straight to full-fledged socialism"[24] or to the total destruction of individual liberty or that it can be given meaning only at the cost of "a complete change of the whole character of the social order." It cannot be disputed that individual liberty and the rule of law still form the framework of the social order of Britain today which, with all the extensive welfare services undertaken by the state, still remains a model of a free society.

The necessary balance seems to me to be appropriately expressed in the notion of the open society, that is to say, a society that does not enthrone either individual liberty or social and economic rights to the exclusion of the other, but is open to both. It does not, as under socialism/communism, elevate social and economic rights into a supreme object in the pursuit of which individual liberty must be sacrificed or suppressed. It recognizes man as both a human being and a social being, and that his needs for social services and amenities are entitled to be catered for by the state within the framework of a free society. While according priority to man's humanity, it also recognizes that food, clothing, shelter, health care and other material conditions of a

---

[22] *ibid*, p. 286
[23] *ibid*, p. 287
[24] *The Mirage of Social Justice* (1976) pp. 64-67.

good, decent life are necessary for human existence, and indeed indispensable to make him better able to breathe, think, feel, speak, move about and act, and to realize and develop his human personality more fully. Still, they are not a constituent element of man's humanity but only supplements.

It would of course be a contradiction if the provision of social and economic amenities by the state were to override man's humanity. In an open society, neither should override the other. They must be properly balanced, one with the other. It is the undue emphasis on social well-being at almost the total expense of individual liberty that proved part of the undoing of socialism of the communist type. A rigid, doctrinaire attachment to individual liberty is equally antithetical to the open society. What is needed, in Sir Ralf Dahrendorf's words, is a "combination of democracy and planning, of economic freedom and demand management, of individual choice and redistribution, of liberty and justice."[25] The "social entitlements of citizenship" should be secured by the state at the same time as "the spirit of innovation and entrepreneurship"[26] is being aroused.

The appropriate balance between liberal democracy and social democracy clearly does not admit of too much state intervention in social and economic affairs which poses a real danger for both individual liberty and the Rule of Law, because it unduly increases the size, influence and importance of the state, imparting to the struggle for its control an undue importance, especially in developing countries. Politics or the struggle for the control of the state comes to loom too large in national life, to dominate it so utterly as to submerge everything else. It also gives to corruption, electoral perversion and abuse of power a greatly increased stimulus and incidence. There should therefore be only so much state intervention as is compatible with freedom and the Rule of Law.

---

[25] *Reflections on the Revolution in Europe* (1990) p. 50.
[26] *ibid*, p. 71.

CHAPTER 6

Balancing Human Rights Protection with Effective Government

Maintaining Acceptable Balance Between Constitutional Democracy and Effective Government

Society undoubtedly has an imperative need for effective government of its affairs if social degeneration and instability are not to ensue. It can scarcely be suggested that this vital need of society is to be sacrificed in order that the fundamental rights of the individual may be protected, vitally important as the latter is for the well-being of the individual and indeed for the development and prosperity of the community itself. Certainly, the limiting of government in the interest of the protection of the individual's liberty does not require the weakening of it; it should not result in government being deprived of the capacity to govern effectively.

The vital needs of society that require to be effectively maintained, secured or promoted, during and outside the periods of emergency, are peace and order, security of lives and property, security of the state, health, morals and general material welfare. The ability of government effectively to maintain, secure or promote these vital needs of society is what requires to be balanced and reconciled with the competing claim of the individual for the protection of his fundamental rights. How to do this acceptably is among the perplexing but crucial concerns of constitutional democracy.

Of the public needs mentioned above, state security calls for some comment because of its susceptibility to varied tendentious applications designed to serve the personal political interests of the rulers, especially those of new states in Africa, Asia and Latin America, where the term is often given a wide and elastic scope predicated ostensibly on the newness and underdevelopment of the state.

117

To begin with, state security and public order are not co-terminous terms. The operative idea connoted by state security is the **safety** of the state and society. (The term public or national security is not used in the relevant provisions of the Nigerian Constitution, which only speak of "public safety" — see sections 11, 45, 215 and 305.) Thus, public disorder must be of a kind or magnitude endangering the safety of the state or society before it can be said to impinge on state security, and it must affect either the entire population or a considerable portion of it. Crime too, and its incidence as single acts by miscreant individuals, e.g. the crime of stealing, prostitution, abortion, suicide, forgery, perjury, to mention just a few, committed by such individuals, raise no question touching on public or national security, except when it assumes the character of a public menace, as with the current public menace of armed robbery in Nigeria; except as stated it concerns rather the security of the individual.

There is thus implicit in what is said above the distinction between the security (safety) of the nation (or national security) and the security of the individual. The "nation" refers to the people, not as several individuals, but as an entity distinct and separate from the several individuals that comprise it— i.e. a collectivity. As such an entity, its security or safety is a matter distinct and separate from the security or safety of the individual. This is not of course to say that the security of the individual is not a concern of the state, only that the security or safety of the nation is what needs to be balanced with human rights protection under the relevant provisions of the constitution.

State security has three distinct meanings and applications, viz:

(a)   external security, which concerns the safety of the nation and its government in relation to acts or threats of them, like aggression, emanating from outside the national territory of the state and calculated to weaken or destroy it or its government;

(b)   internal security which relates to the safety of the nation and its government from acts or threats of them, like subversion, emanating from within the national territory of the state and calculated to weaken or destroy it or its government; and

(c)   situational security which concerns the safety of the nation and its government from "the threat of erosion resulting from long-term changes in social, economic, demographic, and political conditions tending to reduce its relative powers."[1]

Of its three dimensions, it is perhaps situational security that gives to national security the widest scope and potentiality as a source of power in new, underdeveloped states. This is because of the tensions and turbulence implied in the absence of "civil order," the process of change from a traditional, backward society to a modern one (modernisation), the lack of social security, and in the general fragility of the state. These concepts, by no means widely understood, require clarification for a better appreciation of their impact on state security in new states.

Lee in his book, *African Armies and Civil Order* (1969), defines "civil order" as connoting a society with a firmly established convention of "respect for the limits of violence as an instrument of politics," a society characterised by a habit of ordered political competition and political succession, and by "a common language of politics."[2] "'Civil order'," he adds, "is the acceptance of certain norms within a broader definition of the state than that provided by the formal institutions of government, which help to remove the high degree of uncertainty that might otherwise prevail in political negotiation. The attempt to create order in Africa is really a fight to define the limits of political action."[3] Political violence, unlimited and unrestrained by any established conventions or other widely accepted rules of the political game, is evidenced by the existence and use of private armies by the contenders for state power. Moreover, "the context in which violence might be used are greatly expanded by the diminished authority of new regimes. Either old antagonisms will re-assert themselves, or new organisations, such as trade unions or security forces, will be tempted to defend their positions by force."[4]

Modernisation is "the complex process of social and economic change caused by and manifested in the growth of new towns and cities, the spread of mass education, the extension of mass communication, and the process of industrialisation."[5] The fragility of the state in Africa is a product of its

---

[1] S. P. Hunington, *The Soldier and the State* (1962), p. 1.
[2] p. 2.
[3] *ibid*, at p. 3.
[4] at p. 18.
[5] Ali Mazrui, "Military Intervention in African Politics," in Ralph Uwechue (ed.), *Africa Today* (1991), at p. 249.

origin as a creation of colonialism; its lack of roots in the life, culture and habits of the people; the consequent lack of identification with, and loyalty to, it on their part; its nature as "the most ... baffling phenomenon of contemporary life,"[6] utterly incomprehensible to the generality of the backward peoples of Africa; absence of the spirit of communal life, of living together as a community with shared ideals; conflicts between diverse ethnic groups and between the newly emergent social classes; absence of "traditions of disciplined class conflicts;" conflicts among predatory elites, etc. The lack of social security refers to the lack of social protection of the individual against want, poverty, destitution, etc. resulting from sickness, accident-injury, invalidity, old-age, unemployment and other causes. The provision of social security is a matter to be tackled by general policy and under a general national scheme. The least required of the state is to regulate by law the way social security is organised and administered, but its responsibility should extend beyond this to involvement in its administration, and in appropriate cases, its funding in whole or in part. Whilst a disproportionate part of national revenue goes to national security in Africa, little or no attention is given to the provision of social security the lack of which is a major cause of national insecurity.

Thus, the absence of civil order, as defined above, the tensions of modernisation, and the strains and stresses resulting from the fragility of the state, the lack of social security all combine together to give to state security a wide and elastic scope in the new states in Africa.

But there is a further element of vagueness and elasticity about the nature and scope of state security and about the extent of the power to preserve it in Africa. The vagueness stems not really from the term nation which simply means the public or any considerable portion of it, nor from the term 'state' which in the context refers to people inhabiting a defined territory conceptualised as a continuing corporate entity (see further chap. 13 below.) It lies essentially with the term 'government' as used in our definition above. Does it refer to the system or form of government instituted by the constitution, with its established institutions, principles and processes? Or does the term extend to the incumbent government of the day, particularly as

---

6   Christopher Pierson, *The Modern State* (1996), pp. 1 and 15.

regards its continued stay in power and the continued tenure of office of its functionaries and of the ruling party?

The meaning that confines the term to the system or form of government established by the constitution seems to be the one adopted for this purpose by the courts in the United States when they affirmed in a series of decisions that the world communist movement and the activities of communist-action organisations, communist-front organisations or communist-infiltrated organisations registered and operating in the United States are a danger to national security because they are subversive of the government of the United States which they identified with the U.S. system of government established by its Constitution;[7] and that, accordingly, congress has the power to protect and preserve the government against the danger of the world communist movement through the enactment of the Subversive Activities Control Act 1950 which, among other things, imposed restrictions on foreign travels by members of the above-named communist organisations.[8]

No doubt, state security is endangered by an attempt, by overt act or in other ways, to remove a lawfully constituted government by subversion or other unconstitutional means, but that is because such a subversive act, if successful, invariably results in the overthrow of the constitution and the system of governmental succession it established; not infrequently the break in governmental legitimacy following upon it also plunges the nation into a situation of widespread public disorder and instability.

Admittedly too, as Lee points out, internal subversion or attempted subversion of an incumbent government by its political opponents sometimes involves outside powers. "Subversion against one regime can be planned in the comparative safety of another. When the borders themselves are so imperfectly defined on the ground, the security forces of one state might invade the territory of another in order to capture any opponents of the regime."[9] Moreover, "political refugees, whether they were small groups of trained men or large numbers of displaced persons, constituted a peculiar kind of security threat."[10]

---

7 See *Kennedy v. Mendoza-Martinez*, 372 U.S. 144, pp. 159-160.
8 *Kennedy v. Mendoza-Martinez, ibid; Communist Party of the United States v. Subversive Activities Control Board*, 36 U.S. 70; *Aptheker v. Secretary of State*, 378 U.S. 500.
9 Lee, *op. cit.*, pp. 9-10.
10 J. M. Lee, *op. cit.*, p. 9.

Yet the question posed is whether state security encompasses within its meaning the security of an incumbent government's rule against removal from office through the lawful activities of its political opponents, as by defeat at the polls or on the floor of the legislative assembly. Can the emasculation or suppression of organised but lawful opposition be said to be among the legitimate concerns of state security? Such a view of state security is certainly subversive of the very concept of democratic government. Surely, when the constitution of a democratic government, which enshrines a guarantee of human rights, provides that nothing in the guarantee "shall invalidate any law that is reasonably justifiable in a democratic society in the interest of defence, public safety and public order," it could not have intended that the overriding interest of defence, public safety and public order should extend to the political interest of an incumbent government in maintaining itself and the ruling party in power by the emasculation or suppression of the lawful non-subversive activities of all organised opposition. It should again be reiterated that the operative idea in the constitutional provision is the safety of the state and society. The continued stay in office of an incumbent government when it is not threatened by subversion by its opponents can have no proximate or rational connection with public safety.

On this point, regrettably, Lee seems to give to state security a meaning patronisingly peculiar to African countries, although his language is not as clear as might be wished. In doing so, he leaves it unclear whether he meant to deny "the essential difference between the security of the state and security of the regime."[11] As he puts it:

> The colonial state represented a body of laws, however illegitimate; the post-colonial state is a body of men which has captured the state apparatus, buttressed by the sanctions which had been expressed in the final stages of the nationalist struggle ... In many cases, the security of the state cannot in fact be separated from that of the regime, because the main weapon in the armoury of the regime is the state organisation itself. Control of the budget and the system of government appointments provides any regime with the means of defeating its opponents. The state sometimes appears to be little more than a description which can be applied to those who succeeded to the public offices vacated by colonial

---

[11] Lee, *op. cit.*, p. 18.

administration ... Circumstances encourage all those concerned in 'nation-building' to place a much greater emphasis on the state as an apparatus for government than on the state as a system of law.[12]

These views, while they accurately reflect political reality in Africa, are conceptually misconceived. State security cannot, in its essence, mean different things in Europe and Africa, although, as earlier noted, differences in circumstances – the absence of civil order, the turbulence of modernisation and the instability resulting from the fragility of the state – give it a much wider ambit or scope in Africa than in Europe. Lee may rightly be charged of failing to keep the essence of the concept of state security – and of the state itself – distinct from what is clearly an abuse or perversion of it. It is simply a perversion for African rulers to equate themselves with the state, or to treat it, in Lee's words, as just "a body of men which has captured the state apparatus."

In this particular matter, as in many others, the African governments are, to some extent, following in the footsteps of the colonial government; for the perverted conception of state security as embracing within its meaning the maintenance of the incumbent government's rule against lawful challenge from competitors is not without antecedent in colonialism. Challenges, including challenges by lawful means, to colonial rule by organised groups of the indigenous population were viewed as serious threats to security meriting repressive action by the colonial authorities. But there is a difference, which needs to be acknowledged. Colonialism is a system of rule in which the colonial functionaries had no personal political interest apart from that of the colonial state; they were purely agents and instruments of the colonial state. The contest was between the colonial state, as represented by the colonial administrators, on the one hand and the colonised people on the other, not between opposing groups of the people for the control of the state. Still the identification of the colonial rulers with the state is an inheritance which the successor African rulers could not readily shed. Paying no regard to the different context of colonial rule, if they actually appreciate it, the African rulers simply view all challenges to their rule by rival competitors for power in the same way as the colonial rulers had viewed challenges to colonial rule

---

[12]   Lee, *op. cit.*, pp. 9-11.

by the colonised people, especially the nascent nationalist organisations. The reason for this lies in large measure in the nature of the system of personal rule prevalent in most countries of Africa during the first three decades after independence, with its inherent vulnerability. The welfare and fortune of the political class and often of the political order itself are bound up with those of the ruler. "If he falls, his relatives, friends, lieutenants, clients and followers also may fall, and the ensuing political disruption may threaten the political peace."[13]

Having identified the vital needs of society which require to be effectively secured, maintained or promoted by the state, we must now consider to what extent, if at all, the individual's fundamental rights may, in a democratic society, justifiably be interfered with for the purpose. This requires that we should, first, identify rights which, by their nature, should be constitutionally protected absolutely free of interference by the state both during normal and emergency periods; second, define, with as much specificity as possible, the permissible extent to which the state may, in normal times when no emergency is declared, interfere with the rights not embraced in the first category in the interest of public order, the security of lives and property, state security, health, morals and general material welfare; and, third, the extent of permissible interference with rights in the residual category during a period of emergency declared in accordance with the provisions of the constitution.

Rights Requiring to be Guaranteed Absolutely

Freedom of thought, choice, opinion, feeling, conscience and religion must, as John Stuart Mill asserts,[14] be recognised as absolute and free from control by the state; only their manifestation in speech, press, assembly, association, movement, religious practices or in some other forms of action or other overt ways may be controlled by the state.

There is good reason for treating freedom of thought, choice, opinion, feeling, conscience and religion not manifested in action, expression or in other overt ways as absolute, and inviolable by the state. First, because they

---

[13]   Robert Jackson and Carl Rosberg, *Personal Rule in Black Africa* (1982), p. 26.

[14]   J. S. Mill, *On Liberty* (1859); reprinted in *Utilitarianism, Liberty and Representative Government*, Everyman's Library (1910).

constitute the essence of the sacredness, inherent dignity and the spiritual or moral integrity of the human person; they are, in other words, the elements or attributes of the human person that confer upon him sacredness, dignity and spiritual or moral integrity, and which therefore entitle them to inviolability. Man's endowment with reason, with the ability to think and reason, to judge between right and wrong, to form or hold opinions and beliefs, and to have feelings and emotions are the elements that distinguish him from non-human living things. The human physical body partakes, **to some extent**, of this sacredness, dignity and integrity because it encases these vital, spiritual elements. Whereas a human person loses his integrity as a human being, whole and entire, if he is not able to think for himself, to feel or believe, his integrity or personality as a human being is not destroyed or lost because he is unable to move about, speak or act owing to the loss of his legs, tongue and hands, even eyes, unless such loss is deliberately inflicted by the state or another person as a punishment or a sheer act of brutalisation. His integrity or personality may well be adversely affected, but certainly not lost or destroyed because of such loss; he remains a human person with all the sacredness, dignity and moral integrity pertaining to the human person. A person disabled by the loss of his eyes, legs, hands or tongue not deliberately inflicted by others as punishment is as much a human being possessed of the same inherent dignity and integrity as one without such disability, and he may indeed be able to develop his human personality better than the latter, depending on the facilities and opportunities available to them both; but destroy his mind, his soul and his capacity to feel and judge, and he ceases to be a human person. He may still be living but he will have become an idiot, a robot or worse.

So, when we speak of the human person as having an inherent dignity and integrity, and as entitled to inviolability, it is the elements of thought, choice, conscience, the ability to form or hold opinions or beliefs and to feel that are primarily referred to as conferring sacredness, dignity and integrity on the human person. Torture, cruel, inhuman or degrading punishment or treatment, servitude, forced labour, arbitrary or wrongful detention or imprisonment, unfair discrimination on such grounds as race, colour, tribe or place of origin are derogatory of the dignity and integrity of the human person essentially because of their depressing and damaging effect on a man's mind, spirit, feelings and his entire psychology. The worst of all tyrannies, it has been truly said, is tyranny on men's minds. Few things depress the spirit as much as the incarceration of a man, by detention or imprisonment, for an offence he did not commit. Racial discrimination is so awfully damaging to the psychology of those subjected to it.

In the second place, it makes hardly any sense that the state should try to restrict human thought, opinion, conscience, beliefs and feelings, partly because they cannot, meaningfully, be controlled or restricted by the state, and partly because it serves no legitimate public interest for the state to try to control or restrict them. For, what a person thinks in his mind or feels or believes in his heart, but does not manifest in speech or action or in any other overt way (e.g. refusal, on conscientious grounds, to do something required by law), cannot be known to others so as to enable them to control or restrict it by legal punishment or otherwise. It is simply futile to prohibit a man by law from thinking certain thoughts, believing in certain things or from having certain feelings. Besides, mere thought, belief or feeling not manifested in some overt way can have no disturbing effect on any legitimate public interest which the state is entitled to protect, whether it be public order, public security, public morality or public health. Of course, as John Stuart Mill says, it is what men think, believe in or feel that determines how they act,[15] yet human thought, conscience, belief or feeling is not for that reason to be controlled before and until it is actually manifested in action or in some other overt way. A man, said Justice William Douglas of the U.S. supreme court, may be "punished for his acts, never for his thoughts or beliefs or creed."[16] Human thought, opinions, conscience, beliefs, feelings and emotions require therefore to be put beyond the reach of governmental power; no room should be given for their control by the state.

The absoluteness and inviolability of freedom of thought, opinion, conscience, beliefs, feelings and emotions is accepted and enshrined in the International Covenant on Civil and Political Rights 1976 of the United Nations, which guarantees freedom of thought, conscience and religion as well as the

---

[15] J. S. Mill, *Representative Government*, reprinted in *Utilitarianism, Liberty and Representative Government* (1910), p. 198.
[16] W. O. Douglas, "The Manifest Destiny of America," article reproduced in *The Freedom Reader* by Edwin S. Newman (1963), p. 26.

right to hold opinions free of any qualifications whatsoever; only the guarantee of freedom to **manifest** one's religion or beliefs and freedom of expression (including freedom to seek, receive and impart information and ideas) is made subject to such limitations as are prescribed by law and are necessary to protect public security, public order, public health, morals and the rights and freedoms of others (arts 18 and 19). Similarly, under the European Convention on Human Rights and Fundamental Freedoms (1954), the guarantee of freedom of thought, conscience and religion is not qualified at all except as it relates to freedom to **manifest** one's religion or beliefs (art. 9). However, under the European Convention, freedom to hold opinion, equally as freedom of expression with which it is lumped, may be restricted by law to an extent necessary in a democratic society in the interest of national security, territorial integrity, etc. (Art. 10).

In the light of the above, it is a grievous error for the constitutions of all (but four) of the countries of Africa, including Nigeria, to lump freedom of thought, feelings, conscience, religious belief and freedom to form or hold opinion together with their **manifestation** in speech, press, assembly, association, movement, and religious practices, and to subject them alike to control or interference by the state by law in the interests of defence, public safety, public order, public morality, public health and economic well-being of the society or the protection of the rights and freedoms of other persons. The four exceptions are Libya, Algeria, Congo (Brazzaville) and Egypt. Their constitutions affirm: "freedom of conscience shall be absolute" (Libya 1951, art. 21); "freedom of conscience and the freedom of opinion are inviolable" (Algeria 1976, art. 35); "freedom of belief is absolute" (Egypt 1964, art. 34); while Congo (Brazzaville)'s Constitution (1963) prohibits the "incommodation" of anyone on account of his opinions "so long as their manifestation does not disturb the public order established by law." (Art. 9). Egypt's Constitution also guarantees freedom of opinion without limitations (art. 35).

However, nearly all African countries with a Bill of Rights in their constitutions guarantee without qualifications freedom from torture, from cruel, inhuman or degrading treatment, and from slavery, servitude or forced labour except forced labour reasonably necessary in the event of any emergency or calamity threatening the life or well-being of the community or which forms part of normal communal or other civil obligations for the well-being of the community. It is gratifying too that, except it is ordered by a court in accordance with the law, arrest or detention by the government is constitutionally permitted in the 15 countries of former British Africa only when a person is reasonably suspected of having committed, or being about to commit, a criminal offence, and even in this case arrest or detention is circumscribed by constitutional safeguard. Sadly enough, however, outside the 15 countries of former British Africa, with the exception of Ethiopia (1955), Somalia (1960) and Congo (Leopoldville) (1964), freedom from arrest or detention is hardly constitutionally guaranteed in the strict sense of the word; no doubt, the right is protected in the constitution in some form, but the protection so provided falls short of a constitutional guarantee of the right not to be arrested or detained except on the order of a court in accordance with the law. The matter cannot be fully discussed here.

Permissible State Interference with the Guarantee of Rights When No Emergency is Declared

Excepting the rights mentioned above as being, by their nature, inviolable and requiring therefore to be guaranteed free of interference by the state – freedom of thought, opinion, conscience, beliefs, religion, feelings and emotions (when not manifested in action or otherwise) as well as freedom from torture, inhuman or degrading punishment, slavery, servitude and forced labour – it should be permissible for the state to interfere with other human rights to an extent necessary in a democratic society to enable it effectively to secure, maintain or promote public order, life and property, state security, public health, morals and general material welfare provided of course such interference is authorised by a constitutionally valid law.

The prohibition in the U.S. Constitution of the deprivation of liberty "without due process of law" is inadequate because it fails to mention specifically the above-named vital needs of society for the maintenance of which the state may justifiably interfere with liberty thus leaving it to the courts to supply the necessary specifications, which they have done in broad terms as follows:

> "There are," says the U.S. Supreme Court in 1905, "certain powers existing in the sovereignty of each State in the Union, somewhat vaguely termed police powers, the exact description and limitation of which have not

been attempted by the courts. Those powers, broadly stated and without, at present, any attempt at a more specific limitation, relate to the safety, health, morals, and general welfare of the public. Both property and liberty are held on such reasonable conditions as may be imposed by the governing power of the State in the exercise of those powers."[17]

In this connection, the constitution of the countries of former British Africa differ markedly in their approach from those of the countries of former French Africa. In the countries of former French Africa, with a few exceptions, constitutional protection of human rights is, in general, made subject to law; the rights are protected except as otherwise provided by law. Clearly, protection that avails against executive interference but which leaves the right entirely amenable to restriction or violation by law made by the legislative authorities of the state is inadequate. For the legislative power is the power against which individual liberty stands in most need of protection.

In the countries of former British Africa, on the other hand, the constitution does make an attempt at specificity. It is provided that the guarantee of private and family life, of thought, conscience and religion, of speech and press, of peaceful assembly and association, and of movement shall not "invalidate any law that is reasonably justifiable (or required) in a democratic society (a) in the interest of defence, public safety, public order, public morality or public health; or (b) for the purpose of protecting the rights and freedoms of other persons." (The guarantee of the right to life, personal liberty, freedom from torture, cruel, inhuman or degrading treatment, slavery and forced or compulsory labour and the right to fair hearing are not subject to these qualifications.) The qualification is open to at least three preliminary comments aside from the error, mentioned earlier, of extending the state's power of interference to freedom of thought, opinion, conscience, beliefs, feelings and emotions as distinct from their manifestation in action or some other overt ways.

In the first place, the wording seems to shift the emphasis from liberty to the state's authority to interfere with it, from protection of liberty to qualifications on it. It fails to emphasise as clearly as would be desired that liberty is the rule and governmental interference the exception. It seems to place on the individual the onus of showing that an interfering law is not reasonably justifiable in the

---

[17] *Lochner v New York*, 195 U.S. 45 at p. 53 (1905).

specified public interests rather than on the state to show that it is. In short, it fails to strike the balance in favour of liberty which, says Lord Devlin, is "the true mark of a free society".[18] The onus of proving the reasonable justifiability of the law would have been cast unequivocally upon the authorities, and the guaranteed right would have been enhanced in value had the wording of the qualifications read instead, "any law derogating from or interfering with a guaranteed right shall be invalid unless it is reasonably justifiable" etc., or, as in the International Covenant on Civil and Political Rights of the U.N. or the European Convention, the rights and freedoms "shall be subject only to such limitations as are prescribed by law and are necessary to protect public safety, order, health, or morals or the fundamental rights and freedoms of others." The wording of the qualification in the Universal Declaration is to similar effect.

In the second place, while public morality (not just any morality) is rightly included as a legitimate ground of control by the state, Mill's objection notwithstanding, it is an error to leave out economic well-being and general welfare. (Some of the latter Bills of Rights of the countries of former British Africa, e.g. Zambia's, include economic well-being and development).

In the third place, the provisions fail to specify in explicit terms the kind of relationship that must exist between an interfering law and the prescribed public interests to make the interfering law reasonably justifiable in a democratic society in those interests.

In a case before the high court of Zambia, where the issue was whether the power given by the Exchange Control Regulations of the country to customs officers to open and search, without warrant, postal packets reasonably suspected of containing articles or currency notes being imported into or exported out of the country in contravention of the Regulations was an unconstitutional interference with the freedom of correspondence and expression guaranteed by the Constitution,[19] the court held that, to be reasonably required, the connection between a regulatory legislation and public order, public safety, etc., must be a proximate one; that is to say, its bearing on public order, public safety, etc., must be reasonably close and not too remote or far-

---

[18]　Patrick Devlin, *The Enforcement of Morals* (1965), p. 102.
[19]　*Patel v. Att-Gen of Zambia*, 1968 S.J.Z. 1.

fetched. It must also be reasonable and not arbitrary, as well as rational, in the sense that it must suggest itself to a reasonably intelligent mind.

Now, exchange control, being a very vital aspect of a country's development, has certainly some bearing on public order and safety. The question however is whether this bearing is sufficiently proximate and rational to make exchange control reasonably required in the interests of public order and safety and thereby to justify interference with the individual's freedom of expression. The court held, rightly, that it was not. In the words of the learned judge:

> It could conceivably happen that complete financial anarchy might so weaken the economy that internal disaffection might be caused, leading to rioting and civil disturbance. So might widespread unemployment caused, say, by overpopulation. So might prolonged drought which disrupted agricultural production. One might think of many things which could, ultimately, affect the public safety. None of them would, however, have the quality of proximateness which would justify involving this exception. Nor do I think that exchange control is sufficiently proximate to public safety to warrant the present legislation being adopted in the interest of public safety.

The reasoning in this case is a gratifying repudiation of an earlier decision by another judge of the same court. A regulation made by the Government under the Education Act required children in government or government-aided schools to sing the national anthem and to salute the national flag on certain occasions.[20] The requirement was challenged on the ground that it was an unconstitutional interference with the freedom of conscience guaranteed by the Constitution. This depended on whether the regulation was reasonably required in the interests of public safety and public order. Chief Justice Blagden held that it was. His reasoning was that the singing of the national anthem and the saluting of the national flag were necessary to inculcate among the people, especially among children in their formative age, a love of nation and a consciousness of common belonging. The need for national unity, he further reasoned, was much greater in an emergent state like Zambia with its seventy-three distinct tribal groupings, divided not only by language and culture but also by economic and other interests.

---

[20] *Kachasu v. Att-Gen for Zambia*, 1967/HP/273.

All this must be admitted. Yet the question is whether the compulsion of children to sing the national anthem and salute the flag was reasonably required in the interests, not of national unity, which was not one of the specified public interests, but of national security. The Chief Justice who tried the case had reasoned that since "national unity is the basis of national security" then, whatever was reasonably required in the interests of national unity must also be reasonably required in the interests of national security. But surely the connection between the singing of the national anthem or the saluting of the flag and national security is an ultimate, not a proximate, one. The danger to national security in school children not being made to sing the national anthem or salute the flag is rather remote. Indeed, the U.S. supreme court has held that it was not permissible under the U.S. Constitution to use compulsion to try to achieve national unity. "To believe that patriotism will not flourish if patriotic ceremonies are voluntary and spontaneous instead of a compulsory routine is to make an unflattering estimate of the appeal of our institutions to free minds."[21] Accordingly, it held, reversing its earlier decision,[22] that the compulsory flag salute and singing of the national anthem were unconstitutional.

The limitation thus imposed on governmental control of freedom is all the more remarkable because the "reasonableness of each regulation depends on the relevant facts," with the result that "a regulation valid for one sort of business, or in given circumstances, may be invalid for another sort, or for the same business under other circumstances."[23] In upholding a building zone law which excluded from residential districts apartment houses, business houses, retail stores and shops, and other like establishments, the U.S. supreme court observed that:

> regulations, the wisdom, necessity and validity of which, as applied in existing conditions, are so apparent that they are uniformly sustained, a century ago or even half a century ago, probably would have been rejected as arbitrary and oppressive. Such regulations are sustained, under the complex conditions of our day, for reasons analogous to those which justify traffic regulations, which, before the advent of automobiles and rapid transit street railways, would have been condemned as fatally arbitrary and unreasonable ... A regulatory zoning ordinance, which would be

---

21 *West Virginia State Board of Education v. Bernette*, 319 U.S. 624 (1943).
22 *Minersville School District v. Gobitis*, 310 U.S. 586 (1940).
23 *Nebbia v. New York*, 291 U.S. 502 at p. 524 (1934) – per Justice Roberts.

clearly valid as applied to the great cities, might be clearly invalid as applied to rural communities.[24] This approach to the matter has enabled the court to overrule the line of decisions which invalidated laws fixing minimum wages and maximum working hours or prices, as well as certain laws regulating business activities.[25]

The U.S. supreme court has also laid it down that the test of substantial and rational connection applied in ordinary cases is not enough when freedom of political discussion, press and assembly is concerned. A restriction on these rights, the great political freedoms, is valid only if "the words used are in such circumstances and are of such a nature as to create a clear and present danger that they will bring about the substantive evils that congress has a right to prevent."[26] This has become known as the "clear and present danger" test discussed in chapter 6, vol. 4.

Permissible State Interference with the Guarantee of Rights During a Period of a Declared Emergency

The need for effective government is even greater during a situation of emergency declared in accordance with the constitution. Government must be permitted to take action necessary to deal effectively with such a situation; but emergency does not in itself create power. What it does is to call forth the exercise of existing power to maintain peace and order, to preserve life and property, the security of the state, etc. The exigency or danger arising from an emergency situation creates a proximate and rational connection between the action taken and public order, public security etc. Still, the action taken must not be in excess of what is reasonably necessary and justifiable for dealing effectively with the exigency or danger. Whether the action is reasonably necessary and justifiable depends therefore on the degree of seriousness of the exigency or danger created by the situation.

War actually involving the territory of a country creates perhaps the most serious exigency or danger justifying far-reaching interference with liberty. The constitution in most countries usually authorises elections to be postponed

[24] *Village of Euclid v. Ambler Reality Co.*, 272 U.S. 365.
[25] *Lincoln Federal Labour Union v. North Western Iron and Metal Co.*, 335 U.S. 525 (1949).
[26] *Schenek v. United States*, 249 U.S. 47 (1919), per Justice Holmes delivering the unanimous opinion of the court.

for successive periods of six months at a time if the term of office of members of the legislative assembly and executive expires during a war involving the territory of the country making it impracticable to hold elections.

Also, an interfering action not permitted in normal time may be taken during a period of emergency, e.g. detention for more than a few days without the order of a court or death resulting from an act of war.

The protection of human rights demands not only that the action taken must not be in excess of what is reasonably warranted by the danger or exigency of an emergency situation, but also that an emergency is not to be declared unless the situation actually existing as an objective fact warrants a declaration. This makes it necessary that the constitution should spell out in clear, explicit terms the kinds of exigencies that amount to an emergency situation to justify a declaration. Thus, the 1960 Constitution of Cyprus authorised the proclamation of an emergency only "in the case of war or other public danger threatening the life of the Republic."[27] In line with the Constitution of the Fifth French Republic 1958, the constitutions of the ex-French African countries also define an emergency to be "a clear and present danger" threatening the institutions or independence of the nation, the integrity of its territory, or the carrying out of its international undertakings or other situation when the regular functioning of the governmental authorities is interrupted." The danger or threat must be an imminent one, and the event giving rise to it must involve a considerable section of the public, since only so can public order or public safety be said to be in jeopardy.

The definition in the 1979/99 Constitutions of Nigeria is perhaps the most comprehensive.[28] A state of emergency exists only when the country is at war or in imminent danger of invasion or involvement in a war, or there is:

(a) actual breakdown of public order and public safety in the country or any part thereof to such extent as to require extraordinary measures to restore peace and security;

(b) a clear and present danger of an actual breakdown of public order and public safety requiring extraordinary measures to avert it;

---

[27] Art. 183, 1.
[28] SS. 41 and 265, 1979; SS 45 and 305, 1999.

(c)   an occurrence of imminent danger, or the occurrence of any disaster or natural calamity, affecting the community or a section of the community; and

(d)   any other public danger which clearly constitutes a threat to the existence of the country.

A provision, such as that contained in the Constitutions of Nigeria 1960 and 1963,[29] that an emergency shall be any period during which there was in force a resolution by parliament declaring that a state of emergency exists or that democratic institutions in the country are threatened by subversion merely sacrifices the nation and the liberty of the individual to the whims and caprices of parliament.

The usual practice of course is to vest in the executive (i.e. President or Head of Government) the power to declare an emergency but subject to the safeguards as in the 1979/99 Constitutions of Nigeria, that the declaration shall cease to have effect if within 2 days when the National Assembly is in session, or within 10 days when it is not in session, after the publication of the declaration there is no resolution supported by two-thirds majority of all members of each House of the National Assembly approving it. In any event, the maximum period during which a declaration shall be in force is 6 months unless before the expiration of the period, the National Assembly shall, by resolution passed in like manner, resolve that it shall remain in force from time to time for successive periods of 6 months at a time. The only safeguard in the Constitution of the Fifth French Republic and those of the ex-French African countries is the varying requirement to consult certain authorities such as the president of the National Assembly and of the Constitutional Council, and the requirement that the National Assembly shall meet automatically by right and remain in session throughout the period of the emergency.

---

[29]   S. 70 1963 Constitution of Nigeria.

PART II

EVILS OF AUTHORITARIAN RULE

CHAPTER 7

Nature of Authoritarian Rule

The nature of authoritarian rule is, perhaps, best portrayed by examining its various gradations. But before doing so, two preliminary observations may appropriately be made. First, the account in chapters 8-11 of the atrocities committed under authoritarian rule in the discussion of the evils of authoritarian rule in Africa is intended to serve as a vindication of our thesis in this study that no other system of rule so far devised by humankind conduces more to the realization of the ends of human existence upon this earth than one limited by a guarantee of the liberty of the individual under a constitution that has the force of a supreme, overriding law. The other preliminary observation is in the way of general remarks about the evils of authoritarian rule. We begin with the latter.

General Remarks About the Evils of Authoritarian Rule

It may provide a good introduction to begin by noting what some renowned statesmen and political thinkers have said about the evils of authoritarian rule of the dictatorial or despotic type. Sir Winston Churchill, one of the greatest of statesmen, expresses himself thus upon the matter:

> Something may be said for dictatorships in periods of change and storm; but in these cases the dictator rises in true relation to the whole moving throng of events. He rides the whirlwind because he is a part of it. He is the monstrous child of emergency. He may well possess the force and quality to dominate the minds of millions and sway the course of history. He should pass with the crisis. To make a permanent system of Dictatorship, hereditary or not, is to prepare a new cataclysm.[1]

The great French political philosopher and jurist, Alexis de Tocqueville, in

---

[1] Winston Churchill, *Great Contemporaries* (1990 edn.), p. 23.

139

his epochal book, **Democracy in America** (1835), has said that "despotism, taken by itself, can maintain nothing durable ... Do what you may, there is no true power among men except in the free union of their will." He is re-echoed nearly a century later by Lord Bryce, writing in 1920: "No gains," he says, "compensate for the sufferings it (i.e. despotism) inflicts. The only thing it creates is the will to destroy it and start afresh."[2]

Yet, in spite of its well-attested evils, some people are still sometimes inclined to opt for it, because of its pretended advantages or because of the shortcomings of constitutional government. Denouncing this aberrant inclination, Professor Charles McIlwain has pointedly observed:

> A constitutional government will always be a weak government when compared with an arbitrary one. There will be many desirable things, as well as undesirable, which are easy for a despotism but impossible elsewhere. Constitutionalism suffers from the defects inherent in its own merits. Because it cannot do some evil it is precluded from doing some good. Shall we, then, forgo the good to prevent the evil, or shall we submit to the evil to secure the good? This is the fundamental practical question of all constitutionalism. It is the foremost issue in the present political world; and it is amazing, and to many of us very alarming, to consider to what insufferable barbarities nation after nation today is showing a willingness to submit, for the recompense it thinks it is getting or hopes to get from an arbitrary government.[3]

For him, an "autocracy is worse for mankind than even the feebleness of constitutionalism."[4]

The pernicious evil of tyranny by a dictatorship does not consist solely in the mass killings, murders, disappearances, tortures, etc.; no less pernicious is its effect in eroding the capacity of the people to resist. It is the capacity of society and its various institutions – the press, the churches, professional and trade associations, students' unions and so on – to maintain vigilance at all times, to know at the earliest moment when tyranny begins to rear its ugly head and to be resolute in resisting it, that provides the necessary foundation of freedom.

Tyranny, once allowed to establish itself, deprives the people of the capacity to resist because of the pervasive atmosphere of terror, fear, tension and

---

[2] James Bruce, *Modern Democracies*, vol. 1 (1920).
[3] C. H. McIlwain, *Constitutionalism: Ancient and Modern* (1940), p. 32.
[4] C. H. McIlwain, *Constitutionalism and the Changing World* (1939), p. 268.

insecurity created in them by the mass killings, murders, disappearances and tortures. It cows them, and induces in them a mood of cautiousness so as not to risk one's life or liberty: an attitude of resignation, submissiveness and even timidity. This evil effect is tragically brought home to us by Idi Amin's brutal tyranny in Uganda. Subjected to one of the bloodiest of tyrannies imaginable, the people of Uganda, while they were inside the country, were rendered impotent to resist, and were forced into silence, believing in the truth of the age-old adage that discretion is the better part of valour. "As Amin picked them off one by one they continued to entertain the illusion that after one wave of atrocities the country would return to normality."[5] Even the non-brutal, bloodless tyranny of Nkrumah in Ghana produced much the same effect in its people. Its effect on the Christian churches there has drawn tellingly sarcastic remarks from Dr. Conor Cruise O'Brien, former Vice-Chancellor, University of Ghana. "It is," he wrote after Nkrumah's overthrow,

> a joint achievement of the Tudors and the Convention People's Party that in all Anglican churches in Ghana the congregation had prayed each Sunday, up to last Sunday, that Kwame Nkrumah may have victory over his enemies 'spiritual and temporal.' In accordance with a tradition which is as Anglican as it is African, it will be for the victory of his enemies that they will pray henceforward.[6]

But that is not all. Tyranny is, after all, an incident, an extreme manifestation, of absolute power, and must therefore be viewed in the light of the evil of absolute power in corrupting a people and its cherished values and virtues. The wielder of absolute power is of course the first to be corrupted. No ruler in all history has been known to be above the corruptive influence of absolute power. It transforms a person's natural disposition; the wielder becomes a quite different person after some years in the enjoyment of absolute power. Exposure to the arrogance and adulation of absolute power invariably turns even a person of a naturally kind, modest and tolerant disposition into a vain-glorious, intolerant, immodest and unfeeling person, suffused with a false belief in his superior abilities and in his infallible wisdom and a desire for unquestioning obedience to his whims and caprices. He comes to think of himself as not only infallible but also indispensable, a demi-god without whom

---

[5] Ralph Uwechue (ed.), *Africa Today* (1991), p. 1921.
[6] Quoted from T. Peter Omari, *Kwame Nkrumah: The Anatomy of an African Dictatorship* (1970), p. 9.

the ship of state would become rudderless, floundering sooner or later.

Those around the wielder of absolute power are also corrupted into fawning sycophants. Indeed, one of the worst tragedies of absolute power is the large number of people it turns into sycophants and praise-singers, and the longer a dictatorship endures, so do more and more people take to sycophancy as a way of feathering their own nest. They see nothing wrong in taking advantage of the current of events in national life, even when the current is something as immoral and hideous as a dictatorship.

The adulation of a leader or the worshipping of him as a hero is not a bad thing in itself, but in the context of a dictatorship, it easily turns into the deification of him. This is especially the case where such deification is consciously inspired, encouraged or even promoted by the dictator himself, as by Nkrumah speaking approvingly about the "inevitability of deification." It was natural, he told his audience, for the masses to think of their leader as a messiah, a god, likening it to the worship and deification of Jesus by Christians.[7] Now, a people deifying its leader loses the capacity for criticism, for critical appraisal of his performance as ruler, not to talk of resistance to tyrannical rule. They would have bonded themselves to him, becoming mere slavish, obsequious followers, ready to invest him with infallibility and to accept, without question, his idiosyncratic whims and caprices, even those destructive of their liberties. Such was the tragic fate that befell the people of Ghana under the dictatorship of Nkrumah.

Absolute power corrupts the values and virtues of a people in that the standards of integrity, probity, fairness and morality of the absolute ruler set the moral tone of the whole society. Moreover, absolute power induces indifference, apathy and passivity in the people, which is the inevitable result of the lack of popular participation in government. In a state of government-induced indifference, apathy and passivity, people concern and busy themselves, both in their thoughts and sentiments, only in their private affairs, in "the amusements and ornamentation of private life."[8] As John Stuart Mill pertinently observed, "a good despotism is an altogether false ideal ... It is

---

[7] T. Peter Omari, *op. cit.*, p. 144.
[8] Alexis de Tocqueville, *Democracy in America* (1835), ed. Richard Heffner (1956), p. 194.

more noxious than a bad one, for it is more relaxing and enervating to the thoughts, feelings, and energies of the people."[9]

Gradations of Authoritarian Rule

There are four main gradations of authoritarian rule, differing according to the degree or enormity of the evil they permit or are susceptible to, viz: (i) authoritarian rule that is less than an absolutism, as typified by the African one-party system; (ii) an absolute government, as typified by an absolutist military regime; (iii) a fascist government which is an authoritarian system of a type that has not been defined with precision beyond the generalisation that it is a form of dictatorship with socialist, totalitarian orientation and tendencies, such as existed in Italy under Mussolini between 1926 and 1945 and in Germany under Hitler from 1933 to 1945; it is opposed alike to uncontrolled capitalism, political freedom for the individual and communism; and (iv) totalitarian government, as typified by the defunct socialist/communist regimes of Eastern Europe and former Soviet Union.

An absolute government needs no expatiation; it is a government whose powers are not limited by the supreme, overriding law of a constitution through the mechanisms of a guarantee of individual liberty, separation of legislative, executive and judicial powers or in any other institutional way. A totalitarian government is also a government unlimited in its powers by a constitution as a supreme, overriding law. Both an absolute and a totalitarian government are therefore dictatorships, autocracies; often, if not almost invariably, the absolute powers of an absolute or totalitarian government are employed oppressively.

The two differ, however, in that a totalitarian government is a despotism, and one with a vengeance. Total rule implies a government not bound by any law at all, a lawless government, which is what a despotism connotes. The absolute monarch of the past in England, says Professor Charles McIlwain, "may be legally an autocrat but he is no despot,"[10] because he was, in his executive capacity, bound by the common law not to interfere with the private

---

[9] J. S. Mill, *Representative Government*, reprinted in *Utilitarianism, Liberty and Representative Government* (1910), Everyman's Library edn, p. 209.

[10] C. H. McIlwain, *Constitutionalism and the Changing World* (1939), pp. 249 and 252.

rights of individuals. By the concept of socialist legality applied in the totalitarian regimes of Eastern Europe and the former Soviet Union, law is simply an instrument and the expression of socialist totalitarianism, of unfettered arbitrariness by the state in the administration of public affairs. And, according to the Nazi concept of legality, "all means, even if they are not in conformity with existing laws and precedents, are legal if they subserve the will of the Fuhrer." "Totalitarianism simply magnifies the elements of autocracy to their farthest limits"[11] — to the point of despotism.

However, the autocracy of an absolute government may be carried to a point that makes it look like a totalitarian one, as in the case of the absolutist regime of Idi Amin in Uganda (January 1971 — May 1979) where "the law is the gun in the hands of a soldier,"[12] which may be used to kill or maim people as ordered by the dictator at his arbitrary will and pleasure or often as pleases the soldier holding it – sometimes an illiterate, undisciplined soldier at that.

Tyranny scarcely qualifies as a form of government in the modern sense of the term; it implies the absence of government, being simply the extreme of control exercised arbitrarily and brutally. In a full-blown tyranny, government or "the state in effect ceases to exist and civil society is displaced by a system akin to Hobbes's 'state of nature.'" The term 'tyranny' is used here simply to refer to a capriciously oppressive and brutal use of power in its farthest extremity, which may characterise totalitarian as well as an absolute system of government to a varying degree.

The despotism or extreme autocracy of a totalitarian regime rests in part on the fact that, whereas an absolute government is subject to the limitations implied in the separation between civil society and the individual on the one hand and the state on the other, total rule is not. It is in the context of this separation that an absolute government exercises its absolute power. While an absolute government impinges drastically on the domains of civil society and of the individual, if it is of the autocratic, unlimited type, the separation between it and them nevertheless remains as the basic framework of the

---

[11] Eckstein and Apter (eds.), *Comparative Politics* (1965), p. 433; see also Jackson and Rosberg, *Personal Rule in Black Africa* (1982), pp. 236-244.

[12] Thomas and Margaret Melady, *Idi Amin Dada: Hitler in Africa* (1979), p. 47.

polity, operating to inhibit its powers. Total rule, on the other hand, is a system of government in which the separation of the individual and civil society from the state and the limitation on power implied in such separation practically disappears, with civil society and its variegated institutions being integrated into the state. It is a form of rule that tries to integrate, regiment and control "so many aspects of human existence: family life, friendship, work, leisure, production, exchange, worship, art, manners, travel, dress – even that final assertion of human privacy, death."[13]

The nature and character of fascism has been described by Andrew Haywood in terms that can hardly be improved upon, and which, rather than paraphrase, we feel compelled to quote in full. According to him:

> Fascism was anti-rational, anti-liberal, anti-capitalist, anti-bourgeois and anti-communist ... It addresses the soul, the emotions and the instincts (rather than the rational mind) ... while liberals preached the primacy of the individual, fascists wished to obliterate the individual altogether and establish the dominance of the community or social group ... Fascism also stands apart from conventional political thought in its hostility to the very idea of equality ... Fascists were attracted to the idea of a supreme and unquestionable leader ... They believed that society was composed broadly of three elements. First, a supreme and all-seeing leader who possessed unrivalled authority. Secondly, an elite, exclusively male and distinguished by its heroism, vision and capacity for self-service ... Finally, there was the masses, who sought guidance and direction, and whose destiny was unquestioning obedience ... The "leader principle", or *Fuhrerprinzip* is the guiding principle of a fascist state ... In fascist theory, 'true' democracy is therefore an absolute dictatorship. In this way, fascist fused the notions of absolutism and popular sovereignty into a form of 'totalitarian democracy' ... Fascism and capitalism are ideologically incompatible ... Capitalism was thought to be 'plutocratic', dominated by wealth and money, while fascist believed that leadership should be based upon nobility, honour and a sense of duty ... But its brand of socialism was also profoundly anti-communist. ... Fascists were dedicated to national unity and integration, they wished the allegiances of race or nation to be stronger than those of social class ... In relation to the state, fascist ideology embraces two traditions, one, following Italian fascism, has emphasised the role of an all-powerful state, while the other, reflected in Nazism, is built upon the doctrine of racialism.[14]

---

[13] Harry Eckstein and David Apter, eds. *Comparative Politics* (1965), p. 431.
[14] Andrew Heywood, *Political Ideologies: An Introduction* (1992), pp. 174-192.

The system of government in apartheid South Africa cannot be neatly categorised. Alex Callinicos says of it that "it is not a fascist state, but rather 'a racially exclusive bourgeois democracy'... involving a parliamentary system of government in which blacks are denied the vote."[15] The system is perhaps best regarded as a dual system: one for the whites and another for the blacks. As concerns the white minority of 4.8 million people (1984 census), the system might well be described as a parliamentary democracy, but as regards the black majority of 24.1 million, the system was characterised not just by their total disenfranchisement; the powers of the white minority government over them were absolute and total, which justifies a description of it as a totalitarian regime. Without a Bill of Rights in the Constitution or other constitutional safeguards for blacks, e.g. the safeguard implied by the political responsibility of the government to the black majority, the power of the white minority regime over the latter was absolute, indeed total, and was exercised tyrannically. The tyranny of this system is fully discussed in chapter 10.

The system was also fascist in that the power wielded by the government was based entirely on race. A minority government based on race and possessed of absolute, total power over the majority, also defined by race, is certainly a fascist regime for, as Albert Memmi remarked, "what is fascism, if not a regime of oppression for the benefit of a few" defined by race.[16] The fascist character of the system as regards the blacks is reflected in its connection with the German fascist doctrine of the superiority and supremacy of a "master race" identified with the Aryan race, particularly the Germanic people, its destiny to dominate and exploit other races and the necessity for measures to preserve its purity against contamination by the inferior races, which was carried into execution by Hitler's persecution of the Jews and the killing of six million of them.

The emergent banner of fascism in Germany under Hitler in the 1930s had drawn a new generation of Afrikaner graduates to Germany for doctoral studies who, while there, had absorbed fascist ideas about national pride, about an all-powerful state, and about the superiority of the Aryan race and

---

[15] Alex Callinicos, *South Africa between Reform and Revolution* (1988), pp. 28-29; for other critiques of the theory of South African fascism, see Harold Wolpe, *Race, Class and the Apartheid State* (1988), esp. Pp. 40-47; M. Murray, *South Africa: Time of Agony, Time of Destiny* (1987), esp. pp. 107-9.

[16] Albert Memmi, *The Coloniser and the Colonised* (1957), pp. 62,

its destiny to dominate and exploit other races, ideas which they had felt deep in their own bosoms even before going to Germany. Armed with doctoral degrees as a badge of intellectualism and respectability, they returned to South Africa to propagate in the universities and colleges the new fascist ideas in collaboration with young theologians of the Dutch Reformed Church, "so that in time a new generation of urbanised, educated Afrikaners arose steeped in the values of the new nationalism and the new politics,"[17] a radically new idea of how to re-structure the South African society by "dividing it into separate living areas, separate towns, separate economies, separate 'nations.'"[18]

An authoritarian government of the African one-party type is not an absolutism because it is limited by a constitution as a supreme law, though not to anything like the extent required by constitutional democracy, nor does the executive under it possess an independent power to make or suspend laws on its own authority, without reference to a legislative assembly. Its character as a system of authoritarian rule owes to two main factors: the absence (except in Zambia, Kenya and, to some extent, Malawi) of the restraints of a bill of rights enforceable by the courts at the instance of an aggrieved individual; and the dominating position of a single party that integrates the government, both its legislative and executive arms, into itself, with a resultant concentration and personalisation of all powers in the party leader/chief executive/head of state.

The position of the monopolist ruling party differs, however, from that of its counterpart in the totalitarian regimes of the socialist/communist countries of Eastern Europe and former Soviet Union in that, unlike the latter which recasts and remoulds the society, the economy and the polity, integrating them into itself, the African one-party system retains them more or less as they were, merely superimposing the party upon them.[19] Neither the socialist socio-economic order nor the concept of "socialist legality" is an element of the system. The individual under the system is not so regimented in his life as he is under the one-party regimes of the socialist state; he is free to choose his occupation, to indulge in as much leisure as is available and within his means

---

[17] Allister Sparks, *The Mind of South Africa: The Story of the Rise and Fall of Apartheid* (1990), p. 149.
[18] Allister Sparks, *op. cit.*, p. 150.
[19] Ernest Barker, *Reflections on Government* (1942), pp. 285-286.

to afford, to form friendships and business associations. It leaves quite ample scope for the enjoyment of personal and associational autonomy in non-political matters. (This might need to be qualified in relation to Tanzania. The control which President Banda exercised over dress and manners in Malawi was almost totalitarian.)

However, significant associations of a largely non-political character are rigidly controlled. The system does not tolerate independent pockets of power within the state, even when their purpose is essentially non-political. Control is maintained by integrating or affiliating to the ruling party, every organisation or institution of any public significance like the traditional authority and its institutions, trade unions, co-operative societies, farmers' associations, women's and youth associations, ex-servicemen, professional societies, etc.

With three exceptions (the one-party regimes of Kwame Nkrumah in Ghana, Kamuzu Banda in Malawi and Mobutu Sese Seko in Zaire), government under the African one-party system is not a tyranny. No doubt, all the regimes were guilty, to a greater or lesser extent, of human rights violations on a considerable scale involving ban of opposition political parties and other groups, orders restricting the movement of persons, surveillance of the activities of opponents and critics of government by security agents, arrests and detentions without trial for long, indefinite periods, harsh conditions in which detainees were held, forced labour exacted on detainees, denial of fair trial, etc.

Yet, whilst the dividing line between human rights violations of the type just noted and tyranny is a somewhat jagged one, it is nonetheless true to say that "there is a real difference between authoritarian rule and tyranny" and that "most of the Third World countries faced with the battle against the triple curse of poverty, illiteracy, and disease have adopted authoritarian systems of government so they can win the battle quickly, but they still have a fundamental respect for human rights."[20] Whilst the extent human rights are respected or not respected varies from country to country, many of the one-party civilian regimes in Africa may truly be categorised as "moderate" authoritarian regimes in which basic respect for human rights forms part of

---

[20]   Thomas and Margaret Melady, *op. cit.*, p. 175.

the framework of rule, and in which violations of them are not a pervasive feature but only an aberration dictated by the exigencies of the "war" against poverty, illiteracy and disease.

Lying close at the border of an absolutism, the one-party regimes of Kwame Nkrumah in Ghana, Kamuzu Banda in Malawi and Mobutu Sese Seko in Zaire have been described as a "constitutional dictatorship." The notion of a constitutional dictatorship may sound like a contradiction in terms. And, conceptually, it is. For, to merit being so called, a constitution has to be, in Friedrich Hayek's apt expression "a constitution of liberty, a constitution that would protect the individual against all arbitrary coercion."[21] A constitution as a supreme, overriding law hardly merits to be so called if it only grants power in all its plenitude, without limitations designed to safeguard the liberty of the individual while also maintaining appropriate balance between liberty and the safety of the state and society. The liberty of the individual is protected through the constitution by limiting governmental powers by means of a guarantee of civil rights, separation of the three functions of legislation, execution and adjudication, and the guarantee of the right of the people to elect and dismiss the rulers. With such a conception of the nature and function of a constitution, a constitutional dictatorship would be clearly a contradiction in terms.

In practice, however, a constitution, having the force of a supreme, overriding law, does sometimes grant power in its full plenitude with only slight limitations; by so doing, it creates an absolutism, which is then quite appropriately called a constitutional dictatorship. Such was the republican Constitution of Ghana 1960 which invested the "First President", meaning Kwame Nkrumah for as long as he continued to be re-elected president, with executive as well as supreme legislative power. Parliament had of course power to make law concurrently with Nkrumah, yet a law made by him might alter (whether expressly or by implication) "any enactment other than the Constitution." Besides, parliament under Ghana's one-party system was entirely subservient to the president and his government. Remarkably, the centralising design of the Constitution stopped short of subsuming judicial power in the president's and parliament's legislative power. Judicial power

---

[21] F. A. Hayek, *The Constitution of Liberty* (1960), p. 182.

was expressly vested in the courts, which secured its existence as a separate and independent power. But the Constitution might just as well have omitted an express or implied vesting of judicial power in the courts, which would then have subsumed it in legislative power, and so make the absolutism more complete. But while judicial power was separated from legislative power by being vested in the courts, its independence was seriously attenuated by the power invested in the president to appoint and dismiss judges in his unfettered discretion, a power of which he made quite an oppressive use.

Not only were legislative and executive powers united in Nkrumah as president, but also the limitation on power implied by a constitutional guarantee of liberty was absent. The Constitution guaranteed no rights. It only required the president on assumption of office to make a declaration of directive principles of government in terms therein prescribed, a declaration which the country's supreme court has rightly held not to constitute a bill of rights or even a part of the general law of Ghana, being in its form merely a personal declaration of the president's.[22] Also absent were the restrictions on legislative power implied by the provisions relating to chiefdoms and regional assemblies embodied in the independence Constitution of 1957.

Furthermore, the people of Ghana were effectively denied the right to elect their chief ruler at periodic intervals of time and to remove him by refusing to re-elect him if they thought his management of affairs unsatisfactory. This result was brought about by the entrenchment of the Convention People's Party (CPP) in the Constitution as the only legally permitted political party. Taken together with the fact that Nkrumah was the life chairman of the party, indeed he was the CPP, the effect was to guarantee him re-election without opposition or contest, whenever the occasion arose for a presidential election. Thus, Nkrumah as president was practically as irremovable through the electoral process as if he had been proclaimed president for life in the Constitution.

In the executive field, the Constitution assured the president near-absolute power and control. Not only was executive power vested in him, but it was provided that, **"subject to the president's power in that behalf,** the cabinet, consisting of himself and the ministers, shall have the general direction and

---

[22]   *Re Akoto* (1961) GLAIR' 523.

control of the government."[23] It follows that, since the direction and control of the cabinet in Ghana was subject to the powers of the president, the latter had the overriding voice. It needs to be emphasised further that the general direction and control of the cabinet was at the level of the government and not of individual ministries. The ministers, individually, were under the direction of the president for the work of their respective ministries, and it was entirely to the discretion of the president what functions and the extent of such functions to assign to any minister. Herein lay the lever held by the president over ministers and the cabinet.

The cabinet and the individual ministers were neutralised and turned into an appendage of Nkrumah through the manipulation of the **letter** of the provisions of the Constitution, which was a perversion of their spirit, which perhaps justifies the assertion that Nkrumah had raised "extra-constitutionality to the level of an art."[24] (A similar provision in the constitutions of Tanzania and Gambia was not manipulated in the same way to neutralise the cabinet and individual ministers.) It was his power to appoint and assign functions to ministers and the lever it gave him over them, which Nkrumah adroitly harnessed to absorb in himself personally the functions of the cabinet, thereby reducing it to a mere tool for the attainment and furtherance of his ambition for one-man rule. There was, of course, established a full complement of ministries to which were appointed separate ministers, but the critical aspects of the functions of most of them were detached from the minister and given to the president. For example, armed forces were detached from defence, commerce from trade, banking and foreign exchange from finance, major contracting from all departments, police from interior, development expenditure from all departments, radio and television from information and broadcasting, and higher education and research from education.[25] The president also had responsibility over a wide range of other matters: regional organisation including regional and district commissioners, local authorities, regional party organisations and propaganda; establishment, auditor-general's department; African affairs; development planning and certain development projects; all state enterprises

---

[23]   Art. 16 (2).
[24]   Henry Bretton, *The Rise and Fall of Kwame Nkrumah: A Study of Personal Rule in Africa* (1966), p. 148.
[25]   Henry Bretton, *op. cit.*, p. 18.

such as Ghana National Trading Corporation, Ghana National Construction Corporation, Ghana Aluminium Product, State Cocoa Marketing Board, State Tele-Communication Corporation, and Guinea Press. The full list was quite formidable.[26] For many of these functions and others appropriate secretariats were organised, all responsible to the president, e.g. publicity secretariat, African affairs secretariat, establishment secretariat, state enterprises secretariat, etc.

Denuded of the vital aspects of their functions, the ministries were left as mere "hollow shells."[27] The minister was deprived of initiative and autonomy, which necessarily followed from the transfer to the president's office of the vital functions of the ministry. Since the function so transferred must impinge on the work of the ministry, very little scope was left for independent action by the minister. He could hardly initiate policy entirely on his own. By their nature and importance, the functions vested in the president were bound to be the factors controlling policy, which meant therefore that the president was to be the source of initiative in departmental policy as well as in general policy. Without the power to initiate policy for his ministry, a minister can be little more than an administrator concerned in the main to ensure that policy decided elsewhere is properly executed.

Nor was he allowed a free hand even in matters of pure administration. Here too the minister in Nkrumahist Ghana was under the thumb of the president. By law the president could, by legislative instrument, amend a statute so as to transfer to himself, to another minister or to a public officer, any functions conferred upon a minister by that statute.[28] The description of Dr. Lee that ministers in Ghana under Nkrumah were "little more than presidential secretaries who represent the leader in departments of state"[29] therefore seemed apt. With obvious exaggeration Henry Bretton also described them as "no more than highly paid messengers who drove be-flagged automobiles to and from the President's office, carried orders, made enquiries and sought to resolve impasses stemming from the ambiguities surrounding their own position and the apparatus of government in general."[30]

---

26   Henry Bretton, *op. cit.*, p. 180-182; also Ruben and Murray, *The Constitution and Government of Ghana* (1961), Appendix 5, pp. 273-83.
27   Henry Bretton, *op. cit.*, p. 183.
28   The Presidential Affairs (Amendment) Act 1963, s. 4.
29   J. M. Lee, "Parliament in Republican Ghana," *Parl. Affairs* (1962-3), vol. xvi, p. 382.
30   Henry Bretton, *op. cit.*, pp. 97- 8.

The president's office was, of course, well equipped for its extensive functions. Flagstaff House, as it was called, was a vast establishment, staffed by skilled, hand-picked officers chosen both for their ability and for their loyalty to the president.

The cabinet could not but reflect the emasculated power and status of the individual ministers who composed it. It too was reduced to a mere tool, existing just to echo the master's voice.

Nkrumah's powers under the 1960 Constitution (as amended) were thus near-absolute, and his regime is rightly categorised as a constitutional dictatorship. Kamuzu Banda's dictatorship in Malawi was even more squarely based in the Constitution than Nkrumah's in Ghana was, so also was Mobutu's in Zaire, but an examination of the relevant provisions of the constitution in the two countries will overburden the discussion without adding much further illumination of the concept of a constitutional dictatorship. Given that the three regimes border on absolutism, it seems appropriate to treat their evils according as their enormity classifies them with African civilian one-party regimes or with the absolute governments. (Kamuzu Banda frankly admitted being a dictator but maintained that he was such by the permission of the people.)

Authoritarian rule of the African one-party state type differs also from an absolute government in that, it does permit, or is susceptible to, the emergence of personal rule, but not its extreme manifestation: the privatisation of the state. This is attested by the fact that of all the 41 African civilian one-party states, the privatisation of the state occurred only in the near-absolute regimes of Kwame Nkrumah in Ghana and Kamuzu Banda in Malawi. Though power was concentrated in the executive president in the other countries, and even personalised in him in some of the countries, yet the governmental institutions established by the constitution – the cabinet, parliament, judicature, armed forces, police, the civil service and even the party – and their functionaries retained a measure of autonomous existence and role, however minimal, in the actual administration of government; the concentration of powers in an executive president was not turned into a one-man rule. This is accounted for by two main reasons: none of the leaders had Nkrumah's or Banda's extraordinary taste and passion for extreme personalisation of power nor, more importantly, their near-absolute powers under the constitution. (Mobutu's one-man rule and the privatisation of the state in Zaire arose from military absolutism, which was later converted to a civilian one under a supposedly supreme Constitution.)

CHAPTER 8

Repressions and Oppressions under Authoritarian African One-Party System

The atrocious (perhaps better, the tyrannous) repressions and oppressions under authoritarian African one-party system, as exemplified by the regimes of Kwame Nkrumah in Ghana (from 1958 - 1966), Kamuzu Banda in Malawi (1964 - 1994) and Mobutu Sese Seko in Zaire (1964 - 1997), will be here examined under five heads:

    (i)   Detention without change or trial

    (ii) Repression of freedom of speech

    (iii) Interference with due process of law in the courts

    (iv) Interference with the legislative assembly and its autonomy

    (v)   Acts of repression and oppression generally.

Detention without Charge or Trial

Nearly all authoritarian African one-party regimes have used detention without charge or trial as an instrument of repression, but none as extensively as the regimes of Nkrumah in Ghana, Kamuzu Banda in Malawi and Mobutu Sese Seko in Zaire.

Detention without Trial under Nkrumah's Regime

After the Preventive Detention Act (PDA) came into force in Ghana in August 1958, the first wave of detentions under Nkrumah took place in November, involving forty persons alleged to be the organisers of violence and terrorism, From terrorists, it was next the plotters of coups, then the top leadership of the opposition parties and finally the members and ministers of the ruling party. In

155

August 1962, for example, the minister of information and broadcasting, Mr. Tawia Adamafio, the minister of foreign affairs, Mr. Ako Adjei and the general secretary of the CPP, Mr. H.H. Cofie-Crabbe, were detained for their alleged involvement in the attempt on Nkrumah's life. The minister of finance, Mr. Gbedemah, narrowly escaped detention by fleeing the country.

It has been estimated that from August 1958 to February 1966 when Nkrumah was overthrown, over 1,000 Ghanaians were detained under it for periods ranging up to ten years in conditions of severity worse than those laid down by law and accorded to convicted prisoners.[1] The PDA was undoubtedly a most far-reaching instrument of coercion from the standpoint of personal power over lives, property and political behaviour.[2] The Act, Henry Bretton had pertinently observed, "revealed the extent to which government by law had been replaced by government by one man."[3] Everyone's liberty depended on the subjective satisfaction of the President as to whether or not detention was necessary to prevent them "acting in a manner prejudicial to the security of the state;" in other words, it all "depended on the assumed 'humanitarianism' of the President, or more important, on the chance that the details of a miscarriage of justice came to the attention of the President, that he was not too busy, that he listened to the right people, that the right person had last had his ear."[4]

Detention without Trial under Banda's Regime

The principal legal instrument for the repressions used by Banda to maintain his one-man rule in Malawi was the Preservation of Public Security Act, an enactment of the colonial government but never invoked during the colonial period. It is not a preventive detention law in the same sense as the Ghanaian, Tanzanian and Ugandan preventive detention laws because, although it is permanently on the statute book, it needs to be brought into operation by notice in the gazette as and when it is required but there are no limiting conditions as to the kind of situation that must exist before it can be brought into operation.

---

1. International Commission of Jurists Report. According to Harvey, "estimates range from a few hundred to thousands"- *Law and Social Change in Ghana* (1966), 0. 285
2. Henry Bretton, *The Rise and Fall of Kwame Nkrumah: A Study of Personal Rule in Africa* (1966), pp. 45-46
3. Henry Bretton, *op. cit., p. 58*
4. Henry Bretton, *loc, cit.*

All that it requires is for the Minister to be satisfied that it is necessary for the preservation of public security to bring it into operation by gazette notice. It was brought into operation soon after independence.[5] But the Act nevertheless envisages a situation out of the ordinary as showing that it is necessary to bring it into operation.

It is this little obstacle posed by the above requirements and his own autocratic ego that made Banda want to have a preventive detention law in the ordinary sense. And he did have his way. The Constitution of Malawi (Amendment) Act, passed on 30th October, 1964 empowered him, as Prime Minister, to detain anyone "in the interest of defence, public safety or public order," but, being part of the independence Constitution, the power lapsed when that Constitution was abrogated and replaced by the republican Constitution of 1966. In any case, the power conferred by the amendment was no longer needed, since any restrictions on the application of the Preservation of Public Security Act arising from the guarantee of rights in the independence Constitution were removed by the omission of the guarantee in the republican Constitution. So the coast was clear for a regime of unbridled repression based on the Act. Brought into operation soon after independence, the Act, together with the regulations made under it in 1965[6], remained in force throughout Banda's thirty years rule.

The regulations not only authorise detention or restriction of persons but they also authorise any authorised officer, pending the decision of the Minister, to detain or restrict for twenty-eight days any person of whom he has reason to believe that there are grounds which would justify his detention.

The provisions peculiar to Malawi's Preservation of Public Security Act relate to the prohibition of any act or publication, written or oral, likely (a) to be prejudicial to public security; (b) to undermine the authority of, or the public confidence in, the government; (c) to promote feelings of ill-will or hostility between any sections or classes or races of the inhabitants of the country; or (d) to promote industrial unrest in any industry in which the person concerned had not been genuinely engaged for at least the previous two years. The Minister is empowered to declare any district a special area, upon which any person in the

---

5. Gazette Notice 70/1964
6. G.N. 43/1965; 70/1965, 127/1965; and 38/1966

area becomes liable to an arbitrary search and to be shot if he resists; seven districts were declared special areas in 1965.[7] Power is also given to disconnect telephones, or to require any person to furnish or produce any information, article, book or document in his possession or power which is considered necessary for the preservation of public security. It is made an offence, punishable by seven years imprisonment, to consort with or harbour (for example, by giving shelter, food, drink, money, clothing, medicine or any other valuable commodity or giving any other kind of assistance) a person intending or about to act or who had recently acted in a manner prejudicial to the preservation of public order. Any building, hut or other structure which an authorised officer reasonably suspects is being used or intended to be used for the purpose of harbouring such a person may be dismantled or destroyed. Independent Malawi had clearly surpassed in the severity of its security measures anything that the colonial government had done anywhere in Africa when no emergency had been declared.

Banda's regime of repression consisted, for the most part, of detention without charge or trial pursuant to the power conferred by the regulations. To detain a person without charge or trial is clearly oppressive. But the detentions without charge or trial under Banda were not just oppressive; they were tyrannical because of the number of persons affected; the long, indefinite periods of detention; the flimsy, trifling grounds for most of the detentions; the harsh conditions in which detainees were held; the ill-treatment of detainees, sometimes involving torture; the denial of review of continued detention or of other safeguards to secure the release of detainees. (Contrast Philip Short, who wrote in 1974 that Banda's "despotism was in the main benevolent, not tyrannous.")[8] These tyrannical aspects of detention without trial under Banda's regime of repression must now be expatiated upon.

Figures of the number of people detained without trial by Banda to maintain his one-man rule in existence are based mostly on informed estimates, but we know as a fact that 1500 political detainees were released in 1969 to mark his 65th birthday. Seven years later, in August 1976, an estimated 1000 persons were again in detention without trial on political grounds. In early 1977, some

---

7. GN. 55/1965; 251/1965
8. Philip Short, *Banda* (1974), p. 266

2000 political detainees were released.[9] More releases were announced in July 1981 to mark the 17th anniversary of independence. Considering that detentions without trial marked the entire thirty years of Banda's rule, no doubt ebbing considerably at certain periods, the total number involved must run into several thousands. Banda was quite unabashed about the large number of detainees. Announcing the establishment of a detention camp at Lilongwe, the new capital, in January 1965, he declared that "the world can howl dictatorship. I am going to rule this country," and that he might find it "necessary to imprison one thousand people to stamp out subversion."[10] He repeated the warning on April 1, 1965 on the occasion of the anniversary of his release from detention by the colonial government: "If, to maintain political stability and efficient administration, I have to detain 10,000, 100,000, I will do it. I want nobody to misunderstand me. I will detain anyone who is interfering with the political stability of this country."[11]

Detainees were held for indefinite periods, sometimes for a couple of months, but for years in the vast majority of cases: 10, 15, 20 and, in one case, 27 years. The political detainee held for 27 years was only released in 1992.[12] A former cabinet minister and opponent of Banda, who was detained since 1969, died in April 1990 while still in detention.[13]

Detention for such a long time is outrageously inexcusable where the reason for it is something as trifling as showing disrespect to, or making disrespectful remarks about, the president.[14] But Banda, apparently, had no compunction about a person being kept in detention for 20 or 27 years. Referring to detained supporters of Chipembere, he said they "are now rotting at Dzeleka and they will rot at Dzeleka until Doomsday."[15] The fact that there was no regular review procedure to determine the necessity or desirability of continued detention meant that some detainees were simply forgotten and left to rot away in prison for years.

More than anything else perhaps, it is the grounds of detention that starkly

---

9. Amnesty International Report 1978, p. 58; 1979, p.24
10. Hansard Report, 26 January 1965, p. 459
11. Philip Short, *op.cit.,* p.256
12. Amnesty International Report 1993, p. 19
13. Amnesty International Report 1991, p. 150
14. Amnesty International Report 1991, p. 149
15. Banda, Broadcast, 23 April 1967

expose its tyrannical nature. Detentions based on acts subversive of, or prejudicial to, public security actually committed were comparatively few; they were based mostly on mere suspicion of intention, or likelihood, to commit such acts, lawful opposition to, or criticism of, government or some aspects of its policies or actions; mere association or blood relationship with an opponent or critic; merely belonging to an ethnic group or region suspected of wanting to undermine the government; a behaviour or remark that was offensive, disrespectful or insulting to Banda; or some such other grounds with no real substantial relation to the preservation of public security. Some concrete examples will serve to show how really tyrannical these detentions were.

Remarks or statements considered to be an insult, disrespectful or offensive to Banda provided the ground for many detentions, but they make such detentions so absurdly abhorrent because the remarks or statements were often so utterly trifling to be grounds for detention. They included a reference in a speech to the president by name only instead of by the official title and style: Life-President, *Ngwazi* Dr. Kamuzu Banda; a remark in a speech at a political meeting praising a former minister, then an exile outside the country, for his achievements in helping bring development in the southern province; and other similarly harmless but discourteous references to the president for which the speakers, a teacher in one case and a medical instructor in a mission hospital in another, among such cases, were detained for 12, 10, 15, and 5 years respectively. But ludicrous as it may seem to detain a person for not addressing Banda by his official title and style, yet its unfailing use, as well as the pomp and ceremony which attended his public appearances were exceedingly important to him. He was conscious of his dignity in everything he did.[16]

In yet another case, the country's only neurosurgeon was detained for more than 3 years for his effrontery and temerity in challenging the truth of the president's accusation about northerners being disaffected towards the government, and for refusing to apologize to him.[17] Three journalists were detained for more than 2 years for reporting a speech in which the Official Hostess, Cecilia Kadzamira, during a conference on "Women and Development," had said that "man cannot do without woman." She

---

[16.]	Philip Short, *op., cit.,* p. 282
[17.]	Amnesty International Report 1990, p. 154

subsequently denied the statement, although it was recorded in the official U.N. transcript of her speech. The remark gave offence to Banda who has remained unmarried.[18]

A considerable number of people had also been detained for nothing more than that they had ties of blood, marriage or friendship with known or suspected opponents or critics of government, even although they might not have shared in or might have been opposed to their relative's or friend's political opinion and activities. Thus, the brother of a Malawian foreign-based journalist whose political writings about Malawi were critical of government and had caused displeasure to Banda was detained indefinitely for years; so was the son of a former minister dismissed by the president, just for being the son of a discredited minister.[19] Following the president's accusation of northerners as being disaffected towards the government, dozens of them were detained, not because they as individuals were disaffected, but just because they happened to be northerners.[20]

A usual ground for detention was for utterances or acts embarrassing to the government or capable of undermining public confidence in it. Such was the ground for the detention of the son-in-law of the once powerful Alake Banda, cabinet minister and secretary-general of the MCP, who was thought to be the president's heir apparent but was dismissed from his posts for a public statement by him which lent credence to this general belief, and who was later detained in 1980 for criticizing the president's financial management of a state-owned company. The son-in-law's specific offence was that he gave an interview to a British radio station drawing attention to his father-in-law's poor health in prison, thereby causing embarrassment to the government.[21] Some journalists were detained for years for reporting a clash between military forces and FRELIMO guerillas inside Mozambican territory at the time the latter were fighting for liberation from Portuguese colonial rule.[22]

A common ground of detention was criticism by any kind of statement, oral or in writing, which reflected adversely on Banda or the government,

---

[18.] *Ibid,* 1987; p.69
[19.] *Ibid.* 1988, p. 53; 1987, p. 69
[20.] *Ibid.* 1990, p. 154
[21.] Amnesty International Report 1993, p. 200
[22.] *Ibid.* 1978, p. 58

notwithstanding that the statement merely called for change by lawful means or that it contained nothing that might be construed as an incitement to violence. Thus, a teacher, who criticized the president's order that teachers should be transferred to their areas of origin, was detained for some years; so was Malawi's best known and internationally acknowledged poet for his book of poetry, *Of Chameleons and Gods*, considered critical of government.[23] In March 1992, the eight Roman Catholic bishops in Malawi were held under house arrest for issuing a pastoral letter in which they criticized the government for its human rights record, corruption and lack of popular participation in public life. The government then declared the letter seditious making possession of it a criminal offence; many hundreds of people were arrested or detained for this offence, and for the offence of duplicating and distributing the pastoral letter.[24] The pastoral letter did not of course specifically call for the abolition of the one-party system, only for an end to the restrictions on freedom of expression and other civil liberties. Mention should also be made of the detention of a pastor for preaching a sermon critical of the government.

Lastly, detentions for political opposition, for which hundreds were incarcerated. Detentions on this ground were not confined to politicians or political activists. It was extended to civil servants opposed to the practice of making financial contributions to Banda; members of Jehovah's Witnesses religious sect who, on religious grounds, refused to salute the flag or to belong to a political party, including the MCP, a doctrine that characterises members of the sect everywhere else in the world (Banda had also banned the practice of the religion); and to anyone in possession of, "subversive letters distributed by infiltrators masquerading as religious leaders."[25]

The latent forces of opposition to the government were at last unleashed by the Roman Catholic Bishops' pastoral letter, the harassment of the bishops by the government, the dastardly talk by senior officials of the MCP about whether or not the bishops should be killed and the burning down of the press that printed the pastoral letter by the paramilitary Malawi Young Pioneers. In the spontaneous mass uprising in May 1992, sparked by these events and by an

---

[23.]   *Ibid.* 1990, p. 154; 1988, p. 32
[24.]   *Ibid.* 1993, p. 198
[25.]   Amnesty International Report 1979, p. 24; 1987, p. 70; 1988, p. 53; 1982, p. 56

industrial dispute about poor working conditions, low wages, etc., hundreds of people were arrested and 40 were shot dead by the police. The situation was exacerbated by the continued detention of Chihana, a trade unionist and a leader of one of the pro-democracy groups operating from abroad, who had arrived in the country earlier in April 1992 and was still being held in detention without charge in July 1992, despite repeated orders by the high court for the government to produce him in court and to furnish legal authority for his detention. Chihana was later charged with sedition in connection with speeches he had made calling for a multi-party system; and was convicted and sentenced to two years imprisonment at the high court trial in November. His conviction and sentence sparked off another wave of demonstrations and rioting, resulting in the arrest and detention of some 260 people. The demonstrators both in May and now had demanded a multi-party system and an end to one party rule. The demonstrations and rioting were "the first large-scale expressions and spontaneous outburst of discontent with the Banda regime."[26]

As earlier stated, detention without trial as a method of repression for the maintenance of Banda's one-man rule must be considered from the standpoint not only of the large number of people detained, the long, indefinite periods of detention and the fact that the grounds for it had in most cases no real or substantial relation to the preservation of the public security but also the harsh conditions in which detainees were held and the ill-treatment of detainees. Harsh conditions of detention were a feature of Banda's tyrannically repressive one-man rule constantly reported upon by Amnesty International. So harsh were the conditions that several detainees became seriously ill or died as a result of prolonged exposure to harsh, overcrowded and insanitary prison conditions.[27a]

The situation became thoroughly inhuman in 1992. According to Amnesty International:

> Crowded and insanitary prison conditions appear to have been used as a form of deliberate ill-treatment. Many of those arrested for suspected involvement in the multi-party movement were taken to Chichiri Prison Blantyre or Maula Prison in Lilongwe which were already the most overcrowded in the country. Previously, prisoners in Chichiri spent the

---

26. Denis Venter, "Malawi: The transition to multi-party politics", in John Wiseman (ed), *Democracy and Political Change in Sub-Saharan Africa* (1996, p. 158)

27a. Amnesty International Report 1977, p. 80; 1990, p. 155; 1991, p. 150

night sitting back-to-back because there was insufficient room for them to lie down. After the new wave of arrests, prisoners were reportedly forced to stand through the night as there was not enough space for them to sit. One cell in Chichiri prison, measuring 5 meters by 4 meters, was reported to contain 285 prisoners. Former prisoners estimated that on average one prisoner in the cell died every two nights. When a prisoner died he was immediately replaced by another, suggesting that overcrowding was being used as a deliberate form of ill-treatment.[27b]

Ill-treatment by means other than overcrowding was of course common.[28] It consisted of severe beatings, permanent chaining of detainees and deliberate denial of medical treatment. Torture, too, was often applied by means such as electric shocks, suspending of detainees upside down for half an hour and squeezing of genitals. Police interrogators reportedly used pliers to inflict sexual abuse on women detainees. "One woman was alleged to have been stripped naked, beaten and poked with an electric cattle prod."[29] There had been numerous cases of detainees dying from the ill-treatment and torture.

Banda's tyrannical use of detention without trial as an instrument of political control — in order to maintain his one-man rule in existence — was a perversion, an abuse, of power, but the perversion was made worse by manifold illegalities. Hundreds of people detained under the part of the regulations which empowered an authorised officer, pending the decisions of the Minister, to detain them for 28 days continued to be held for years thereafter without their continued detention being regularized by an order made by the Minister.[30]

Secondly, detainees were denied the right to have their continued detention reviewed periodically, although the regulations provided for such reviews. It was only in July 1992, following the mass uprisings, that Banda introduced for the first time a detainees review tribunal chaired by a high court judge to review the reasons for the detentions and the necessity for continuing them, but the tribunal hardly functioned as government stopped referring cases to it later in the same year; instead, suspected opponents were held for weeks without charge and then released or were charged with sedition which in Malawi was committed merely by making "statements likely to undermine public confidence in the Government."[31]

[27b.]   *Ibid.* 1993, p. 199
[28.]   *Ibid.* 1984, p. 65; 1986, p. 66; 1987, p.70; 1990, pp. 154-166; 1993, p. 199
[29.]   *Ibid.* 1993, p. 199
[30.]   Amnesty International Report 1997, p. 80
[31.]   *Ibid.* 1993, p. 198

The successor government of Bakili Mulusi, who defeated Banda at the multi-party presidential election in May 1994, was thus saddled with the responsibility of having to pay out heavy amounts of money as compensation to people unlawfully detained and for the ill-treatment of detainees by Banda's government, and has appealed for international aid for this purpose.

The picture of President Banda emerging from the above account of his repressions in Malawi is that of a monster, a hydra-headed monster. Not unjustifiably therefore, Malawi, under him, has been described as "an archetype of the 'Leviathan' state" whose monstrous one-man despotism had created "a climate of fear almost unparalleled anywhere in Africa, even in countries wracked by violence."[32]

It has been suggested that Banda was personally unaware of many of the atrocities and that "the **de facto** rulers of the country" were John Tembo and his niece, Cecilia Kadzamira, Banda's former private secretary, who constituted Banda's "family." Tembo, as Minister of State in the Office of the President, handled all the important ministries the President had allocated to himself, which, it is said, made him in effect "Prime Minister" and, to all intents and purposes, the real ruler of Malawi.[33] Cecilia Kadzamira, as official hostess, was the person closest to the President, and "was believed to have had the President's ear and therefore had the greatest influence on him."[34] (The contrast between Banda and the woman who was always at his side is interesting: he was a diminutive, unsmiling man while she was a "large woman with a flashing smile.") Powerful as the **duo** of John Tembo and Cecilia Kadzamira certainly were, and while Banda might not personally have been aware of the details of all government decisions and actions, it seems that he, even as old age increasingly took a toll of his mental and physical power, still had a grip on how the affairs of government were handled. The autocratic, repressive style was very much a reflection of his character and personality. In any case, he was the person who created the one-man rule machine and set it in motion, and must therefore answer for the atrocities committed by it and in his name.

But be that as it may, the curtain, happily, was brought down on this tragic

---

[32] Denis Venter, "Malawi: The transition to multi-party politics", in John Wiseman (ed), *Democracy and Political Change in Sub-Sahara Africa* (1996, pp. 155 & 156)

[33] Denis Venter, *op. cit.*, p. 155

[34] Denis Venter, *loc. cit*

phase of Malawi's post-colonial history when, in the multi-party election in May 1994, he was rejected and humiliated by the people of Malawi whose admiring support and worshipping adulation he had so grievously abused. He scored 996, 363 votes (or 33.45 per cent of the total votes cast) against Bakili Muluzi's 1,404,754 votes (47.16 per cent), with Chihana coming third with 552,862 votes. He subsequently died in a South African hospital in 1996 at the age of about 100 years.

Detention without Trial under Mobutu's Regime

The first decade after Mobutu's seizure of power (1965-75) was one of comparative peace and order, when Mobutu could justifiably claim that "political stability had returned," and that "peace, calm, tranquillity reign." The regime seemed to enjoy general acceptability, which had the effect of muting criticism and opposition, though pockets of disaffection were simmering beneath the placidity that was at the surface. Brutal repressions in the period up to 1978 were thus directed in the main against those accused or suspected of involvement in alleged abortive plot to overthrow the government; plot to disrupt the economy, kill members of Mobutu's family and force him to resign; armed invasion from outside the country; or internal armed rebellion in disaffected districts. A notable case of large-scale arrests and detentions with several people killed by both sides occurred during the two invasions of Shaba province (formerly Katanga) in 1977 and 1978 by insurgents based in neighbouring Angola. Certainly, in a situation of attempted coup d'etat or insurgency and counter-insurgency and counter-insurgency operations, killings, arrests and detentions without trial are inevitable and excusable.

Apart from those accused and convicted for the parts they played or were alleged to have played in the insurgencies, it is to be expected that the Shaba invasions and the Banbundu rebellion would give rise to large-scale detentions without trial. A large number of people from all ranks of society, including students, and from different parts of the country, mostly from the two provinces affected, were in fact detained for varying periods of time. According to Amnesty International:

> in June 1978, some 1,300 detainees were transferred from Lubumbashi, the capital of Shaba province, to Lokandu military camp near Kindu in Kivu province where they were detained without trial for several months. In late

July 1978, 27 people detained in this camp were reported to have been executed. Conditions at the camp were extremely harsh and detainees received little food, some dying from starvation.[35]

Of course, detention without trial of opponents not connected with a coup plot or armed insurgency was widely used mostly in the period from 1978. But before examining the detentions without trial and the grounds for them, it is fair to mention at the outset that detentions on flimsy and ludicrous grounds, such as those that grounded many of the detentions in Malawi, were rare. There were only one or two reported cases approaching—but not equalling — the flimsiness and ludicrousness of the Malawian grounds for detention. A university professor was detained for "impudence" for filing his dossier as a candidate for the presidential election; it was an act of temerity on his part to have challenged the Father of the Nation, the Messiah, to an electoral contest. The consecration of Mobutu as the "Founding President" in the Constitution, whilst it fell short of proclaiming him president for life, was as good as conferring on him immunity from opposition for the office. Also, a former government minister and professor of law at Kinshasa University was detained for five months for refusing to speak at an MPR congress in May 1984 on the topic, "Zaire as a State of Law."[36] There was also the case of two leaders of the illegal opposition party, the Union for Democracy and Progress (UDPS), convicted by the state security court of insulting President Mobutu.[37]

Although not bordering on the flimsy or the ludicrous in terms of the Malawian grounds, mere criticism of government not amounting to sedition or other criminal offence is hardly a sufficient reason for detention. And yet it accounted for a good many detentions, usually for a short time, as in the case of a doctor detained for criticizing the country's nationality law. More frequently, mere criticism was punished, not by detention, but by internal banishment, a sanction unique to Zaire and which was visited on 13 elected members of the national assembly and one political bureau member for signing an "open letter" criticizing President Mobutu. They were arrested in January 1981, deprived of their civil and political rights, then banished to isolated villages under a 1961 law, and kept there under restriction until December 1981 when the banishment and

---

[35.] Amnesty International Report 1979, p. 40
[36.] Amnesty International Report, 1985 pp. 109-110
[37.] *Ibid,* 1987, p. 119

restriction were lifted. Banishment of critics or opponents of government to remote villages became fairly frequent from 1983/84, increasing greatly in scale in 1987/88.

Apart from such cases as mentioned above, detentions in Zaire were, in general, for reasons that might be considered sufficient because they constituted a criminal offence against the security of the state: involvement or suspected involvement in subversive activities or in acts otherwise inimical to state security, like having links with subversive organisations in exile; being supporters of such organisations existing within the country; being in possession of subversive documents; or helping a restricted person to flee the country. They do not of course justify detention without trial.

The more usual and frequent ground for detention was organised opposition through the medium of an opposition political party formed in violation of the prohibition in the country's one-party Constitution which was sanctioned by a provision in the Criminal Code making it a criminal offence to conspire to destroy or change the form of government established by the Constitution (art. 196). The formation in 1982 of such an opposition party, the Union for Democracy and Progress (UDPS), constituted a special source of worry for the government, and its supporters or suspected supporters were specially targeted for incarceration.

In March and April 1982, shortly after its formation, 45 alleged supporters were arrested. After investigation, 26 of them were released in June (1982), while the remaining 19, including 12 of the 13 elected parliamentarians and one political bureau member mentioned earlier, were charged before the state security court. All, except one who was acquitted after apologizing for his action, were convicted, the 12 parliamentarians and the political bureau member being sentenced to 15 years' imprisonment, the maximum penalty prescribed for the offence charged.[38] According to Amnesty International, many suspected supporters of UDPS arrested between July and November 1982 were still being detained without trial at the beginning of 1983,[39] but were all released in May 1983 under a general amnesty granted by Mobutu. Fresh arrests and detentions or internal banishment of UDPS supporters took place thereafter

---

[38]   Amnesty International Report 1983, p. 98
[39]   *Ibid* 1984. p. 115

and, indeed, intensified. The same fate was visited on supporters of the Congolese National Movement/Lumumba (MNC/L), dissolved after the 1965 coup but illegally resurrected in 1984.

Students were another group whose militancy and its supposed impingement on state security constituted a troublesome thorn in the government's flesh, marking them out for stern repressive actions. They were viewed as constituting "islets of resistance." The first major confrontation occurred in 1969 when students at the Catholic mission-owned Lovanium University demonstrated over their demand for a share in university government and army units swooped on the demonstrators, resulting in several dozens killed and many more arrested and detained. Following upon this, all students' organisations, except the MPR youth wing, the JMPR, created in July 1967, were dissolved. Another violent encounter with the army occurred in 1971 during the ceremony commemorating the second anniversary of the 1969 demonstration. Many students were again arrested and detained. As a consequence of this second encounter, all students of the Lovanium University were conscripted into the army and all universities and institutions of higher education, both private and state-owned, were turned into campuses of the government-controlled National University of Zaire, constituted as the sole university in the country

But how widely, it may be asked, was the detention dragnet spread in terms of the number of people affected when compared with its scale in Malawi under Banda or Ghana under Nkrumah? The concern of Amnesty International about the "widespread use of detention without trial" may have been expressed with particular reference to the detention in the aftermath of the Shaba invasions, the rebellion in Banbundu and the troubles that led to parts of Kivu province being designated a "military operation zone." Apart from these, the number of people in detention rarely exceeded about 100 at any one given time.[40] The largest number of politically motivated arrests and detentions, reckoned at several hundreds according to Amnesty International, occurred during 1985. "Most of those arrested were apparently released after a few weeks or months in custody,"[41] and the numbers were kept down by releases under a general amnesty granted from time to time by Mobutu. The long and

---

[40.] Amnesty International Report 1984, p. 114
[41] *Ibid* 1986, p. 110

short of all this is that the detention did not approach the magnitude of the detention in Malawi or even Ghana.

There is another aspect in which the detentions contrast markedly with those in Malawi and Ghana: they were mostly for short periods ranging from some days or weeks to up to a year or so. Detentions for longer periods certainly did take place but they never exceeded two or three years at most. There were no known cases of detentions for the outrageously long period of ten years, as in Ghana, or 15, 20 or 27 years, as in Malawi.

Over the years since 1978, Amnesty International has repeatedly reported cases of ill-treatment of political detainees and the use of torture on them by such methods as: severe beating, burning the body with matches, suspending persons upside down, electric shock, piercing with needles and tying a cord tightly around the testicles.[42] Again, the incidence of ill-treatment and torture appears not to have reached the scale it did in Malawi.

Mention may also be made of one further point that seems to put Zaire's detention system in a favourable light. In contrast to Banda's regime in Malawi which regarded Amnesty International as a meddler in its internal affairs, refusing it the favour of a response to its requests for information or access to the country to check on the number of people in detention and the conditions under which they were detained, Mobutu, in July 1981, invited an Amnesty International mission to visit the country to discuss its concerns on these matters with the appropriate government authorities and even allowed it to visit various prisons and other detention centres. An invitation for a second visit, issued in December 1981, was later withdrawn because, according to Mobutu in an interview on French television, his "was the only government in Africa to have twice invited Amnesty International to its country." However, several Amnesty International missions were allowed to visit the county in subsequent years.[43]

An aspect of the Zairean system that seems to have given it a bad image, and for which it has been justly criticised, was the multiplicity of agencies involved in the arrest and detention of critics and opponents of government. There were the Military Intelligence and Security Service — later renamed the Military Intelligence and Action Services (SRMA) — the National Research and

---

42. Amnesty International Report 1986, p. 114
43. *Ibid* 1990, p. 268

Investigation Centre (CNRI) and the National Intelligence Services (SNI): all three operated with ill-defined, overlapping powers, often arbitrarily and without legal authority for their actions. In addition, various army units also illegally carried out arrests of suspected opponents, detaining those arrested in their respective military camps and extorting money from them as a condition for releasing them, sometimes even summarily executing those unable or refusing to pay.

In response to an Amnesty International Report highlighting the grievous human rights violations being committed by these agencies and the unwholesome overlap in their actions – Mobutu himself confirmed that some of these violations had been verified as true by a commission of inquiry – the CNRI and SNI were merged together in November 1983 to form the National Documentation Agency (AND) and the SRMA was disbanded in October 1986. At the same time, a new Department for Citizens' Rights and Freedom was established, charged with the function of dealing with complaints by victims of human rights violations, and with power to refer any official accused of torture for prosecution.[44] The new department opened offices in a number of Kinshasha districts where complaints were to be submitted, and immediately began investigations into them. By a government decree of September 1989, the decisions of the department were made unchallengeable in the courts, but its powers were limited in that it could not challenge cases where people were kept in detention longer than the prescribed period without being referred to the procuracy as required by law, which happened and continued to happen frequently. Early in 1987, 12 members of the disbanded SRMA were tried by a military court on various charges, including the illegal detention of citizens. All were convicted and sentenced to various terms of imprisonment: two years for the most senior of them.[45]

As part of the democratic reforms introduced in July 1990, detentions without trial and internal banishment of political opponents of government were supposedly brought to an end and most of those in political detention, internal banishment or under house arrest were released. However, as the political situation again deteriorated from 1991 following the forcible suspension of the

---

44. Amnesty International Report 1987, p. 118; 1990, p. 266
45. *Ibid* 1988, p. 84

national conference by the government, several arrests and detentions without trial were made when political gatherings and demonstrations were broken up by the security forces. An abortive coup in 1991 led to many more arrests and trials by court-martial. The repression of opposition grew increasingly worse, now also featuring "disappearances" of persons abducted in their homes or in the streets by armed men in civilian clothes as well as extra-judicial execution of arrested political opponents by the security forces. With marauding soldiers on the streets, looting property and killing innocent people, Zaire was again approaching a state of lawlessness and anarchy reminiscent of the early 1960s.[46]

Repression of Freedom of Speech
Repression by Nkrumah's Regime

The widespread use of detention without trial in Ghana operated inevitably to repress freedom of speech among the population. In 1961, another measure designed to repress freedom of speech still further was enacted by way of an amendment to the Criminal Code, which made it a criminal offence to publish by writing, word of mouth or in any other manner whatsoever, any defamatory or insulting matter concerning the President with intent to bring him into hatred, ridicule or contempt.[47] The justification for this is questionable. The Ghanaian Minister of Justice, Mr. Ofori Atta, had defended the provision on the ground that the "Head of State of Ghana is a sacred person, irrespective of the party to which he belongs".[48] Ideally, a Head of State should be above politics in order that his embodiment of the state and its majesty should attract maximum respect. However, an apolitical Head of State is possible, if at all, only if he is a titular head. Such a head can be above partisan politics because he exercises no political function and belongs to no political party. An executive Head of State is in a different position. The exercise of executive powers necessarily invites criticism. One should not accept the office and refuse its price: that would be like eating one's cake and having it. Moreover, an executive President is not just the chief functionary of the government; he is the government itself. To ban criticism of him is to inhibit undue criticism of government. Where an executive

---

[46.] Amnesty International Report 1993, pp. 317-318
[47.] S. 183A
[48.] National Assembly Debate 13 Oct. 1961, col. 32

President is a partisan leading a political party in a two or multi-party system, as in Ghana in 1961, the protection becomes even more objectionable. Such a system necessarily implies political compensation. The President should not be a partisan in politics and at the same time refuse to accept its price. Verbal attacks, sometimes of a very derogatory kind, are inseparable from political competition. Within reason, it is legitimate for politicians to try to discredit each other as part of the effort to enhance one's standing and undermine that of opponents. The leader of the opposition in Kenya, Mr. Ngala, put the point aptly when he said that, as a political head, the president is "a person who throws mud at other fellow politicians and mud can be thrown at him and he can have political fights with other leaders."[49]

Considering, therefore, that Nkrumah was executive President of Ghana and, in 1961, leader of the ruling party in a two-party parliamentary system, the effect of criminalising abuse or insult of him was to raise "the person and activities of the President in all respects, official and unofficial, above all criticism,"[50] as well as to invest him with infallibility and build him up into a cult, the personality cult. The analogy with the maxim on which Mussolini based his rule in Italy is striking – "*Il Duce ha sempre ragione*" ("The leader is always right.")[51] In effect, the person of Nkrumah, having been endowed with sacrosanctity in popular myth, was elevated above the law.[52a]

It is not being suggested, of course, that freedom to criticise the president and the policies and actions of his government should be turned into a licence for vulgar insult; though the danger in prohibiting vulgar insult which is not an offence by the ordinary law of libel or sedition lies in the difficulty of drawing the line between it and permissible criticism. Nor does the use made of the prohibition in Ghana lead one to believe that the law was aimed against vulgar abuse only. For example, a man who, in a conversation with a friend, said that Nkrumah's doctorate degree was an honorary one was prosecuted under the law; the prosecution was later withdrawn and the man was detained instead.

During the debate on the bill in parliament, the disgraced former minister of finance, Mr Gbedemah, had drawn attention to the inhibiting effect the

---

[49.] House of Reps Debate, 27 October, 1964, col. 3910
[50.] Henry Bretton, *op.cit.,* p.53
[51.] Quoted from Bretton, *op. cit.,* p. 56
[52a] Bretton, *loc. cit.*

amendment would have on "free criticism of government policies in parliament."[52b] This danger was demonstrated by the way a similar amendment in Zambia in 1965,[53] which was inspired by the Ghanaian amendment, was applied by the speaker of the Zambian National Assembly.

In October 1969 during the debate in the Zambian National Assembly on an amendment to the Constitution, the speaker repeatedly reminded opposition M.P.s of his earlier ruling that the president should not be made the subject of debate. For, he said, "a Head of State is a Head of State for everybody"[54] and is "the nucleus of the pride of the nation, whether he be UNIP, Congress or otherwise."[55] "If," he continued, "honourable Members wish to attack each other politically, there are many official Members here, Ministers, to attack, rather than attacking a person who is not connected with the debates of this House".[56] The particular amendment under debate was that which sought to abolish the Barotseland Agreement. In opposing the abolition, an opposition member recalled President Kaunda's assurances to the chief and people of Barotseland on the eve of independence that the Agreement would be respected, and how the president had turned round in 1969 to denounce the Agreement at a UNIP meeting. This drew from the speaker a warning that the member was violating his ruling not to involve the president's name in debate; upon which the member protested that the political activities of a president who is also the secretary-general of the ruling party ought not to be above discussion in parliament. The speaker then rose in anger and adjourned the house. The member was arraigned before the Standing Orders Committee, and found guilty of a most serious offence of a nature rendering him unfit to be a member of the house, and for which therefore severe punishment was demanded. However, as the offending member had only recently been discharged from hospital after an operation, the Committee felt disposed to be lenient with him, and accordingly imposed only an apology. Thus condemned, the member was ordered the following morning to stand at the bar of the house and 'register my sincere apology and say that I never intended to be

---

[52b.] National Assembly Debate, 13 Oct. 1961, cols. 25-36
[53.] S. 69 Criminal Code Act 1965
[54.] Zambia Hansard No. 19, 7-17 Oct, 1969, col. 135
[55.] *Ibid*, col. 144
[56.] *Ibid*, col. 135

disrespectful to His Excellency the President. My loyalty to His Excellency the President and Government is unquestionable'[57] In discharging the member after his apology, the speaker further warned that:

> a time might arise in the future when I will not inconvenience the whole
> House by adjourning it, but I will be forced to mete out immediately some
> punishment to an honourable member who does not heed the ruling of the
> Chair, like naming him[58]

Was all this really warranted by what the member said? The assurances given by the president in 1964 to the chief and people of Barotseland were very much relevant to the debate on the proposal to abrogate the Agreement, and it was legitimate, for the proper discharge of his duty to his constituents (the Barotse), that the member should criticise the president for denouncing what he had previously praised publicly and undertaken to respect.

A new security outfit, the state security service, replacing the Criminal Investigation Department of the police, was created in Ghana in 1963 to give teeth to the various repressive laws, and was made 'responsible directly to the president.'[59] The new outfit was designed, and its personnel trained, largely by experts from Russia and other communist countries. It was:

> exclusively at the disposal of the President, completely independent from
> the party, the Central Committee of the party, the cabinet, the armed forces
> and the police. It was meant to be the backbone of the personal political
> machine[60]

It employed 'the whole ugly apparatus of the Police State, complete with ... its intricate mechanism of telephone tapping and censoring of mails and the planting of spies and *agents provocateurs.*'[61] Nkrumah was thus able to control even private conversation.

The press had also been brought under the personal control of Nkrumah. By January 1965 all the daily newspapers belonged either to government or the CPP anyway. Editorial comments, press criticisms and all other publications, both local and foreign, critical of Nkrumah or his government were censored.

---

[57]. *Ibid.,* col. 143 (personal statement by the member for Mongu, Mr. Mumbuna)
[58]. *Ibid.,* col. 145
[59]. S. 1. (1), Security Service Act 1963
[60]. Henry Bretton, *op. cit.,* p.59
[61]. Quoted from T. Peter Omari, *Kwame Nkrumah: The Anatomy of an African Dictatorship* (1970), p. 151; Bretton, *op. cit.,* p. 103

A non-Ghanaian deputy editor, Bankole Timothy, of one of the independent newspapers before the takeover of the press, *Daily Graphic,* was deported for writing an article protesting the suppression of free speech; and several foreign newsmen were also deported on short notice.[62]

Repression by Banda's Regime

Also in Malawi, a tight control of the press – and of freedom of expression generally – was a crucial part of Kamuzu Banda's repressive arsenal. To begin with, all news media in the country were owned entirely by government and published only what complied with the wishes and interests of the government. It was unlawful to circulate within the country any publication not submitted to, and approved by, the censorship board, which had the power to ban or limit the circulation of any publication critical of government: it banned Jack Mapanje's *Of Cameleons and Gods,* among many others. On 14 August, 1978, foreign journalists were banned from entering the country; as the president himself explained, the action became necessary because of the false reports in some foreign news media of conditions in Malawi and of election abuses. Malawi was thus screened off by an iron curtain from the prying eyes of foreign journalists, and news reports by locally-based journalists were strictly censored.

Interference with Due Process of Law In The Courts
Interference by Nkrumah's Regime

The courts too did not escape the enclosing repressive machine of Nkrumah's regime in Ghana. The most abhorrent manifestation of this was the use of legislation to secure the conviction and punishment of persons accused of an attempt to assassinate him in August 1962 as he was returning from a state visit to Upper Volta. The first step in this assault on the judicial process was taken earlier in 1961 through an amendment to the Criminal Procedure Code. The amendment created a special criminal division of the high court for the trial of offences against the state, offences against the person and such other offences as the president might specify by legislative instrument. The court, consisting of a judge and two other members, was to be constituted by the chief justice in accordance with a request made to him by the President. Trial was by a summary

---

62. Bretton, *op.cit.,* p. 89

procedure and the decision of the Court, to be arrived at by a majority, was final. By legislative instrument made by the president, the trial procedure was changed so as to deprive the presiding judge of the power to rule that there was no case to answer; he must call upon the accused person for his defence, 'whether or not a *prima facie* case was made out against him. The intention was, of course, to facilitate the conviction of persons charged with these offences. It did not however guarantee conviction, and failed indeed to secure it in respect of those charged with involvement in the abortive assassination attempt. Their acquittal provoked a second amendment, which authorised the President, if it appeared to him that it was in the interest of the state so to do, to declare by an executive instrument the decision of the court to be of no effect, the instrument to be deemed a *nolle prosequi* entered in terms of section 54 of the Criminal Procedure Code by the Attorney-General before the decision in the case was given. The operation of the Amendment was backdated to 22 November, 1961, the date of the first Amendment. The acquittal of the accused persons having been nullified by the President in pursuance of this power, a third Amendment was brought in which re-constituted the special division. It was now to consist of the chief justice or one other judge, sitting with a jury of twelve whose verdict was to be by a majority. The re-constituted court then re-tried and convicted the accused persons (they had been kept in prison all the time under the Preventive Detention Act) and sentenced them to death, later commuted by the President to a prison term.

The earlier acquittal led to the dismissal of all three judges involved in the trial, including Chief Justice Sir Arku Korsah. Nkrumah had the Constitution amended to give him a completely unfettered power in the appointment and removal of judges.

Interference by Banda's Regime

Interference with the due process of law by Banda in Malawi took the form of the creation in 1969 of traditional courts[63] which were, for all practical purposes, President Banda in a judicial garb. These courts were hierarchically graded – from the local through the regional courts to the national traditional court at the apex – and formed a system parallel to, and independent of, the supervisory or

---

63. Traditional Courts Act 1969

appellate jurisdiction of the ordinary courts[64] and with no right of audience for legal practitioners. Their jurisdiction, which was limited to black Malawians, extended to offences carrying the death penalty as might be specified in a warrant issued by the President, which was the constitutive document designating the members of each court, mostly tribal chiefs with no legal qualification, defining the area of its jurisdiction, etc. Chiefs in Malawi were government agents appointed and removable at will by the President. The creation of the courts, which caused four expatriate judges to resign in protest against what was clearly a retrogressive measure, was in response to a number of acquittals by the high court, on legal technicality, of persons accused of murder by ritual means alleged to be connected with opposition to President Banda.

These traditional courts were used for the trial of some detainees, after some years in detention, who were alleged to have been involved in treasonable acts, plotting to assassinate President Banda and to overthrow the government, subversion or sedition. Five notable trials before the traditional courts may here be noted.

Orton Chirwa, one of the three rebellious ministers dismissed by Banda in the 1964 cabinet crisis, was abducted with his wife and 26-year old son in 1981 from Zambia where they were on a visit to a relative. The couple (but not the son who was kept in detention until he later died) were put on trial for treason before the Blantyre Regional traditional court and sentenced to death, which was confirmed by the national traditional court of appeal. The sentence was later commuted to life imprisonment in June 1984 after an intensive international appeal campaign on their behalf.[65] (Chirwa had formed the Malawi Freedom Movement in Tanzania where he was resident as an exile and from where he went to visit relations in Zambia.) He died in prison in October 1992 from an unknown cause and his wife was refused permission to attend his burial. Considering his age (he was in his mid-60s) and the ill-treatment he received in prison, it bears testimony to his fortitude and unconquerable spirit that he was alive until 1992. For some period during his imprisonment he was 'manacled for long periods each day and handcuffed to an iron bar at night. Although he could lie down to sleep, he could not move freely even in his own cell.'[66]

[64.] Section 70 (3), Constitution
[65.] For details, see Amnesty International Report 1983, pp. 56-58, 1984, pp. 65-66; 1986, p.6.
[66.] *Ibid.*, 1988, p. 53

Earlier in February 1977, a former cabinet minister, Albert Nqumayo, and the head of the security police, Martin Gwede, had also been convicted and sentenced to death by a traditional court for plotting to assassinate Banda and to overthrow the government. Their appeal to the national traditional court of appeal was dismissed. Nqumayo was executed in September 1977 while Gwede's sentence was commuted to life imprisonment. Another former cabinet minister, Gwanda Chakuamba, and a former nominated member of parliament, Faindi Phiri, were convicted of sedition and sentenced to 22 years and 5 years respectively by the Blantyre regional court in March 1981.[67]

Interference by Mobutu's Regime

Trial by court-martial or state security courts was a conspicuous feature of Mobutu's regime in Zaire. Thus, it was they (i.e. military or state security courts) that tried, convicted and sentenced to death for treason those connected with the invasion of Shaba province (formerly Katanga) in 1977 and 1978 by insurgents based in neighbouring Angola. Those so convicted and sentenced included the paramount chief of the province's dominant ethnic group, the Lauda, several army commanders and leading political figures from the province: one of them being Nguza Karl I Bond, minister for foreign affairs and second most powerful figure in the government after Mobutu. The latter's sentence was, however, later commuted to life imprisonment following international appeals on his behalf. The earlier trial and conviction in 1966, of prime minister-designate, Evariste Kimba, and three former minister — Jerome Anany, Emmanuel Bamba and Alexandre Mahamba — and the death sentence passed on them for their involvement in an abortive coup plot, the Pentecost plot, as it is called, were also by military tribunals: they were publicly executed in May 1966.

A military war council was also the tribunal that tried and convicted 79 people (62 armed forces personnel and 17 civilians) accused of involvement in the plot to disrupt the economy, kill members of Mobutu's family and force him to resign. The trial resulted in 19 death sentences (five of them **in absentia**) while 51 of the accused persons were sentenced to terms of imprisonment ranging from 1 to 20 years. Thirteen of the 19 sentenced to death were executed

---

[67.] Amnesty International Report 1987, p. 70.

by firing squad the day after the sentences were pronounced. Mobutu had announced in a national broadcast that he "will no longer tolerate actions to stop Zaire punishing criminals in the way they deserve under the pretext of safeguarding human rights."[68]

Interference with the Legislative Assembly and Its Autonomy
Under the Regime of Nkrumah

As was to be expected, the PDA had a very restrictive effect on the M.P.'s freedom of debate and criticism in Ghana. The mere thought of prison is apt to inhibit freedom of speech. An M.P., of course, enjoys immunity from criminal and civil process for anything he says in parliament; the immunity is considered essential to the effective exercise of his freedom of speech and action in parliament. Seizing a member by means of a criminal process while he is in the house or on his way to it is as derogatory of his freedom of speech as prosecution for a critical speech; the former may indeed be more derogatory, since it prevents him from delivering the speech at all. Immunity, therefore, extends to a member while he is in the house or while he is proceeding to or from it. It is a collective privilege of the house, which a member enjoys by virtue of his membership of the house. Enacting this immunity, Ghana's National Assembly Act 1965 declared that "there shall be freedom of speech, debate and proceedings in the Assembly, and that freedom shall not be impeached or questioned in any court or **place** out of the Assembly",[69] and then went on to prohibit the institution of any civil or criminal proceedings against a member in respect of anything said by him in the assembly or any matter or thing brought by him before it by petition, bill, motion or otherwise, and the service or execution on a member of any civil or criminal process issuing from any court or **place** outside the assembly while he was in the house or within its precincts or on his way to, attending at or returning from any proceeding of the assembly.[70]

These immunities are unquestionably very wide, but the question is whether they avail a member against the power of preventive detention under the PDA. If a member can be detained or restricted under the PDA while he was in the

---

68. Amnesty International Report 1978, p. 94
69. S. 18; (emphasis supplied)
70. SS/ 19 and 20

assembly or going to or returning from its meetings, or for something said in it, will this not amount to questioning the member's freedom of speech in a "place out of the assembly"? And is not a detention or restriction order a **process** issuing from a "place out of the assembly"? The rule of interpretation in cases of conflict between two statutes, one of which is general and the other special, is that the latter constitutes an exception to the former. The PDA is a general statute relating to persons generally, while the immunities statute is a special Act affecting only M.Ps. Accordingly, in a conflict between them, the immunities Act will prevail, notwithstanding that it is earlier in time. This, however, was not likely to be of any avail to a member, since it would be almost impossible to prove that he was being detained or restricted for something he said in parliament and any reasons which the government might state as ground for the detention would be of such a general nature as not to refer specifically to things said in a debate in parliament; nor could the courts compel it to particularise the reasons for the order. Several members were in fact arrested and detained even while parliament was sitting, though their arrest took place in their homes or other places outside the house. One of such arrests provoked some hot exchanges in the house on 24 August, 1960.[71] The government's answer was that the member in question was arrested outside the precincts of the assembly, and that "the immunity of Members of Parliament should not be used as a cloak to protect or shield any Member whose act is prejudicial to the security of the state." If the case was that a member was arrested for purposes of detention or restriction under the PDA while he was in the house or on his way to or from it, there would be no room for equivocation that a contravention of the immunities statute had been committed.

Then there were the measures directed specifically at members of parliament and aimed at securing its subservience to the executive arm of government. Even before the enactment of the PDA, opposition political parties had been subjected to various forms of repression, both subtle and blatant which, coupled now with the PDA and other repressive enactments already noted or to be mentioned shortly, took quite a heavy toll of their following in the country and in parliament. Thus, of the thirty-three opposition members elected to parliament in 1956 (as against seventy-one CPP), only seven were left by the end of 1963,

---

[71.] National Assembly Debate, 24 August, 1960, cols. 899-902; 25 August, 1960, cols. 903-904.

the rest having either joined the CPP, been detained under the Preventive Detention Act or left the country and thereby vacated their seats under the disqualifications introduced in 1959.[72] "By 1960," writes Dennis Austin:

> the effect of the combination of threats and blandishments was plain to see; of the thirty-two opposition members at independence, three were being held in detention, one was in exile and twelve had crossed to the government side. A number more were to take the same road under the republic: some to prison, some abroad and others to the sanctuary of the ruling party.[73]

Opposition political parties in Ghana seemed to have over-indulged boycotts and walk-outs as a method of demonstrating and dramatising their opposition to Nkrumah's government — boycotting constitutional conferences, elections and meetings of parliament. Nkrumah sought to curb this by imposing the forfeiture of seat upon any M.P. who, in the course of a meeting and in the hearing of the speaker or other person presiding, made a public declaration of intention to be absent systematically from meetings of the national assembly.[74] It is not clear when a boycott becomes a systematic absence. Whilst the opposition parties may have over-indulged this method of protest, the idea of suppressing it by a compulsory forfeiture of a member's seat seems too harsh and undemocratic. Now and again, a boycott or walkout may have a real value in dramatising and so bring to the attention of the public an oppressive measure or some other type of abuse of power. The argument of Nkrumah's government that it was derogatory of the prestige and dignity of the assembly for a member to declare publicly before the speaker and in his hearing that he intended to boycott its meetings[75] does not justify the repressive implication of the law.

Forfeiture of a member's seat on the ground of a publicly announced intention to boycott meetings of the legislative assembly is different from forfeiture because of absence from meetings for a specified period. The latter also attracted the forfeiture of seat under the same law, if the absence was for **twenty** consecutive **sittings**.[76]

[72.] J. M. Lee "Parliament in Republican Ghana", *Parliamentary Affairs* 1962-3; vol. XVI. p. 376; Harvey, *op, cit.*, p. 323; Dennis August, *Politics in Ghana* 1946-60 (1964), p. 386

[73.] *op. cit.*, p.386

[74.] National Assembly Act 1961, s. 2 (1) (e) - consolidating earlier Acts on the matter.

[75.] See National Assembly Debate March 17, 1959, col. 359

[76.] National Assembly Act 1961

There seems to be nothing intrinsically reprehensible in penalising repeated and unauthorised absences from meetings by means of the forfeiture of seat. Such a penalty is not uncommon in the rules governing even purely social and cultural associations and whatever justification there is for it in that case must be more in the case of members of a national assembly entrusted with such a weighty responsibility as the government of the nation. The nation ought not to keep or pay for an M.P who does not bother to attend meetings. Yet the origin of the penalty in Ghana seemed to have had a political motivation, being designed as part of a whole network of repression, of which preventive detention was the hob. To escape the dragnet of the PDA, many opposition M.Ps and one or two government ones, like Gbedemah, had been forced of flee the country. The aim seemed to have been to complement the effect of the PDA by visiting loss of seat upon the exiles. Every hole was plugged in a way that left no avenue of escape; if an opponent stayed in the country he might be detained and thereby lose his seat for absence for twenty consecutive sittings, if he fled the country he lost his seat just the same.

Indeed the mere fact of detention under the PDA, irrespective of absence from meetings, had the effect of vacating a member's seat automatically; it also disqualified a person for election to parliament where the detention or restriction occurred within five years immediately preceding the date of the election. [77] Backdated to 1958, the relevant statute enabled Nkrumah to unseat those members of parliament, mostly opposition members, against whom preventive detention orders had been made since the passing of the PDA in 1958. The impact of this, particularly on members of parliament, was to inhibit criticisms of President Nkrumah and his government. From that date on, debate in the Ghana national assembly became, in the words of an opposition M.P., Joe Appiah, more of a ritual dance,[78] in which the government M.P.s, like gagged captives, merely nodded their assent to every government measure, raising their voices only to interrupt opposition speakers. The justification proffered for the disqualification was that it would be "unfair in the extreme to the constituents"[79] for them to be without representation even for less than twenty days, but especially ⁻

---

[77]   National Assembly (Disqualification) Act 1959
[78]   National Assembly Debate, July 14, 1959, col. 457
[79]   National Assembly Debate, March 17, 1959, cols. 357 ff – per Kojo Botsio, Minister of External Affairs

where the detention was for a longer period, say, five years or more. The last of these measures was that enacted by the National Assembly (Amendment) Act 1965 which authorised the recall of a member by either the electorate or the party if the member had "abused the confidence reposed in him at the election."

Interference with the autonomy of the assembly is also exemplified by the encounter of its speaker, Mr. Asiedu, with Nkrumah, as recounted by him (the speaker) in the April 12, 1966 issue of *The Evening News*. The speaker had gone to Nkrumah to protest about an order from the President that he should not go ahead with his announced decision to give a ruling on a breach of parliamentary privilege committed by the party press. "Mr. Asiedu," Nkrumah had said to him, "in Ghana there is only one President. If you think your position as a speaker can challenge me, then try it."[80] That was the end of the matter, and the ruling was never given. Mr. Asiedu further testified in the same newspaper article:

> At this period Kofi Baako, former Minister of Defence, was appointed Leader of the House, and became virtually the Speaker. He openly sought to influence rulings in the House. I offered to resign, but this was turned down by the deposed President.[81]

In spite of occasional noises made by members showing themselves off as "independent," not a single government measure had ever been voted out since 1956.

Under the Regime of Banda

Kamuzu Banda, a notable disciple of Kwame Nkrumah, had followed in that great master's footsteps not only in the use of detention without trial as an instrument of coercion and control, but also in the use of his other repressive measures or devices: the recall of a member of the legislative assembly by the party, the vacation of his seat in the event of his resignation or expulsion from the party and the forfeiture of his seat following upon his detention or his absence for a specified number of meetings.

---

[80]   Omari, *op. cit.*, p. 68, pp. 67-68 reproducing part of the article
[81]   Omari, *loc. cit.*

Under the Regime of Mobutu

The legislative assembly in Zaire under Mobutu was first made impotent, later dissolved in March 1966 and remained dissolved until mid-1970 when a new Constitution, adopted in 1967, came into force. Under the 1974 Constitution, President Mobutu was invested with the right to preside over the legislative assembly; its members were in effect to be named by him and were subject to his control and direction. The so-called election of the deputies was merely nominal, and farcical too, since, until 1977, they were submitted to the voters as a single slate approved by the political bureau which meant, in reality, by Mobutu as the President of the sole party, and then adopted by the voters by acclamation. The position was much the same in Ghana under Nkrumah and in Malawi under Banda, with slight variations. An account of the post-1976 changes in the method of election in Zaire, which were introduced in response to pressures, mainly by Mobutu's foreign sponsors, is omitted here.[82]

Acts of Repression and Oppression Generally
Under The Regime of Nkrumah

The initial emergence of Nkrumah's one-man dictatorship in Ghana involved no widespread state-organised violence and brutality and no mass killings. It is a reflection of his abiding respect for the sanctity of human life that Nkrumah never intentionally caused the death of a single person either by execution after trial and conviction by a court or by extra-judicial killing. No doubt, some of the people detained by him, including his arch-rival, old Dr. J.B. Danquah, died while in detention, but their death was not intentionally caused by Nkrumah. This is a redeeming aspect of Nkrumah's tyranny which, as the International Commission of Jurists remarked, is "an example that should be reflected upon by political leaders facing internal dissent both in Africa and elsewhere." The absence of killings of opponents by the government and of state-organised bloody violence was thus a feature of Nkrumah's regime of repression that distinguished it from those of Kamuzu Banda in Malawi and Mobutu Seso Seko in Zaire. Nkrumah's tyranny consisted essentially of severely repressive laws and other measures of a legislative kind by the use of which all opposition

---

[82] See on this, Crawford Young and Thomas Turner, *The Rise and Decline of the Zairean State* 1986, pp. 201-207

and criticism of his regime were ruthlessly suppressed; and all institutions of government and their functionaries were neutralized and reduced to mere malleable and manipulable tools in the service of his one-man dictatorship.

Under the Regime of Banda

In contrast to Nkrumah's, Kamuzu Banda's regime of repression and oppression in Malawi was, as just stated, brutal and bloody. It predated the introduction of one-party system. In the belief, apparently, that as leader of the nationalist movement who saved the country from the stranglehold of the white-dominated Federation of Rhodesia and Nyasaland (December 1953 — December 1963) and won independence for it, Malawi (formerly Nyasaland) was his to rule as he liked, Banda had, directly after independence, begun to conduct its affairs as sole personal ruler quite unabashed and uninhibited by the system of cabinet government instituted by the independence Constitution under which the authority for government belonged to him and the other ministers equally as co-repositories thereof, although as Prime Minister he was first among equals. For him, such constitutional niceties had been set at naught by the popular will which idolized him as the *Ngwazi* (Lion), the destroyer of the hated federation, and which was sloganised in the party's song *Zimene Nza Kamuzu Banda* (everything belongs to Kamuzu Banda.) He regarded and treated the ministers not as colleagues in the government, but as emissaries, calling them patronisingly as "my boys" in his public speeches and addresses. As he said of them in the legislative council in 1961, "I talk to them like children and they shut up."[83] He made himself feared by the ministers and almost unapproachable, so that they could not relate to him as members of the government; "his legendary temper permeates the civil service" too.[84] He developed an awe-inspiring, intimidating "presence."[85]

The policies of the government, domestic as well as foreign, were decided by him alone, and any opposition or disagreements by the ministers were brusquely and contemptuously brushed aside. It is a mark of the contempt with which he regarded his ministers that he put more reliance on the advice of expatriate civil servants and other Europeans.

---

83. Philip Short, *Banda* (1974), p. 198
84. Carolyn McMaster, *Malawi – Foreign Policy and Development* (1974), p. 169
85. Philip Shot, *loc. cit.*

He found the dispatch of his Ministers to various parts of the globe on study tours and aid-seeking visits a useful means not only of creating valuable contacts, but also of removing them from the active scene of Nyasaland politics.[86]

The ministers were abroad almost all the year round; one particular minister was recorded to have gone on visits to nine foreign countries in one year. Besides, most vital government functions, including the administration of departments, were under his direct responsibility.

Remarkably, unlike in the case of Nkrumah in Ghana under the system of cabinet government (1957 — 60), Banda's arrogation to himself of the authority of sole personal ruler did not go unchallenged by his cabinet colleagues who, increasingly resentful of what was clearly a perversion of the Constitution, accused him of treating the government as his personal estate. The challenge erupted into a major political crisis in September 1964, just two months after independence.[87] Apart from the general accusation of unconstitutional arrogation of authority as sole personal ruler, the crisis was sparked by the ministers' refusal to go along with Prime Minister Banda's plan to introduce a preventive detention law on the same lines as Nkrumah had done in Ghana; his foreign policies as they affected Malawi's relations with the white racist regimes in South Africa, Southern Rhodesia, the Portuguese colonial government in Mozambique and the People's Republic of China; and his rejection of proposals for the Africanisation of the civil service.

Banda's response to the challenge was typically high-handed. He dismissed three of the ministers while three others resigned in sympathy with their dismissed colleagues. All six were suspended from the ruling party, the Malawi Congress Party (MCP). Next, he recalled the national assembly from prorogation to a special session and got it to give him a unanimous vote of confidence. The rebellious ministers then had to flee the country for their own safety. In February 1965, there was an invasion led by one of them, Henry Chipembere, who had crossed the border into Malawi with 200 armed men, and had marched as far as the Shire river, but had to retreat because of difficulties in securing a crossing. Three were killed and seven captured by the pursuing security forces. Chipembere was declared a wanted person. "I want him back," Banda had announced in

---

[86.] Carolyn McMaster, *Malawi – Foreign Policy and Development* (1974), p. 45
[87.] For a full account of the cabinet crisis, see Philip Short, *op.cit.*, pp. 197-230

parliament, "alive if possible, if not alive, then any other way."[88]

On hearing that Chipembere was in the United States, he said in a nationwide broadcast that Malawians would have liked "to see him hanging and his legs dangling and swinging from a pole."[89] From his place of refuge in Zambia, another of the ministers, Yatuta Chisiza, crossed into Malawi with a band of twenty-five men. He and one of his men were killed in the fighting, while most of the others were captured and later hanged.

By the Constitution of Malawi (Amendment) Act passed in October 1964, the seat of a member of parliament was forfeited:

> if, having been elected as a candidate representing a political party established in Malawi, he subsequently ceases to represent or to be a member of that party or claims to represent another political party.

Thus, all the rebellious ministers and other MPs expelled from the party by Banda lost their parliamentary seats.

The crisis had a profound effect on Banda's approach to government and politics in the country. From his point of view, Malawi was "at war" with the rebels, and all means were fair in war. Hence, he spared no means to crush it, and he did crush it decisively.

By the beginning of 1965 one-man rule was firmly and securely on the ground. Banda moved to give it solid constitutional basis. On 20 July, 1965 he announced that Malawi would become a republic on 6 July 1966 under a new constitution; a ministerial constitutional committee was set up to prepare a draft, which was approved by a congress of the ruling party meeting from 13 — 17 October. Thereafter it was passed into law by parliament as the Republic of Malawi (Constitution) Act 1966. Tailor-made to suit the aspirations of Banda, the Constitution had no basis whatever in popular approval expressed through a referendum or otherwise. When, therefore, Banda, frankly admitting to being a dictator, maintained that he dictated "by permission, by consent," his claim was obviously not well-founded, considering that the Constitution under which he exercised his dictatorial rule was not popularly adopted, and that from 1962 to 1994 he never submitted himself to any popular election.

[88.]   Hansard Report, 28 October 1964

[89.]   Philip Short, *op. cit.*, p. 230

Under the Regime of Mobutu

Repression and oppression in Zaire under Mobutu after the first ten years of relative peace and stability were pervasive. His treatment of students' militancy bears this out. With the suppression of all other youth organisations, as noted above, the efforts to organise strong JMPR units within the institutions of higher education and to coerce students to join led to minor conflicts, which were again repressed. The organisation of JMPR units within the institutions of higher education, it has been said, "wholly failed to mobilise real support outside the realm of ritual and ceremony."[90] The next major confrontation was sparked in January 1982 by a strike of students at the Kinshasa campus of the National University and two other institutions of higher education over their demand for higher grants. The three institutions were closed down, and the organisers of the strike, some 95 of them, described as "subversives," were conscripted into the army, but instead of being deployed to military service, they were detained in a military camp under very harsh conditions from January to November (1982) when they were released and allowed to go back to their studies.[91]

Severe acts of repression were also exacted on religious sects whose religious doctrines and practices were considered to be inimical to the hegemonic interests of the regime. The Jehovah's Witness sect was banned in March 1986. Several of its members were arrested and detained in 1989: six of whom were put on trial for insulting the national flag by failing to salute it and for insulting the nation's emblem by refusing to wear the ruling party's badges or to chant party slogans. [92] They were acquitted. The hammer of repression had earlier fallen on the millennial sect in Bandundu in January 1978. Fourteen of its leaders were publicly executed while hundreds of its followers were killed in a violent encounter with the army.[93] Perhaps the regime might have suspected the sect to have had a hand in instigating the rebellion in Bandundu; that might explain in part the severity of the repressive action against it.

The older Christian churches, in particular the Catholic Church whose adherents accounted for 40 per cent of the population, had had a running battle

---

90. Crawford Young and Thomas Turner, *op. cit.*, p. 199; see generally pp. 62, 194-199

91. Amnesty International Report 1983, p. 97

92. *Ibid* 1990, p. 267

93. Crawford Young and Thomas Turner. *op. cit.*, p. 74

with the regime over many aspects of its rule: its dictatorial tendencies; the pervasive corruption; the closure of the seminaries on account of the Catholic Church's initial refusal to accept JMPR branches there; the suspension for six months of the Catholic weekly *Afrique Christienne* for its criticism of the concept of authenticity and the ban of Christian forenames; the absorption of Lovanium National University of Zaire; the eviction of the Catholic prelate, Cardinal Malula, from the residence built for him by the regime because of his criticism; the banning of all religious broadcasts; the dissolution of church-sponsored youth organisations or movements; the state take-over of all mission schools (the schools were returned after 18 months as the government found itself incapable of managing them); and the stoppage of the observance of Christmas as a public holiday![94]

The circumstances of the emergence of Mobutu's one-man despotic rule in Zaire present an interesting contrast to Banda's in Malawi; an account of them might perhaps not be out of place here.[95] It was not, as with Banda's, a product of brutal repression but rather of a combination of military absolutism arising from a bloodless military *coup d'etat* and sheer resourcefulness and ingenuity in the exploitation of situations and the manipulation of people and relationships. Brutal repression came, not at the initial stage, but after the one-man dictatorship had been established and been consolidated.

Independence from Belgian colonialism in June 1960 had sparked a chain of chaotic events: inter-ethnic violence, mutiny by a section of the army, secession bid by the mineral-rich province of Katanga (later renamed Shaba), rebellion by insurgents in the provinces of the northeastern third of the country, conspiracies by different groups of predatory politicians and, above all, a paralysing stalemate arising from a personality clash and conflict of interests and ideological orientation between, on the one hand, the nominal head of state, President Joseph Kasavubu, conservative, enigmatic and uninspiring, and on the other, the effective head of government, Prime Minister Patrice Lumumba, volatile, charismatic and radical. With the authority of the central government eliminated in more than one-third of the country and further undermined by the conflict between president and prime minister, by the mutiny of a section of the army and by the machinations

---

[94.] Crawford Young and Thomas Turner, *op. cit.*, pp. 66-68
[95.] For a full account, see Crawford Young and Thomas Turner, *op. cit.*, pp. 51 ff.

of predatory politicians, the country stood precariously on the brink of collapse and disintegration, from which, happily, it was rescued by the timely intervention of an international military force comprising troops contributed by various countries under the United Nations command, the first such operation in which the world body had been involved since its inception in 1948. From this tragic experience, centralised power and unity of command were posited as an imperative necessity as being the form of government organisation best calculated to prevent a recurrence of these tragic events.

Mobutu, as commander of the army, had played a crucial role in rescuing the country from governmental paralysis consequent upon these events. He first intervened in September 1960 to end the stalemate created by the conflict between President Kasavubu and Prime Minister Lumumba by installing a "College of Commissioners" to rule the country for a period of five months, thereby neutralising the two antagonists. When another stalemate occurred in 1964-65 following President Kasavubu's dismissal of Moise Tshombe from the premiership and the failure of the new premier-designate, Everista Kimba, to secure the necessary parliamentary approval because of opposition by Tshombe's supporters – Kasavubu's renomination of Kimba after his defeat in the first balloting heightened the sense of impasse – Mobutu again intervened in a bloodless military *coup d'etat* to take over the government on 25 November, 1965.

With parliament now in total disarray, President Kasavubu and his rival, Tshombe, accepted the power seizure without demur as did some of the political parties, thus themselves helping to discredit the parliamentary system in favour of military absolutism. On his part, Mobutu, like the astute political strategist that he was, was able to win support among other African countries by appropriating "symbols of Zairean nationalism cherished elsewhere in Africa, particularly those associated with the name of Lumumba."[96] In a move quite untypical of African armies after the seizure of power, parliament, the provincial assemblies and presidents and other institutions of the 1964 Constitution were continued in existence and confirmed in the continued exercise of their functions. While political activities were suspended, political parties were not initially

---

[96] Crawford Young and Thomas Turner, *op. cit.*, p. 53

dissolved, and some issued communiques supporting the power seizure. Respect for constitutionally guaranteed rights was also assured. All this was, however, part of Mobutu's strategy to win support for his regime. By March 1966, these institutions had all been progressively dismantled, with Mobutu, his position as president now consolidated, assuming full executive power, untrammelled by the limitation on presidential power in favour of the government and the premier under the 1964 Constitution as well as power to legislate by edicts; and, although parliament continued to meet until March 1966 when it was dissolved, it had been rendered powerless even before then.

"Political decision, policy initiative and its public presentation were firmly seated in the presidency."[97] The ministers (the premiership was formally abolished in October 1966) functioned merely to execute the decisions and policies of the president. Initially, Mobutu used to listen carefully to daily briefings on policy by the presidential staff comprising "young university graduates assembled together as a technocratic brain trust," but "by 1968 these sessions were less frequent, and the task of the presidential staff became the faithful interpretation of presidential thought rather than participation in the definition of policy".[98]

Thus emerged Mobutu's personal hegemony, anchored as it was in a pervasive "image of force, power and strength." It was also an exclusive hegemony, none being "permitted to claim political roles on the basis of autonomous political power."[99] Until 1970, the basis of Mobutu's personal hegemony still lay in military absolutism. For, although a constitution for a civilian government was adopted by referendum by 98 per cent majority in 1967, its commencement was postponed to 1970 to await Mobutu's attainment of the age of forty required for the presidency. The conversion of the regime from a military to a civilian one under this 1967 Constitution was further consecrated by the popular but uncontested election of Mobutu as president in 1970 with a majority of 99.9 per cent

Having established his personal hegemony by exploiting the situation in the country, marked as it was by factionalism, disorder, chaos and fratricide, which dictated popular acceptance of the absolutism of a military government, Mobutu

---

97.   *Ibid.,* p. 55
98.   *Ibid.,* p. 61
99.   *loc. cit.*

next resorted to manipulation to sustain it in existence. African tradition, in particular the supposed monistic nature of leadership in African traditional society, was also invoked and used as a slogan in support of one-man rule. "A village," so went the slogan, "has only one chief;" "our ancestors were ruled by an unchallenged chief." A chief in African traditional society, Mobutu pontificated, must "seek counsel among the elders. He must inform himself, but after having taken counsel and informed himself, he must decide and resolve the issue alone, in full cognisance of the problem. The tradition, assuming it to be as asserted, cannot be determinative with respect to the management of an organism with such complex affairs and relations of which were largely unknown in African traditional society.

The precedent of the first era of colonial rule when the country was treated as a personal fiefdom of the Belgian King and was ruled by a monistic patrimonial system under which high offices of state were bestowed in return for personal services to the ruler was also invoked and developed to a caricatural extent where, by 1970:

> there was literally no one in the state domain who held a position other than through presidential grace. Once in office, the incumbent has little choice but to conform to the patron-client role prescribed by the basic framework of the system... The prison gate was too close to permit incurring presidential disfavour by deviation from the norm of faithful clientage.[100]

Even for non-office-holders, the ability to acquire wealth in private business and the high social standing that went with it was largely determined by state favour or proximity to state power, and "opposition by deed or even word ran the risk of loss of class standing."[101] Under the system, everything of importance, in particular every policy decision, emanated from the president personally who was serviced by a secretariat composed of courtier-technocrats, and which was "above all the instrument for the transmission of presidential will."[102]

A personality cult was yet another means used to maintain Mobutu's one-man rule in existence. An image of Mobutu as the embodiment, the incarnation, of the nation was built up in the public consciousness. He was erected into an

---

[100.] Crawford Young and Thomas Turner, *op. cit.,* pp. 165, 168 and 398
[101.] *Ibid.,* p. 398
[102.] *Ibid.,* p. 167

ideology, "Mobutism," an ideology with no easily discernible and intelligible meaning or content. An array of praise-names reflecting his crucial role in rescuing the country from the jaws of factionalism, disorder, chaos and fratricide as well as his other great accomplishments and acts of heroism were daily echoed and re-echoed in the media: Guide of the Zairean revolution, Helmsman, Father of the Nation, Founding President, National Hero, Messiah. This was complemented by songs in salutation of him chanted at political gatherings. An article in 1975 by Mr Engulu, minister of the interior, typifies the deification which the officially-backed public glorification of Mobutu had assumed:

> In all religions, and at all times, there are prophets. Why not today? God has sent a great prophet, our prestigious Guide Mobutu —— this prophet is our Liberator, our Messiah. Our Church is the MPR. Its chief is Mobutu, we respect him like one respects a Pope. Our gospel is Mobutism. This is why the crucifix must be replaced by the image of our Messiah. And party militants will want to place at its side his glorious mother, Mama Yemo, who gave birth to such a son.

All this clearly indicates a conscious effort, officially promoted, to garner for Mobutu as a life-sustaining device for his one-man rule, the respect, dignity and authority commanded by a deity, even the attributes of divinity which, not surprisingly, drew from the Catholic Church the charge of sacrilege. (Whilst all gods are divinities, the word divinity is here used in a restricted sense to refer only to God or to Jesus as God.) If not a deity or a divinity, Mobutu had at least been elevated into a superhuman person endowed with infallible wisdom, whose decisions must be accepted and obeyed without question.

> By enshrouding the state in the political personality of Mobutu, criticism was made extremely difficult; anyone identifying policy flaws ran the risk of *lese mejest* ... Those wishing to draw presidential attention to policy difficulties had to preface their carefully formulated observations with ritual flattery about the inspired genius reflected in the policies, then suggest through subtle indirection that some minor difficulties might be removed at the working level. By the early 1970's there was almost no one who could speak openly to the president.[103]

Symbols, concepts and even words, like the term revolution, were also skilfully manipulated to strengthen and sustain Mobutu's personal power. The legend of Lumumba and the symbols associated with his passionate vision of

---

[103.] Crawford Young and Thomas Turner, *op.cit.,* p. 171

Congolese and African nationalism were harnessed for the purpose. Lumumba was declared a "National Hero." But " as the ascendancy of Mobutu consolidated, the Lumumba legend was allowed to slip slowly into the shadows," and was replaced by that of Mobutu; "the national pantheon had room for only one hero."[104]

Mobutu next invoked and harnessed for the same purpose the vague and superficial concept of "authenticity" in pursuance of which the country's name was changed from the Congo to Zaire, and people were forced to drop their Christian forenames in favour of Zairean ones, and to change from Western-style suits with tie to collarless safari suits without tie, called **abacos.**

On 30 November, 1973, Mobutu, the master strategist and manipulator, announced in the national legislative council his decision that "farms, ranches, plantations, concessions, commerce, and real estate agencies will be turned over to sons of the country": Zairenisation, as the measure was called. In fact only the politico-commercial class comprising a tiny proportion of the population benefited from it. This measure which also covered many small industries, construction firms and transportation, was aimed at putting "an end to exploitation" in the country, which Mobutu described as "the most heavily exploited in the world." He followed this up on 30 December, 1974 with another measure dubbed "radicalisation of the Zairean revolution" which, shorn of its rhetorical pretensions, only involved the take-over by the state of the larger business enterprises, mostly Belgian-owned, which had not been covered by the Zaireanisation measure of 30 November, 1973.

With his personal hegemony firmly consolidated, Mobutu next embarked upon the stage of brutal repression, the main features of which have earlier been described.

---

[104] *Ibid.,* p. 169

CHAPTER 9

Privatisation of the State and Bloody Reign of Terror under One-man Dictatorship

The absolute governments that exist or have existed in Africa are for the most part military governments established following a successful *coup d'etat* and take-over of the state by the military. Altogether, 32 countries have been affected by such take-overs to date; the tally of military coups (excluding abortive ones) stands at 82 as at now (June 2001), many of them being coups against an incumbent military government while many of the countries affected have experienced it more than once, some as many as five or six times.

As a system of rule of a higher authoritarian order than the African one-party state type, an absolute government partakes of the evils noted in the last chapter in relation to the former. It erodes democratic governance, the rule of law, separation of powers and civil liberties. Being a dictatorship or an autocracy by definition, it permits or is susceptible to a much greater oppressive use of powers. Its worst evil has manifested itself in two main forms in Africa, viz the privatisation of the state and the establishment of a reign of terror, and a bloody one at that.

Privatisation of the State and Evils Associated with It

"When," writes Alexis de Tocqueville, "the same individual was the author and the interpreter of the laws, and the representative of the (nation) at home and abroad, he was justified in asserting that he constituted the state."[1] Tocqueville was writing with reference to the absolute monarch in Europe, especially Louis XIV of his own country, France, who asserted that he was

---

[1] Alexis de Tocqueville, *Democracy in America* (1835), ed. Richard Heffner (1956), p. 63.

196

the state. However, the privatisation of the state does not just refer to the notion of an absolute ruler as the embodiment or personification of the impersonal entity called the state, which is what Tocqueville was attacking i.e. the ruler as **embodying** the idea, dignity and power of the state. It refers to the much wider and infinitely more pernicious notion of the state under an absolute one-man rule being treated by the ruler as if it were his private estate – as if he owned it, with state affairs becoming practically indistinguishable from the strictly personal affairs of the ruler, with all institutions and powers of government being absorbed in him, and with impromptu decisions and actions based on his personal whims and caprices being substituted for regularised government decisions-taking procedures and processes. What is more, state money and other property are treated as if they were his, personally, to dispose of and be dealt with as he likes, with little or no restrictions on the obligation of accountability, with scant regard indeed to laid-down financial regulations or budgetary controls, breeding in the process utter indiscipline in the expenditure of public funds and of course corruption. Life President Macias Nguema as sole ruler of Equatorial Guinea (September 1968-August 1979) kept the state treasury in notes stored in a building near his house; Field-Marshal Idi Amin, the brutal dictator of Uganda (January 1971-May 1979), kept a huge sum of American dollars, money belonging to the state, in his house; Gen. Sani Abacha, absolute military ruler of Nigeria (November 1993-June 1998), had a small central bank office set up in the presidential villa to facilitate personal dealings with public money; President Mobutu, autocratic sole ruler of Zaire (November 1965-1997), kept with him the cheque books of the state bank accounts, which he carried along whenever he travelled.

The privatisation of the state under a one-man rule is thus an abuse in an extreme degree of absolute power, and a perversion of the concept of the state as a body of laws, not a body of men, as an organisation whose "activities are systematised, co-ordinated, predictable, machine-like and impersonal."[2] One-man rule is arbitrary rule because the course of governmental actions is often based, not on pre-determined general rules applying to all alike, but rather on the ever-changing whims and caprices of the ruler – on "*ad hoc* impromptu directives, reflecting spur-of-the-moment interests, a sudden burst

---

[2]   Poggi, *The Development of the Modern State*, p. 75.

of enthusiasm, or an instinctive urge to appease a given faction, to please an interest group, or to punish a rebellious or recalcitrant" individual or group.[3]

Nkrumah, for example, as sole personal ruler of Ghana (1960-66), was known to order instant promotions, increases of salary, transfers or allocation of government accommodation on feminine appeals to him made by wives on behalf of their husbands without regard to laid-down civil service procedures and to the embarrassment of the proper bureaucratic administration of government. Of the about 20 per cent of public funds disbursed by Mobutu of Zaire outside the normal framework of budgetary control, a significant portion was given out as personal gifts made on the spot during his meet-the-people tours in the interior. "Mobutu always tries to resolve on the spot as many problems as possible. If a given community lacks an indispensable vehicle, if the budget of a school or dispensary has been forgotten, the credits are at once accorded" — a practice which, despite external criticisms, he clung tenaciously to as "an essential ingredient of Mobutu politics.[4] The expropriation of commerce and plantations was meant in part to provide "a huge new pool of resources for patrimonial distribution."[5]

The whims and caprices of the one-man ruler are bad enough as a basis for the administrative actions of the type ordered by Nkrumah and Mobutu in the cases mentioned above, but they are fraught with grave dangers of gross misrule when made a basis for law-making. The making of laws to govern the lives of an entire people is too serious a business, with far-reaching consequences, to be based on the whims and caprices of one man or to be done in a haste. It requires the interaction of many minds in a legislative assembly and its various committees.

The interaction of many minds is indeed necessary in other areas of government. The cardinal evil of one-man rule is that it hinders the development and the maximum utilisation of "the society's critical faculties and collective brain power and the ability to bring that power to bear on the governmental functions."[6] Under one-man rule, the cult of the infallible wisdom of the ruler becomes the governing principle; his decisions are invested with

---

[3]   Henry Bretton, *The Rise and Fall of Kwame Nkrumah: A Study of Personal Rule in Africa* (1966), p. 113.
[4]   Crawford Young and Thomas Turner, *The Rise and Decline of the Zairean State* (1985), p. 168.
[5]   *loc. cit.*
[6]   Henry Bretton, *op. cit.*, p. 140.

sacrosanctity, and must be accepted and complied with without question. Critical discussions of governmental measures are forbidden. Intellectualism is disdained. The intelligentsia are shunned, and kept away from public affairs, with the result that the nation is deprived of the benefit of their knowledge, skills and insights, leading to sterility in leadership and in the administration of government.

Isolated by his high office, with all its comforts, and surrounded by praise-singers and flatterers, the ruler's perception of the needs, aspirations and interests of the people, of events and their social or economic effects, and even of the physical environment, is often distorted or flawed by his personal value system, his biases, attitudes and by the influence of sycophants around him. The risk of error of judgment arising from misperceptions and miscalculations is thus magnified. "At times, the entire apparatus was directed to pursue a whim suggested to the ruler by whoever happened to have his ear," or by "real and imagined threats to the security of the political machine."[7] In the result, "the state and society are irretrievably committed to disastrous policies" dictated by the ruler's wrong perceptions.

The imperfections of the ruler's perceptions and his limited perspectives are entrenched beyond correction because one-man rule hinders "the ability of a government and an administration to improve, or innovate, to modernise, in all spheres of responsibility" which, it has been rightly said, "depends on the extent to which information is received by the decision makers, the quality of that information and the extent to which it is blocked or lost in transit as it passes through the channels of communication."[8] Under one-man rule, the two-way process of communication is largely stultified. Decisions are usually made by the ruler without input from functionaries below him and are just passed down from top.

The plain fact, which must be accepted, is that the government of the affairs of our modern society, in all the complexities of its needs, aspirations and relations among its members, is simply beyond the capacity of any one single individual, however well-endowed he may be intellectually as well as in physical energy and ardour. No nation should allow it, for it leads assuredly to disastrous failure.

---

[7]   Henry Bretton, *op. cit.*, pp. 141-161.

[8]   *ibid*, p. 140.

The truth and logic of this fact has been realised from the early stages of the development in Rome of the complex organism, the state. From the emergence in the first century A.D. of imperial absolutism, the Roman emperor, on whom had devolved the law-making power hitherto in the republican period exercised by the whole citizenry assembled in the Centurial Assembly or Tribal Assembly, did not attempt to shoulder alone such "a prodigious burden of toil and responsibility." Lord Bryce has described for us the system evolved in response to the sheer enormity of the task:

> A Council soon grew up ... At first it was a fluctuating body, composed of ... some of the ablest and most trusted men ... But under Trajan and Hadrian it became a regularly organised chamber ... Among the duties of the Emperor's legal councillors, that of prompting, directing and shaping legislation must have been an important one.... How much the Emperor himself contributed, or how far he examined for himself what was submitted to him, would depend on his own special knowledge and industry. Rude soldiers like Maximin, debauchees like Commodus, would leave everything to their advisers, and if these had been wisely selected by a preceding Emperor, things might go on almost as well as under a capable administrator like Hadrian or a conscientious one like Sexerus Alexander.[9]

If the Roman rulers realised nearly 2000 years ago when social and economic relations among the people were not yet as complex as they have become today that the management of the affairs of the state requires the interaction of many minds in a council, the African rulers of the modern state have a duty to their citizens not to jeopardise their welfare by attempting the impossible task of governing alone.

The privatisation of the state under a one-man rule gives rise not only to intellectual decay but also to political decay[10] through the state institutions – the cabinet, the legislative assembly and (in a one-party system) the party – being deprived of their independence and turned into mere tools to carry out the wishes and dictates of the ruler who becomes the virtual sole legislature, sole executive and sole embodiment of the party, and through the civil society and its institutions – the press, the churches, the trade unions, women's associations, professional associations, students' unions, etc. – being deprived of their autonomy as centres of political power and turned into fawning,

---

[9]   James Bryce, *Studies in History and Jurisprudence*, Vol. 2 (1901), p. 314.

[10]   Samuel P. Huntington, "Political Development and Political Decay," *World Politics*, xvii, No. 3 (April 1965), pp. 386-430.

slavish and obsequious followers of the ruler.

One-man rule has a tendency, perhaps more than other forms of government, to give rise to moral decay too. The ruler in a regime of one-man rule is both political and moral leader of his people – and more beside. The society takes its moral tone from the moral standards of the ruler; his standards of integrity, probity and morality generally filter down the entire body of the society, setting the standards for the people who simply take their cue from him. If he is unjust, unscrupulous, unprincipled, self-centred and grabbing, as nearly all such rulers are (or they will not aspire to be sole personal rulers), these negative qualities would become the vogue among the general run of the citizenry. All other individuals and agencies who in other societies serve as sources of moral leadership and inspiration – churches, philosophers and writers, historical and mythical figures[11] – are effectively neutralised by the ruler's monopolisation of that role.

The moral decay resulting from one-man rule manifests itself most tragically in the vastly heightened scale of misappropriation of public funds, an inexorable concomitant of the fact that the ruler's dealings with public funds are not subject to any controls or checks. That he is a person of integrity may minimise, but it cannot remove completely, the incidence of such abuses, so high and irresistible are the opportunities and temptations for such abuses. The revelations after the downfall of such sacred sole personal rulers like Nkrumah in Ghana and Banda in Malawi popularly believed to be above corruption attest to how impossibly difficult it is to resist the temptations of corruption in a situation where the entire funds of a country are at the absolute disposal of one individual as sole ruler, with no checks and no obligation to account to anyone. The only way to avoid it is not to have a situation of one-man rule at all.

When the sole personal ruler is a person of not such high moral fibre, the scale of corruption is vastly increased; where he is a kleptomaniac, it becomes boundless. Gen. Sani Abacha, Nigeria's military dictator (November 1993-June 1998), exemplifies, in a really astounding degree, boundless kleptomania in his dealings with public funds. The full extent of misappropriations of

---

11   Henry Bretton, *op. cit.*, p. 166.

public funds under his regime may never be known, but the little that is known, which may be taken to represent perhaps only a tip of the iceberg, is beyond belief in our modern state, conceived as an organisation characterised by systematised and regularised procedures. The successor military regime of Gen. Abdulsalam Abubakar announced in November 1998 that a total of ₦125.2 billion of misappropriated funds had as at that time been recovered.[12] This figure included $700 million (₦60.2 billion) of a total sum of $1.331 billion withdrawn from the Central Bank of Nigeria (CBN) "ostensibly for security purposes" but which was thereafter transferred to a private bank account in Beirut, thus leaving $631 million (roughly ₦54 billion) still to be recovered.

The recoveries did not also include ₦8.6 billion which had disappeared from the "National Security Adviser's Special Forex Account" in which it was kept at the CBN, nor the sum of $2.5 billion (₦172 billion) taken from the national coffers to buy-back the discounted debt owed to Russia. Also not included was the value of 37 houses (28 in Abuja, 5 in Zaria and 4 in Kano) and five vehicles illegally acquired with misappropriated public funds by Abacha's national security adviser, Alhaji Gwarzo.

Taking the recovered and the yet to be recovered misappropriated funds together, the total misappropriations so far identified stood at well over ₦351 billion (over $4 billion at the exchange rate of ₦85 to $1.00). Such incredibly high scale of misappropriations could only occur under a one-man regime where the ruler is subject to no controls and checks of any kind, but it still staggers the mind why any ruler under any form of government should want to pillage the nation's treasury of amounts not explicable by any conceivable motive for wealth acquisition by man, unless it be the mere love of accumulating it. In our experimentation with the alien state system, African rulers need constantly to bear in mind the words of the emperor of the great Roman Empire, as he breathed his last: "I have been everything and it is worth nothing."

Similar mind-boggling misappropriations of public funds, albeit on a somewhat lesser scale, had also been reported to have taken place under Abacha's predecessor as head of the military government, Gen. Ibrahim Babangida. It involved the sum of $12.4 billion (₦272 billion at the then

---

[12]   Ebere Ahanihu, "Abacha and the Stolen Billions," *The Guardian on Sunday,* 14 November, 1998, pp. 20-21; Austin Edemodu, "Year of Kleptomaniacs," *The Guardian on Sunday,* 27 December 1998, p. 18.

prevailing exchange rate of ₦22 to $1.00) which accrued to the country from the sharp increase in the prices of petroleum products as a result of the Gulf war in 1990. A panel appointed by Gen. Abacha under the chairmanship of Dr. Pius Okigbo found that the money ($12.4 billion) was paid, not into the proper account stipulated by the law, but into special dedicated accounts, from which it was drawn out and "spent on what could neither be adjudged genuine high priority, nor truly regenerative investment." Further, "that neither the President (Babangida) nor the Governor (of the CBN) accounted to anyone for these massive extra-budgetary expenditures." "These disbursements," said the panel, "were clandestine while the country was openly reeling with crushing external debt overhang. They represent a gross abuse of public trust."[13]

The experiences of Ghana under Kwame Nkrumah's one-man rule and of Malawi under Kamuzu Banda's attest to the intellectual, political, ideological and moral decay which the privatisation of the state under a one-man rule inflicts on a country. These two regimes together with Mobutu Sese Seko's in Zaire are the three most notable civilian one-man regimes in Africa.

It must be acknowledged, as even his most bitter critics acknowledge, that Nkrumah achieved a lot in Ghana,[14] but, given his enormous goodwill both within Ghana and in the international community (the goodwill had by 1965 been dissipated to a considerable extent), we venture to suggest that he could have achieved a great deal more had the policies and actions pursued had the benefit of critical discussions by, and the collective wisdom of, a cabinet and a legislative assembly whose members enjoyed the freedom of independent thought and expression, instead of being the product of his supposedly infallible wisdom and had those policies and actions not been largely pre-determined by his egocentrism, vanity, biases, intellectual arrogance, obsession with grandiose schemes connected with his dreams of the unity of Africa under his leadership, his illusions of grandeur and his personal political interests. As a result of the overwhelming influence of these personal factors in decision-making, "the learning and correcting capacity of the government

---

13 Quoted from Austin Edemodu, "Looting as an Art of Governance," *The Guardian on Sunday*, 22 November, 1998, p. 28.

14 Henry Bretton, *op. cit.*, pp. 150-151; T. Peter Omari, *Kwame Nkrumah* (1970), p. 13.

and administration of Ghana was submerged in a welter of irrational, contradictory, erratic, highly emotional perspectives concerning events at home and abroad. The learning capacity of Ghana was reduced to the learning capacity of Kwame Nkrumah."[15]

Nkrumah, it has been rightly said, inflicted political decay on Ghana by "reducing the capacity of party leaders to generate their own political force and influence. He accomplished that by selecting only mediocres for sub-leadership functions, by devising obstacles to freedom of movement, by monopolising all sources of prestige, and by keeping all leadership elements constantly off balance."[16] Even law and justice, as well as its guardians, the courts and the legal profession, "had been reduced to little more than handmaidens of personal rule."[17] His bid to provide ideological leadership for Ghana also failed because "all ideas, good or bad, soundly conceived or naive, are filtered through only one mind before gaining political acceptability." Furthermore, "the exigencies of personal rule operated inexorably to restrict the flow of ideological activity to a trickle. Everything of substance was measured against the security requirements of the political machine."[18]

The evils of one-man rule had also manifested themselves tragically in Nkrumah's dealings with state property and funds. His numerous admirers, including the present writer, were astounded by the revelation after his overthrow that Nkrumah, who over the years had skilfully nurtured and forced on the public an image of himself as "fount of honour" and "paragon of virtue", had vast amounts of misappropriated public funds secreted in various hidden foreign accounts. The misappropriations had been done in a variety of ways. Many of the major public contracts were awarded by him alone without reference to the cabinet, the appropriate minister, the cabinet contract committee, and without regard to laid-down procedure for the award of such contracts. He created a company, the National Development Company (NADECO) through which public funds were diverted into "whatever channels and for whatever purposes he wanted"[19] without any form of

---

[15]   Henry Bretton, *op. cit.*, p. 142.
[16]   Henry Bretton, *op. cit.*, p. 144.
[17]   *ibid*, p. 147.
[18]   *ibid*, p. 159.
[19]   *ibid*, p. 66.

accounting – mostly no doubt for party purposes, which meant in effect for Nkrumah's personal political machine.

Malawi's experience under Banda's one-man rule had been even more tragic than Ghana's. All the evils noted above with respect to Nkrumah's one-man rule in Ghana, including corruption involving Banda personally, were also present there, and in a magnified degree. The stability (Banda's rule lasted more than thirty years) and progress achieved was at an exceedingly high price in terms of the intellectual, political, moral and ideological decay wrought on the country. Remarkably, his anti-intellectualism was openly avowed. "All these grey-haired professors or bald-headed professors at the University," he once exclaimed, "making all this mysterious lingo, Socrates, Demosthenes, Solon, Edmund Burke and Rousseau, and all that. Talk about democracy, socialism, African socialism. What is African socialism? It makes me sick."[20] Also he was openly disdainful of experts – "so-called experts," as he used to refer to them; any experts whose views conflicted with his own "do not know what they are talking about."[21]

Banda's precepts on morality, like his banning of the wearing of mini-dresses and trousers by women, were "motivated by the need to assert political control than by the desire to exert moral control."[22] He had no use for the arts either, which could not, therefore, develop under him. His pronouncements on the matter are quite outlandish:

> In the West now there exists a permissive society. Do you know what I call it? Depraved society — that's all it is. It is, it is. Women going unspeakably in public like that, and then in New York on the stage doing unspeakable things, and they call that art ... Call it art! You call that civilisation? You call that Christianity? No, to me, if that is civilisation, if that is Christianity, then keep it in Europe, keep it in America.[23]

He had Malawi's best known and internationally acknowledged poet, Jack Mapanje, detained for years, and his book of poetry, *Of Chameleons and Gods*, banned.[24]

---

20   Hansard, April 1966, p. 563.
21   Quoted in Philip Short, *Banda* (1974), p. 279.
22   Philip Short, *op. cit.*, p. 279.
23   Hansard, 24 March, 1976, p. 489.
24   Amnesty International Report, 1988, p. 52; 1990, p. 154.

Banda's policy of co-operation with the white racist regimes in Rhodesia (now Zimbabwe) and South Africa as well as the Portuguese colonial government in Mozambique[25] had brought upon Malawi isolation from virtually the rest of the countries of Africa, and an image of an unprincipled, opportunistic country that had betrayed its Africanism by flirting with an evil racist system of rule, just for the economic benefits it derived from those racist regimes. Banda had tried to justify his policy as having been dictated by Malawi's best interests. No doubt, a small, poor, landlocked country, helmed in by Rhodesia and Mozambique in the south and east, Zambia in the west and Tanzania in the north, Malawi faced dire prospects of economic strangulation and even damage from military attack by the racist regimes. The dire prospects that thus faced the country clearly imposed serious constraints on policy options open to her. Yet, what was determinative was not the constraints resulting from these factors as Banda's perception of their seriousness. As with Nkrumah, his perceptions were grievously distorted and made deficient by his egocentrism, intellectual arrogance, his personal value system, his biases, attitudes and his personal political interests. It is these personal factors that largely determined his policy of co-operation and accommodation with the racist regimes as well as his friendly and welcome attitude towards the West and his hostility towards the communist countries.

In a succinct but devastating commentary, Carolyn McMaster has said of Banda that he was his own legitimacy, a legitimacy that rested entirely on a cult of infallibility that he built around himself – "Kamuzu knows best," as the party's song carelessly proclaimed. But his knowledge and experience of government administration was very limited and deficient indeed – he was invited home to take over the leadership of the nationalist movement in 1958. What is worse, he was not open to the influence of the critical views of his ministers, the legislative assembly and the party. He dismissed three ministers who dared oppose his policies, prompting three others to resign in sympathy, which then culminated in a crisis of temporarily destabilising proportions. The end result of his more than thirty years autocratic one-man rule was a disastrous failure.

---

[25] For full discussion, see Carolyn McMaster, *Malawi — Foreign Policy and Development* (1974), pp. 70-176; Philip Short, *Banda* (1974), pp. 231-250; 283-316.

The epitaph of Emperor Joseph II of the Holy Roman Empire, (i.e. the Romano-Germanic Empire which claimed to be the successor of the Roman Empire in some parts of Germany[26]), written by the emperor himself, seems to fit Kamuzu Banda: "Here lies a man whose intentions were pure but who had the misfortune to see all his plans fail." Banda had the misfortune to see the pillars of his foreign policy collapse. In his lifetime and while he was still in office as president, Mozambique won its independence from Portuguese colonial rule (1975), Rhodesia became the independent black state of Zimbabwe (1980), communism disintegrated in the Soviet Union and Eastern Europe (1989-90) and black majority rule was attained in South Africa (1994). There could be no more telling testimony of Banda's inability to take a far-sighted enough view of things and to provide visionary leadership. He was just a conservative, reactionary ruler with warped and severely limited visions. At home in Malawi itself, his one-man rule, entrenched in the Constitution to last for the duration of his life, crumbled like a pack of cards between 1993 and 1994 when the people of Malawi, now driven to a point where not even the pervasive fear could hold them back any more, rose to assert their freedom from autocracy. But was his failure mitigated by the purity of his intentions? Banda was too self-centred and too self-opinionated for his intentions to have been entirely pure, his oft-repeated assertions of the purity of his intentions notwithstanding.

The decay accompanying the privatisation of the state under a one-man rule sometimes goes beyond intellectual, political, ideological and moral decay, as noted above, and becomes general, permeating the very existence of the state itself. Such general decay occurs when the ruler is not a person with outstanding capabilities to an extent enabling him to attempt, with some measure of success, the impossible task of governing a country alone, as did Nkrumah and Banda. With a much less capable ruler, the decay, sooner or later, permeates the entire fabric of the state itself, in the sense, not just of its malfunction, of deterioration in its ability to discharge its functions effectively, but of its atrophy through an inability to maintain its existence in a recognisable form necessary to fulfil its essential purposes, namely: maximal utilisation of national resources for the welfare of the people, provision of adequate security for life and property,

---

[26]   The Holy Roman Empire, described as neither holy nor Roman, was destroyed in 1806 by Napoleon.

securing its territory against armed incursion from outside and effective execution of its policies, so as to thereby command public confidence in its guardianship of the overall interests of the citizenry. For, though weakened and diminished by the malfunctioning of its instrumentalities – the government and its institutions – the state in the hands of a capable sole personal ruler still continues to exist and to function tolerably well; with a ruler not so outstandingly endowed or a kleptomaniac, it still continues to exist but only more or less as a mere verbal expression, or what John Ayoade aptly calls a "state without citizens."[27]

What this means, in more explicit terms, is that, of the three component elements of the state – people, government and territory – the first two are largely denuded of all practical meaning as functional entities. Divorced and alienated from the state, the people exist, not as citizens with a claim against the state for protection and to be catered for, matched by reciprocal duties to it, but simply as individuals struggling for survival on their own. A state without citizens is like a disembowelled person hanging precariously to life or, to borrow John Ayoade's other metaphors, a "bed-ridden state" functioning by "fits and starts" on the way to becoming an "expired state" or a "morbid state."[28] Government too, as earlier noted, ceases to exist as an organisation whose activities are "systematised, co-ordinated, predictable, machine-like and impersonal," and is absorbed in the person of the ruler and subjected to all his personal whims and caprices, his misperceptions and miscalculations. "State agencies become involuted mechanisms, mainly preoccupied with their own reproduction. Their formal activity tends to become symbolic and ritualistic"[29] and so arises the tragic phenomenon of a state existing only as "an idea without an existential content."[30] Even territory is not effectively policed and controlled, making possible incursions by exiled insurgents operating from neighbouring countries as well as mass movement of refugees across the porous borders from or into the state and its boundaries are often disputed.

Yet, as an idea, the state remains very much part of the social order of African countries. "So deeply rooted is this notion that the state is taken for

---

[27] John Ayoade, "States Without Citizens: An Emerging African Phenomenon," in Donald Rothchild and Naomi Chazan (eds), *The Precarious Balance: State and Society in Africa* (1988), p. 100.

[28] *ibid*, pp. 100-101.

[29] Crawford Young and Thomas Turner, *op. cit.*, p. 399.

[30] Basil Davidson, *The Black Man's Burden* (1992), p. 255.

granted both as empirical fact and normative expectation. The idea of state is ritualised in innumerable ceremonies, small and large ... The banal artifacts of everyday life – coins, banknotes, stamps, party buttons worn by officials – image the state."[31]

Such was the state to which the Zairean state was reduced by Mobutu's one-man rule. It was bled to near-death by Mobutu's unbridled kleptomania and by the sheer ineptitude of his one-man rule in the management of public affairs. From all accounts, Mobutu was a clever, intelligent man, with an "unusual combination of psychic energy and personal resources."[32] Yet he did not belong in the same class with Nkrumah or Banda either in terms of ability to govern a complex modern state or integrity and probity. His conception of the state seemed to have derived from the early beginnings of the colonial state when the Congo was a personal fiefdom of the Belgian king and his notion of government was entirely in terms of patrimonialism, a primitive system in which public office is bestowed in return for personal service to the ruler, and is held on condition of continued personal loyalty to him in a patron-client relationship determinable at the pleasure of the ruler. Patrimonialism went hand-in-hand with the cult of personality – "Mobutism" – which was elevated to a height that stifled rationality, initiative, creativity and the exercise of critical faculty by the people. Yet, the infallibility with which Mobutu was invested in popular belief and by his active prompting and unremitting urging was a complete farce totally unrelated to his actual intellectual capability. In the result, most government policies and decisions were based on Mobutu's misperceptions, miscalculations, whims and caprices, and his personal political and economic interests, giving rise to incessant errors of judgment — such as his Zaireanisation, "authenticity" and radicalisation measures — and to disastrous failures. All Mobutu could offer Zaire by way of ideological leadership was the vague, superficial concept of "authenticity" in the name of which Zaireans were compelled by law in 1972 to discard their Christian names in favour of Zairean ones, and the ban on Western-style suits with tie in favour of collarless safari suits without ties called abacos; when both measures were later abrogated in 1990, Zaireans quickly and joyfully

---

[31]   Crawford Young and Thomas Turner, *op. cit.*, pp. 403-404.
[32]   Crawford Young and Thomas Turner, *op. cit.*, p. 165.

reverted to their Christian forenames and to Western-style suits, which demonstrates the silliness of the measures. (Mobutu's wife had defiantly refused to drop her Christian forename, and no action was taken against her.)

But worse still was Mobutu's utter lack of public probity, of a sense of rectitude in public life. He was simply a charming rogue, a downright kleptomaniac, whose formal education stopped at the level of junior secondary in a mission school from which he was expelled for burglary of the mission library. His piratical misappropriations of public money were so colossal as to be unbelievable. In 1975 a journal in Brussels listed him as holding assets abroad valued as follows:[33]

Residence and estate in Switzerland near Lausanne	$3,750,000
Chateau at Nammur	$1,625,000
Villa at Rhode-St-Genese	$875,000
Estate, and football field at S.A. Royale Belge	$1,500,000
Ten-storey building, Boulevard Reyers, Brussels	$2,000,000
Building on Boulevard Lambermont, Brussels	$1,000,000
Other properties in Belgium	$12,500,000
Residence in Paris, Avenue Foch	$750,000
Residence in Nice	$1,250,000
Residence in Venice	$625,000
Chateau in Spain	$1,250,000
Building in Bangui, Central African Republic	$250,000
Villa in Abidjan, Ivory Coast	$500,000
Funds on deposit in Swiss banks	$125,000,000
Total =	$152,865,000

The list does not of course include foreign property holdings acquired after 1975; these include three hotels in Dakar, eight houses and three castles in Brussels as well as properties in Paris, Lucerne, Ndjamena, Abidjan and Dakar. From 1977 to 1979 he illegally withdrew $150 million in foreign exchange from the Bank of Zaire for his private use. In September 1981 another $30

---

[33]   Crawford Young and Thomas Turner, *op. cit.*, p. 197.

million was, on his order, transferred to his personal account abroad by the Bank of Zaire. Proceeds from the sale of the country's minerals (copper, cobalt and diamonds) worth scores of millions of U.S. dollars were paid direct into his foreign accounts from time to time. His foreign wealth was estimated at about $5 billion in 1984. His private wealth within Zaire itself almost rivalled that of the state: his conglomerate employed 25,000 persons, including 140 Europeans, ranking as the third largest employer of labour in the country after the state and a state-owned company.

Lacking a sense of integrity and rectitude, Mobutu as sole personal ruler of Zaire had completely abandoned morality not only by these huge misappropriations of public funds but also by the corrupt manner in which expropriated foreign enterprises were distributed. By his repeated preachings he had led the people into believing that the expropriations were intended for the betterment of the lot of the suffering masses when in reality it was meant for the enrichment of himself and his collaborators. By garnering to themselves most of the enterprises, leaving the masses more impoverished than before, Mobutu and his top aides had sacrificed their duty as guardians of the interests of society as a whole to their selfish desire for their own enrichment, thus dramatising most starkly "the moral vacuum in which the state operated."[34] For people who did not benefit from the distribution, the deceit and corruption of the exercise "tended to dissipate whatever scruples might remain"[35] Morality had been completely jettisoned from public life.

By the 1980s, the Zairean state, bled white by Mobutu, drifted towards bankruptcy; constitutional institutions other than the presidency had been jettisoned. There was a general decay which permeated all state apparatuses and processes; the state now existed more in name than in reality.[36] Exiled insurgents based in neighbouring Angola had taken advantage of the situation to invade Shaba province (former Katanga) in 1977 and again in 1978; the state only managed to survive with the help of troops sent by Morocco, France and Belgium, supported by French and British aircraft, later replaced by an inter-African force, including a Moroccan contingent, with US transport

---

[34]   Crawford Young and Thomas Turner, *op. cit.*, p. 344.
[35]   *ibid*, p. 345.
[36]   Crawford Young, "Zaire: Is there a State?" *Journal of African Studies* vol. 18, No. 1 (1984), p. 80; Crawford Young and Thomas Turner, *op. cit.*, pp. 71-77; 396-406.

and equipment.

The general decay which befell the Zairean state under Mobutu's one-man rule starkly reveals the limits of any one individual's capacity to govern the affairs of a modern state. One-man rule under Mobutu "consumed the national wealth without producing justice, welfare or security to the helpless and demoralised bewilderment of the populace."[37] The state existed solely for the benefit of Mobutu and a small class of the politico-commercial bourgeois class who had fed themselves fat upon the wealth of the nation and the spoils of the Zaireanisation measure – "an insecure predator upon civil society."[38] They are reckoned to have numbered just about 300,000 in all.[39] After 32 years of his one-man rule, Mobutu was finally chased out by invading exiled insurgents led by Laurent Kabila and died of cancer shortly after. The new regime refused to allow his body to be brought home for burial.

Bloody Reign of Terror

An absolutist military regime is a dictatorship and is not infrequently tyrannical. All are repressive, of course, but some are known to have been highly repressive, characterised as they were by arbitrary detention without trial on a large scale for long, indefinite periods of time, torture of detainees by various cruel methods such as electric shock and physical assault and other inhuman or oppressive treatment of detainees, criminal trials by military or special tribunals often conducted in camera, press censorship, widespread feeling of fear and insecurity among the population, etc. Such regimes are rightly classified as tyrannical, albeit comparatively "moderately" so (not tyrannies in the conceptual sense of the term).

Among such highly repressive military regimes may be cited those of Lt-Col. Seyni Kounteche in Niger (April 1974-November 1987), Major-General Buhari in Nigeria (January 1984-August 1985), Gen. Sani Abacha in Nigeria (November 1993-June 1998), Gen. Samuel Doe in Liberia (April 1980-

---

[37]   Crawford Young and Thomas Turner, *op. cit.*, p. 77.
[38]   Crawford Young and Thomas Turner, *op. cit.*, p. 399.
[39]   Jules Gerard-Libois, "The New Class and Rebellion in the Congo," in R. M. Liband and J. Saville (eds), *The Socialist Register* (1966), pp. 267-280.

September 1990), Gen. Siad Barre in Somalia (October 1969-January 1991). The regimes of Lt-Col Seyni Kountche and Gen. Samuel Doe were characterised additionally by killings and summary executions just falling short of mass massacres, as well as state terrorism involving harassment, brutality and disappearances of people.[40] These additional characteristics made the two regimes more than moderate tyrannical regimes.

The really full-blown brutal tyrannies were the bloody reigns of terror of Field Marshal Idi Amin in Uganda (January 1971-May 1979), Field Marshal (Emperor) Jean-Bedel Bokassa in Central African Empire (December 1965-September 1979), Life President Macias Nguema in Equatorial Guinea (September 1968-August 1979) and Col. Mengistu Haile Mariam in Ethiopia (February 1977-May 1991). Tyranny in apartheid South Africa is so large a subject as to require treatment in a separate chapter of its own (chapter 10 below).

Col. Mengistu's "revolutionary red terror" has been described as the bloodiest in Ethiopia's 3000 years of recorded history.[41] Although the tyranny had begun before he acceded to the headship of the Provisional Military Administrative Council (Derg) in 1977, he was the moving spirit behind the tyrannical actions of the *Derg* right from its inception in 1974. Moreover, before his accession to the headship, the tyranny was relatively moderate, being then limited to detentions without trial on political grounds, which involved about 8,000 people by March 1976, and to the execution, after trial by military tribunals, of many (50 in November 1976 alone) for a wide range of political offences, including in particular "sympathising with counter-revolutionary organisations." There were also widespread extra-judicial killings of real or suspected counter-revolutionaries. The political detainees at this time included members of the family of the late Emperor Haile Selassie (suffocated to death by Mengistu personally), his ministers, some members of the nobility, members of parliament, senior civil servants, diplomats, high-ranking military officers and top officials of the Ethiopian Orthodox Church,

---

[40] Jibrin Ibrahim, "From Political Exclusion to Popular Participation: Democratic Transition in Niger Republic," in B. Caron *et al* (eds), *Democratic Transition in Africa* (1992), pp. 58-60; Ralph Uwechue (ed.), *Africa Today* (1991), pp. 1121-1125; 1424-1426.

[41] Samuel M. Woldu, "Democratic Transition in Africa: A case study of Ethiopia," in B. Caron *et al* (eds), *op. cit.*, p. 70.

the established church. This group of detainees were held in the dark unlit underground cellars of the *Derg's* headquarters in the former Menelik Palace.

But it was after Mengistu's accession to the headship of the *Derg* on 3 February, 1977 that the tyranny took on an extremely brutal flavour. His accession was marked by the execution of the former head, Brigadier Feferi Bante, and six other members of the *Derg* ironically for "collaborating with counter-revolutionary organisations." This was followed in November by the execution of the vice-chairman of the *Derg* under Mengistu, Lt.-Col Abate, for various counter-revolutionary offences. The real brutal tyranny began with the launching shortly after his accession of his notorious "red terror" campaign avowedly for the purpose of protecting the revolution. The army and the newly formed people's militia were directed to "dispense revolutionary justice" and to "liquidate counter-revolutionaries," by which was meant the summary killing without any form of trial of all real or suspected opponents of the regime. So began the slaughter of thousands and thousands of people, whose only offence was that they were opposed to tyranny.

Students, being in the vanguard of the opposition through their various public demonstrations, were specially targeted for the exaction of Mengistu's revolutionary justice, the worst incident involving them being, according to Amnesty International, the massacre on 29 April, 1977 of about 500 youths by the army and the people's militia; 300 more of them died in detention later in October of the same year (1977). Also specially targeted were members of opposition political groups, like the Ethiopian People's Revolutionary Party (EPRP), the Oromo Liberation Front (OLF), the banned All-Ethiopia Socialist Movement and the Tigre Liberation Front (TLF).

The "red terror", which began with the massacre of youths, continued into the week after 29 April, when the death-roll rose to around 1,000;[42] it reached;

> a peak during December 1977 and January 1978 when killings of up to a hundred were common in Addis Ababa each night; bodies were exposed in public and a reasonable estimate of deaths would be in the region of 2,500 to

---

Amnesty International Report 1977, p. 71.
[43] Amnesty International Report 1978, p. 49.

3,000. The campaign extended to the rest of the country but without such large scale killings as in Addis Ababa.[43]

Under the "red terror" campaign, mass arrests and detentions without charge or trial also vastly increased. The detainees were held incommunicado in dirty over-crowded cells without medical treatment or proper sanitary or toilet facilities; many died as a result. Arrests and detentions without charge or trial continued every year for the whole duration of Mengistu's rule. Among the detainees were thousands of members of minority churches – the Ethiopian Evangelical Mekane Yesus Church (EEMYC), the membership of which consisted mostly of people of the Oromo ethnic group, the *Falashas* or Ethiopian Jews, the Meserete Christos Church, Kale Hiwot Church, Baptists and Jehovah's Witnesses. Not only were thousands of their members detained without trial, some of their churches and schools were closed, religious worship was restricted or banned, many of their workers were killed, and the headquarters of the EEMYC in Addis Ababa was confiscated in November 1981.

The detention of, and other repressive acts against, members of the minority churches were mostly on account of their ethnic or suspected political links with opposition groups, like the Oromo Liberation Front. Some of the *Falashas* were detained on the additional ground of attempting without permission to leave the country for emigration to Israel which, by an amendment to the criminal code in 1982, was criminalised as the offence of "betraying the revolution" and made punishable by lengthy imprisonment – or death if committed "under grave circumstances."[44]

Although mass summary killings and executions after secret trials by military or special tribunals abated somewhat with the end of the "red terror" campaign in May 1978, the tyranny still continued, now characterised by a new feature: the disappearance from their places of detention of an increasing number of people whose whereabouts or fate remained unaccounted for, but who were believed to have been secretly executed soon after their "disappearance". They included the former Patriarch of the Ethiopian Orthodox Church, nine members of the ousted government of Emperor Haile Selassie and the General

---

[44] Amnesty International Report 1983, p. 32.

Secretary of the Ethiopia Evangelical Mekane Yesus Church. The abatement of summary killings did not of course mean their complete stoppage; they continued but on a reduced scale right up to the end of Mengistu's regime in May 1991, and increased again after the May 1989 attempted *coup*. A considerable number among the hundreds of people detained in connection with the coup attempt were summarily executed. Twelve army generals involved in the *coup* were executed after trial by a special military tribunal.

Torture of detainees was a regular feature of Mengistu's tyranny. The methods of torture used include: electric shocks; submersion in cold, dirty water until the prisoner nearly lost consciousness, severe beatings on the head, shoulders, buttocks or the soles of the feet while the prisoner was suspended from an iron bar; tying a heavy weight to the testicles; burning parts of the body with fire or hot oil; and crushing the hands or feet.[45] Many detainees died as a result of the torture.

Torture was often used to extract confessions from detainees. According to Amnesty International;

> confessions of counter-revolutionary sympathy were demanded and refusal to confess was often taken as evidence of guilt. Thus, confession was preferable to further interrogation. It was much serious for one person to be denounced by another – which could lead to interrogation process. Confessions and denunciations of this kind led to instances of children denouncing their parents who were consequently killed.[46]

Mengistu's tyranny must also be seen in terms of the number of people forced into exile as refugees – estimated at 4 million – or facing starvation from famine caused by a ruined economy as well as drought: another estimated 7 million.[47]

At long last the tyranny was terminated when Addis Ababa was overrun on May 28, 1991 by the Ethiopia People's Revolutionary Democratic Front (EPRDF), a civilian armed force, forcing Mengistu to flee the country into exile. From a report in November 1999,[48] the trial *in absentia*, begun some

---

[45]   Amnesty International Report 1978, p. 49; 1979, p. 19; 1984, p. 44; 1985, p. 42; 1986, p. 46; 1988, p. 40; 1991, p. 90.

[46]   Report 1978, p. 49.

[47]   Samuel M. Woldu, *op. cit.*, p. 70.

[48]   *The Guardian*, November 10, 1999, p. 10.

five years ago, is continuing in the high court, Addis Ababa, of some 3,000 former government officials (some 2,000 more have been held in custody awaiting trial since the fall of Mengistu's regime in 1991) for their part in the killing of tens of thousands of people during the red terror campaign of 1977/78, and sentence of death has been passed on one of them, a lieutenant Getachew.

Together with Mengistu's, the tyranny of the trio of Jean-Bedel Bokassa, Macias Nguema and Idi Amin – three men united in friendship by common personal characteristics of sadism, bestiality and barbarism – constituted a dreadful excrescence on Africa's battered human rights image. In the case of Bokassa, the sadistic and cruel streak in him was displayed by his ordering the public mutilation of thieves before the press as well as by personally killing some himself and by personally assaulting and inflicting serious injuries on a British journalist arrested in Bangui, the capital. But the most notorious of his acts of bestiality was the killing, on his orders, of dozens of school children, some under ten, arrested and detained in prison following a protest demonstration against the compulsory wearing of uniforms made by a factory belonging to his family.[49] According to the report by a team of investigators from five African countries, Bokassa "almost certainly took part personally in the killing of the children." The report of the investigating team was followed by the murder of those who testified against him before the international investigating team.

His sadism and cruelty were matched by his comic display of vanity to the point of absurdity. In December 1976, he proclaimed the Central African Republic an empire and himself Emperor Bokassa I, and decreed the use of or any reference to the country's former name a criminal offence. For this offence, three students, just arriving from France, and a teacher who put them up, were sentenced to ten years imprisonment after trial in *camera* at which access to lawyers was denied them.[50] His coronation in 1977 was a lavishly extravagant display of vanity costing £14 million. The coronation crown, studded with 2,000 diamonds, which he put on himself with his own

---

[49]   Amnesty International Report 1979-80; Ralph Uwechue (ed.), *Africa Today* (1991), pp. 686-688.
[50]   Amnesty International Report 1977, p. 40.

hands at the ceremony, cost an additional £2.7 million. He always appeared in public in the uniform of a field-marshal bedecked with a fantastic array of medals. A very small man in stature, he could hardly stand at attention under the weight of so many heavy medals.[51] By 1979 not even his sponsors, the French government, could tolerate his bestiality and absurdity any more. His removal had become imperative and, on September 20, 1979, while on a visit to Libya to seek aid, he was overthrown in a military coup believed to have been master-minded by the French government.

Macias Nguema was a tyrant with the instinct of a wild untamed beast who should never have occupied the exalted office of president of any country, even one as backward and as small as Equatorial Guinea, with a population of 430,000 (1989 estimate). The tyranny of his regime was characterised by the terrorisation of the community by members of the militia known as **"Youth Marching with Macias;"** by mass summary killing of thousands of opponents, many of whom were members of a rival ethnic group, as well as former associates who disagreed with him; by mass arbitrary arrest and detention of thousands more; and by the systematic torture and ill-treatment of detainees. According to Amnesty International,

> prisoners in the country are divided into three categories: 'Brigade A' consists of political opponents (or suspected opponents) of the President, and although they receive no trials, they are all considered to be under sentence of death. 'Brigade B' prisoners have committed no major offence against the President, but are considered a threat and detained indefinitely. 'Brigade C' prisoners are common-law criminals, many of whom are persuaded to help the prison guards beat and maltreat the Brigade A and B prisoners. One former detainee at Blabich Prison in Malabo (formerly Santa Isabel) reported that, during his four years in prison (1971-1975), he counted 157 prisoners beaten to death in the yard outside his cell.[52]

The tyranny also featured a crackdown on religious activities, with the arrest of priests and nuns in Rio Muni during church service, the deportation of expatriate bishops and climaxed with the outlawry of Roman Catholic worship in a country 90 per cent of whose population were Roman Catholics.

Such was the terror unleashed on the community that thousands, some

---

51   Thomas and Margaret Melady, *Idi Amin Dada: Hitler in Africa* (1977).
52   Amnesty International Report 1978, p. 46.

150,000—accounting for between one-third and one-half of the population at independence (1968) — were forced into exile as refugees. Nigerians living and working at cocoa plantations in Fernando Po had to be evacuated back home in ships sent by the Nigerian government to rescue them from the terror. By 1979, *Africa Today* reports, "the toll of Macias' victims was thousands, possibly tens of thousands",[53] i.e. excluding the 150,000 who fled the country into exile as refugees. When he was finally overthrown on August 3, 1979 after 11 years rule, Macias Nguema held out for ten days at a prepared heavily guarded fortress at Mongomo, his home town, in Rio Muni, where "the treasury was kept in notes stored near his house".[54] Found guilty of genocide, treason, embezzlement and systematic human rights violations, he was executed on September 30, 1979.

As if by conspiracy, during the same period another tyrant, by far more deadly than Bokassa and Nguema and surpassing them both in sadistic cruelty and savagery, had thrust himself upon the African political scene – Major-General Idi Amin, commander of the Ugandan army, who had overthrown the civilian government of President Milton Obote on 25 January, 1971. In its extent and sadism, his cruelty surpassed that of Mengistu too. Writing from the vantage position of one who, as American ambassador, was in Uganda during part of Amin's reign of terror and so watched it at close quarters, Thomas Melady, in a book co-authored with his wife who was also present with him in Uganda, has said that "even among the group of rulers who are continually violating the human rights of their own people, Amin still leads all others in the scale of his brutality."[55] The horror of his tyranny simply cannot be conveyed adequately in words.

The *coup d'etat* itself was almost bloodless but was immediately followed by "a massive blood-letting;" the bloodiest in the history of military take-overs in Africa, involving the brutal massacre of thousands of people, soldiers and civilians alike, in Amin's effort to consolidate his seizure of power. Among the victims of this first phase of massacres was Obote's minister of internal affairs, Mr. Basil Bataringaya, who was dismembered alive and his head put

---

[53]   *Africa Today*, ed. Ralph Uwechue (1991), p. 875.
[54]   *Africa Today, loc. cit.*
[55]   Thomas and Margaret Melady, *Idi Amin Dada: Hitler in Africa* (1977), p. 160.

on display on a pole at the garrison town of Mbarara in south-west Uganda. In order not to waste bullets, an expensive commodity, the victims were, for the most part:

> choked with their genitals, their heads bashed in with sledgehammers and gun butts, hacked to pieces with *pangas*, disembowelled, blown up with explosives, suffocated in car boots, burned alive in cars and houses after being tied up, drowned, dragged along roads tied to Land-Rovers, starved to death, whipped to death[56] or beheaded.

It was a great mercy to be shot dead instantly. Apart from those killed in this way, by late March 1971, two months after the *coup*, about 1,000 were being held without trial in various prisons throughout the country, almost all of whom were later to be slaughtered after severe beating and other forms of torture.

Amin's atrocities during this first phase of repression had an added revolting dimension – ritual killings and cannibalism. The army chief of staff, Brigadier Hussein, a professional rival whom Amin resented bitterly, was clubbed with rifle butts, his body hideously mutilated and his severed head taken to Amin at home and put on his table where he ritually addressed it and then kept it in the fridge overnight. Apparently for ritual and fetish purposes too, the dead bodies of two other top army officers, Colonel Arach, commander 1st Infantry Brigade, and Colonel Langoya, commandant, School of Infantry, were also taken to Amin, with the severed penis of the former pushed into his mouth, and the stomach of the latter split open. What he did with the bodies is not known. Considering that Amin was illiterate, primitive, superstitious and without exposure to the liberating influence of education, it should perhaps not surprise us that he believed so much in fetish and occult powers, and consulted regularly with soothsayers and witchdoctors. According to reports, Amin ate human liver which had been prescribed for him by his witchdoctor to ward off evil spirits.[57] His mother, "a camp follower," lived by the practice of witchcraft.[58]

After the first phase of massacres in the aftermath of the coup and take-

---

56   Manifesto entitled "An Indictment of a Primitive Fascist," issued by a guerrilla organisation, The Front for National Salvation (Fronasa); quoted in David Martin, *Idi Amin*, 1994), p. 228; see also p. 134.

57   Thomas and Margaret Melady, *op. cit.*, p. 136.

58   David Martin, *op. cit.*, p. 15.

over, a second phase was launched in late September 1972 ostensibly as a reprisal for the abortive invasion of Uganda earlier that month by Obote and his supporters. It was characterised mainly by secret abductions and "disappearances" of hundreds of prominent people accused or suspected of collusion with the invaders; they were officially declared "missing" or that their whereabouts could not be traced. They included the vice-chancellor of Makerere University, the former governor of the Bank of Uganda and the chief justice of the country, Justice Kiwanuka. In fact, all these people whose whereabouts were officially declared to be unknown had been brutally murdered. Chief Justice Kiwanuka, while he was still alive, had his ears, nose, lips and arms chopped off, his private parts severed and pushed into his mouth, and was then disembowelled; after this, the brave chief justice writhed in agony for some two hours before he finally died. The repression during this phase was further characterised by the depredations of special elimination squads of which there were ten who carried out the murder of hundreds and hundreds of people, among whom were several of Obote's ministers and army officers; unlike the "disappearances," the fate of these people was not camouflaged with the words "missing" or "whereabouts unknown."

The killings, tortures and other types of repression continued until the end of Amin's regime in 1979. The brutal episode in March 1976 involving students of Makerere University was one of several such massacres in the later period of the reign of terror. The students had demonstrated in connection with the killing of a male student shot by an army captain because of their rivalry over a female student. Following upon the demonstration, the police raided the campus and took away hundreds of students. The dead bodies of 130 of them were later found dumped near the campus. Eighty others were also killed in prison.

By the end of Amin's 7½ years reign of terror (January 1971-May 1979), the final death toll from the massacres, murders, disappearances and tortures had been put at 300,000 according to estimates by Amnesty International.[59] In 1977 the International Commission of Jurists put the deaths conservatively at well above 100,000. They and the methods used clearly show that Amin's disregard for human life was total.

---

[59]   Amnesty International Report 1978, p. 38.

The disposal of all these dead bodies created quite a problem in itself. Various methods of disposal were again used, beginning with burial in mass graves. As "too many details of this got out they were thrown in rivers and lakes for the crocodiles. But this proved unsatisfactory as the crocodiles could not eat all the bodies and the bloated carcases attracted vultures. Next they were dumped in the bush to be eaten by predators or burned with petrol."[60] They provided "good meat" too.[61] The mind simply boggles at the incredibly staggering enormity of the brutal repression. Little wonder that for the first two years of Amin's rule, stories about his murders and tortures were treated with scepticism and disbelief by a world that has left behind it the bestialities of the Dark Ages of more than a millennium ago. How could such sadistic cruelties have occurred in any society in the 20th century?

From the massacre of fellow black countrymen, Amin moved against brown-skinned Asians, expelling some 40,000 of them including some with Ugandan citizenship; the Ugandan Asians not expelled he threatened to send to the rural areas to farm. The businesses and properties of the expelled Asians were seized. He claimed that he had been directed to do this by God in a dream for the benefit of the economic emancipation of Uganda. Forced to leave their homes and the country of their birth or adoption, the departing Asians were often mercilessly beaten, money and other valuables seized in the course of harassing searches and women were sometimes raped.[62] The expulsion of Asians and the confiscation of their businesses coupled with the general situation in the country caused by Amin's reign of terror brought about a sharp decline in coffee and cotton production, a massive depreciation of the currency, fuel shortages, empty shop shelves, the close-down of the big industrial and commercial establishments and the consequent ruin of the economy.[63]

Amin, a moslem of Nubian/Kakwa origin, also moved against the Christian churches. Their priests were subjected to harassment of various types. A Dutch Roman Catholic Bishop was stripped naked at Makindye Prison and kept for twenty-four hours without food or water. The Anglican

---

[60]   David Martin, *op. cit.*, p. 225.
[61]   David Martin, *op. cit.*, p. 151; Thomas and Margaret Melady, *op. cit.*, p. 173.
[62]   Thomas and Margaret Melady, *op. cit.*, pp. 70-93.
[63]   *Africa Today* (1991), ed. Ralph Uwechue, p. 1921.

Archbishop of Uganda, Janani Luwun, was murdered in February 1977; several priests were also murdered. Fifty-five missionaries were expelled and those remaining were subjected to physical searches for suspected subversive activities. The entire Christian community was thrown into a state of intense fear; "many seemed to wait in expectation of arrest."[64] The murder of the Anglican Archbishop was such a critical event that it led to the regime's diplomatic isolation and to increasing international awareness of its brutalities. At the same time, forced conversion to Islam was mounted in the army.

The Jews and Zionists too came in for merciless verbal battering by Amin and even violence: as in the brutal killing of Mrs Dora Block, a Jewish passenger in a hijacked Air France plane, who had been to a Kampala hospital for treatment when the 82 other Jewish passengers in the plane were rescued by Israeli commandoes who, in a lightning operation, had raided the Entebbe Airport where the hijacked plane was taken to by its Palestinian hijackers. Mrs Block was dragged, screaming, away from the hospital and murdered.

All this created fear, tension and a feeling of insecurity among the population, it hung over them as in a nightmare. "The people had been so tensed up that a mere rumour was able to cause panic,"[65] as happened often from time to time in the capital, Kampala. Flight into exile abroad seemed the only practical way of escape from the terror, and thousands— estimated at 60,000 —[66] did so. But the exiles were divided against themselves mainly by tribal and ideological considerations and so could not band together to move against Amin. However, in October 1978 Amin himself took the fatal step of invading and occupying part of Tanzania; large numbers of Tanzanian civilians were tortured and murdered and some 31,600 had to move out of the occupied areas to other parts of Tanzania. This provided President Nyerere a perfect, internationally-accepted justification for a counter-attack aimed at ridding Uganda and Africa of a barbarous and despicable murderer. Goaded by Nyerere, the various groups of Ugandan exiles, some 18 of them, now came together under a common banner, called the Ugandan National Liberation Front (UNLF), and joined forces with the Tanzanian People's Defence Force

---

[64] Thomas and Margaret Melady, *op. cit.*, p. 126.
[65] Thomas and Margaret Melady, *Idi Amin Dada: Hitler in Africa* (1977), p. 45.
[66] Amnesty International Report 1978, p. 39.

in a massive and sustained attack on Uganda. By the end of April 1979 the whole of Uganda had fallen to the invading forces. In their retreat, Amin's soldiers committed large scale massacres of civilians in the east and north of the country. Amin himself fled to Saudi Arabia as an exile after a spell in Libya and so Uganda and Africa were rid of the infamy of his presence.

Like Bokassa, Amin's vulgarity was revealed in his ludicrous antics, his illusions of grandeur, his absurd love of vanity and his "primitive art for words."[67] Again like Bokassa and in imitation of him, Amin often appeared in public bedecked with an array of medals on a Field-Marshal's uniform. Funnily theatrical, he "had an unusual desire to be at the centre of the stage,"[68] even the international stage where he liked to portray himself as the equal of great world leaders. After the coup, he promoted himself from Major-General to full general, then to field-marshal; and he took on the style and title of President for Life, Lord of All the Beasts of the Earth and Fishes of the Sea and Conqueror of the British Empire in Africa in General and Uganda in Particular.

Certainly, the likes of Idi Amin – as well as Bokassa, Nguema and Mengistu – do not typify the blackman, as the white racialists think; they rather degrade him as indeed they degrade all humanity. As stated in chapter 12, illiteracy and lack of exposure to the liberating influence of proper education is a crucial factor in their abnormal behaviour. A revealing insight as to why Amin behaved the way he did as ruler of Uganda is provided in a memorandum written by a man who served under him as a minister for two years. Amin, the memorandum states:

> cannot concentrate on any serious topic for half a morning. He does not read. He cannot write. The sum total of all these disabilities makes it impossible for him either to sit in the regular cabinet, to follow up the Cabinet minutes, or to comprehend the briefs written to him by his Ministers. In short he is out of touch with the daily running of the country, not because he likes it but because of illiteracy. He rarely attends Cabinet, and even then it is only when he is giving directions about problems concerning defence or 'security' of the country or when he is sacking more civil servants. So the only means of getting information

---

[67]   Thomas and Margaret Melady, *Idi Amin Dada: Hitler in Africa* (1977), p. 9.
[68]   Melady, *op. cit.*, p. 16.

about the country which he rules is by ear from various sources, mainly fellow illiterates in the security forces. Information is rarely checked and statements are contradictory either through genuine lapses in memory or deliberately.[69]

Yet Amin's bloody reign of terror was not a peculiarly African phenomenon. As Thomas and Margaret Melady observed in their book, *Idi Amin Dada: Hitler in Africa* (1977), "there are so many comparisons to be made between the Amin regime and Nazi rule – the cruel tortures, the killer squads, the anti-intellectualism, the reprisals, the aggressive war posture, and above all, racism," as manifested in the expulsion of 40,000 Asians and Amin's anti-Semitic statements.[70] The conclusion suggested by the authors' insightful account giving details of the similarities in the mass killings, tortures, cruel methods and false, propagandist cover-up stories, under both regimes[71] as well as Amin's open endorsement and praise of Hitler and his actions, particularly the extermination of six million Jews and the expulsion of other millions, is that Amin's tyranny in Uganda was inspired by, and deliberately patterned upon, Hitler's, which justifies the authors' labelling of him as "Hitler in Africa." But whilst indisputably both were holocausts of heart-chilling magnitude, still Amin's tyranny was a less grievous imitation of Hitler's.

---

[69] Quoted from David Martin, *op. cit.*, p. 223.
[70] Thomas and Margaret Melady, p. 46.
[71] *ibid*, pp. 152-174.

CHAPTER 10

Tyranny by Apartheid (Fascist) Regime in South Africa*

Introduction

The cruel oppression of the black, "coloured"[1] and Indian majority in South Africa by the white minority rulers dates back to the establishment of European colonialism over it in 1652 by the Dutch who were later supplanted by the British. British colonialism in South Africa ended in 1910 and was replaced by what is known as settler colonialism (i.e. rule by minority white settlers), which continued until replaced by black majority rule in 1994.

Abuse of the Black Africans in South Africa

By the 1984 population figures, South Africa consisted of 24.1 million blacks (or roughly 70 per cent of the population), 4.8 million whites (or roughly 15 per cent), 2.8 million half-castes or coloureds, and 0.9 million Indians. Fascist racism in South Africa was manifested in the unjust privileges of the whites, secured by the cruel exploitation of the blacks and maintained by an overwhelming coercive force. There was, first and foremost, the wholesale domination of the entire apparatus of government (including a large police force, about 55,000 strong in 1989, and a well-armed, well-equipped army of 480,000 men, the largest and most powerful on the African continent) and

---

* For anything near a complete picture of the evils of authoritarianism in South Africa, this chapter should be read together with chapter 11 of volume 1 of the companion study, *Colonialism in Africa: Ancient and Modern.*
1. "Coloured" is a peculiar South African nomenclature for people of mixed blood or half breed; with a European population of 128 men and 6 women in 1657, native women and imported female slaves provided the only sexual outlet for most of the white men, from which originated what later grew into a sizeable population of persons of mixed race.

226

the domination of the electoral process, to the total exclusion of the blacks, who were thus denied all political rights of whatever kind, be they rights of suffrage or representation, membership of executive and legislative organs and even the right to organise politically in opposition to the white-dominated government – in short, the right of citizenship, of belonging.

The privileged position of the whites under the system was further manifested in the way they (i) controlled the land, apportioning only 7 per cent of the 1,221,037 square kilometres total land area to the blacks (increased to 13.6 per cent in 1936) and forbidding them to acquire land beyond the limits of the area allocated to them, the so-called "native reserves," except by the special permission of the white government under the Native Land Act of 1913 and the Development and Land Act of 1946, an apportionment that meant that "each white person gets twenty times more land than each black person;" (ii) appropriated 70 per cent of aggregate personal income as against the black majority's share of only 29 per cent; (iii) dominated virtually all mining, industrial and commercial enterprises of any size; whites controlled 95 per cent of industrial enterprises – racial capitalism; (iv) exploited the labour of the blacks, paying for it less than subsistence wages; (v) repressed the languages, traditions and cultures of the blacks in favour of the white man's culture and languages (Afrikaan, which was defined to include Dutch, and English were made the official languages); (vi) lived in ease and comfort, waited on by differential black servants and surrounded by other trappings of affluence, with all the amenities provided by the state in highly developed white urban centres and their suburbs while the blacks lived in degrading poverty caused by unemployment, illiteracy and low wages resulting in malnutrition, disease and high mortality, which was further aggravated by overcrowding in squalid slums, ghettos and resettlement camps, with their mud shacks, matchbox huts and shanties devoid of modern amenities. Alexandria, one of the black townships outlying the city of Johannesburg, has been described as a slum, with no electricity, its unpaved and dirty roads were dotted with stinking, stagnant water full of maggots, and were "filled with hungry, undernourished children scampering around," "the air was thick with the smoke from coal fires in tin braziers and stoves."[2] In Sophiatown,

---

[2] Nelson Mandela, *The Illustrated Long Walk to Freedom — An Autobiography* (abridged edn 1996), p. 29.

another of Johannesburg's outlying black townships, "every plot was filled with dozens of shanties huddled close together" and several families were crowded into each shanty.[3]

Such was the overcrowding in black homes – countless numbers of blacks were without homes at all – that the average floor space per person was three square metres; a man returning home from work in the evening had hardly enough floor space to rest his legs because there were "children and adolescents and middle-aged aunts sleeping on the floor, under the kitchen table, and between the beds."[4]

The social and economic privileges and opportunities of the white settler minority in South Africa were still more starkly revealed by more individualised statistics, viz:

(i)   average individual income in 1984: R273 per month for blacks and R1,834 per month for whites;

(ii)   expenditure on education per head in 1983/84 – R234 for blacks and R1,654 for whites; R476 for blacks and R2,508 for whites in 1986/87 – excluding black children in the homelands where much less was spent per child;

(iii)   teacher-pupil ratio in 1984: 1 teacher for 41 black pupils and 1 teacher for 19 white pupils (52 per cent of urban and 79 per cent of rural blacks were illiterate in 1984);

(iv)   medical care: 337 blacks as against 61 whites per hospital bed; and

(v)   infant mortality in 1982: 80 deaths in urban and 190 in rural areas per 1,000 live births for blacks as against 14 deaths for whites.

Not only political rights but also the right, enjoyed by white workers, to form or be members of a trade union, with all the benefits that go with it, in particular, the benefits of collective bargaining and other collective actions, were denied to blacks. As late as 1964, the Minister of Labour said that blacks had not yet reached the stage where they could exercise the functions and rights of trade unions with   out harmful results. However, without official recognition, black trade unions nevertheless grew up and steadily increased both in the number of unions and in membership, becoming a powerful

---

[3] Nelson Mandela, *op. cit.,* p. 52.
[4] *Rule of Fear: Human Rights in South Africa* (1989), p. 49; a publication of the Catholic Institute for International Relations in association with the British Council of Churches.

force in the liberation movement. The fact of not being recognised by the statute law and therefore operating outside it left the black trade unions more or less free to engage in politics unaffected and untrammelled by some of its restrictions and prohibitions. Only in 1979 were black unions granted recognition and registration under the statute law.[5]

The privileged position of whites *vis-a-vis* the blacks, which characterised virtually all spheres of life in South Africa, was also manifested in racial segregation in post offices, railway stations, airports and other public places, involving the use of separate schools and colleges, separate hotels, restaurants, clubs, buses, beaches, reservation of better paid jobs for whites and lower paid ones for blacks, etc. Needless to say, the separate amenities for blacks were patently inferior to those for whites.

Thus subjected to white minority political rule, socio-economic domination and discrimination in all spheres of life, blacks of South Africa were made a subject people under a special type of colonialism, white settler colonialism, as it is aptly called. As the African National Congress (ANC) put it, black South Africa was made a colony of white South Africa, a special form of colonisation, since "the coloniser and the colonised live side by side in the same geographical area."[6] The conditions of the blacks under the system, in particular, the merciless exploitation, oppression, humiliation, deprivation, abuse and de-humanisation, tantamounted to semi-slavery. Blacks were indeed like slaves in their own country, with no control over their own destiny.[7]

The Segregation of Blacks in Distinct Black "States"

Yet all this discrimination, exploitation and oppression only represented what was called "petty apartheid" which, increasing in extent and intensity over the years, was as old as the white settlement in South Africa. But real apartheid or the physical separation of whites and blacks into different states, a white state, still to be called by the name South Africa, and several black states or "Bantustans" to be called by appropriate ethnic names, was a phenomenon

---

[5]   Industrial Conciliation Amendment Act 1979.
[6]   Francis Meli, "South Africa and the Rise of African Nationalism," in Maria van Diepen (ed.), *The National Question in South Africa* (1988), p. 68.
[7]   Nelson Mandela, *The Illustrated Long Walk to Freedom*, p. 16.

of later origin, dating from the 1950s. Real apartheid differed therefore from pre-1948 apartheid, not from the standpoint of mere racial discrimination, exploitation and oppression in their varied manifestations noted above, which of course continued and intensified, but rather in the radical idea of the physical separation of whites and blacks into different states, and in the methods and strategies employed to propagate and implement it.

To begin with, the new apartheid system called for the rigorous enforcement of racial segregation and discrimination by law rather than by mere practice and convention, as before 1948. "Except in employment, little of this (pre-1948) segregation was enforced by law. It just happened ... What happened automatically before was now codified in law and intensified wherever possible."[8] Codification by law ended the flexibility and pragmatism of mere social practice, which allowed exceptions and local modifications, as with the mixed townships that grew up in some places. In the second place, while racial segregation in the period before 1948 was thus merely a manifestation, by practice and convention, of racial prejudice and discrimination more or less characteristic of white-black relationship in other colonial territories in Africa, apartheid in South Africa since 1948 was a thorough-going doctrine sanctioned by law, propagating, as a categorical imperative, and with the fervour of a religious dogma, the preservation of the racial integrity of the whites as a superior race, somewhat in the fashion of Hitler's doctrine of the Germanic people as a master race whose identity must be preserved against Semitic contamination.[9] To quote Allister Sparks again, racial segregation after 1948 "became a matter of doctrine, of ideology, of theological faith infused with a special fanaticism, a religious zeal."[10]

The doctrine of the physical separation of whites and blacks into different states or "separate development," as it is euphemistically called, was rationalised upon the theory that:

> whites and non-whites are so dissimilar in culture that they can never live together as a community. If they were to try, either the numerically stronger non-whites would swamp the whites or the white minority

---

[8]   Allister Sparks, *The Mind of South Africa: The Story of the Rise and Fall of Apartheid* (1990), p. 190.
[9]   Edgar H. Brookes, *Apartheid: A Documentary Study of Modern South Africa* (1968), p. xxviii; Allister Sparks, *op. cit.*, pp. 161-175.
[10] Allister Sparks, *op. cit.*, p. 190.

would have to suppress the majority by force in order to preserve its own identity. Where people of different colours inhabit the same country ... the sensible thing is to divide the country into areas where each group alone would have the rights and privileges of citizenship.[11]

The object, therefore, was, by promoting in each group a separate sense of identity, to prevent their integration into a multi-racial state. Its purpose, in the words of the Minister of the Interior, Dr. T. E. Donges, while introducing the Group Areas Bill in the South African Senate in June 1950, was "to preserve a White South Africa, while doing justice to the non-European elements and allowing them to develop each within his own area to the fullest extent of their capabilities."[12]

There is a certain vagueness in the statements quoted above which need clarification to make more precise what is meant by "a white South Africa." It does not mean simply a South Africa controlled by whites as the ruling population group, which had always been the case since the creation of the South African state in 1910. It means, more importantly, a state, called by the name, South Africa, the majority of whose citizens were whites. It was this latter meaning that formed the true essence of apartheid.

The scheme devised by the architects of apartheid for making whites the majority racial group in the South African state contemplated, firstly, the removal of ALL blacks physically from it into separate states of their own, the so-called black ethnic "homelands". The "homeland" was conceived as a state, a black state, separate from the white South African state and every black man was regarded as belonging to a "homeland" as a citizen thereof. When the removal of all blacks to the "homeland" would have been accomplished and the black townships lying mostly outside the "homelands" had thus withered away, the South African state, now rid of all blacks, would then comprise only whites, coloureds and Indians, with the whites out-numbering the coloureds and Indians together by as much as 1.1 million according to the 1984 census figures.

That was one leg of the plan. While the removal of the blacks to the homelands would be going on, their presence in the South African state was

---

[11]   Marquard, *The Story of South Africa* (1968), pp. 249-250.
[12]   Senate Debates, Hansard, 14 June, 1950.

regarded as non-permanent; in the contemplation of the system, their residence there was merely the residence of migrant aliens; the over ten million blacks residing outside the "homelands," but right within the boundaries of the South African state, were not to count as part of the civic population, the citizenry, of the South African state. The Minister of Bantu Administration and Development put it bluntly in 1972. A black man, he said, was a citizen only in his ethnic "homeland," to which he will always continue to be attached, wherever he might be resident; and notwithstanding that he was born in the white South African state or had lived and worked there for many years under a permit granted by the white state, his status there was only that of an immigrant alien, with no citizenship rights whatever, a "statutory foreigner in the land of his birth."

The doctrine on which the system was built was that, while the whites were so heavily dependent upon black labour, the presence of blacks in white South Africa was to be tolerated only so far as their labour was needed to "minister" to the needs of the whites; "blacks must therefore be confined in their 'homeland' until they were requisitioned and recruited under the migratory labour system,"[13] but not as settled workers with rights of permanent residence.

As an initial step, the Bantu Authorities Act 1950 created a new system of local administration for the African "native reserves" with enhanced powers for the traditional authorities. Nine years later when it was felt they had gained experience in the exercise of limited authority, the "native reserves" were constituted into eight (later increased to ten) self-governing "Bantustans" or black states – Transkei,[14] Bophuthatswana, Ciskei, Venda, KwaZulu, KwaNdebele, Lebowa, Qwa Qwa, Kangwane and Gazankulu[15] – and granted powers to govern their own internal affairs under a constitution enacted for each of them by the parliament of the white South African state, with all the paraphernalia of a flag, anthem, homeland citizenship, a chief minister, ministers, a cabinet, a legislative assembly containing in nearly all cases more traditional chiefs (appointed and dismissable by the white government) than elected members and empowered to make laws on an extensive range of listed

---

[13] J. Kane Berman, *The Method of the Madness* (1979), p. 244.
[14] Nelson Mandela, a Xhosa, is from Transkei.
[15] Promotion of Bantu Self-Government Act 1959.

subjects, etc.[16] By reason of the blacks now being regarded as citizens of states separate from the white South African state, the separate roll and the special representation for them (represented by whites of course) in the central parliament became unnecessary, and were abolished.

The plan was that all ten "homelands" should become not merely self-governing but independent, four having already become so by 1981 – Transkei in 1976, Bophuthatswan in 1977, Venda in 1979 and Ciskei in 1981.[17] (The independence of the six other "homelands" was prevented by stiff opposition.) By the provisions of the enabling law enacted by the white Parliament, each of them was declared "a sovereign and independent state" and as no longer forming "part of the Republic of South Africa." "The Republic of South Africa," it was further declared, "shall cease to exercise any authority over" it. The independence not recognised by the United Nations, the OAU or by any the individual countries of the world, has no reality anyway. As a consequence of the so-called independence of the four "homelands," their indigenes, numbering millions, about one-third of South Africa's total population, were by the express stipulation of the enabling law, divested of the citizenship of South Africa and left with only the citizenship of their "homelands".

The apartheid system had also a narrow ethnic goal. Its aim in this narrow perspective was that the Afrikaners, accounting for 60 per cent of the total white population, should constitute both the **nation** and the ruling group in white South Africa by virtue of being the majority group. Hence the exclusively Afrikaner party, formed in 1914 and which had ruled the country continuously from 1948 to 1994, was called the **National** Party. In this narrower perspective, therefore, apartheid was aimed at a.radical restructuring of South African society in order to ensure that "the white Afrikaner nation would have a home for posterity, even into the remotest future in this continent of swelling black numbers,"[18] the "black peril" of Winston Churchill. The Afrikaners had thought of themselves as the "chosen people", and South Africa as their

---

[16] Transkei Constitution Act 1963 and the Constitution Acts for the other Bantustans; Homeland Citizenship Act 1970; Bantu Homelands Constitution Act 1971, later renamed the Black States Constitution Act.

[17] Status of Transkei Act 1976; Status of Bophuthatswana Act 1977; Status of Venda Act 1979; Status of Ciskei Act 1981.

[18] Allister Sparks, *op. cit.*, p. 147.

promised land. But the goal of an Afrikaner nation right in the bosom of Africa was feared to be endangered by the phenomenon of the cohabitation of the races in mixed-race ghettos, an evil which,

> if allowed to continue, would contaminate the blood-purity of Afrikanerdom's posterity, destroying its national identity and submerging it in a single unidentifiable 'mishmash' race. So if the long-term survival of the *volk* was to be ensured, there would have to be not only a home for posterity but safeguards for its racial purity as well. That meant its home would have to be separated from that of the black.

As separate "homelands" could not be created for the coloureds and Indians, they were, by the 1983 Constitution, co-opted into the government of white South Africa to share power with the whites in a curious arrangement under which Parliament consisted of three houses, one for each of the three population groups: whites, coloureds and Indians. The new scheme, details of which cannot be discussed here, represented a certain amount of concession on the part of the whites. For the first time they were accepting to share power with the coloureds and Indians. But the new scheme did not really change much, inasmuch as the separateness of the three population groups was maintained and control still remained in the hands of the whites as firmly and effectively as before. The elaborate and complex power sharing arrangement was simply a facade to mask this fact.

The exclusion from the new power-sharing scheme of the over 10 million blacks living permanently outside the boundaries of the "homelands" and forming a mixed society with whites, coloureds and Indians reflects the unyielding determination of the Afrikaner nationalists to maintain South Africa as a white state; a state in which the whites constituted the majority group and entitled to rule by virtue thereof – as earlier stated, the whites out-numbered the coloureds and Indians together by as much as 1.1 million (1984 figures). The explanation given by the Minister of Co-operation and Development (the new name for Minister of Bantu Administration) in the House of Assembly at the time was that, apart from considerations of practicability and logistics, the inclusion of the blacks would "destroy the whole process of self-government for the Black nation of South Africa". (The only political concession to the blacks in the new dispensation was the setting up by an ordinary Act of Parliament of black municipal councils to run the "own affairs" of the black townships.)

As far as the Afrikaner nationalists were concerned, the 10 million blacks resident in white South Africa belonged, not to it, but to the black "homeland" states and their residence there, being merely the residence of migrant aliens and therefore notionally non-permanent, was discounted. It was discounted, since, to accept its permanence was "to accept another string of implications – from finding some way to accommodate them politically (other than through the homelands) to improving the physical amenities of the townships."[19] Yet "the permanence of the urban blacks was ... a reality that could not be denied."

We must next consider how the Afrikaner architects of apartheid set about implementing the physical removal of all blacks to the black states, the "homelands" or "Bantustans," in order to accomplish their scheme of a white South Africa, a South Africa comprising only whites, coloureds and Indians, with the whites as the majority group and entitled to rule by virtue of being the majority group. (As earlier noted, what this meant was perpetual Afrikaner rule, they being 60 per cent of the white population.) The idea being monstrous, pernicious and iniquitous in itself, its implementation necessarily involved the infliction of repressive brutalities and untold sufferings on the blacks.

The central legal plank in the implementation programme was the Group Areas Act 1950. Before that Act, the only land reservation for blacks was limited to 13.6 per cent of the total land area. The rest of the land lying outside the "native reserves" (86.4 per cent of the total land area) was not set aside exclusively for the whites nor were the blacks completely excluded therefrom. They could acquire land there with the special permission of the government or, in areas regarded as special areas, e.g. the Cape Province, without such permission. And so had grown up in different parts of the country, areas occupied by a mixture of the races, the townships outlying the cities.

All that was changed by the Group Areas Act 1950 with its numerous amendments over the years since then. Using the machinery and procedures provided in the Act, the territory of the Union was demarcated, ie. partitioned, into **exclusive** areas, and each component race, whites, blacks and coloureds (Indians were lumped with coloured for this purpose), had separate areas

---

[19] Allister Sparks, *op. cit.*, p. 315.

demarcated for its exclusive occupation for residential, farming and business purposes (ownership was dealt with in a different way.)

Here, then, was a land partition between races in which one race alone did the partitioning and decided the share and the locations of what each race was to have. As Senator Dr. Edgar Brookes remarked during the debate in the Senate, "this is a Bill in which the white man is to divide up the land between himself and the others and he is going to decide which part each shall get ... We know ... that what you get for a Native location in an urban area is a bit of land which nobody else wants."[20] The Bill, he went on, was in the nature of "compulsory segregation administered by one race," who, in the nature of things, could not be trusted to "hold the scales equally between the races."

In introducing the Bill in parliament, the Minister of the Interior had rationalised the demarcation of separate exclusive areas for each race as being to "eliminate friction" by reducing, to the minimum, "points of contacts" between them. For "contact brings about friction, and friction brings about heat, and may cause conflagration."[21] Certainly, as Senator Dr. Brookes countered, it is far from being the case that separation, especially when it is forced on people against their will, brings harmony in the relations between different races living in the same country. Challenging and even daunting as the problem of race relations in the peculiar circumstances of South Africa is, given the length of time the whites have been living there (more than four centuries), the considerable size of their population (4.8 million in 1984) and the fact that they have no other country that they can call their own and to which they can go — connection with their original home, Holland, having been all but lost — yet it seems a rather cynical view of the human specie to think that no *modus vivendi* could be devised that would enable all the different races in the country to live together in reasonable harmony as one community.

In conception and in execution as well, separation of whites and blacks was to be total; it was not to stop with the separation of the main living areas, the native reserves or "homeland" on the one side and the white areas on the other. The black townships until they could be completely obliterated and

---

[20] Senate Debates, Hansard, 14 June, 1950.
[21] Senate Debates, Hansard, 14 June, 1950.

even the residential areas housing farm workers and such like must also be at a sanitary distance. Allister Sparks describes the system of separation with telling effect:

> It was not enough simply to segregate living areas; a law of 1954 required that there should be a buffer strip at least five hundred yards wide between any black quarter and the (white) town it served. Five hundred yards of bare windblown veld littered with trash to mark the boundary between the 'nations', between civilisation and barbarism, between Van Riebeeck's white descendants and the black people of Africa[22] ... The strip of bare veld ... is more than just a physical barrier, it is a mental barrier, too, ... isolating them psychologically from the people who live there. As a reporter, shuttling between the black townships and the white suburb where I live, I have often felt as though I were crossing some invisible Berlin wall between different perceptions and different realities. One can spend the day witnessing events in one place and then cross the barrier into another only a few miles away but as distant as another planet.[23]

Removal to the "homelands" posed very grave problems and tribulations for the blacks. It meant that millions of them living or carrying on business outside the "homelands" had to re-locate or be forcibly re-located. Re-location from an urban area to a rural "Bantustan" was viewed as an affront to "black pride." Secondly, re-location disrupted the settled pattern and rhythm of life of those affected. "What this Act means," said Helen Suzman in the House of Assembly in 1961, "is the mass uprooting of settled communities. It has also entailed the disruption of commercial life ... The most crushing anxieties are introduced into the lives of law-abiding citizens, who know that any time in future the permits under which they carry on business may be withdrawn," and they and their families forced to move to a black "homeland." It had meant the demolition of whole black settlements needed for white occupation and resettlement in new black areas.

The traumatic impact on the life of those affected was exemplified by the experience of an old coloured couple forced suddenly and unexpectedly to move from their 150-year-old family home with spacious grounds and a well-tended garden and orchard to a strange new, low-class resettlement estate where they were condemned to a life of solitude and misery, torn away from friends

---

[22] Allister Sparks, *op. cit.*, p. 189; Van Riebeeck was the leader of the first group of Dutch settlers to arrive at the Cape in 1652.

[23] *ibid*, p. 215.

and from everything they had been accustomed to. As they awaited death,

> fear and isolation had become the essence of their lives, fear of practically
> everything: their neighbours, the people who pass by in the street, fear of
> venturing out of the two small rooms that now confine them, fear of
> their loneliness, fear of losing their last hold on respectability, fear of
> looking too far into the future or even back into the past, even fear of
> nothing.[24]

The demolition of Sophiatown and the uprooting and re-location of its 60,000 black inhabitants to what became known as Soweto is among the numerous cases of the social devastation wrought on blacks by apartheid.[25]

Understandably, therefore, blacks were unwilling to re-locate. They did so only "under considerable duress, because they are too old to continue, ill, or simply despair of finding work. Many born in town are forced into rural areas they have never seen before."[26]

Thirdly, there was the problem of keeping in the rural "Bantustans" those blacks already there before the new apartheid system. It was the unshakeable desire and determination of blacks to move to the urban areas in search of livelihood and in the hope of escaping from the degradation of unemployment and poverty in the rural areas. The choice for many was between death by starvation in the poverty-stricken rural areas and the risk of incurring the sanctions of the law for moving to townships or urban areas in violation of the prohibition of such movement; the latter was chosen as the lesser evil. "Influx control legislation did not stop people coming to town. They came anyway in the search for economic survival and, in spite of constant arrest and imprisonment, they stayed."[27] There were 278,887 arrests for violations of pass laws in 1978 alone.

Moreover, the "homelands", covering only 13.6 per cent of the country's land area, were insufficient to absorb the 24.1 million blacks and to meet their needs for residence, farming, pasturing, business, etc. Heavily dependent on inadequate financial allocation from the white government — up to 80 per

---

[24] Article titled "Group Areas Anniversary," by Brian Barrow, *Cape Times*, 26 Nov., 1966; reproduced in Edgar Brookes, *op. cit.*, pp. 173-178.

[25] Nelson Mandela, *op. cit.*, pp. 53-59 for an account of the demolition of Sophiatown and the removal of its black inhabitants.

[26] *South Africa in the 1980s*, a publication of the Catholic Institute for International Relations, 4th edn (1987), p. 37.

[27] *Rule of Fear: Human Rights in South Africa* (1989), *op. cit.*, p. 45.

cent of their budget in some cases, e.g. Ciskei, one of the independent ones — the "homelands", supposed to be self-governing, lacked resources for the provision of welfare services, such as education, health, pipe-borne water, housing, electricity and other development projects, and had therefore remained undeveloped. There was the further fact that their boundaries "were so drawn as to exclude almost all the economic (industrial and infrastructural) resources of South Africa, e.g. cities, harbours, mines and dams."[28] Such was the land scarcity and poverty in the "homelands" that collectively they accounted for only 3 per cent of the country's gross national product.

Nor was there anything that could properly be called a "homeland" economy. From the economic standpoint, they (the "homelands") were primarily intended and were more properly regarded, as labour reserves to provide "a pool of cheap black labour power for the white-owned factories, mines and farms, and at the same time serve as dumping grounds for 'surplus' workers and the 'superfluous appendages' of the workforce in white areas – the unemployed and the unemployable."[29] Some 60 per cent of the male labour force in the "homelands" were engaged as migrant contract workers in white areas while much of the overcrowding in them was caused by resettlement of blacks from white areas.[30]

A "homeland" could not function as an integral economy because in the majority of cases it consisted, not of a continuous stretch of territory, but of scattered, uncontiguous pieces of land here and there, "dusty little patches of leached soil and overstocked veld." For example, KwaZulu comprised seven scattered areas of territory separated by white areas and Bophuthatswana had six of such.

Re-location or re-settlement of blacks away from white areas was not the sole means employed to try to accomplish their physical integration into the "homelands". As a considerable number of blacks were resident outside the "homelands", in the townships particularly, the boundaries of the "homelands" were being constantly re-drawn to incorporate such black settlements or communities. Forced incorporation by this method met with

---

[28] *Rule of Fear: Human Rights in South Africa* (1989), *op. cit.*, p. 37.
[29] Alex Callinicos, *South Africa Between Reform and Revolution* (1988), p. 21.
[30] Alex Callinicos, *op. cit.*, pp 20-21.

resistance in nearly every case. In the face of such resistance, violence, involving in some cases the demolition of homes, was often used to enforce incorporation. But violence only increased resistance, which took on a national character in October 1989 when eight communities threatened with forcible incorporation organised the "Stop Incorporation Campaign" and a threatened incorporation was frustrated in one case by a successful application to the court. New legislation was passed to impede the chances of such applications succeeding and generally to facilitate the process of forced incorporation.

In spite of all the measures taken to remove blacks to the "homelands" in accordance with the apartheid scheme, a massive influx of blacks into the urban areas meant for whites only continued and increased as a result of the factors noted above. "Blacks sleeping rough in white areas looking for work increased to a point where Bantu Administration officers were obliged to turn a blind eye. The attempt in 1986 to remodel influx control may be seen as a response to a virtual collapse of previous mechanisms."[31] In the event, more than 10 million blacks were still to be found outside the "homelands" as rightless, landless migrants, some as workers, some as squatters and others as "vagrants". Squatter settlements had sprung up all over the country. The ramshackles that sheltered them "are often demolished by the police. The people are arrested and charged with trespass or illegal squatting, but they continually rebuild in the same place or in the vicinity because they have no alternative." Those labelled as "vagrants" lived "where they can without even rudimentary shelter.[32] They settle in the parks, golf courses and backyards of white city suburbs, under freeways and in doorways in the city centres, in public lavatories and railway station waiting rooms."[33] It was the insufficiency of land allocated to blacks that had greatly contributed to the problem of black homelessness and no solution was possible without the re-distribution of land by the state. There were an estimated five million homeless blacks in 1989.[34]

---

[31] *South Africa in the 1980s, loc. cit.*
[32] *Rule of Fear: Human Rights in South Africa, op. cit.,* p. 46.
[33] *Rule of Fear: Human Rights in South Africa, loc. cit.*
[34] Review of 1989: Repression and Resistance in South Africa and Namibia (1989) — an IDAF publication, p. 15.

Besides the Group Areas Act, there were numerous other laws that provided the legal framework for the scheme to separate the whites and blacks into different states, to preserve the identity of the white race uncontaminated by too much contact with blacks, and to repress resistance to the scheme. These laws, which were of course rigorously enforced by repressive actions by the police and the army, must now be noted.

Of the principal apartheid measures enacted since 1948, we may here note influx control through the requirement of a permit to enter an urban area for the purpose of employment; control of squatting; control of black labour generally, including refusal (until 1979) of recognition to black trade unions; the classification of persons by race to be identified by a number in a register and by a "pass"; prohibition of marriages between whites and non-whites with the object of preserving the purity of the white blood by preventing its admixture with non-white blood (sexual relations between whites and blacks without marriage were prohibited in 1927 and extended to such relations between whites and coloureds by a 1950 amendment.)[35]

Also deserving to be noted was the prohibition, except under a permit, of mixed amenities, now extended to all facets of life and all social, cultural, economic and scientific activities – mixed choirs, orchestras, ballets and other dance groups, soccer and other sporting teams or clubs, mixed trade unions, even mixed scientific societies or organisations, etc.; mixed audiences, gatherings, functions or celebrations in cinemas, music or concert halls and theatres, stadiums and other public (but not private) places of entertainment, etc.[36] – "absurd nonsense" as such extensions of the prohibition were called by Helen Suzman.[37] The cases and the manner in which the prohibition had been applied in practice simply caricature reason, they "surpass belief", as where permission for coloured people to watch rugby was granted on condition that a 6-foot wire fence be built between them and the white spectators, or

---

[35] Group Areas Act 1950, as amended; Urban Areas Act 1952: Prevention of Illegal Squatting Act 1989; Labour Relations Amendment Act; Labour Regulations, Govt. Gazette Extraordinary, 3 Dec., 1965; Population Registration Act 1950; Prohibition of Mixed Marriages Act 1949; Immorality Act 1927, as amended in 1950.

[36] The Reservation of Separate Amenities Act 1953. The extensions were mostly in pursuance of Proclamation R. 26 made under the Group Areas Act 1950.

[37] House of Assembly Debates, Hansard, 2 June, 1965.

where permission for white children to take part with non-white children in a Red Cross pageant was refused. Segregation in schools and colleges was also maintained and extended to university education[38] against the protest of the universities in the country. The prohibition of the registration or attendance of non-whites as students in white universities and *vice versa*, without ministerial approval, said the Minister of Education, Arts and Science during the debate on the Bill[39] in the House of Assembly, was so as "not to estrange people from their own national group. It is fatal, and it will always remain fatal, to try to turn a non-White into a White and conversely to try to turn a White into a non-White. Consequently we must ensure that the racial groups are separated on racial basis and that their education fits in with their own national character."[40]

Not only were the schools, colleges and universities racially segregated, not only were the facilities in the segregated educational institutions patently unequal, but also the medium of education, based as it was on the Afrikaan language, its content and the control over teachers were intended to create a culturally and mentally subservient black population. "It is a system that inculcates a sense of superiority into some, whilst denying the vast majority what is their fundamental right – an education of decent quality."[41] The psychological impact of apartheid in the educational sector was such that the spirit or motivation to learn or teach was killed amongst black students and teachers alike. The white children and youth were also harmed by their minds being indoctrinated with the doctrine of "a God-ordained superiority" of their race. Such, indeed, was the tyranny and inhumanity of the system of Bantu education introduced by the Bantu Education Act 1953 under which the white minority government took over the ownership and control of most black primary and secondary schools in the country, with a view to ensuring, as the Minister of Bantu Education, Dr. Hendrik Vervoerd, explained, that black education was designed to "train and teach people in accordance with their opportunities in life," implying that black education must be limited by the limited opportunities open to the blacks.

Thus, under apartheid the whole life of the black man was hedged round

---

[38]   The Extension of University Education Act 1959.
[39]   Originally called the Separate University Education Bill 1959.
[40]   House of Assembly Debates, Hansard, 8 April, 1959.
[41]   *Rule of Fear: Human Rights in South Africa, op. cit.*, p. 61.

with restrictive regulations and permits. He required a permit at every turn –
a permit to enter an urban area, to seek employment or to work there, or to
be admitted to a white university. These restrictions on the life of blacks were
the point in Nelson Mandela's rejection of the amnesty offered him by President
Botha on condition that he "unconditionally rejected violence as a political
instrument."
"What freedom am I being offered," he said,

> when I may be arrested on a pass offence? What freedom am I being
> offered to live my life as a family with my dear wife, who remains in
> banishment in Brandfort? What freedom am I being offered when I must
> ask for permission to live in an urban area? What freedom am I being
> offered when I need a stamp in my pass to seek work? What freedom am
> I being offered when my very South African citizenship is not respected?[42]

No less restrictive of the life of the black majority was the control of the
right to assemble peacefully together or to march in procession to protest
against oppression. "Since 1976 there has been a nationwide prohibition on
outdoor gatherings. Emergency powers have extended this prohibition to
ban a number of indoor gatherings."[43]

These restrictions combined with the penal sanctions for violations of
racial segregation laws to make the black man's life most precarious indeed.
For, it was a crime punishable by imprisonment or fine to:

> walk through a Whites Only door, a crime to ride a Whites Only bus, a
> crime to use a Whites Only drinking fountain, a crime to walk on a Whites
> Only beach, a crime to be on the streets after 11 pm., a crime not to have
> a pass book and a crime to have the wrong signature in that book, a crime
> to be unemployed and a crime to be employed in the wrong place, a crime
> to live in certain places and a crime to have no place to live.[44]

But perhaps the most ridiculous of the apartheid measures, the *reductio ad*
absurdum, was the prohibition of mixed membership in a political party or
other political organisation.[45] Even more ridiculous was the provision in the
same statute making it an offence for a person of one racial group to "address

---

[42] The full text of the response to the conditional offer is reproduced in *South Africa in the 1980s,*
op. cit., pp. 64-66.
[43] *Rule of Fear: Human Rights in South Africa* (1989), *op. cit.,* p. 34.
[44] Nelson Mandela, *op. cit.,* p. 52.
[45] Prohibition of Political Interference Act 1968.

any meeting, gathering or assembly of persons of whom all or the greater majority belong to any other population group or groups, for the purpose of furthering the interests of a political party or the candidature of any person who has been nominated or may be nominated as a candidate for an election," or to give financial or other assistance or to make, prepare or disseminate propaganda in support of or in opposition to such a political party or candidate. (Mixed membership of a trade union was also prohibited.)[46]

Four laws provided the main legal plank for the repression of resistance to apartheid, viz: the Suppression of Communism Act 1950, the Terrorism Act 1967, the Internal Security Act 1976 (all three of which were consolidated and superseded by the Internal Security Act 1982) and the Public Safety Act 1953. The Suppression of Communism Act, the most notorious of all, not only outlawed the Communist Party of South Africa and made it a crime, punishable with a maximum of ten years' imprisonment, to be a member of the party or to further the aims of communism, it also empowered the government to ban any organisation or individual opposed to its policies. Thus, opposition to apartheid by anyone branded the person concerned with the label of a communist, a "statutory communist", that is. It was under this Act and the Internal Security Act 1976, as consolidated and replaced by the Internal Security Act 1982, that the African National Congress (ANC), the Pan-African Congress (PAC), the Congress of Democrats, the South African Indian Congress, 56 other organisations (including 42 in the independent "homelands") and hundreds of people were banned. For nearly five years, until February 1988, the United Democratic Front (UDF), launched in August 1983, escaped the dragnet (only its activities were restricted), because it was not a political organisation in its own right, but rather a broad front of some 1,200 independent church, women's, trade union, students', youth and community organisations.

An individual banned under the Acts (as consolidated by the 1982 Act) was restricted in his movement within a specified area and barred from engaging in certain activities, such as speaking at public meetings, writing in a newspaper, and might be required to report personally to the police at regular intervals,

---

[46]   Industrial Conciliation Amendment Act 1979.

usually once a week. Hundreds had also been banished from their ethnic area to a remote ethnic area. But the most widely used power of repression under the Acts was detention without trial which had netted thousands of people: some 73,000 since 1960 plus 21,863 detained by the independent "homeland" governments between 1963 and 1988. Repression under the Acts reached into all areas of South African life – trade unions and their members, schools, colleges and universities and their students and teachers, the churches and all political, social, civic and professional organisations engaging in resistance activities.

Having decided to counter resistance to apartheid by still more repressive action, the Botha Government, on June 12, 1986, declared, and renewed annually thereafter, a state of emergency under the Public Safety Act 1953, accompanying it with draconian emergency legislation (an earlier state of emergency was declared on 21 July, 1985, but was lifted seven months later.) With this, the security forces, aided by special constables and vigilantes, hurriedly recruited and trained, mounted a ferocious reign of terror, which was again rationalised upon the demands of national security. In the desperate effort to crush all resistance to apartheid, in particular the growing black control of the black townships, the South African state was thoroughly militarised, with human life, individual rights and economic life increasingly subordinated to national security and military requirements. The black townships were occupied by troops and put in a state of siege. Twenty-six thousand (26,000) people were detained without trial in 1986, 10,000 of them in the first three weeks of the state of emergency, and over 50,000 between 1986 and 1989. Powers of detention without trial under the Internal Security Act remained, now reinforced by the much wider powers of detention under emergency power. A detainee might be released only to be put on restriction instead. 17 organisations, including the UDF, were banned in February 1988.

Repression of opposition was accompanied by suppression of press reports of what was going on. There were, for example, 417 listed persons in 1988 whose utterances, speeches and statements were not to be published or disseminated without ministerial permission. And from 12 June 1986 under the state of emergency, a blackout on information, as in wartime, was imposed and rigorously enforced. The object of all this censorship of the dissemination of information and ideas was of course to suppress the articulation of opposition.

Caged-in by various ouster provisions and hamstrung by the absence of a bill of rights in the constitution, the courts too were greatly incapacitated to protect the individual from governmental oppression and tyranny. The freedom of the courts in apartheid South Africa, about which the government boasted so much, was no greater than the freedom of a fish to "swim in a net." Yet hamstrung as the judges no doubt were, the overall impression created by many of their decisions was, lamentably, that of a judiciary more in sympathy with the executive than with the oppressed individual, a judiciary prepared, as the International Commission of Jurists observed, "to adopt an interpretation that will facilitate the executive's task rather than defend the liberty of the subject and uphold the Rule of Law."[47]

Repression necessarily involves violence by the state. Resistance to apartheid, organised or spontaneous, — violent or non-violent-riots, uprisings in black townships, strikes, stay-aways, protest marches, boycotts, civil disobedience campaigns, guerilla actions, etc. – was met with violence by the state, reaching horrifying proportions by steady progression. Among the forms taken by this violence were shooting of protesters, bombing of properties, arson, kidnappings and violent attacks on individuals.

State violence under apartheid was indeed ever-present and all-pervading. Repression, it has been rightly said, cannot exist without violence. The words of Allister Sparks describing state violence in South Africa are revealing and telling:

> Pervasive, everyday, institutionalised violence, built into the polity and made part of the law, is the essential element by which a minority can hold power over a majority, and it is fundamental to the apartheid system. It is there in the compulsion and regulation, in the vagrancy laws and the squatter laws, in the forced removals and the police raids, in the daily confrontation between white authority and black subject. It is there in South Africa's overcrowded prisons (which hold a daily average of 110,000 people, the vast majority of them black, for a population of under 30 million.) Television viewers around the world have seen glimpses of this violence on their screens, with police lashing out at fleeing demonstrators

---

[47]   Quoted in *Rule of Fear: Human Rights in South Africa* (1989), *op. cit.*, p. 8.

with what sometimes seems almost sadistic relish, and unleashed violence that goes beyond what is required to maintain order, even by authoritarian standards ... In the interrogation cells this mutually destructive violence of oppressor and oppressed reaches its apex ... The interrogator's power is absolute. He has the power to hold, the power to torture, the power to kill even ... Torture has become routine, a standard tool employed in the name of state security ... There is the helicopter, when a handcuffed prisoner is hung from a stick thrust between the folds at his elbows and knees and lashed with *sjambok* whips as he is twirled around. There is the submarine, when his head is held under water until he nearly drowns, or, as a refinement, when he is suffocated by having a wet sack pulled over his head. There is the telephone, when electric wires are attached to his nipples or genitals and he is subjected to repeated shocks. Often, too, prisoners are made to stand for hours on end, even days, sometimes on bricks that are placed on edge, sometimes in squatting positions with their arms outstretched, sometimes naked and blindfolded with creeping things sent crawling over their bodies.[48]

Nothing could be more barbarous, yet all this atrocious violence was perpetrated by white men who claimed to be civilised and to have come to Africa on a "civilising mission." But the enumeration above does not exhaust all the forms of violence employed by the white minority regime in South Africa. Detainees were also tortured by beating, forced gymnasium-type exercises, strangulation, pulling out or burning of hair, heating or burning soles of feet, being thrown in the air and allowed to fall, being given salted water to drink, being set alight, squeezing of breast, being placed in the boot of a car, cutting of hands with a knife, burning of fingernails, being tied to a tree and many other forms of violence designed to break down the will of the victim.[49] Still, the violence of apartheid fell far short of Hitler's sending six million Jews to the gas chamber.

As to be expected, this overwhelming violence resulted in wanton destruction of lives, with 2,400 killed between September 1984 and February 1987 plus the considerable number of deaths by torture or poisoning in detention places, "disappearances" and political murders.

Commenting on this tragic phenomenon of pervasive, everyday violence, Allister Sparks had feared about

---

[48] Allister Sparks, *op. cit.*, pp. 219-222.
[49] *Rule of Fear: Human Rights in South Africa* (1989), *op. cit.*, p. 14.

the possibility of a Khmer Rouge generation emerging, generation of black youth so brutalised and desensitised by its violent encounter with white South Africa's repressive forces that it would lose all sense of life's value, a generation grown up in the institutionalised violence of apartheid and the endemic violence of the ghetto, that was having superimposed on that the violence of street rioting and of bloody clashes with the police and the army.[50]

He then adds the question: "What happens to a ten-year-old who is put in jail, threatened, abused, beaten, tortured, tear-gassed in the street, shot at, who sees his friends killed, learns to throw stones at an armoured car, set fire to a house, maybe kill a cop if he can."[51] The child will certainly grow up imbibing brutal, violent behaviour as part of his personality. That is part of black South Africans' inheritance from apartheid.

Despite all this violence backing up repression of resistance to it, the apartheid system eventually collapsed in 1994. (With the collapse, the four independent "homelands" were re-incorporated into the South African state.) Its collapse shows it to have been an exercise in sheer folly and futility. In a country inhabited by different races who have become so intermingled and interdependent by the forces of urbanisation and industrialisation, as was the case in South Africa, total, rigid territorial separation is not just impracticable, it is "beyond the bounds of possibility." As Allister Sparks observed, "the inherent unreality of the programme that caused apartheid's crisis of practicality in the 1970s should have been obvious from the beginning," had "idealism not already taken leave of reality".[52]

The Legacy of Apartheid

The discussion above shows apartheid as an unmitigated tragedy both for the mental and emotional pain and despair it caused its victims and for the physical suffering inflicted by its brutal repressions. In the telling words of the Report of a visit to South Africa by representatives of the British Churches in 1985:

the essence of apartheid is not separate seats and entrances, nor even separate townships or separate school systems, all of which can be subject to reform, but the ingrained assumption that Blacks must remain

---

[50] Allister Sparks, *op. cit.*, p. 267.
[51] Allister Sparks, *loc. cit.*
[52] Allister Sparks, *op. cit.*, p. 181.

subservient, at best to white paternalism, or at worst to white tyranny ... Whenever the legitimate nonviolent dissent of Blacks, Coloureds or Indians had achieved any strength and coherence, instead of being heard it had been maligned as treasonable or communist, its organisation banned, its leaders detained or eliminated, and its active following harassed with shocking brutality."[53]

Apartheid is thus rightly denounced as "intrinsically evil",[54] and the apartheid state as "morally illegitimate and tyrannical."[55] The regime was illegitimate because its rule was not based on the consent of the majority and was maintained over that majority by violence through the brutal application of the organised, institutionalised force of the state.[56] It was tyrannical because it governed in the interest of a small minority of the people identified by race, and asserting an inherent superiority, to the detriment of the overwhelming majority whose legitimate right to share in the benefits of democracy, freedom, justice and the good life it ruthlessly repressed merely because they were of another, supposedly inferior, race. As a system which accorded the ultimate value of the human being, namely the dignity of the human person, only to whites, and denied it to non-whites, apartheid palpably contradicted the common basic humanity and natural equality of all men and women as being created in the image of God, which therefore gives it the taint of a heresy.[57] (It was so declared by the World Alliance of Reformed Churches at a conference in Ottawa in 1982.) The doctrine of a master race, proclaiming itself the guardian of other races, is inimical to the peace of the world, as is amply demonstrated by the case of Nazi Germany.

The apartheid system has indeed ravaged the blacks of South Africa. It has blighted the black's entire personality: his individuality, initiative, perspicacity, self-confidence, self-esteem. It did this not only by the sense of insecurity that pervaded his life from childhood to adulthood – lack of job and other opportunities, the intimidating presence of the police everywhere, the ever-present threat of eviction from home or forced re-location to a re-settlement

---

[53] Report reproduced in *South Africa in the 1980s, op. cit.*, pp. 79-88, quotation from pp. 79-80.

[54] United States Catholic Conference Administrative Board Statement on South Africa, Sept. 11, 1985; reproduced in *South Africa in the 1980s, op. cit.*, pp. 74-78, at p. 74.

[55] The KAIPOS Document, a Christian, biblical and theological comment on the political crisis in South Africa; reproduced in *South Africa in the 1980s, op. cit.*, pp. 66-70, at p. 69.

[56] Allister Sparks, *op. cit.*, p. 211.

[57] John de Gruchy and Charles Villa-Vicencio, *Apartheid is a Heresy* (1983).

camp or to a homeland, etc. – but also by all forms of humiliation and degradation. "How," asks Allister Sparks, "does one learn to feel pride in oneself, in one's race, in one's heritage, when one's earliest childhood memories are" of one's own parents cringing before the wanton abuse of the police, fawning in their pleas for work, and of other kinds of humiliation and debasement by a white master?[58] The psychological damage was simply incalculable. But the whites themselves were not entirely free of the ravages. "Apartheid, brutalising the whites as it destroys the self-esteem of the blacks, robs both of their humanity."[59]

The separation of the different peoples or races comprised in a country is bad in itself, but what makes it monstrously so is the inevitable inequity and injustice it involves, since the development of the races and the separate areas they occupy, and of the separate amenities in mixed areas are bound, in the nature of things, to be unequal. "Destroying separation," a leading member of the African National Congress (ANC), Francis Meli, has said,

> is relatively very easy. We take over and do away with racial laws. But how do we destroy (the results and effects of) inequality? When people have been disadvantaged for 300 years, this must affect their culture, the economy, their interests and needs, aspirations and levels of development, education and skills – in fact everything.[60]

Herein lies a major part of the monstrous legacy of apartheid; it has left behind a legacy of unequal development and inequality in conditions of the whites and blacks in South Africa as well as the legacy of its embittering effects on relations between them. Apart from the land question, how are the privileged position of whites and the manifold deprivations, the disadvantages and legal disabilities of blacks, like the resettlement camps, the ghettos, pass laws, influx control, impoverished homelands, neglect of black education, black unemployment and other instances of unequal development and general inequality between whites and blacks be dismantled or redressed to secure a fair measure of equity and justice for blacks in a post-apartheid South Africa? "One cannot hobble people for centuries, give others every possible advantage

---

[58] Allister Sparks, *op. cit.*, p. 225.
[59] Allister Sparks, *op. cit.*, p. 218.
[60] Francis Meli, "South Africa and the Rise of African Nationalism,": in Maria van Diepen, (ed)., *op. cit.*, p. 75.

for generation after generation, then put both in the same starting blocks for a flat race and say piously, 'May the best man win'."[61] As he boasted, the chief architect and ideologue of apartheid, Dr. Hendrick Verwoerd, had indeed seen to it that the system was so firmly and deeply entrenched that its complete unscrambling by any future government might be well-nigh impossible. That is the great challenge posed to a black majority government in South Africa.

---

[61] Allister Sparks, *op. cit.,* p. 388; who states that "South Africa has the widest gap between rich and poor of any country in the world for which data are available".

CHAPTER 11

Unmitigated Evils of Socialist Totalitarian Rule

Perhaps it is appropriate to begin with a caveat. Whilst there have, at various times, been eleven countries in Africa that formally proclaimed themselves socialist states in their constitutions (Algeria, Angola, Benin, Congo (Brazzaville), Egypt, Ethiopia, Madagascar, Mozambique, Somalia, Sudan and (since 1984) Tanzania) – this is exclusive of countries which have pursued a socialist path of development within the framework of the African one-party system but without formerly transforming themselves into socialist states in their constitutions, e.g. Cape Verde, Guinea, Guinea-Bissau, Seychelles and (before 1984) Tanzania – none of them can properly be described as totalitarian states and therefore characterised by the elements and evils noted hereafter. For example, the integration of the individual and society into the party-state is hardly true of any African socialist state. The character of the socialist constitution as just a political charter of government and the complete jettisoning of the Rule of Law in favour of the concept of "socialist legality" are also not true of all African socialist states (e.g. Tanzania and Algeria whose 1976 Constitution proclaims "the primacy of law"); some of the other elements (like state ownership of the means of production and the empowerment of the masses) have only minimal application in some of the states. Egypt, as a socialist state, is remarkable in two main respects. First, the principle of a single vanguard party is excluded in favour of a multi-party system (art. 5, 1980 Constitution). Secondly, the concept of socialist legality is also excluded. In a part of the Constitution (1980) headed "Sovereignty of the Law" it is provided that "sovereignty of the law shall be the basis of rule in the state," and that "the state shall be subject to law" (arts. 64 and 65).

The evils of a socialist totalitarian government go far beyond those of an absolutist one. A totalitarian government is, as stated in chapter 7, a despotism with a vengeance, an extreme form of autocracy worse than fascism, because it is "more ruthless, barbarous, unjust, immoral, anti-democratic, unredeemed by any hope or scruple."[1]

Socialist totalitarianism does not merely curtail liberty, as does the African one-party authoritarianism or an absolutism, it destroys it totally, and, with it, individuality. Respect for man as man, his personality, his impulses and emotions, is almost totally destroyed. Man is treated like a disposable property, his life is subordinated to the state and may be taken at the arbitrary whim of the state. The security of his person counts for little. A regime of terror and of total arbitrariness is unleashed on the society, a terror in which travel restrictions, internal exile, constant surveillance, a terroristic secret police and other instruments of coercion, the concentration camp, executions and frequent use of armed force against the population are all extensively employed. The sheer brutality of the socialist/communist regimes, often involving torture, is simply inhuman and degrading to the human personality. And the abolition of private property meant the total destruction of individual liberty of action, for it is the desire for private acquisitions that provides the motif force, the *raison d'etre*, for most of our actions.

No less pernicious an incident of total rule under socialism/communism is the fact that it is always accompanied by a totalitarian control of human thought and the expression of opinion. It deprives the people of the capacity for independent and rational thought. The goals of the socialist socio-economic order are erected into a creed which everyone, willy-nilly, must not only work for but must also believe in, not from a rational conviction of its validity, but as something sacrosanct and never to be questioned, an article of faith. Socialist goals and ideas become the only line of thought permitted to the people, deviation from which, as by criticism of the system, is treated as an act of disloyalty or sabotage punishable by death; it is for that offence that many, nay millions, were executed during the great purges of the Stalin era in the USSR.

Belief in socialism and its principles is instilled in the minds of the people and entrenched as part of the public values of the society not only by coercion

---

[1] Marx Eastman, *Stalin's Russia and the Crisis of Socialism* (1940), p. 82.

but also by indoctrination by means of propaganda, harnessing for its effective propagation the state's monopoly of all the instruments of mass communication (television, radio and the print media) and all the apparatus for spreading knowledge (the schools, colleges, universities, academies, etc). Its monopoly of the instruments of propaganda enables the state to mould the minds of the people to believe in socialism as the best way of life and not to think of any other alternative way of organising society. Human thought and opinion become thoroughly collectivised in the manner directed by the state—what has been aptly called the "nationalisation of thought." Next to the wanton taking of human life, totalitarian control of human thought is the worst type of tyranny imaginable.

The propaganda does not stop at indoctrinating the people with a belief in socialist values so as to make them the shared values of the community which, as an imposed system of belief, is bad enough in itself. It is also used to manipulate facts in order to maintain or win public loyalty to the system. Facts likely to weaken such loyalty are suppressed or misrepresented.

> The basis of unfavourable comparisons with conditions elsewhere, the knowledge of possible alternatives to the course actually taken, information which might suggest failure on the part of the government to live up to its promises or to take advantage of opportunities to improve conditions will be suppressed.[2]

And so we find that, as part of their ruling technique, socialist/communist regimes everywhere indulge in mass falsehood or suppression of facts partly as a way to cover up their failures and shortcomings. Thus, in the midst of an all-pervading poverty, chronic shortages of the essentials of life and a general economic stagnation and decline, and in spite of the frequent conflicts, uprisings and revolts, socialist/communist governments still claimed, and had it proclaimed to the world in the constitution, that "rapid and all-round development of the country" had been achieved, that "our economy is expanding as never before," that "production is increasing from year to year and living standard of all working people is constantly rising", that "class antagonisms" have been put to an end, and "rapprochement of all classes and social strata" attained. They not only claimed that the system is guaranteed

---

[2]　F. A. Hayek, *The Road to Serfdom* (1944), p. 119.

to free the individual from "the despotism of physical want" but also indulged the deceit that freedom from want had been achieved for all.

Mass falsehood or suppression of facts indulged in by the state as a deliberate technique of rule is, as Hayek points out, particularly evil because it undermines, if it does not destroy, the sense of, and respect for, truth in the society. Even

> the word truth itself ceases to have its old meaning. It describes no longer something to be found, with the individual conscience as the sole arbiter of whether in any particular instance the evidence (or the standing of those proclaiming it) warrants a belief; it becomes something to be laid down by authority, something which has to be believed in the interest of the unity of the organised effort, and which may have to be altered as the exigencies of this organised effort require it.[3]

With this mass falsification or suppression of facts went the perversion of language, the tendentious use of words by giving them completely different meaning, with the result that rational discourse between socialists and non-socialists was made virtually impossible. Thus, socialist governments claimed to govern by the Rule of Law and to practise democracy when in reality only a perverted version of these concepts, "socialist legality" and "socialist democratism" as they are deceptively called, was maintained while equality by means of a planned economy is held out to the people to disguise an officially enforced inequality.

Next, there is the total arbitrariness of socialist rule. Socialist rule, like all total rule, is arbitrary because it necessarily precludes the Rule of Law whose central principle is that the government cannot take away or curtail the rights of the individual or otherwise frustrate or stifle his freedom of action except in so far as, and only to the extent that, its action is authorised (not merely permitted) by, and is strictly in conformity with, the existing law, either the law of the constitution or the ordinary law validly made or deemed to be made by the legislature, with the object of reducing the amount of discretion exercisable by government in the administration of the state and the extent it can act in an unpredictable, *ad hoc* manner, and thereby enabling the individual to conduct his affairs with the foreknowledge of what to expect and how he stands in relation to the coercive powers of the state.

---

[3] F. A. Hayek, *op. cit.*, p. 121.

Under socialist rule, the exercise of the sovereign law-making power, the greatest of all discretionary powers, is not limited by a supreme constitution. Likewise, the executive government is conducted according to a system in which decisions and actions are taken, not within the framework of pre-determined and known rules of law applicable in all circumstances and to all and sundry, including the government itself, but according to what the rulers consider to be necessary for the realisation of the goals and objectives of the socialist socio-economic order, which simply is tantamount to total arbitrary rule. It is just not possible to direct and manage centrally according to pre-determined rules, the activities and affairs of the members of society in all their variegated ramifications. Within the ambit of the general law, the individual can conduct his affairs as suits him. He can slave himself and be as austere as he likes, he can deny himself certain wants or needs in order to achieve other ends, but to subject him to such a regime at the will of others in order to achieve ends determined by them is a form of oppression altogether intolerable to the nature of man. For, as far as the individual is concerned, any decision to deny him those wants or needs in order to attain ends chosen without his agreement or against his will is arbitrary, and will be looked upon as an unfair discrimination in aid of those favoured by it. Where the government undertakes to provide for the actual needs of people as they arise and has to choose deliberately between them, its decision or choice cannot but be arbitrary, since it is not determined by formal rules of law applicable in all circumstances and to all persons without distinction, but by the momentary will of the rulers, which leaves the door open to caprice and arbitrariness.

In this sense, as Hayek pertinently observes, the Rule of Law has

> little to do with the question whether all actions of government are legal in the juridical sense. They may well be and yet not conform to the Rule of Law. The fact that somebody has full legal authority to act in the way he does gives no answer to the question whether the law gives him power to act arbitrarily or whether the law prescribes unequivocally how he has to act.[4]

Under the constitution, the socialist government has full authority to implement the socialist socio-economic order by means of a central direction of all

---

[4]   F.A. Hayek, *op. cit.*, p. 61.

economic activities, which means in effect that its actions in this behalf are legal (socialist legality), but since the power, by its nature, does not admit of being circumscribed by pre-determined rules of law, total arbitrariness is built into the system. The position is thus as if the law authorises the government to act in all matters just as it pleases. In communist thinking, the Rule of Law makes the state "unfree," a "prisoner of the law;" in order, therefore, to be able to act justly, the state has to be "released from the fetters of abstract rules. A free state was to be one that could treat its subjects as it pleased."[5]

Among the worst evils of socialist/communist rule is the total denial of individual freedom of choice and action: freedom to decide what to do with oneself, whether not to work at all, to be self-employed or to work for an employer and, if so, to choose an employer to work for and to agree on the terms of such employment. The individual is obliged to work for no one else but the state, and only in the kind of job assigned to him and on terms dictated by it; a professional or other highly trained person may be assigned to work as a road sweeper, a stoker or to perform some other menial job, often by way of victimisation for disobeying orders. The system is thus one of forced labour amounting in Friedrich Hayek's words to "serfdom" or "a new form of slavery."[6]

Forced labour is evil because it leaves the individual no choice but obedience to the orders of a superior, and it is no less evil because the new master is the state. "The defence against oppressive hours, pay, working conditions or treatment," said the U.S. Supreme Court, "is the right to change employers. When the master can compel and the labourer cannot escape the obligation to go on, there is no power below to redress and no incentive above to relieve a harsh overlordship or unwholesome conditions of work."[7] Whilst, even in a free enterprise system, few people have ever an abundance of choice of occupation,

> what matters is that we have some choice, that we are not absolutely tied to a particular job which has been chosen for us or which we may have chosen in the past, and that if one position becomes quite intolerable, or if we set our heart on another, there is almost always a way for the able,

---

[5]   F. A. Hayek, *The Constitution of Liberty* (1960), p. 239.
[6]   F. A. Hayek, *The Road to Serfdom* (1944), p. 10.
[7]   *Pollock v. Williams*, 322 U.S. 4 (1944).

> some sacrifice at the price of which he may achieve his goal. Nothing makes conditions more unbearable than the knowledge that no effort of ours can change them; and even if we should never have the strength of mind to make the necessary sacrifice, the knowledge that we could escape if we only strove hard enough makes many otherwise intolerable positions bearable.[8]

Forced labour is inherently exploitative, and its exploitation is inexorable. The form of exploitation involved in this case is one more intolerable than capitalist exploitation, which it was meant to eradicate. Under capitalism, the state is interposed between the private capitalist employer and his workers, and its interventions, through the enactment of such measures as minimum wages, maximum working hours, humane working conditions, collective bargaining and other social justice legislation, serves to moderate the exploitation, to democratise the relationship and to hold the balance between the two, whereas under socialism/communism there is no power above the state to play such a moderating role between it, as sole employer, and the workers. Without any democratic institutions for its control, exploitation by the socialist state is total. It is all the more odious because it is perpetrated by a class that comprises a large number of political bureaucrats (reckoned at hundreds of thousands in each country), the *nomenklatura* as it is called. A privileged group, self-perpetuating, parasitic and corrupt, the *nomenklatura* has been described as holding the communist society in fief.[9] They manipulated the workers for their own benefit. One had to be connected with the *nomenklatura* or to bribe them to obtain any benefit or advancement under the system. The existence of such a large group with special privileges and exploitative tendencies makes nonsense of socialism's claim to be a more just system, which is really its sole justification.

Any system that totally destroys man's individuality and human liberty is utterly repugnant to human nature, and is therefore inherently evil. Liberty is natural to man because

> the ability to be, think, and act was part of man's endowment as a whole, sane, normal human personality... The ability to be was the ability to live and to enjoy life. The ability to think and act was the ability to protect life more securely, to expand liberty more generously, to safeguard property

---

[8] F. A. Hayek, *The Road to Serfdom*, (1944), pp. 70-71.
[9] Z.A.B. Zeman, *The Making and Breaking of Communist Europe*, (1990), p. 250.

more adequately, to ensure conscience more liberally, and to advance happiness more easily.[10]

Take these away, and man ceases to be human. The almost total destruction of man's individuality and human liberty under socialism/communism has two disastrous consequences. First, it renders the regime so susceptible to popular resistance and violent uprisings, since individuals, deprived of liberty of action and forced into a common mould and a regimented existence, would always try to break free of it. The belief that the elimination of bourgeois ownership of the means of production would abolish all conflicts in the state between the ruling bureaucrats (i.e. the government) and the governed, between different classes *inter se* and between different racial or ethnic groups comprised in the state is an illusion.

> Revolts and uprisings are endemic to societies in which those at the bottom of social hierarchies including labour are no better than anywhere else, the place of capital is taken by a new class of political bureaucrats, and that of wage disputes and strikes, or elections and changes of government by complex procedures of unwilling adaptation which are always liable to break down.[11]

Hence the frequent uprisings in the communist countries of East Europe, such as occurred in East Germany in 1953, Hungary in 1956, Czechoslovakia in 1968 and Poland in 1980, to mention but a few.

In the second place, total rule breeds economic stagnation and decline by the near-total state monopoly of industrial activity (amounting to about 90 percent of all such activity) and by state ownership of the means of production. The collectivisation of farming had meant that those

> who remained on the land no longer owned it and were alienated from their work. A haphazard and unpopular collectivisation led many people to concentrate on their gardens and allotments, which ensured food supplies for them, and for family members who had migrated to the towns and cities,[12] but not for the market which was disallowed.

State monopoly of economic activity and ownership of the means of production are inherently bad because they abolish or, at any rate, severely restrict the institutions of contract, the market and, above all, competition.

---

[10] Neal Riemer, *James Madison: Creating the American Constitution,* (1986), p. 34.
[11] Ralf Dahrendorf, *Reflections on the Revolution in Europe* (1990), p.17
[12] Misha Glenny, *The Rebirth of History* (1990)

An economy organised on such lines is bound to stagnate and decline. Economic growth and prosperity is the product of individual entrepreneurship, individual initiative, an enterprising spirit and of individual inventiveness and self-reliance – the very things that socialism/communism seeks to smother totally. Without them, growth and prosperity is hardly possible. The individual needs an environment of freedom and free competition to be able to blossom and organise his life for his maximum comfort and happiness.

"Competition is not only the life of trade, it is the trade of life."[13] Life is about competition for survival in all fields of human pursuit. An enterprise shielded from the stimuli of competition cannot be fully efficient or maximise its productivity. The consumer too needs to have competitive sources of supply from which to choose, based on the quality and prices of their products, otherwise he would be entirely at the mercy of the monopolist who would thus be enabled not only to "decide what commodities and services were to be available, and in what quantities; it would be able to direct their distribution between districts and groups and could, if it wished, discriminate between persons to any degree it liked."[14] What is more, the monopolist would be able to dictate price, unlike in a competitive system where the price is not determined by the conscious will of anybody, so that its operation cannot therefore be manipulated to favour or disfavour any particular persons or groups; and it does not discriminate between people according to anyone's views of their merits or demerits nor can it be predicated in advance which persons will gain or lose by it. Competition has thus the merit of impersonality and impartiality. Given an appropriate framework of laws and provided that it is properly controlled by the state to check some of its unjust effects, it is perhaps the only mechanism known to mankind for regulating economic activities in a society and adjusting them so as to maintain an acceptable balance between the various elements in it.[15]

Stagnation or decline of the economy means, of course, misery and suffering for the individual. When the state, having reduced the individual to a state of utter dependence by undertaking to be responsible for all the needs

---

[13] Will and Ariel Durant, *The Lessons of History* (1968), p. 19
[14] F. A. Hayek, *op. cit.*, p. 70
[15] See Hayek, *The Fatal Conceit* (1988), where the argument is extensively canvassed.

and wants of society and each and every one of its members, proves incapable of fulfilling its undertaking, economic misery and suffering become the inexorable lot of the individual. The undertaking by the state to be a general provider is simply impossible of fulfilment, for the simple reason that there is just no way the state, socialist state no less than any other, can adequately discharge it in the sense of being able to cater for the needs and welfare of each individual as well as the general welfare of society. It is alright for the state to undertake to cater for the general welfare of the society. But the welfare and happiness of the members of a community, considered as individuals, depend, not alone on the satisfaction of needs common to all and which can be collectively planned for and provided by the state; it depends even more on the satisfaction of those desires that are peculiar to each individual and different from everyone else's and which can be satisfied only by the individual being left to organise his life and his affairs in his own way, not by the state assuming onto itself the central direction and management of all the activities and affairs of one and all according to a single plan, which necessarily means a regimented existence for everybody.

Prevented from helping himself by his own private enterprise and initiative, the suffering of the individual is made inexorable, one from which there is no escape however much he wills to improve his lot. "While people will submit to suffering which may hit anyone, they will not so easily submit to suffering which is the result of the decision of authority."[16]

Perhaps it can be said that economic stagnation and decline, while inevitable under socialism/communism, led to such devastating misery and suffering for the individual because the system had been applied in places for which it was not intended in Marx's theory. Socialism/communism, as conceived by Marx, was meant for an industrialised society, not a poor agrarian one. The class struggle on which his theory and prediction were premised is an industrial phenomenon resulting from the exploitation of the industrial worker by the industrial capitalist. It is a system "conceived in the womb of capitalism," and which could only lead to intolerable misery and suffering if it is delivered in a poor agrarian society lacking adequate capital assets (means of production) to be taken into socialist ownership; to nationalise poverty is simply to entrench

---

[16]   F.A Hayek, *The Road to Serfdom*, p. 80

and perpetuate it. Now, Russia in 1917 and most of the countries of Eastern Europe in 1948 were just or nearly as agrarian as were Ethiopia, Angola, Mozambique and Tanzania at the time they embraced socialism.

The misery of the inhabitants of the socialist countries is brought home more starkly because of their close proximity to the prosperous countries of the Western democracies. Closely juxtaposed as the two are, and separated only by a thin, narrow border, a short day's shopping trip across the border from Eastern Europe to Central Europe or from Dar-es-Salem to Nairobi is almost like a glorious transition from misery to comfort and excitement. In their depressed societies the inhabitants of the socialist countries were made painfully aware that "life was passing them by."[17]

Not the least of the evils of socialist/communist rule is the fact that, by investing supreme authority in an unelected bureaucratic body, the communist party, which is thus elevated above the elected political organs of government––the legislature and executive––the democratic principle of the popular mandate as the basis for government is thoroughly eroded and emptied of all meaning. The institution of elections itself loses meaning as elections are no longer fought over issues sponsored by competing political parties.

On the moral plane, total rule has again had a negative and destructive effect. An organisation of society in which the state directs everything, plans our lives for us and takes all the decisions about means and ends and about all the problems of social life cannot but deprive the individual of that sense of responsibility, that consciousness of duty, on which the development of morality depends. As already implied, it also destroys independence of mind, self-reliance, the spirit of enterprise and of freedom which are all moral virtues vital to the development of a healthy social morality. In the absence of the interplay of individual conscience from which the common morality of the community is formed, public morality is thus what the rulers decide and impose on the people. The subjective judgment of the rulers, and not any objective norms of public morality, is the only yardstick that determines equality and justice in the assignment of work among various people and the distribution of income between different classes of producers: between hand-workers and brain-workers, the skilled and the unskilled, the strong and the

---

[17]   Z.A.B. Zeman, *op. cit.*, p. 12

weak, the industrious and the indolent. And the assumption, which underlies the system, that the rulers would be entirely unselfish in making these determinations, has proved to be mistaken. Lord Bryce has summed up the moral divergence between the two systems thus: "Communism regards (the nation) as primarily an Economic whole existing for the purposes of production and distribution, while the apostles of Democracy regarded it primarily as a Moral and Intellectual whole, created for the sake of what the ancient philosophers called the Good Life."[18]

What clearly emerges from all that has been said is that there is an irreconcilable conflict between democracy and socialism/communism; the one is an individualist and moralist institution resting on the will of the people, the other, a collectivist, materialistic and bureaucratic one.

Just as it originated in revolution in most of the countries (Eastern Europe excepted), socialism/communism was brought to an end in the revolutionary events that took place in 1989-1990 in Eastern Europe. Its evils made the collapse predictable, perhaps inevitable, but they were not the immediate reason for it. The collapse is attributable to three main immediate causes: the emergence of Gorbachev as Soviet leader, with his open and liberal style of rule; the change in Soviet policy under Gorbachev from interference in the internal affairs of the satellite states in order to keep them in line, to complete freedom for them to go it their own way, even to the extent of deviation from the communist party's monopoly of power; and the economic situation of the 1980's which brought prosperity to the West and greater depression to the communist block thereby making the disparity in standards of living in the two blocs more intolerable to the populations of the latter. The revolution succeeded partly because, as Timothy Garton Ash stated, the communist rulers themselves seemed to have lost faith in the system and in the legitimacy of using armed force to maintain and preserve their rule.[19]

What is more important for us, however, is not so much the reasons for the eventual collapse as that the world should be rid of what was clearly a misfortune for the millions enslaved under it and a potential danger for the

---

[18] James Bryce, *Modern Democracies* (1920), Vol. 2, p. 654; also F.A. Hayek, *The Fatal Conceit* (1988) where the moral issue is extensively examined.

[19] T.G. Ash, *We the People* (1990), pp. 141-142

rest of us in view of its ambition to become the order for the entire world. "To follow socialist morality," as Hayek wrote just a year before the collapse, "would destroy much of present humankind and impoverish much of the rest."[20] Its collapse was therefore a welcome release for its subjects and a good riddance for the rest of us.

The collapse of socialism/communism invites one final observation. Writing in 1835, Alexis de Tocqueville remarked that, while men have a love of both liberty and equality, their love of equality was stronger than their love of liberty and that they "prefer equality in slavery to inequality with freedom."[21] Nearly a century later, in 1920, Lord Bryce wrote that "nothing has happened since his (Tocqueville's) day to contradict, and some things to support, this view."[22] There can be no more unequivocal contradiction of this view than the forcible overthrow of socialism/communism in the revolutionary events of 1989-1990, which were a clear rejection of "equality in restraint and servitude," to use Tocqueville's phrase in his other writing, and which bear out eloquently man's preference for "equality in liberty." The clear lesson of the socialist/communist experience is that equality is meaningless without liberty.

---

[20] Hayek, *The Fatal Conceit* (1988), p.7

[21] Alexis de Tocqueville, *Democracy in America* (1835), ed. Richard Heffner (1956), p. 55

[22] James Bryce, *op. cit.*, vol. 1, p. 77

CHAPTER 12

Factors Contributing to the Authoritarianism of African Rulers

Introduction

The authoritarianism of African rulers and their role as intellectual leaders are a product of a complex of causative factors which (or some of which) are here examined. The discussion should, at the highest, be taken as an explanation or rationalisation, but not a justification, of the behaviour of these rulers.

Innate Character of the African

A ready, easy and tempting explanation of the authoritarianism and the aberrant behaviour of African rulers is to say that Africans are, by nature, unfit for liberty, democracy and self-government. Even the great Thomas Jefferson, third President of the United States, had permitted himself this "racist nonsense," as Philip Alston rightly castigated the argument which sought to explain the prevalence of authoritarian and paternalistic regimes in Asia as being the form suited to the authoritarian and paternalistic character of Asian societies.[1]

Jefferson had adumbrated the view that negroes "are inferior to the whites in the endowments both of body and mind." This view has certainly no more objective basis than mere racial prejudice. The black peoples of Africa, in the words of Liberia's Declaration of Independence (1847), possess with other peoples "a common nature, are with them susceptible of equal refinement, and capable of equal advancement in all that adorns and dignifies man." The

---

[1] Philip Alston, in Report of ICJ Conference on Development, Human Rights and the Rule of Law (1981), Pergamon Press, p. 55

so-called inherent superiority of the whites *vis-a-vis* the blacks is a myth. The success of white states is not due to the inherent superiority of the whites, neither is the failure or the poor performance of the black states the result of the inherent inferiority of blacks.

The repressions of African governments are not due to an inherent lack of respect for human dignity and human life. Far from it! Africans do, by nature, have a deep respect for human life and human dignity. It could not be otherwise in a man-based community in which, moreover, the web of kinship ties are all-encompassing and in which members accept it as an obligation to be their brothers' keeper. However, this respect for human dignity and human life was largely limited to members of the community, and those of neighbouring communities sharing common ties, and hardly extended to complete strangers from outside. This is the result of backwardness—lack of communications, particularly—which confined them and their outlook within a severely narrow world.

But backwardness, whilst undeniably a conspicuous feature of pre-colonial African societies, is not a peculiarly African characteristic, nor is it a reflection of a people's innate character or a permanent condition for any people. It is perhaps enough to rebut the claim of an in-born racial superiority of the whites to recall that they have not always been in their present civilised state; that they were once, for long centuries indeed, as backward and barbarous as the blacks were at the time Africa was colonised. After all, the word "barbarian" was originally applied by the ancient Greeks and Romans to almost the whole human race outside themselves, including almost the whole white race, especially some of the Germanic races of Central Europe, the Goths, the Vandals, etc. Europe had passed through its Dark Ages: a period of real darkness, marked by unimaginable barbarism and bestiality, which spanned some five centuries from the collapse of the Roman Empire in Western Europe in 476 A.D. to the end of the 10th century A.D. This was followed by another six centuries, characterised by little development and by the decline of the state itself with the attendant insecurity and instability in society. In the 14th-16th centuries A.D. followed the Renaissance or the revival of art and literature in the old classical traditions of ancient Greece and Rome. The Industrial Revolution, which ushered in the present high level of advancement in Europe, only began in the early part of the 19th century, and took the better half of that century to run its full course.

Personal Characteristics of Individual Rulers

It is not intended to suggest by what is said above that personal characteristics of individual rulers are not a factor in their repressive and authoritarian style of rule. Far from that being the case, they are, in many cases, a major causative factor. Indisputably, there are among African rulers, as elsewhere in the world, those who, by nature, are inclined to be domineering, egotistical and dictatorial, and who have a predilection for personal rule and for the arbitrariness that is inseparable from it. The overwhelming dominance of authoritarian regimes— – from the moderate ones, through the "constitutional dictatorship," the autocracies characterised by the privatisation of the state, to the highly repressive and red terror military regimes— is, to a considerable extent, attributable to the personal characteristics of individual African political leaders.

In a careful and insightful study of personal rulers in Black Africa, Robert Jackson and Carl Rosberg have identified many whose personal characteristics can fairly be said to have been a major factor in their authoritarian and repressive style of rule, men disposed by nature towards repression. Kwame Nkrumah of Ghana is a notable case. He was a man characterised by a passion for personalised power and the arbitrariness that goes with it; a man so egotistical and domineering, overbearingly arrogant towards his fellow countrymen; intensely intolerant of opposition and criticism; a man suffused with a belief in his infallible wisdom, his indispensability, his messianic role and unique place in history as well as a desire to be worshipped, adulated and deified as a hero; a man with an intense passion for vanity and self-exaltation. Near-absolute power in the hands of such a man seems a clear recipe for one-man rule and oppression. "If one is driven by the love of power and the passion to dominate, one may very well be driven to kill in order to retain power."[2]

Yet, although Nkrumah's character and personality had inclined him to an oppressive use of his near-absolute power under Ghana's 1960 Constitution, the oppression was somewhat moderated and restrained in that it involved

---

[2] Robert Jackson and Carl Rosberg, *Personal Rule in Black Africa* (1982), p. 239.

no widespread state-organised violence and brutality and no mass killing. It is a reflection of his character, his abiding respect for the sanctity of human life, that Nkrumah never intentionally caused the death of a single person either by execution after trial and conviction by a court or by extra-judicial killing. His oppression consisted essentially of severely repressive laws and other measures of a legislative kind by means of which all opposition and criticism of his regime were ruthlessly suppressed, and all institutions of government and their functionaries were neutralised and reduced to mere malleable and manipulable tools in the service of his one-man rule.

Like Kwame Nkrumah, Kamuzu Banda of Malawi also had a passion for personalised power, but his seemed to border on psychosis, for he lacked Nkrumah's fundamental respect for the sanctity of human life. He was, by nature and disposition, autocratic, egoistic and domineering, but without Nkrumah's charismatic personality. He was a Christian and yet with cruel repression and vengeance in his instincts and with no forgiveness or compassion in his heart. He was cynical and ruthless without Nkrumah's disarming charm and affability; overbearingly arrogant and contemptuous of the capability of his fellow countrymen; and intensely intolerant of opposition and criticism. Again like Nkrumah, he was suffused with a belief in his infallible wisdom—–"Kamuzu knows best," the party's song went—his indispensability, his messianic role, his unique place in history and his claim to immortality by virtue of his achievements as the redeemer of his people from colonial bondage. He also shared with Nkrumah a deep-rooted desire to be worshipped and adulated as a hero and his passion for self-exaltation was almost megalomaniacal. "When I was negotiating a constitution," he said in May, 1964, "before my men knew what I was doing I had finished everything. I said: 'well, boys, I've done this, that and that, finished." The similarities in character traits and his close friendship with Nkrumah had made him to admire Nkrumah and to want to follow his personalised style of rule.

As Henry Chipembere said, Banda's temperament was such that "whenever you criticised him, he flared up so violently that you had to consider your own position. You didn't want to be dismissed from the Central Committee of the Party or from the cabinet."[3] A further testimony of his autocratic

---

[3]   Quoted from Philip Short, *Banda* (1974), p. 200.

character is revealed by his own statements: "I say a thing and when I say a thing nobody must say anything else and my ministers must do nothing before I approve of it"[4] or "anything I say is law. Literally law. It is a fact in this country."[5]

Ahmed Sekou Toure of Guinea too had a lot in common with Nkrumah: a fanatical faith in and devotion to the validity of his ideas, such as brooked no disobedience, criticism or opposition and such as disposed him to employ any available means, however ruthless, to repress or eliminate critics or opponents; a love of the political power of the modern state system as an instrument of control and coercion and a source of wealth, privileges, patronage and influence; a love so intense and overbearing as to tolerate no rivalry from individuals, factions or groups; a passion to be adulated, worshipped and deified; a desire for a near-totalitarian control of the individual, society, economy and the state. He indeed surpassed Nkrumah in his "sense and use of personal power."[6]

Love of absolute power exercised personally as sole ruler was also a conspicuous aspect of the character and personality of Mobutu of Zaire; it certainly equalled, if it did not surpass, that of Nkrumah or Banda. He simply loved untrammelled power and glorified in the exercise of it, just as he hungered to be adulated and worshipped. He loved high-ranking titles too: he promoted himself general and later, in 1983, field-marshal. An astute political operator, he displayed immense resourcefulness and ingenuity in political manipulation of situations and men to a degree perhaps rivalling Nkrumah's but definitely surpassing Banda. And he could be ruthless too, although, like Nkrumah, his ruthlessness was often tempered by a forgiving heart, which prevented it from reaching the megalomaniacal proportions of Banda's. He certainly was not cruel, or not nearly as cruel as Banda was. He was a spirited nationalist and Africanist but who, regrettably, was led astray by an unbridled, perhaps uncontrollable, instinct for perversion and manipulation for the attainment of personal power and the amassment of personal wealth. Perhaps his poor, humble origins might have had something to do with this: his father was a

---

4   Hansard 29 May, 1964, p. 93.
5   Quoted from Philip Short, *op. at.*, p. 254.
6   Jackson and Rosberg, *op. at.*, p. 210.

domestic servant, a cook.

Ahmed Ahidjo of Cameroon may fairly be classified with the four above. He was of the political strongman mould: tough, domineering, uncompromising and inclined to use repression to suppress or eliminate rivals. He brooked not even the slightest degree of opposition, and dealt severely with any disobedience to his orders. Lacking charisma and inspirational leadership qualities, but largely "through shrewd manoeuvre, skilful manipulation and timing and the will and ability to use power and force, he has acquired complete personal mastery of the state apparatus," which he turned into "something of a 'police state,'" complete with the instruments of a secret police, security surveillance of persons, informers, press censorship, etc.[7] Such was the measure of his love of unfettered power.

"Cut from a similar cloth,"[8] Omar Bongo of Gabon was more or less like Ahidjo; perhaps slightly less disposed to repression and ruthlessness, but certainly with a love of personal power no less intense. In Robert Mugabe of Zimbabwe we have another ruler driven by love of power to pursue an authoritarian style of rule.

Elevated above all else by common personal characteristics of sadism, bestiality and barbarism, fuelled of course by an inordinate thirst for power, are the trio of Idi Amin of Uganda, Jean-Bedel Bokassa of the Central African Republic and Macias Nguema of Equatorial Guinea. To the trio must be added Mengistu Haile Mariam of Ethiopia, also notorious for insensitivity to the suffering of others—an insensitivity born also of an inordinate love of power. There are four other former military rulers also conspicuous for their passion for power and brutal instincts but who certainly cannot be classified with the four sadists: Sani Abacha of Nigeria, Seyni Kountche of Niger, Samuel Doe of Liberia and Siad Barre of Somalia.

But the majority of Africa's authoritarian rulers are of a different character mould; men whose personal characteristics, though they might have contributed, cannot be said to have been a significant cause—not to say a major cause— of the repressions under their rule. They include Kenneth Kaunda of Zambia, a sincere humanist, described as "a political saint forced to become a Prince";[9]

---

7   Jackson and Rosberg, *op. cit.*, p. 154.

8   *ibid.*, p. 156.

9   Jackson and Rosberg, *ibid.*, p. 87.

Julius Nyerere of Tanzania, another lover of humanity and of human freedom within the framework of his somewhat misguided vision of a socialist society in his poverty-stricken country; a great intellectual and a true statesman who desired power, not for personal aggrandisement, but for the satisfaction of the needs and welfare of the people; Leopold Sedar Senghor of Senegal, a scholarly, refined gentleman-politician obliged to be a consummate political manipulator and manoeuvrer with occasional resorts to repressive methods but nonetheless a statesman who instinctively seems to understand "the strengths and weaknesses of the society he rules, and therefore the possibilities and limitations of rule;"[10] William Tubman of Liberia, a nice, affable but conservative man without ruthlessness in his character, and his successor-in-office, William Tolbert, a Baptist minister of "strong religious faith," a humanist and liberal-minded ruler, with a generous heart and a populist style of rule; Modibo Keita of Mali whose character reflected the "virtues of austerity, discipline, individual responsibility, criticism and self-criticism."[11]

Somewhat on the severe side of the line but not really wicked or power-driven were: Jomo Kenyatta of Kenya, stern, paternalistic, with perhaps an excessive relish for the authority of a father-figure and a *pater familias*, which occasionally inclined him to punish, with undue severity, acts of disloyalty or challenges to his leadership; Felix Houphouet-Boigny of Cote d'Ivoire, an austere, stern but dignified and well-cultivated gentleman/statesman who for so long dominated the affairs of his country and its people so completely as to leave no room for rival contenders, not through the use of brutal and regular repression or state-organised violence, but largely by the success and effectiveness of his government in meeting the needs of the citizenry for employment, welfare, stability and relative prosperity; Gaafar Mohammed Nimieri of Sudan was a well-disposed, benevolent, populist and compromise-type ruler who found himself obliged to take ruthless measures to deal with a recurring series of revolts, plots, coups and conspiracies against his regime.

It is therefore inaccurate and unfair to portray the majority of Africa's authoritarian rulers in the image of rulers driven by a sheer passion and lust for power to repress the human rights of their citizens and to desecrate other

---

[10]   *ibid.*, p. 90.
[11]   *ibid.*, p. 188.

institutions and principles of democracy. This is not, however, to say that the quality of leadership provided by these rulers has been as high as might be wished. Undeniably, lack of the right kind of leadership accounts, to a considerable extent, for part of Africa's problems of governance. With a few exceptions, Africa has not, since independence, had the benefit of a leadership at once dedicated, single-minded, selfless, disciplined, patriotic and highly motivated in the national interest; a leadership prepared, in Amilcar Cabral's famous metaphor, to commit suicide by sacrificing its vested elitist interests in the preservation of the existing social and economic system. Thus, lack of the right kind of leadership is perhaps what is meant when it is said that "in African countries governance is more a matter of seamanship and less of navigation; that is, staying afloat rather than going somewhere."[12]

With respect to such things as peace, order, stability and non-material security, not the maintenance of the institutions, principles and norms of democracy, it may be that the quality of leadership provided by individual African personal rulers, judged as either good or bad leadership, has been "more important than anything else"[13] in securing these things i.e. peace, order, stability and non-material security.

Nonetheless, our thesis is that, however crucially important the personal characteristics of individual African rulers and general lack of the right kind of leadership may be as a causative factor, they are not the **root** cause of the failure of Africa's experiment in democratic governance. The root causes are linked to cultural, sociological and economic factors and more overwhelmingly to Africa's colonial heritage. However, in saying that personal characteristics of individual African rulers are not the root cause of the continent's problems of government, one must not be taken as an apologist for the misrule of African political leaders, both civilian and military. These root causes will now be examined.

Cultural Factor

The African's traditional conception of authority is one important cultural factor. Authority in African traditional society is conceived as being personal,

---

[12] Robert Jackson and Carl Rosberg, *op. cit.*, p. 18.
[13] *ibid.*, p. 3.

permanent, mystical and pervasive.[14] The chief in most African traditional societies is a personal ruler and his office is held for life. His office pervades all the other relations in the community, for he is both "legislator", executive, judge, priest, medium, father, etc. These characteristics of the African traditional political system appear to have contributed significantly to the prevalence of personal rule as a form of government in most of the states in Africa created by colonialism. They also account, in part, for the considerable number of Africa's personal rulers hanging on to power for long, indefinite periods of time, some as life presidents so proclaimed in the constitution.

Felix Houphouet Boigny of Cote d'Ivoire died in office after 34 years as President, William Tubman of Liberia after 28 years, Sekou Toure of Guinea after 26 years, Abdel Nasser of Egypt after 16 years, Jomo Kenyatta of Kenya and Sir Seretse Khama of Botswana after 15 years. Mobutu Sese Seko of Zaire (Congo Leopoldville), Sir Dauda Jawara of The Gambia, Lebua Jonathan of Lesotho, Hamani Diori of Niger and Kwame Nkrumah of Ghana were in office for 32, 29, 20, 14 and 10 years respectively before being overthrown in military coups or armed revolt, while Kamuzu Banda of Malawi and Kenneth Kaunda of Zambia ruled for 29 and 27 years respectively before they were voted out in a free multi-party democratic election. Habib Bourguiba of Tunisia was dismissed after 32 years in office on the ground of senility certified by a group of medical doctors. Julius Nyerere of Tanzania voluntarily retired after 27 years in office as did Leopold Senghor of Senegal after 21 years. Gnassimgbe Eyadema of Togo, Omar Bongo of Gabon and Muamar Gaddafi of Libya are still in office (August 2002) after 31, 31 and 28 years respectively.

Habib Bourguiba of Tunisia and Kamuzu Banda of Malawi had themselves proclaimed life president in the constitution as had Jean-Bedel Bokassa of the Central African Republic before his overthrow by the military in 1972. Other African presidents, like Kwame Nkrumah and Kenneth Kaunda, rejected offers of a life presidency, just as Banda did for some time before finally succumbing to the pressure and the temptation. All had said they would stay in office for as long as the people wanted them, which, given the indefinite

---

[14] Alvin W. Wolfe, "African Conceptions of Authority," unpublished paper (1965); cited by K.W. Grundy & M. Weinstein, "The Political Uses of Imagination"(1966) *Transition* 31, p.5.

eligibility for re-election, meant in effect, for life. The only difference was that every four, five or so years they would have to submit themselves to the ritual of an election. It was the ritualistic nature of the exercise perhaps that finally induced Banda, with his characteristic aversion to hypocrisy, to accept the life presidency.

Now, a life president, or, one who has held office for 20 or 30 years, is a different kind of functionary from one who is limited to a maximum of two terms of four or five years each. His authority is bound to be greater; for after twenty or thirty years in office he is apt to become an institution himself, attracting loyalties of a personal nature.

Related to the African's traditional conception of authority is the traditional African attitude towards power. Tradition has inculcated in the people a certain amount of deference and even adulation for a man of power. The chief's authority is sanctified in religion and it borders almost on sacrilege to flout it, except in cases of blatant and systematic oppression when the whole community might rise in revolt to destool, banish or kill a tyrannical chief. Thus, while customary sanctions against extreme cases of abuse of power exist, there is also considerable toleration of arbitrariness by the chief. The attitude towards power tends to be transferred to the ruler of the modern state. The vast majority of the population, which of course is still illiterate and custom-bound, is not disposed to question the ruler's power, and indeed disapproves of those who are inclined to do so.

In a sense, therefore, the presidency in Africa is regarded by many in the light of the attitudes inculcated in them towards chiefly authority, and its power as the projection of chiefly authority into the national sphere. The president, in effect, is the **chief** of the new nation, and as such is entitled to the authority and respect due by tradition to a chief.

African political ethic also favours and aids authoritarian rule. To begin with, there is the relative impotence of extra-constitutional sanctions against the abuse of power. The social values of the advanced democracies enshrine a national ethic which defines the limits of permissible action by the wielders of power. This national ethic is sanctified in deeply entrenched conventions operating as part of the rules of the game of politics. Thus, although an action may well be within the powers of the ruler under the constitution, still he cannot do it if it violates the moral sense of the nation, for he would risk calling down upon himself the wrath of public censure. The force of public opinion is sufficiently developed to act as a watchdog of the nation's ethic, and no action that seriously violates this ethic can hope to escape public condemnation. More than any constitutional restraints, perhaps, it is the ethic of the nation, its sense of right and wrong, and the capacity of the people to defend it, which provides the ultimate bulwark against tyranny.

Julius Nyerere of Tanzania has underscored the point:

> When the nation does not have the ethic which will enable the government to say: 'We cannot do this, that is un-Tanganyikan'– or the people to say: 'That we cannot tolerate, that is un-Tanganyikan'–if the people do not have that kind of ethic, it does not matter what kind of constitution you frame. They can always be victims of tyranny.[15]

Africa is yet to develop a strong moral sense in relation to the affairs of the modern state. Standards of public morality have not become deeply rooted, nor are they effectively articulated and enforced, partly because the instruments of public opinion are controlled by the very people to be checked. Because of this, an African ruler can get away with a lot of things which an American President dares not venture.

Sociological and Economic Factors

Illiteracy and ignorance are a primary sociological factor underlying the authoritarianism of African rulers. The worst offenders against human rights have been barely educated soldiers who rose from the ranks: Idi Amin of Uganda, Samuel Doe of Liberia, Jean-Bedel Bokassa of Central African Republic, Macias Nguema of Equatorial Guinea and Mengistu Haile Mariam of Ethiopia. Such bestiality as was perpetrated by these men is impossible in a person with the education and refinement of Nnamdi Azikiwe of Nigeria, Leopold Sedar Senghor of Senegal, Julius Nyerere of Tanzania and, the best of them all, Nelson Mandela of South Africa. True, Tanganyika did adopt a Preventive Detention Act in 1962 but its application was moderated by Nyerere's refinement and his civilised view of it as an outrage made necessary only because of the exigencies of the situation in his country and whose

---

[15] National Assembly Debate, 1962, col. 1104.

application must therefore be limited to what was absolutely required to deal with the situation.

But illiteracy and ignorance are significant more as a manifestation of a socio-economic condition of greater impact, namely, underdevelopment. The underdevelopment of African societies forces upon African rulers an interventionist policy. Just as the economic depression of the early 1930s called forth Franklin Roosevelt's New Deal measures, which was perhaps the highest point presidential power has attained in peace time in America, so also does the poverty of African societies aggregate power to the presidency. Given this poverty, and the illiteracy which contributed to it, the challenge and burden of development must rest first and foremost upon the state, since it alone has anything like the type of resources needed for development programmes in industry, commerce and agriculture. The nationalist struggle is an on-going one, its political objective having been won, the next phase is in the economic field. The economic dependence of the new state upon the old colonial business interests must be brought to an end by nationalisation or by the state taking over majority shareholdings. Development through state action and state ownership seemed an inevitable response to the poverty of African societies and to the economic domination of them by foreign business interests, and no president, however moderate, can remain passive and leave development entirely to individual enterprise. Every African nationalist leader is therefore, willy-nilly, an interventionist. Although all African presidents rank as strong presidents in this sense, some are stronger than others. While some are content with establishing new industries, commercial enterprises, agricultural projects and other nation-building schemes, giving private enterprise virtually a free hand, others, notably Tanzania and Guinea, have embarked upon a thorough-going nationalisation of the principal means of production and distribution. Because of the extensiveness of its participatory role in the economy, the state now towers like a colossus over every aspect of economic activity; its size has become indeed over-bloated.

Indeed, most of the first generation African leaders had assumed a socialist posture simply because it seemed to be in consonance with the intellectual climate in Africa at the time.[16] To begin with, among African nationalists,

---

[16]   UNESCO, *General History of Africa*, vol. viii (1993), pp. 486-487.

capitalism had come to be associated with imperialism and colonialism and every progressive nationalist had to be something of a socialist to be true to his anti-imperialist and anti-colonialist sentiments. Moreover, the inadequacy of the capitalist approach to development in the context of the pervading poverty in Africa had predisposed some African leaders to look to socialism as an alternative path to economic development.

There were two further predisposing factors. To many African leaders, the path to social and economic development had seemed to lie in an adaptation of the African traditional communal system in which land, the principal means of production, was owned, and, in some places, farmed, in common by the family, village or community, and in which the well-being of the society and its individual members was a collective responsibility of all: African traditional socialism, as it is called. And to many more, indeed most, the appeal of socialism lay even more in its one-party model which was looked upon as the best organising framework for economic development in the African context. These factors and perhaps others account for the socialist posture of African leaders in the early post-colonial decades.

Nation-building is an objective to which all are committed but it is a task that calls for total mobilisation of the nation if any impact is to be made upon it. An African president is therefore necessarily cast in the role of popular leader. This again makes him a "strong" president in another sense of the American conception of the term. In this sense, American presidents have been rated as strong or weak according to their ability to mobilise the nation. "The greatest Presidents have all ranked high on this scale, whatever their skills as administrators or legislative managers. All have made themselves national symbols; in so doing they have given substance and purpose to the nation itself."[17] But the popular leadership required of an African President is of a much more personal and spiritual kind, for he has to be at once leader, guide and teacher. The leader of a predominantly illiterate, poverty-stricken community has not only to lead, but to guide as well. He has to provide the light so that people may see the road in the first place and then guide and direct them along that road to the ultimate destination of prosperity and progress. He

---

[17] Grant McConnell, *The Modern Presidency* (1967), p. 15; R.S. Hirehfield "The Reality of Presidential Power," *Parl. Affairs* 1967/1968, vol. xxi, p. 370.

may be likened to one who leads a blind man.

The leader of a blind man has to establish an intimate personal identification with him. So it is with the leader of a new nation. Having got the people on the difficult road to development, it is his duty "to propose, to explain, and to persuade,"[18] to preach to them the need for hard work, for self-reliance, and for integrity in order to maximise national productivity. Preaching has to be accompanied by example: as, for example, the leader working with the farmers in the field. "There must be, among the leadership, a desire and a determination to serve alongside, and in complete identification with, the masses."[19] Hence the title *Nwalimu* (Teacher) given to President Nyerere. No other African president has more devotedly discharged this teaching role. Reading his speeches and writings, one is deeply impressed by the fervour and dedication with which he has gone about trying to inform and to educate his countrymen on the needs and requirements of nation-building.

Not the least of an African president's leadership roles is that of a showman. Whatever progress has been achieved needs to be advertised to the people in order to keep up national morale and enthusiasm. The president has therefore to perform the formal opening of completed public projects and launch shows that advertise the national effort, like agricultural and commercial shows and trade fairs. All this is part of the total mobilisation of the nation. It gives to presidential power in Africa a reality that is usually lacking in advanced countries. The inadequacy of the American presidency in providing this kind of leadership is often a source of disillusionment among Americans. The inadequacy results, not from the personality of American presidents, but from the nature of American society as compared with the African.

The African president's role of popular leadership is of course greatly facilitated by the virtual state monopoly of the media of mass information, perhaps the most crucial source of power in modern government. The radio and television are mostly state-owned, as are the most influential newspapers, and a large part of the news items in all three media is taken up by news about the president, his speeches and other activities. The president is always in the news, perhaps inevitably so, since, as has been explained, the functions

---

[18]   Julius K. Nyerere, *Ujamaa: Essays on Socialism* (1968), p. 90.
[19]   Julius K. Nyerere, *op. cit.*, p. 89.

of government in Africa are all-pervading. Either he is laying the foundation stone of, or opening, a new factory, a new school or a new hospital, or he is touring different parts of the country and is preaching the need for unity, hard work or self-reliance. His being constantly in the news immensely enhances his prestige and authority. But the monopoly of the information media is significant also in determining popular consent in government. Whoever has it is put in a position where he can mobilise public opinion and the nation in support of himself and his policies and actions. Such a person can get away even with murder, for murder can be made to wear the appearance of a virtue or be represented as serving the best interest of the nation.

There is yet another respect in which the poverty of African societies is a source of power for the President. In a developing country where there is mass unemployment, where the state is the principal employer of labour and almost the sole provider of social amenities, and where a personal ambition for power and wealth and influence rather than principle determines political affiliations and alliances, power to dispense patronage is a very potent weapon in the hands of the President, enabling him to gain and maintain the loyalty of the people at various levels of society. Water installed in one area, an industry sited in another, a school or hospital built in yet another may capture for the president the support and loyalty of the inhabitants of those areas. Scholarships, roads, government contracts, jobs, etc — all these are crucial sources of power in Africa. Moreover, loyalty of the type secured by patronage can often border on subservience. It produces an attitude of dependence, a willingness to accept without question the wishes and dictates of the person dispensing the patronage. Patronage has therefore been one of the crucial means by which African leaders have secured the subordination of the legislature, the bureaucracy, the police and even the armed forces, and the support and loyalty of various sections of the state.

An African Ruler's Role as Intellectual Leader

An African president also has to try to provide intellectual leadership for the new state. It is true that for the masses ideology has little relevance, their conception of government being in terms of the material benefits it can bring to them: peace and order, employment, medical services, water, etc.

Yet, the African president cannot neglect ideology completely, for a new nation has a great need for it. It needs a national ideology to act as an inspiration and guide for action. "Unless we are so armed and inspired," Nkrumah once told his followers, "we shall find ourselves rudderless. From the lowest members to the highest we must arm ourselves ideologically."[20] Popular leadership in nation-building needs to be buttressed with an ideology if it is to infuse a sufficient sense of purpose and direction in the people, especially the elite. And a sense of purpose and direction has virtue because of its unifying influence upon the actions of the members of the state. Ideology defines specific goals for society, prescribes the institutional forms and procedures for pursuing them, and by so doing seeks to direct and concert the efforts and actions of the people towards the achievement of those goals. In this way it seeks to unite the society into one people bound together by common attitudes, common institutions and procedures, and, above all, an acceptance of common social objectives and destiny.

To quote Nkrumah again, "the dominant ideology is that which in the light of circumstances decides what forms institutions shall take, and in what channels the common effort is to be directed."[21] More succinctly but tellingly, Wole Soyinka has written: "I think, after all, there is only one common definition for a people and a nation: a unit of humanity bound together by a common ideology."[22] Explaining the need for an ideology, Julius Nyerere has said that, despite the many socialist measures launched by his government, "it gradually became clear that the absence of a generally accepted and easily understood statement of philosophy and policy was allowing some government and party actions which were not consistent with the building of socialism, and which even encouraged the growth of non-socialist values and attitudes."[23] It was to meet this need that the Arusha Declaration was issued in February 1967. As a statement of the country's national ideology, it "provided the necessary signpost of the direction in which the nation must travel to achieve its goal."[24]

---

[20] *Evening News*, Accra, 14 June, 1959, Address by Nkrumah.
[21] Kwame Nkrumah, *Consciencism* (1964), p. 57.
[22] Wole Soyinka, *The Man Died* (1972), p. 183.
[23] Julius Nyerere, *Ujamaa: Essays on Socialism* (1968) Preface.
[24] *ibid.*

As leader and father of the nation, an African president of the first generation felt it his peculiar duty to provide the new nation with the much-needed ideology. Hence his role of philosopher and theoretician. There are other reasons why he had to assume this role. First, he was the leader of a revolution and history shows leaders of great revolutions in politics as theorists: Lenin, Mao, Fidel Castro. It is natural that the African leader should see himself in the image of such great political leader-theorists. By so doing he was merely following in the footsteps of history and it is unfair to label him an imitator, lacking in originality."[25] The nationalist revolution in Africa may not have the world stature and impact of the communist revolution successfully launched in Russia by Lenin and in China by Mao, yet it comes close enough to the communist revolution as an epochal event in world history. It has added to international politics a third force.

International politics, hitherto dominated by the struggle for ascendancy between East and West, has today to reckon with this third force: the non-aligned countries of Africa and Asia who constitute the third world. Like the authors of the first world revolution, the leaders of the third world had to expound, defend and consolidate their creation both within their national borders and at the international level. Among the nationalist leaders in Africa, Kwame Nkrumah's position approximated more closely to that of Lenin in the communist revolution. He it was who made black African independence a reality by the liberation of Ghana in 1957, and thereby created a haven for the intellectual protagonists of African independence as well as for the freedom fighters. He gave them both inspirational and material support. His unique position as the leader of the first black independent African country thrust upon him a special responsibility to expound and champion the nationalist revolution in Africa. His theorising may have lacked consistency and sufficient social relevance,[26] yet it cannot be denied that it gave inspiration and stimulated the pride and fervour of Africans in Ghana and elsewhere.

The objectives of the nationalist movement did not end with the achievement of political independence. Africa's cultural past, so badly distorted

---

[25]   See the provocative article by Ali Mazrui, "Nkrumah: the Leninist Czar" (1966) *Transition* 26, p. 9, and the great controversy which it provoked in subsequent issues of the same journal, nos. 27, 29, 30 and 31.

[26]   H.L. Bretton, *Rise and Fall of Kwame Nkrumah* (1966), p. 135.

by colonialism, must be rediscovered and revived. The nationalist movement is viewed as a kind of renaissance, "a rebirth of ideas and actions" in Africa's cultural heritage. Yet this revival cannot be indiscriminate; it must take account of the cross-current of ideas and cultures in which modern Africa is caught. Thus, while preaching the revival of Africa's cultural past, the nationalist revolution has also got to try to reconcile that with the present — with the perhaps more paramount need for modernity. That too is a function of ideology. Part of the objectives of this cultural revival is the restoration of the personality of the African which has been degraded by colonialism. In African society every individual had worth and counted equally with any other individual. "The only political ideology," Kofi Baako has said, "which allows the maintenance of our own traditional beliefs and attitudes appears to be the socialist idea that all men are equal."[27] Then there is the need to rationalise modern government in terms that would make it intelligible to the African masses.

Modern government is impersonal, concerned as it is with roles and a variety of impersonal processes, whereas African traditional government has man as its central object, his needs, his relations with his family, friends and society generally. The ideas underlying modern government are foreign, creating therefore a necessity to try to relate and adapt them to African conditions in order to give them relevance and legitimacy. Thus it has been considered necessary to rationalise the form of government of the modern state in terms of African political organisation and procedures in order to make it understood by the people. The presidency is portrayed in the light of the chief in the traditional system and the one-party state in the light of the consensus procedure of decision-taking in the traditional system. There is also the threat posed to the nationalist revolution by the machinations of imperialism and neo-colonialism, particularly economic imperialism which seeks to maintain its economic stranglehold on the African continent. These are the factors that have thrust the role of philosopher upon African presidents. They have called forth the "Humanism" of Kenneth Kaunda, the "Neo-colonialism" and "Consciencism" of Kwame Nkrumah, the "Ujammaism" of Julius Nyerere

---

[27]   Kofi Baako, Speech delivered at the Conference of Ghana's Envoys, January 1962, reproduced in T.P. Omari, *Kwame Nkrumah: the Anatomy of an African Dictatorship* (1970), pp. 192-193.

and the "African Socialism" of Jomo Kenyatta. Kamuzu Banda has stood outside this current. "All these grey-haired professors or bald-headed professors at the University," he once exclaimed, "making all this mysterious lingo, Socrates, Demosthenes, Solon, Edmund Burke and Rousseau, and all that. Talk about democracy, socialism, African socialism. What is African socialism? It makes m e sick!"[28]

Banda's anti-intellectualism reflects the increasingly materialist role of political leadership in the advanced countries today. Political leaders have become too absorbed in the power struggle and in the practical job of government, which often induce a resort to a kind of hand-to-mouth attitude, characterised by a fondness for expediencies. They have thus tended to lose sight of the ideological function of political leadership. The necessity for a carefully formulated policy is of course acknowledged, but there is progressively less concern for the theoretical foundations of the policy. Intellectualism in politics has thus been submerged. The West in modern times has produced no political leaders who are also great political theorists of the calibre of Lenin and Mao.[29] The explanation for this seems to lie partly in the fact that the need for ideology in the politics and government of the Western countries is perhaps somewhat less compelling than in the emergent states.

Africa's Colonial Heritage

More overwhelmingly than any other causative factor, Africa's colonial heritage is at the root of the authoritarianism of African rulers and of the continent's problems of governance generally, but it seems appropriate to postpone a discussion of it to chapter 11 of volume 5, since it bears more perhaps on the issue there examined, namely: the prospects for the success of constitutional democracy in Africa and of good governance generally. But two aspects of Africa's colonial heritage must be noted here. First is the mystique with which an African president is clothed and the enormous reality which that imparts to his power. This mystical quality derives from the achievement of the past generation of African presidents as the leaders of the nationalist movements

---

[28] Parliamentary Debate, April, 1966, p. 563 (Malawi).
[29] Ali Mazrui laments this anti-intellectual tradition in Western politics in his article, "Tanzaphilia: A Diagnosis," 30, p. 21.

which overthrew colonialism and established the new state. The leader incarnated the spirit of that struggle and the aspirations of those engaged in it. The realisation of those aspirations elevated him to the status of a deliverer, a messiah.

The struggle against colonialism was in large measure a struggle to redeem the personality of the African from the indignities and degradations inflicted upon it by colonialism. The perpetuation of the inferiority of the African was central to the philosophy and technique of colonialism, and anyone who was able to challenge the myth of white superiority was considered a man of extraordinary qualities, and success in overthrowing it was a feat of miraculous proportions. All the awe and mystique associated with the white man was now transferred to the leader. The reality was brought home to the people by the spectacle of the leader occupying the former colonial governor's official residence, that symbol of the glory and glamour of empire. There he now sat, perhaps in the very chair used by the embodiment of white power, directing the affairs of the state, and giving instructions to all functionaries of the state, both white and black. The President thus incarnated power, indeed he was power himself, and Africans admire and respect a man of power. And so it is that the African president is revered. "We are following Nkrumah," a Ghanaian minister once remarked,

> because his achievements are unexcelled in the country. He has done what the Ashantis were unable to do. He has been able to conquer the colonial power which the Ashantis failed to conquer by force of arms, even when the imperialists had not established themselves... But now Nkrumah has been able to defeat the imperialists by word of mouth.[30]

An attribute of mystique is charisma. No leader around whom such a fantastic mystique has been built up can fail to arouse a charismatic appeal among the people. This, by and large, was the basis of the so-called charismatic authority of the first generation of African leaders. It was due largely to their role in the nationalist movement, to the fervent spontaneous and popular enthusiasm which the movement generated. When the movement lost its fervour after having achieved its goal, the charisma remained, but was now sustained largely by manipulation and by the prestige of office. Unlike George Washington, who retired from the presidency after two terms against the

---

[30] Parliamentary Debate, 23 April-12 July, 1957, cols. 438-439.

exhortations of his countrymen and continued to be idolised in retirement, the office is indispensable to the charisma of African leaders, and the possibility of its loss arouses the fear of oblivion. Undeniably some, like Julius Nyerere of Tanzania, did possess a genuine charismatic appeal based partly on the mystique of their achievement in the nationalist movement, and partly on personal charm and selfless, dedicated statesmanship. Yet, whatever its basis, the charisma of these leaders inspired tremendous personal loyalty among the population, which enhanced their authority and prestige. The charisma and mystique engendered the belief that the leader was a kind of demi-god specially commissioned by Providence to deliver the people first from colonial rule and now from the evils of poverty, ignorance and disease; a belief that Providence had endowed him with extraordinary power to divine what was good for the community, so that when he had so divined what should be done, there arose an implied obligation on the part of all to obey. Obedience was enjoined because the leader had ordered it.

An authority based on this kind of charisma needs constant nurture, since the mystique on which it is based is liable to evaporate if exposed to public contact. The cult of personality was resorted to for the necessary nurture. A cult of infallibility and incorruptibility was accordingly built up around the leader. His name and his activities were kept tirelessly in the public view. His image was glorified in songs praising his achievements, in posters showing his photograph, in institutions and streets named after him and in statues of him erected in the most conspicuous centres of the city. His head was engraved on postage stamps, coins and currency notes. The burden of mistakes or harsh decisions was made to fall upon lieutenants in order to create the feeling among the disaffected that the leader could not personally have permitted their plight to go unredressed.

These factors – mystique and charisma as well as tradition – were sources of power which are not easily accessible to a president in America and Europe; they have, however, proved largely ineffective in legitimating the state. It has been said of the American presidency that its essential dimension today is how to "generate sufficient authority for presidential action to match the needs of the nation."[31] No modern American president, with the possible

---

[31]   Grant McConnell, *The Modern Presidency* (1967), p. 15.

exception of Franklin D. Roosevelt, has been able to harness to the presidency a deep, widely-felt personal loyalty based upon charisma. This means that the authority of the American presidency in modern times is in no way comparable to that of its counterpart in Africa. Only George Washington, the first American president, seems to have inspired a personal loyalty comparable to that of the African President. But his too was a loyalty and authority based partly on the father-of-the-nation mystique. Through his achievement in leading his countrymen to victory in the war of independence against England, Washington became a legend. It is true that the wide loyalty which he attracted to himself owed also to his noble character, his humanity, uprightness and wisdom,[32] yet it seems that his elevation into a myth and a cult was more the result of his achievement as founder of the American nation.

Then there is the fact of the newness of the state in Africa, the heterogeneity of its society and the tensions of modernisation. The new state requires a legitimating force. The problem of legitimacy is peculiarly serious in a new state, and is complicated by three factors. An artificial creation of colonialism, the state in Africa has no roots in the traditions or thoughts of the people. Their attitude towards it was that it was an instrument of the white man for the subjugation and exploitation of Africans. To the subject people, therefore, the state was not 'ours' but 'theirs', the white man's state. Such an attitude must be eradicated if the state is to be able to fulfil its purpose. And this requires the fostering among the people of a feeling of identity with the state. (The point is discussed further in chapter 11 volume 5.)

The second complicating factor is that the concept of state is a mere abstraction totally incomprehensible to the simple mind of a peasant. It needs therefore some visible, physical object to symbolise it in the eyes of the people, and no other object can be more readily comprehensible for this purpose than the personality of the President. The President thus assumes a symbolic role as the embodiment of the state. There is here a close parallel with the monarchical device of making the king the personification of the state, though the conception and the implications are different. Third is the fact that the state in Africa has an artificial and heterogeneous social constitution, embracing a large variety of peoples of differing origin, culture, language and character.

---

[32] Marcus Cunliff, *George Washington: Man and Monument* (1960), pp. 20-21.

This heterogeneous collection needs to be integrated into a unity, infused with a sense of common destiny and common national aspirations. It is the role of the President as leader to serve as the focal point of unity around which this heterogeneous mass can be knit together.

This integrating role of an African president involves the exercise of power – power to prevent the inevitable cleavages of tribalism from destroying the state. Tribal conflicts create a condition of instability, which is made worse by the tensions of rapid change from a traditional to a modern economy. In the view of the African leaders the state of affairs is comparable to a state of emergency and a state of emergency, even in the most advanced democracies, demands actions of an authoritarian type to preserve the peace and integrity of the state. The experience of the United States illustrates the great potency of a situation of emergency as a source of presidential power, for it is during such periods that the presidency has attained its zenith of power, as is "illustrated by Lincoln's 'dictatorial' regime during the Civil War, by Wilson's highly-centralised World War administration, and by Franklin Roosevelt's executive-dominated government during the emergencies of domestic depression and global conflict."[33]

The preservation of the state against the insecurity inherent in tribal cleavage and the tensions of rapid social change is perhaps the greatest source of presidential power in Africa. Tribalism may also operate in other ways to put greater power in the hands of the President. In the clash of interests between various tribes and their leaders, an atribal President may become a kind of counterpoise holding the balance of power in the state. President Kenneth Kaunda of Zambia was put in that role in 1968. The unbridled tribal bigotry which attended the elections within the ruling United National Independence Party (UNIP) in 1967 had virtually destroyed the credibility of the party's machinery in the eyes of the losing tribal faction in that contest, with the result that, when the time came for the parliamentary elections in 1968, that faction refused to accept the use of the party machinery for the nomination of candidates. In the event, President Kenneth Kaunda, who is not identified with any particular tribe, became "the fulcrum on which the contending political forces ... are balanced,"[34] and was entrusted with sole power to nominate all party candidates.

---

[33] R.S. Hirchfield, *op. cit.*, p. 382.
[34] R.I. Rotberg, "Tribalism and Politics in Zambia", *Africa Report*, December 1967, p. 34.

PART III

STATISM AND THE EVILS
ASSOCIATED WITH IT

CHAPTER 13

The State: Its Nature, Origins and Development

Introduction

Running through nearly every page of all five volumes of this study is the organism known as the state and its government, together with the institutions, procedures and processes for the administration of government. The concept of human rights, as has been noted, originated as legal claims against the state; constitutionalism is about the limiting of the powers of the state, while authoritarianism connotes the absence or inadequacy of limitations on state power. Thus, everything revolves around the state; its existence and influence permeates every aspect and facet of social life.

The state, in its strict signification, is said to be Europe's great gift to Africa, an inheritance from its colonisation of the continent. At the same time, it (the state) is also at the root of Africa's problems – problems arising, essentially, from the illegitimacy of the state and its constitution in the context of Africa, its lack of roots in the life, culture, traditions and thoughts of African peoples and the difficulty of domesticating it. There is also the problem, among others, of how or by what institutional forms and processes this ubiquitous organism is to be administered and by whom or by what groups – tribes, political parties, civilian politicians or the military, the elite or the common people. Apart from being the illegitimate child of colonialism, the post-colonial state in Africa, as a characteristic stamped on it by European colonialism, functions as an instrument of arbitrary, dictatorial power and of organised violence and oppression in the hands of the rulers, both Africans and their colonial predecessors, as well as an instrument of exploitation and discrimination based on race, ethnicity and political affiliation. (These characteristics of the alien state system brought to African by

European colonialism will be expatiated upon in the next chapter.) It can therefore be asserted that statism, perhaps more than human factors like corruption, chicanery, mismanagement and so forth, is at the heart of African's problems.

It is statism that has brought about the introduction into Africa of pernicious authoritarian forms and practices which no African would have thought of or comprehended, had the state not been transplanted to Africa— the authoritarian African one-party system, military absolutism/despotism and the totalitarian socialist system.

The fault for the introduction of these pernicious authoritarian forms was not entirely that of the African rulers, as is commonly supposed. Here were political leaders groping in an unfamiliar terrain in search of suitable institutional forms for the government of an inherited, sophisticated, alien organism, little understood by them and not at all understood by the mass of the people to be governed under it. Africa is simply passing through an experimental stage, a phase of trial and error, of adaptations of existing systems, during which various forms have been, and are being tried, to be discarded if found unsuitable.

Statism has also bequeathed to Africa the monstrous social constitution of the state composed, as it is, of a mosaic of mutually antagonistic and incompatible social groupings warring among themselves for the right to administer the state, to control its resources and to dispense its vast array of patronages. Associated with "tribalism" are the evils of corruption, clientelism, exploitation, discrimination and oppression. The process of election for the choice of rulers is bedevilled by the trappings of the ballot box and ballot papers, by the winner-take-all form of election and by massive rigging of election. Even the institution of political parties, necessary and desirable as it is for the successful conduct of modern government, has itself proved problematic in Africa for structural more than human reasons. Thus while the development and modernisation of Africa might well be difficult, perhaps even impossible, to realise without the organisational and institutional framework provided by the state, yet it is no less fraught with troubles because of that undoubted advantage. The crisis in which Africa has been gripped since independence is thus primarily, as Basil Davidson says, "a crisis of institutions" and only secondarily one of human failures. These are institutions which, because of their alien character and origin, lack legitimacy and the ability to arouse in the people that sense of identification, loyalty and patriotism necessary for the success of the statist project. Rather than elicit their identification, statism has produced instead the alienation of the people from the state and its government (Davidson sees this "crisis of institutions" as having created an "institutional void concealed for a while behind a political-curtain with parliamentary symbols of European provenance, a mere facade of order on lines drawn by alien cultures.")

What, then, is the nature of this organism? How did it originate and how has it developed to become what it is today? These questions call for examination in order that the discussion in the study may be intelligible and meaningful to the reader.

Definition of the State in General Terms

Although the state is today a common, universal phenomenon, yet there is no agreement on what actually constitutes it, nor are the ideas underlying it widely understood. The different meanings ascribed to it have been stated by the U.S. Supreme Court. Sometimes, said the court, it is used to denote:

> a people or community of individuals united more or less closely in political relations, inhabiting temporarily or permanently the same country; often it denotes only the country or territorial region, inhabited by such community; not infrequently it is applied to the government under which the people live; at other times it represents the combined idea of people, territory and government.[1]

The definition leaves many questions unanswered. To say that a state means one or the other of these three things or all of them combined tells little or nothing about the relation of the state to the people as individuals and as a society, to territory and to government. It says nothing about the relation of the state to law and to force. What is the nature and rationale of the force backing up the state? Then there is the question of the relation of the state to religion. Should religion be part of the structure of the state or not?

We may here venture to define the state as an organisation of people at a certain level of development in various fields of human endeavour, inhabiting a given territory, which through various institutions and instrumentalities, and by

---

[1]   *Texas v White*,   7 Wall 700 at p. 720 per Chief Justice Chase delivering the opinion of the Court. The important elements in the definition of the state are listed and discussed in Christopher Pierson, *The Modern State* (1996), pp. 8-34.

means of laws, particularly legislated law, and executive acts, backed and enforced by organised coercive force— mainly physical force of which it has or claims monopoly – regulates, orders and manages the affairs of its members for the common good or welfare of all as a society of men and women.

Our analysis of the relations implied in this definition proceeds from a historical perspective, and the historical perspective is based largely upon the history of the Roman state, partly because of its long duration spanning over 2200 years, from 753 B.C., the date of its founding, to 1453 A.D. (the Roman Empire collapsed in the West in 451-455 A.D. but continued in the East till 1453); partly because it is the progenitor of many of the modern nation-states which owe much of their character and form to its influence; partly because it is by common consent "one of the ablest and most successful governments that the world has yet known,"[2] (its military conquests and achievements in many other fields are perhaps unsurpassed); and partly because in our experimentation on how to organise a state we in Africa today may yet have something useful to learn from it, notwithstanding the more than 500 years that separate us from it.

The State and the People
The State and the People as Several Individuals

The state is, and cannot be anything other than, an abstraction – "it cannot be seen, touched, tasted, smelled or heard"[3]—from the fact that a multitude of individuals live together in one country (territory) under a common government. It is conceived as an entity, albeit an artificial one, existing separately from those individuals. The idea underlying it is analogous to that of a corporation (statutory or registered corporation). The latter is also an abstraction from the fact that two or more persons, corporators, join together for a common purpose. The corporate concept thus presupposes some natural persons in whom the corporation resides. It is individuals that the law incorporates into a separate legal entity with a personality separate from the personalities of those corporators. Without corporators, the law cannot conjure up a wholly fictitious personality. You do not, indeed you cannot, incorporate the air any more than you can

---

[2] Will Durant, *The Story of Civilisation*, III (1944), p. 25.
[3] C.C. Rodes *et al*, *Introduction to Political Science* 4th edn. (1983), p. 20

create something from nothing. What the law does is simply to deem some corporators as having a single personality separate from their individual personalities. Put simply, a corporation must consist of some individuals (or other persons), it must reside in some persons. As with a corporation, so also must a state consist of individuals by whom it is formed.

Indeed, a state is more dependent upon, more inextricably bound up with, people than a corporation is. For, while, should all the members of a corporation be killed in some accident or other calamity, "the corporation is not dead, but temporarily in abeyance,"[4] the destruction of the entire population of a state erases it completely from existence. The history of the ancient world is littered with instances of states, mainly city-states, wiped out of existence through the decimation of their entire population in a war.

The famous city-state of Carthage (territory in the modern state of Tunisia), founded in 813 B.C. by Phoenician settlers, was a classic case. In what had been described as among the most brutal conquests in history, it was erased from the face of the earth in 146 B.C. in a slaughter and fire that decimated its 500,000 population, leaving only 55,000 survivors who were then sold into slavery by the conquering Romans. Carthage was refounded in 30 B.C. by Augustus, and again grew to become, within a century of its re-founding, the largest city in the Roman Empire next to Rome, and ranking after Athens and Alexandria as a university town. It was again completely destroyed and erased by the Arabs in 698 A.D. The city-state of Corinth was also completely destroyed and erased by the Romans in the same year, 146 B.C. and was re-founded by Caesar, becoming, within half a century of that, the wealthiest city in ancient Greece. Going farther back into antiquity, the famous city-state of Sparta was virtually erased from existence in the battle at Leuctra in 371 B.C.; so overwhelming was her defeat and so total her fall that today "hardly a torso or a fallen pillar survives to declare that here there once lived Greeks."[5]

The inextricable linkage of the state with people does not, however, mean that, as Rudolf von Ihering maintains, the state and its citizens *(civitas)* are one and the same; that it is "no abstraction apart from the people," and that therefore rights belonging to the state "inhere in the people and what is more, in each of them individually." Such a view of the state seems completely at variance with

---

[4] Carr, *The General Principles of the Law of Corporation* (1905), p. 127
[5] Will Durant, *The Story of Civilisation*, II, p. 87.

all experience and practice. Surely, if the state is one and the same with its citizens, it would need no one individual to **personify** it; the institution of monarchy would have lost its entire basis and the notion of civil society, its whole meaning and relevance. We must therefore reject Rudolf von Ihering, influential as his views upon jurisprudence and law are.

People are indispensable to the concept of the state for another reason: they are the source from which the main aspect of its sovereignty is derived. (The other aspect of a state's sovereignty, which derives from territory, territorial sovereignty, is considered later.) Sovereignty may here be defined simply as the highest power in a state. The human component of sovereignty is predicated upon the power inherent in each individual to dispose of himself as he likes. "By nature," writes Walter Berns, "everyone is sovereign with respect to himself, free to do whatever in his judgment is necessary to preserve his own life."[6] In this view, what is called the sovereignty of the people is simply the sum total of the natural sovereignty inhering in each individual member. In the act of constituting a state, however, each individual, acting in concert with others, is said to surrender to the state "his natural and sovereign powers."[7]

Perhaps the most significant result of the American Revolution of 1776-1783 is the reversion to the people of the sovereignty said to have been surrendered to the state. With this development, the people are now generally recognised as sovereign and as entitled to exercise the powers incident to sovereignty, including constituent power. The people as sovereign is not any more a mere matter of political theory. "We the People," the opening words of the U.S. Constitution, "does not merely echo revolutionary sentiment, it reflects a common practice."[8]

From the time of the American Revolution, writes Alexis de Tocqueville in 1835:

> the doctrine of the sovereignty of the people ... took possession of the state. Every class was enlisted in its cause; battles were fought and victories obtained for it; it became the law of laws... Sometimes, the laws are made by the people in a body, as at Athens; and sometimes its representatives, chosen by universal suffrage, transact business in its name... The people

---

6. Walter Berns, "Do We Have a Living Constitution?" *National Forum, The Phi Kappa Phi Journal*, Fall 184, Vol. LXIV, No. 4, p. 31
7. Walter Berns, *loc. cit.*
8. David Mathews, "We the People," *National Forum, op.cit.*, p. 46

reign in the American political world as the Deity does in the universe. They are the cause and the aim of all things, everything comes from them and everything is absorbed in them.[9]

But, whether sovereignty is in the people or in the state, it is held and exercised by the state for the benefit of the people. Yet the location of the **title** of sovereignty, as distinct from the possession and exercise of it, is important as determining the character and form of a state as either a republic or a monarchy. Where the title of sovereignty is in the people, then, the state is a republic, regardless of how or by whom sovereignty is exercised, whether by an usurping dictatorship of one man, by right of birth (aristocracy), by virtue of wealth (plutocracy) or by the people themselves directly (direct democracy) or by the elected representatives of the people (representative democracy). Thus, the character and form of a state as a republic rests solely and entirely on whether the bare title of sovereignty (as distinct from the **substance** of it which is connoted by the power to exercise it) is in the people; it (i.e. the character and form of a state) has nothing at all to do with how or by whom sovereignty is actually exercised — how or by whom government is actually conducted. A republican state does not therefore necessarily imply a popular or democratic government, as is commonly supposed. The rise of popular or democratic government, as we know it today, is after all, largely a development of the 20th century whereas the notion of a republic dates back to antiquity (the monarchical form of state in Rome was abolished and a republic established in its place in 508 B.C.) There are even today, as Lord Bryce, writing in 1920, rightly pointed out, many republican states that do not have a popular or democratic government.[10] A democratic republic is a state in which the title of sovereignty is in the people and its exercise is by them or by persons elected or mandated by them.

On the other hand, where the title of sovereignty is in the state as personified by an individual, then, again regardless of how or by whom it is exercised, the state is a monarchy. A monarch, as head of state, does not merely **represent** the state, as does the head of state in a republic, he **personifies** it in a real, not merely symbolic sense. The effect of this personification is to transfer the title

9.   Alexis de Tocqueville, *Democracy in America* (1835) ed. Richard Heffner (1956), pp. 56-58
10. James Bryce, *Modern Democracies* (1920) Preface

of sovereignty from the state to the monarch, thereby making him the sovereign, and the government his own; allegiance is owed to him personally, and not to the state, as in a republic, public functionaries being required to swear that they will be faithful and bear true allegiance to him and will well and truly serve him. The personification means that he is indeed the state, a fact which is acknowledged in the national anthem and in various other ways.

Being thus invested with the title of sovereignty, the monarch as sovereign and as the state attracts greater pre-eminence in society than the head of the state in a republic. He is set apart from the rest of the community; as between him and them the relationship is one of sovereign lord and liege, a relationship that demands from the subject not only allegiance and obedience but also a reverence that borders on obsequiousness. He is "his majesty," which again expresses his claim to be the state. His person is inviolable. He is above the law. "The king can do no wrong" is a well-recognised maxim of law. The only redress against an erring king is to force him to abdicate or have him impeached and dethroned, but not to put him on trial in his own courts.

Whilst the theory about the individual members of a state having surrendered their natural sovereignties to the state under a social contract may be tolerated, the idea of an individual personifying the state is difficult to accept. An individual may represent the state, but to equate him with it or to regard him as owning it or to invest him with the sovereignty surrendered to it by the people seems to make nonsense of the concept. Monarchy is simply subversive of the state concept. Yet it was, from the cessation of the republican era in Rome (508-49 B.C.), the universal form of the state as well as the universal form of government, and only began to crumble with the American and French Revolutions in 1783 and 1789 respectively. Happily, it now survives only in a comparatively limited number of states.

The foregoing discussion shows that the character and form of a state is something to be distinguished from the character and form of its government. (The latter is considered below.) How or by whom powers of government implied in sovereignty are actually exercised only define the character and form of a government, not the character and form of the state, which rests solely and entirely on whether the bare title of sovereignty is in the people, or in the state as personified by an individual.

The State and Society

In contradistinction to the people as several individuals, society means the people collectively; it is a collection of individuals associating and sharing life together as a community. As an organised group or association of individuals, is society, then, one and the same with the state?

Before the Stoics (301 B.C.), writes Professor Charles McIlwain, the "Greeks apparently drew no clear distinction between society and the state, between the social and the civil." From this, the inference was drawn that "institutions that are thus identical must also be coeval," and that "theoretically at least, the state must be as old as human association; there is no science of society apart from politics."[11] It is remarkable that a people as sophisticated and advanced in their thinking upon human institutions as the ancient Greeks were, should fail to perceive the clear, inescapable logic of the distinction between society and the state. The distinction flows logically and necessarily from the fact that, in the nature of things, the state can only be the product of organised human society; it is an entity brought into existence by the act of organised society. As an entity created by society, it cannot be identical or coeval with its creator. "The state is a brash new comer in the long history of organic and social development."[12]

From the conception of society as an organised group or association of individuals, separate from, and anterior to, the state, three important implications follow. First, given that society existed before the state, it must have had rules of social life older than the state — laws of humanity (or the law of nature, as they are more commonly called) and the customs of the community. What is the relation of this older law to the state after its creation? Is this older law, particularly the component of it embodying the laws of humanity, a higher law to which the state must conform, with the consequence that any of its acts inconsistent therewith is null and void?

The second implication is more crucial to the conception of the state. It concerns its relation to what, since 1787, is called a constitution — by which the people construct a frame for the government of their affairs and also for the regulation of the relation of the government to the individual. Does such a

---

11. Charles McIlwain, *Constitutionalism in the Changing World* (1939)
12. Rodes *et al, op. cit,* p. 21; see also Christopher Pierson, *The Modern State* (1996) "it is clear that, for most of its history, humankind functioned without even a very primitive form of state" at p. 2.

constitution also embody a higher law binding on the state with an overriding force? These two issues are considered below in the section dealing with the relation of the state and law.

The third implication is that society, as an organised group or association of individuals existing separately and autonomously from the state, serves, or at any rate, is supposed to act, as a counter-force against possible despotism by the state through its instrumentalities. The notion of civil society, to employ a somewhat technical term, conceives society as one single national body which, assisted by its variegated organisations, associations, interests and classes, which, may be national, regional, local, professional or occupational, serves as a centre of power and is able, independently of the state, to act as a check against any usurpation of power and violation of individual liberty by government.

The character of a state as a totalitarian state is defined by the absence of civil society as defined above. The communist totalitarian state affects civil society in three ways. Whereas in an absolute government, the individual and society remain separate and distinct from the state, and the separation provides the context within which the government exercises its absolute powers, with civil society operating to limit those powers, under communist totalitarianism, on the other hand, the separation and the limitation upon governmental powers which it implies practically disappear, with civil society and its variegated institutions being integrated into the state. Secondly, the objective of the communist social order of eliminating the division of society into classes, the replacement of class divisions by a classless society with the communist party as the "vanguard and guiding force," the "effacement of ...the essential differences between town and country, and between mental and physical labour,"[13] seem to spell the virtual destruction of society as an autonomous force capable of acting as a check on government. Thirdly, the communist totalitarian state is subversive of the notion of civil society because it is a form of state that tries to integrate, regiment and control "so many aspects of human existence: family life, friendship, work, leisure, production, exchange, worship, art, manners, travel, dress – even that final assertion of human privacy, death."[14] It is a despotism with a vengeance.

The African one-party state differs from the communist totalitarian state in that, unlike the latter which recasts and remolds the society and the economy, integrating them into the state and the monopolist party, it maintains the separation between them (society and economy) and the state (social and economic

---

[13.] S. 19 USSR Constitution (1977).
[14.] Harry Eckstein and David Apter, (eds.) *Comparative Politics* (1965), p. 434.

organisations of political significance are of course integrated into the party-state) and the limitation which the separation imposes on state power, merely superimposing the monopolist party upon them. The absence of civil society in the new African states owes, not to its absorption by a totalitarian state, but to the fact that it did not exist as a national entity before the modern state was created by forcibly bringing together different peoples of disparate cultures. It has to be created anew from this agglomeration of peoples.

The State and Territory

When we speak of territory as an essential requirement in the concept of the state, we mean, not an uninhabited expanse of territory, a *territorium nullius*, but a more or less defined area of territory of a certain size under effective occupation by a settled population also of a certain size. What size of territory and population, then, is required by the concept of the state? We must consider first the nature or character of the population. It must be a settled population. A state cannot exist among a wandering band of nomads with no fixed habitat, such as the medley of independent Germanic tribes of Central Europe, known in ancient times as the barbarians. These were a band of migratory hunters and herdsmen; a race of tall, fierce and martial men, who fought naked in battle in demonstration of their martial prowess (war was said to be their meat and drink), and whom the all-conquering Romans chose for whatever reason not to subdue and bring into the Roman Empire — failure to subdue them proved ultimately to be Rome's undoing, for it was these same barbarians who, in invasion after invasion in 400-455 A.D., overran the Empire in the West, and hastened its collapse there. (The more settled, civilised parts of what we know as Germany today were of course subjugated and incorporated into the Empire.)

Even when a people has progressed beyond the nomadic stage, and has evolved some form of political organisation, a certain level of civilisation and development would seem to be implied by the state; it is a necessary foundation for statehood. The state is an advanced, sophisticated organisation of society; it is an organisation of society at an advanced stage of intellectual, technological, economic, institutional, social and cultural development. Statehood also requires certain habits among the people. That is to say, it requires a population habituated to: order, obedience to law, respect for constituted authority, discipline, public service, loyalty and love of country. It is on these grounds, among others, that backward peoples everywhere and in all ages are considered not to possess the status of a state, strictly so-called; quite often of course, the term 'state' is loosely applied to them.

We are accustomed today to think of a state in terms of a country of fairly large territory and population, and it might be said that a small face-to-face community of a few thousand people inhabiting a small area of territory, with only a rudimentary social organisation, does not constitute a state in the strict, meaningful sense of the term. Yet, we know that the better-known states of the ancient world were not large countries but one-city communities, city-states as they were called. Indeed, the Greek world of antiquity consisted almost entirely of independent city-states, 158 of them in Greece itself and hundreds founded by emigrant Greek settlers outside Greece — on the islands in the Aegean and Ionian seas, Asia Minor, North Africa, Sicily and on the coastlines of Italy, France and Spain. It would suffice to mention only a few of the leading ones: Athens, Corinth, Delphi (in Greece), Byzantium (renamed Constantinople by the Romans, now Istanbul), Rhodes, Syracuse, Nice, Monaco, Marseilles, Naples. Phoenicia too consisted almost entirely of city-states, notably Tyre, Sidon, Bibylus; among the principal Phoenician city-states in North Africa were Utica and Carthage. The greatest of all the city-states of antiquity was Rome. Monaco is, apparently, the only one of the ancient city-states still surviving today with its independence intact, all the others having been absorbed as part of larger states.

Being a one-city state, and not a conglomeration of villages, towns and cities, the ancient city-states were relatively small in population—Rome, 260,000 in 560 B.C.; Syracuse, 500,000 in 500 B.C.; Corinth, 110,000 in 480 B.C.; Sparta, 376,000 in the sixth century B.C.; Carthage, 500,000 in 146 B.C. They also covered relatively small areas; Rome, for example, covered an area of 350 sq. miles (roughly 19 miles by 19 miles) while Syracuse was 14 miles in circumference.

But the significant fact about these city-states of antiquity is that, despite their limited size in population and territory, they were prosperous and powerful, with well organised systems of government and law and a civilised culture that enabled them to exert a dominant influence on the affairs of the then known world. Significantly, one of them, Rome, became, by peaceful colonisation but mainly by territorial conquests, the largest empire the world has yet known, embracing within its jurisdiction and power, the population and territory (as at that time) of the present states of North Africa, the Middle East, Asia Minor, Britain and much the greater part of Europe outside Russia and Scandinavia.

From an area of 350 sq. miles and a population of 260,000 in 560 B.C., Rome and its empire covered 3,340,000 sq. miles and a population of about 120 million at the death of Emperor Augustus in 14 A.D. It was further expanded under later Emperors, mainly under Claudius (41-54 A.D.), Nero (54-68 A.D.), Domitian (86-96 A.D.) and Trajan (98-117 A.D.); the additions being the province of Britain which was conquered and annexed to the Empire after a war of about forty years (44-84 A.D), "undertaken by the most stupid, maintained by the most dissolute and terminated by the most timid of all the emperors"[15] (the references are to Claudius, Nero and Domitian who terminated Agricola's successful campaigns in 81-84 A.D., leaving the northern extremity of Scotland unsubdued) and the province of Dacia (about 1,300 miles in circumference) conquered and annexed, after five years of war (101-107 A.D.), by Trajan, whose death while on military expedition ended his grand design to push the eastern frontier of the Empire as far as India. Trajan's other notable conquests — Armenia, Mesopotamia and Assyria, each of which was constituted a province— were, after his death, given up by Emperor Hadrian (119-138 A.D.), who preferred security of frontiers to the prestige of extensive new dominions that were insufficiently conquered.[16]

Such was the vast extent of the Roman Empire. In the words of Edward Gibbon in the opening sentence of his great classic, *The Decline of Fall of the Rome Empire* (in six volumes), "in the second century of the Christian era, the Empire of Rome comprehended the fairest part of the earth, and the most civilised portion of mankind."[17] The Empire crumbled in part because it had grown too vast in territory and in the diversity of peoples comprised within it for effective administration under one central authority. The vastness and diversity

---

[15] Edward Gibbon, *The Decline and Fall of the Roman Empire* (1776-88); Everyman's Library edn (1910), Vol. 1 chap. 1, p.4.

[16] The victories of Marcus Aurelius Antoninus (161-180 A.D.) did not really bring additions to the Empire, as he was fighting in defence.

[17] See pp. 20-28 for a detailed description of the extent of the Empire. The figure of "sixteen hundred thousand square miles" given by Gibbon as the area of the Empire in 98-180 A.D. is a gross under-estimate, but as he himself said at p. 28 (footnote), he distrusted both the learning and the maps of Templeman's Survey of the Globe from which the figure was taken.

of her territorial conquests had become a major factor in the long process of her decline and fall. Professor J.S. Reid has observed that the greatest problem in history is to explain how a city-state of 260,000 people inhabiting an area of 19 by 19 miles was able to conquer the world and rule it for more than 1,000 years.[18]

From the ashes of the Roman Empire and after many territorial re-organisations and re-alignments over the centuries, the various peoples or nationalities comprised within it eventually emerged as the territorial units of the modern state organisation. Thus were born the modern nation-states, each composed of people of one common culture inhabiting one contiguous territory. The fellow-feeling, the sense of common nationality, existing among people of the same cultural identity— common indigenous language, custom and tradition— has shown the nation-state as the ideal basis for organising a state. Yet the emergence of successful new states in the American Hemisphere, containing a conglomeration of different peoples, precludes us from positing a nation as a requirement of the concept of the state.

Equally, it seems that the ability to exert international personality and diplomatic pressures in all the complexities of modern international relations is a pre-requisite for statehood. This presupposes a state of a certain size in area and population and possessing an organisational form adequate for this purpose.

As earlier stated, a state's sovereignty derives partly from the people and partly from its territory, both complementing each other; sovereignty is thus inseparable from ownership of territory. But the term territorial sovereignty is used and, it seems, quite aptly used, to embrace the entirety of a country's sovereignty. Power and jurisdiction over persons only, even to the fullest extent, acquired by one country in another country confers authority only for a limited amount of control. Full control of the affairs of a country in all matters connected with its peace, order and good government can only lawfully be assumed and exercised when jurisdiction over both persons and territory (though not necessarily the title of sovereignty) is acquired. Annexation, following a conquest or following a treaty of cession, is the means by which the territorial sovereignty of a country is acquired. Territorial sovereignty connotes, therefore, dominion over both persons and territory.

---

18.   J.S. Reid in *Cambridge Medieval History 1,*.p. 54

The terms of a typical treaty of cession of territorial sovereignty underline the cardinal significance of territory in the concept of the state and its sovereignty. The treaty by which the island of Lagos in Nigeria was ceded to Britain in 1861 is typical enough. It reads:

> I, Docemo, do, with the consent and advice of my council, give, transfer, and by these presents grant and confirm unto the Queen of Great Britain, her heirs and successors for ever, the port and Island of Lagos, with all the rights, profits, and revenue as the **direct, full, and absolute dominion and sovereignty of the port, Island and premises**, with all the royalties thereof, freely, fully entirely, and absolutely ...; **the inhabitants of the said Island and territories, as the Queen's subjects, and under her sovereignty, Crown, jurisdiction, and government, being still suffered to live there.** (emphasis supplied).

But though the dominion implied in territorial sovereignty connotes absolute ownership, it does not carry with it beneficial ownership of land (except in conquered territories), only the power of administrative control by means of legislation, which may be exercised to bestow beneficial ownership and generally to regulate the tenure of land.

Sovereignty over territory implies independence from external control. 'The doctrine of sovereignty, in its external dimension, prescribes independence as the fundamental norm of true statehood.'[19] It also implies the ability to maintain the integrity and security of the territory against external interference.

The State and Government
The State as Government Transmuted into a Corporation

The relation of the state to government is of such intricacy as makes it difficult to explain intelligibly. This is because the state is merely a concept, a contraption, artificially invented to give government a 'corporate halo'[20] or, more precisely, to give it a corporate existence. Government, on the other hand, is not just a concept; it is the practical exercise, through various organs and instrumentalities, of political power, direction and restraint over the activities and affairs of the inhabitants of a community or society; it is the practical conduct, the administration in actual practice, of public affairs through various organs and instrumentalities,

---

[19] Crawford Young, "The Colonial State and Its Political Legacy," in *The Precarious Balance: State and Society in Africa*, edited by C. Young and Naomi Chazan (1988). p. 31

[20] Carl. J. Friedrick, *Constitutional Government and Democracy*, revised edn. p. 16

although in popular usage, the organs and instrumentalities that carry on the conduct of public affairs are usually referred to as the Government, thus transferring the emphasis from what is really a conduct or a process to the organs and their functionaries. Government being really a conduct or a process the necessity was felt by political theorists of giving it a distinct legal personality capable of bearing rights and duties, of owning property and generally of acting and being treated in like manner as a physical person. As a corporate entity capable of bearing rights and duties, the powers exercised by government belong to the state, and are exercised in its name and on its behalf for the benefit of the people.

Thus, a state represents the idea of incorporation in the realm of government. It is a device which enables the machinery of government evolved by a political community for its own administration to be given a separate existence for the purpose of performing legal acts. For all legal and other purposes, therefore, the device enables the state to be separated from the members of the community generally, and from the persons who control the government machinery from time to time. The death of any one such member or functionary (not of all the members though), be he even the head of state, leaves the existence of the state unaffected. The members and rulers may come and go, but the state endures or is supposed to endure for ever. The state, of course, exists for the members of the community by whom, after all, it has been created; it also exists and operates upon territory inhabited by them. It is therefore necessarily linked to people and territory, but in a strict legal sense it is government conceived as a distinct legal, if a disembodied, entity.

The next development in the concept of a state was its linkage to the idea of sovereignty, a process of thought which was progressively developed to a point where the state itself was proclaimed sovereign. This is not unintelligible. Legal sovereignty is an attribute of government, and since the state is government transmuted into a corporation, the sovereignty associated with government must enure to the state.

Important implications flow from the conception of the state as a distinct corporate entity separate from the organs of government. It creates the necessity for someone to represent it or even to personify and embody it, although, as earlier remarked, the idea of someone personifying and embodying the state is unnecessary and subversive of the concept. Secondly, invested, as it is, with perpetuity, the state does not derive its existence from the constitution of the government; it is independent of it, with the result that the destruction of the constitution and of the organs of government established by it leaves the state unaffected, but this is disputed in some quarters. [21] As the repository of the title and ceremonies of the sovereignty associated with government, the state has invested in it the symbolic authority and majesty that go with them.

The separateness of the state from government is underlined not only by the greater authority and majesty inhering in it (the state) but also by the fact that the headship of the state is a position distinct and different from that of head of government, and carries with it a certain inherent authority and dignity not possessed by the head of government. He embodies the majesty of the state. The position of head of state has been aptly described by Oppenheim as follows:

> As a State is an abstraction from the fact that a multitude of individuals live in a country under a sovereign government, every State must have a Head as its highest organ which represents it within and without its borders, in the totality of its relations ... The Head of a State as its chief organ and representative in the totality of its international relations, acts for his State in its international intercourse, with the consequence that all his legally relevant international acts are considered to be acts of his State. [22]

The separateness of the state from the government has tended, in practice, to be blurred by the union of the two offices of head of state and head of government in the same person in most countries, and, in countries where they are not so united, by the virtual reduction of the head of state to a figurehead, implying that only the government, but not the state, has an effective, significant existence. This should not be so. A head of state is a position that implies more than a figurehead. It is a position that conceptually and logically ought to be, and function as, a moderating agency; as "a balance sheet to the constitution intervening when the political authorities or forces seem to be out of alignment with one another." [23]

The concept of a head of state as a moderating agency is perhaps best effectuated by the provision in the Constitution of the French Fifth Republic

---

21. See B. O. Nwabueze, *Constitutionalism in the Emergent States* (1973), p. 238 for the argument.
22. Oppenheim, *International Law*, 8th edn, ed. Lauterpacht, Vol. 1, p. 757.
23. S. E. Finer, *The Man on Horseback: The Role of the Military in Politics.*

(1958) and the Constitution of Romania (1991) under which the President of
the Republic, as Head of State, is invested with power to 'secure respect for the
Constitution,' to 'secure, by his arbitration, the regular functioning of the governing
authorities as well as the continuity of the state,' and to serve as 'guarantor of
national independence and territorial integrity.'[24] To this end, he is to take all such
actions as may be required for dealing with a grave and immediate danger
threatening the integrity of the state or its institutions and authority.[25] Had his
powers under the Constitution stopped there, there would have been no blurring
of the line separating the offices of head of state and head of government. But
he is clothed with many other powers and functions that seem to leave it in no
doubt that the preponderance of the power to execute the government lies
with him, and not with the premier or head of government.[26]

In our conception of the state as government transmuted into a corporation,
two other matters falling for consideration are:

(i)   the function and purpose of government;

(ii) the organisation, form, powers and processes of government and
      adequate to an effective exercise of its functions.

Functions and Purposes of Government

Aside from the conduct of relations with other states, the functions of the state,
exercised of course through the government, is to govern the affairs of the
people, both as individuals and as a society — the maintenance of law and
order, peace and public security, including the settlement of disputes; protection
of life and property; regulation of the affairs of the community by means of
legislation; the provision of the infrastructure needed to enable individuals to
develop by their own efforts and the promotion of development generally;
and the defence of the community against foreign interference.

However, as Lord Denning observed in 1977, while "a century ago no
sovereign state engaged in commercial activities," "in the past fifty years there
has been a complete transformation in the functions of a sovereign state. Nearly

---

24. Art. 5; art 80 Constitution of Romania (1991); under the latter, he is also to "mediate between the state and society".

25. Art. 16, France

26. For details, see B. O. Nwabueze, *Ideas and Facts in Constitution Making* (1993), pp. 182-186

every country now engages in commercial activities."[27] This development has necessitated a line being drawn between two types of activities undertaken by modern states, between those of a **governmental nature** called *acta jure imperii* and those of a **commercial nature**, *acta jure gestionis*.

The distinction has not escaped criticism. It is contended that every activity of a government, even when it is carried on purely for profit, is a governmental function. A government, it is argued, may deem it as essential to its economy that it should own and operate a railway, a mill, electricity generation and supply or an irrigation system as it does deem it essential to own and operate bridges, street lights or a sewage disposal plant.[28] The argument is not without merit altogether. It must be conceded that a view of governmental functions based upon their usual, traditional or historical forms or manifestations is rightly condemned as upon a static concept of government which denies its essential nature.

Yet a line must be drawn somewhere between "a government as government and a government as trader."[29] Perhaps a more satisfactory approach would be to distinguish between the constitutional and extra-constitutional functions of a government, i.e. between functions required of a government by the constitution and those which, while not so required, are nevertheless not prohibited to it and which may therefore be pursued by government alike with individuals and other juristic persons. When a government acts under its constitutional powers, then, any act done in the exercise of those powers is governmental.

The government functions of the state have but one end or purpose — the public good.[30] As, however, the end or purpose of government is not an attribute necessary to the definition of a state, a discussion of it is inappropriate here.

Organisation, Form, Powers and Processes of Government

Taking government as being concerned with the **exercise** of sovereignty, regardless of where the **title** to it resides, whether in the state or in the people,

---

27. *Trendtex Trading Corpn Ltd v Central Bank of Nigeria* (1977) I ALL. E.R. 881; (1977) 1 Q.B

28. See the minority judgment in *New York v United States*, 326 U.S... (1946) at pp. 590-598

29. *New York v. United States, ibid* at p. 591.

30. *ibid,* at p. 597.

we may say that the only requirement regarding its organisation, powers and processes is that it must be sufficiently organised and must be possessed of powers and a force adequate and conducive to the effective discharge of governmental functions and the responsibilities of the state to the people.

Adequacy is determined by the existence of;

(a) a system of conscious law-making by legislation for the regulation of social life and relations as well as for the enactment of the necessary framework and authorisation of measures for securing the welfare of society and development generally;

(b) a coercive force, more or less organised, for the enforcement of the law, the maintenance of order in society, and the protection of life and property;

(c) an organised machinery for the execution of laws providing for welfare services as well as the execution of the business of government generally; and

(d) courts, with compulsive jurisdiction, for the administration of justice according to law in disputes between parties, the settlement of disputes according to law by courts with compulsory jurisdiction rather than by private force being a necessary condition of order in society.

Without these, a state can be said to exist only in the loose sense but not in the strict, meaningful sense of the word. It is the change from the rule of custom to the rule of legislated law in permanent form and from the settlement of disputes by private force or feud vengeance to the arbitrament of law, that heralded the emergence of the state in the strict sense. Hence state power (or political power) is defined by John Locks as "a **Right** of making Laws ... and of employing the force of the Community, in the Execution of such laws, and in the defence of the Commonwealth from Foreign Injury."[31] And to John Austin, law, strictly and properly so-called, is not custom, but obligatory rules of behaviour of action "commanded" by the sovereign (i.e. the state) in the form of legislation; "laws which are not commands," he maintains, "are law improper, or improperly so-called."[32]

---

31. John Locke, *Second Treatise of Civil Government* (1690), p. 268.
32. John Austin, *Lectures on Jurisprudence*, 5th edn (1885) Vol. 1 p. 79

Conscious Law-Making by Legislation as a Necessary Attribute of the State

Legislation as an instrument of government is by no means a recent phenomenon. It dates back indeed to antiquity. The first written code of laws in Greek history goes as far back as 664 B.C. — disregarding for the present purpose earlier codes, like those of Lycurgus,[33] Minos, Hammurabi and Numa, said to be revelations by the gods, and not the product of conscious law-making by human reason. This 664 B.C. code was followed in 610 B.C. by the laws made for the city-state of Catana (in Sicily) by Charondas, which became "a model for many cities in Sicily and Italy, and served to create public order and sexual morality."[34]

Then followed the famous laws of Solon at Athens in 594 B.C.— the Solonian laws were preceded by those of Draco in 620 B.C.—which blazed a revolutionary trail in government. It revolutionalised the Athenian system of government by injecting into it a significant element of both direct and representative democracy and the participation of the people, as jurors, in the administration of justice; economic and social relations among the people were also revolutionised through the cancellation of all existing debts, the abolition of servitude for debt, the reform of the coinage, the individualisation of land-holding, the recognition of testamentary disposition of property and the stimulation of commerce and industry. The code also sought to reform morals and manners through the punishments of idleness and the violation of women, the regulation of prostitution and the limitation of dowries and of goods that might be buried with the dead. Quite significantly, the Solonian laws were sanctioned by remarkably humane penalties, unlike the draconian penalties of Draco's earlier laws in 620 B.C.

But legislation in the ancient Greek world consisted of merely isolated single instances rather than a system. It was in Rome that it attained that character and became a regular, leading instrument of rule. Government by legislated law was Rome's supreme legacy to the world. Legislation in Rome consisted of laws passed by the Assemblies or by the Senate, the edicts of the municipal magistrates and the provincial praetors, the statutes of the principates and the emperors *(edicta, decreta, rescripta and mandata)* and the opinions *(responsa prudentium)*

[33.] The Lycurgus code at Sparta, Greece, has been described as "the most unpleasant and astonishing body of legislation in all history." Will Durant, *The Story of Civilisation*, II. p. 77.

[34.] Will Durant, *ibid*, at p. 170

of great jurists, all of which were codified by Emperor Justinian in 529-533 A.D. in the manner described below. Codification in Roman law had begun in 451 B.C. with the Twelve Tables of Decemvir which transformed the old customary law. The codification of praetorian edicts, begun in 117 A.D. under the principate of Hadrian (117-138 A.D.), the Perpetual Edict, as Hadrian's codification is called, was continued under the principate of his successors, Antoninus Pius (138-161 A.D) and Marcus Aurelius Antoninus (161-180 A.D.) — the two Antonines.

Initially, laws made for Rome and its citizens, the *jus civile*, did not apply to the inhabitants of the provinces who were not Roman Citizens; the latter were governed by different laws, the *jus gentium*, made for them by their provincial governors and by the aediles and, more importantly, by a *praetor peregrinus* by virtue of power given to him to marry the rules of the *jus civile* with the varied pre-existing laws and customs of the provinces. But as Roman citizenship was gradually extended to all free inhabitants of the empire, this duality in the laws for citizens and for non-citizens lost its rationale. The emperors now legislated directly for the provinces (as well as for Rome) by rescripts, decrees and edicts, supplemented by the edicts of the provincial governors.

Over the centuries, an increasing divergence and conflict had occurred in the enormous body of legislation and had created a clear need for reform that would trim down the vast accumulations of centuries into one coherent system of law and rid it of the manifold contradictions, with their resultant confusions and chaos. The necessary reform was effected by the **Code** of Justinian of 529 A.D. which codified all existing legislation from a given date (the time of Emperor Hadrian, 117-138 A.D., was chosen as the base-line), with modifications necessary to "purge the errors and contradictions, to retrench whatever was obsolete or superfluous," retaining only such laws as were "wise and salutary and best adapted to the practice of the tribunals and the use of the people."[35]. The **Code** was declared the law of the Empire, nullifying all previous legislation not re-enacted therein, and was "transmitted to the magistrates of the European, the Asiatic, and afterwards the African provinces."[36] And despite "its rigid

---

35. Gibbon, *op. cit.* IV, p. 397; and pp. 374-444 for an extended account of the history and development of Roman law.
36. Gibbon, *op. cit.,* IV. p. 397

orthodoxy, its deeper obscurantism, its vengeful severity... the Code for some generations gave order and security to a motley assemblage of people..., and entered like a scaffolding of order into the structure of many modern states,"[37] Being too laborious a volume, it was later in 533 condensed into a handbook under the title of the **Institutes.**

The Code was supplemented by a **Digest** of the *responsa* or commentaries on the statutes and other laws by the great Roman jurists, which were considered deserving to be given continued application. Two thousand treatises of forty most eminent jurists were abridged into the fifty books of the Digest (533 A.D.). The Digest was then approved and given force of law by the emperor, forming with the Code and the Institutes the only laws to be admitted in the tribunals as the legitimate system of civil jurisprudence throughout the Empire. It has been said that the great attribute of Roman law, as contained in the Code and the Digest, is that it embodied generalisations framed with "extreme clarity and sharpness" to meet " the problems which arose in civilised society, rather than drawing on principles conceived in a theocratic or ideological mould."[28]

The laws enacted by Rome provided not only an "imposing architecture of government," but also a sublime instrument for order, peace and regularity — the famed *Pax Romana* — which served perhaps more than anything else to unify the provinces of the Empire.[39] The peace and security established by Roman law and maintained by the Roman government within its borders and throughout its far-flung Empire, is acclaimed "the supreme achievement in the history of statesmanship."[40] Under the *Pax Romana*, every part of the Empire had unprecedented prosperity, advancement and contentment, so much so, it is said, that "today our highest labours seek to revive the *Pax Romana* for a disordered world."[41] (Foreign envoys in Rome had reportedly sought admission for their countries to the "boons of the Roman yoke."[42])

In the form as codified in Justinian's Code, Digest and Institutes, Roman law was transmitted to medieval and modern states. In this form and

through a hundred lesser channels, and the silent tenacity of useful ways,

37. Durant, *op. cit.,* iv. p. 114
38. Wilfrid Knapp, *Tunisia* (1970), p. 30.
39. Edward Gibbon, *op. cit.,* vol. 1, p. 28
40. Will Durant, *op. cit,* III p. 232.
41. Will Durant, *ibid,* p. 670.
42. Will Durant, *loc. cit.;* Edward Gibbon, *ibid, p.* 9.

Roman law entered into the canon law of the medieval Church, inspired the thinkers of the Renaissance, and became the basic law of Italy, Spain, France, Germany, Hungary, Bohemia, Poland, even — within the British Empire — of Scotland, Quebec, Ceylon, and South Africa. English law itself, the only legal edifice of comparable scope, took its rules of equity, admiralty, guardianship, and bequests from Roman canon law.[43]

And so it was that, from the Roman legacy, the state came to conceived as a legal order consisting of a body of laws, mostly legislated laws, regularly enforced by a coercive agency (the police and the army) and by courts with compulsive jurisdiction, for the maintenance of peace and order in society, and the regulation of human activities and social life generally, which is the basis of a civilised society as distinguished from one in a state of barbarism. The inculcation among a people of the habit of law and order, the habit of obedience to law as the basis of orderly life, is a further step in the evolution of the concept of the state.

The fall of the Roman Empire in the West in 451-453 A.D. and the general disorder and chaos that followed in its wake had as one of the consequences that law enacted by the state as the expression of its sovereign will declined drastically to the extent where the state itself was considered almost non-existent to all intents and purposes, except under Charlemagne (768-814 A.D.), who still made considerable use of it, with his quite significant output of capitularies, as his legislations were called, some 65 of them in a 46 years rule, all of which manifested "a conscious effort to transform barbarism into civilisation."[44] Legislation gave way to the rule of custom. The medieval notion of law in Europe, we are told by D'Entreaves:

> corresponded to an extremely simplified and archaic view of social institutions, a view that can be found only among primitive peoples, where customs and immemorial traditions are surrounded, as it were, by a religious halo, and are the object of veneration and of respect bordering on fear. Such notions were further characterised by a markedly static conception of social life, in consequence of which law, instead of being regarded as an instrument placed at man's disposal for betterment and change appeared rather as a limit imposed by a mysterious and transcendent force on the expression of their references and on the choices dictated by their needs.[45]

[43.] Will Durant, *ibid*
[44.] Will Durant, *op. cit,* 464: pp. 461-471
[45.] D' Entreaves, *The Notion of the State* (1967), p. 85.

Legislation again emerged in the 17th century as a leading instrument of government, and was reinforced by the reception of Roman law, as codified by Justinian, in several of the countries.

It may safely be concluded that the function of the state cannot be adequately discharged, and a state cannot therefore exist in any meaningful sense, in the absence of conscious law-making by legislation. This has particular relevance to the status of pre-colonial African communities which, not having evolved a system of conscious law-making by legislation, are not states strictly so-called. (The status of pre-colonial African communities, whether or not they are states strictly so-called is extensively discussed in chapter 3 of the companion study, *Colonialism in Africa*.)

Form of Government

Given the adequacy and conduciveness of the organisation and form of government in the sense noted above, no particular form of civil government is implied or required by the concept of the state and so violation of the ideas underlying the concept necessarily flows from the adoption of any one of the various forms or a combination of them — rule by a hereditary monarch or other unelected individual (a monarchy may be elective), by an aristocracy, a plutocracy, by the whole people directly (direct democracy) or by representatives duly mandated or elected by them (representative democracy). We are not here concerned with the goodness or badness of particular forms of government.[46] (Both an aristocratic government and a plutocratic one are an oligarchy, i.e. government by a few.)

The government of most states has passed from one form to another at different stages in their history. As a classic example, the Roman State passed from rule by a monarch (753-508 B.C.), to rule by a mixture of royal, aristocratic, plutocratic and democratic elements interspersed by brief periods of one-man dictatorship (508-27 B.C.), to the rule of a one-man principate, described by Edward Gibbon as "an absolute monarchy disguised by the forms of a commonwealth" (27 B.C.-192 A.D.), and back again to undisguised monarchy (192 A.D.-1453). We are told by Will Durant that by 31 B.C., the date of the

---

[46.] As to this, see J. S. Mill, *Representative Government,* reprinted in *Utilitarianism, Liberty and Representative Government* (1910), Everyman's Library edn. pp. 198-217

decisive battle of Actium between Octavian, Julius Caesar's adopted son and heir (better known by his later name Augustus), and Mark Antony, "Rome had completed the fatal cycle known to Plato and to us: monarchy, aristocracy, oligarchic exploitation, democracy, revolutionary chaos, dictatorship."[47]

The collapse of the Roman Empire did not mean the end of monarchy, which persisted until the peculiar feudal system of rule in the Middle Ages in Europe, becoming again thereafter the universal form until the American and French Revolutions in 1783 and 1789 respectively. It is often not readily realised that the U.S. was the first example in the modern world of a non-monarchical, representative democratic government, although universal adult suffrage came by stages and was not fully achieved until the 20th century. Its attainment in Britain was by a gradual process of piece-meal extensions in 1832, 1867, 1885 and 1918. Today, government by representatives elected on a universal adult suffrage at periodic intervals of time has established itself as the universal form. Lord Bryce, writing in 1920, has spoken of "the universal acceptance of democracy as the normal and natural form of government". "Seventy years ago," he wrote:

> the approaching rise of the masses to power was regarded by the educated classes in Europe as a menace to order and prosperity. Then the word Democracy awakened dislike or fear. Now it is a word of praise. Popular power is welcomed, extolled, worshipped. The few whom it repels or alarms rarely avow their sentiments. Men have almost ceased to study its phenomena because these now seem to have become part of the established order of things.[48]

The State and Law

The concept of the state is bound up with that of law in an inextricable tangle. Law is a necessary attribute as well as a necessary instrument of the state; law is made by the state but the state itself is grounded on law, i.e. law considered as a body of laws or in totality. The state is characterised by power and force. State power, the power to govern the affairs of men in society, is not just arbitrary power but rather one exercised in accordance with definite procedures and rules. Force, which is the central attribute of the state, and without which it cannot exist — "states exist or not according as they have the force to impose

---

[47.] Will Durant *The Story of Civilisation*, III, (1944), p. 208
[48.] James Bryce, *Modern Democracies*, Vol. I (1920), p. 4.

their commands"[49] — is also not just brutish, unregulated force but rather "force displayed in a regular and uniform manner" in accordance with law that regulates, conditions and therefore qualifies it.[50] In more succinct language, the state denotes power and force exercised "in the name of the law;" it connotes a legal order, a body of laws that regulates, conditions and qualifies the exercise of power backed by force within a given community.

It follows that the state, as an organisation of power and force, can no more be defined apart from law. While law is created by the state, and is "an instrument more or less necessary for carrying out the state's activities and attaining its ends,"[51] the state, in its turn, is grounded upon law; it is the law that imparts to the state its character as an organisation whose "activities are systematised, co-ordinated, predictable, machinelike and impersonal."[52] Law and the state are thus correlative entities neither of which can be properly conceived without the other. Each is conditioned by the other in the sense that the existence of each is a condition for the existence of the other. The state cannot exist apart from or without law any more than law can exist apart from or without the state. Accordingly, force or power and, *ipso facto*, a state not regulated and conditioned by law, that is to say, a lawless state, is a perversion, a complete distortion, of the state concept.

Law, as a necessary instrument of the state for carrying out its activities and attaining its ends, raises an issue which also bears significantly on the nature of the state, viz: whether the power of the state to make law is or is not subject to any limitations, inherent or extrinsic. The nature of the state appears to have, inherent in it, the principle that its powers, including the law-making power, are only to be exercised in accordance with definite, regular procedures and with known rules, among which in particular is the requirement that coercive commands should apply uniformly to the generality of the people and should not single out named individuals or groups for selective or discriminatory treatment.

Aside from the limitation inherent in the nature of the state and its powers, the awesomeness of the law-making power seems to create a necessity for

---

49. D'Entreaves, *The Notion of the State* (1967), p. 8
50. D'Entreaves, *op. cit.,* p. 2
51. D'Entreaves, *op. cit.,* p. 71
52. Poggi, *The Development of the Modern State*, p. 75

further limitation. The questions raised by this have been posed earlier but may, for convenience, be repeated again here. What is the relation of the state to the rules of social life existing in society before the establishment of the state? Is this older "law", particularly the component of it embodying the laws of humanity, a higher law to which the state must conform, with the consequence that any of its acts inconsistent therewith is null and void? What is the relation of the state to the instrument by which the people construct a frame for the government of their affairs and the regulation of the relation of the government to the individual? Does such an instrument also embody a higher law binding on the state with an overriding force?

Theory aside, no legally binding and enforceable limitation on the power of a sovereign state can be derived from or be based on the law of nature or on the customs pre-existing in a community before the emergence of the state. Natural law can have no more than a moral force, providing merely "a basis of comparison ... an intellectual standard."[53] Rightly therefore has the contention that a sovereign legislature is limited in its law-making power by the law of nature been rejected on the highest judicial authority.[54]

Yet, without elevating it into a rule of law enforceable by the court, limitation derived from the laws of humanity should be accepted and form part of the conventional norms of moral code governing the exercise of power by the state. Sanctioned by the force of tradition and public opinion, such a moral code or conventional norms should serve to guide and control the state as to what laws to make or how the laws should be framed to be effective in curbing the arbitrariness of executive power. In this sense, as Friederich Hayek observes, the rule of law should be conceived as both a rule of the law as well as "a meta-legal doctrine or a political ideal." In the sense of a meta-legal doctrine or political ideal, however, the rule of law will be:

> effective only in so far as the legislator feels bound by it. In a democracy this means that it will not prevail unless it forms part of the moral tradition of the community, a common ideal shared and unquestioningly accepted by the majority.[55]

---

[53] C.H. McIlwain, *Constitutionalism: Ancient and Modern* (1940), p. 37
[54] *Liyange v. R.* (1967) 1 A.C. 259 (Privy Council on appeal from Ceylon, now Sri Lanka).
[55] F.A. Hayek, *The Constitution of Liberty* (1960), p. 206

But we are concerned here with the relation of the state to law as a legally binding and enforceable limitation on state power, and not so much with merely conventional or moral limitation, however efficacious that may be in actual practice. Is the state free of all legal limitation in the exercise of its law-making power? Happily, the need for a legally binding and enforceable limitation had, to a large extent, been realised in the notion of a written constitution, operating, not merely as a normative code like the constitutions of the socialist/communist countries, but as a supreme law with a coercive overriding force.

The idea of a constitution is of course not new; it as old as government itself. In its original meaning, a constitution refers simply to the rules implied in the **actual** frame or composition of a government; to the way in which a government is **actually** structured in terms of its organs, the distribution of powers within it, the relations of the organs *inter se,* and the procedures for exercising powers. Putting it differently, it refers, in the words of Professor Charles McIlwain, to "the substantive principles to be deduced from a nation's actual institutions."[56] It is this sense that the term was used and understood by the ancient Greeks and Romans, and is still used in Britain today.

What is new and revolutionary is the idea of a constitution as something separate from, and external as well as anterior to, government, and from which government derives its existence and powers, as a code or charter embodying the fundamental principles according to which a state and its relations to the individual are to be governed. A constitution in this sense was unknown before the American Revolution of 1776-87. It was a distinctly American innovation which, in the words of Chief Justice John Marshall in the great case *Marbury v Madison,* represented "the greatest improvement on political institutions."

From its origin in the U.S. and as a result of armed rebellion against the tyranny and arbitrariness of monarchical absolutism — a rebellion inspired in many cases by the revolutionary teachings of doctrinaire philosophers proclaiming the message of liberty, equality and fraternity — the old conception of a constitution as referring simply to the rules and principles implied in a nation's actual institution of government, with its corollary of the absolute, unlimited sovereignty of the government, has become discredited and has given place to written constitutions consciously framed as a code or charter by which

---

[56]   C. H. McIlwain, *Constitutionalism: Ancient and Modern* (1940), p. 5.

government is instituted as a deliberate contrivance. The United States Constitution was followed by: Poland on 3 May, 1791; France on 3 September, 1791; Sweden 1809; Venezuala, 1811; Ecuador, 1812; Norway, 1814 (the second longest surviving constitution in the world); Mexico, 1824; Central American Federation, 1825; and Argentina, 1826. Liberia's Constitution of 1847, which lasted until it was overthrown in a military coup in 1980, was the first written Constitution in the African Continent.

This development had been given a new boost by the emergence from colonialism of a host of new nations in Africa and Asia which needed written constitutions to launch them into their new, independent existence and to impose checks against the abuse of majority power in the interest of tribal, racial or religious minorities. So much has the development encompassed the world that only six countries are today without written constitutional codes as against 160 with such codes.[57]

The emergence of a written constitutional code was accompanied by the even more revolutionary notion of a written constitution as law — a supreme law binding on the state and making null and void any state-made law inconsistent with it. With the establishment of the U.S. Constitution in 1787 the notion of a constitution as law — a supreme, overriding law — was born. The subjection of the state to a higher law embodied in a constitution ordained by the people — the constitutional state — was indeed an epochal event in the development of the concept of the state. From the U.S. the notion has again been transmitted to most but not all countries of the world today. Further discussion of this revolutionary development is not appropriate here.

The State as an Organisation of Coercive Force
Nature and Rationale of the Force Backing up the State

The state is, by the very nature of the functions required of it, an organisation of force. An organised force is needed for the protection of the life, liberties and property of the individual in society, the enforcement of the laws of society, the maintenance of order among its members and the safeguarding of the society's collective security. This is the very *raison d'etre* for men joining together

---

[57] See A.P. Blaustein and G.H. Flanz (eds) *Constitutions of the Countries of the World* (1982); A.J. Peaslee (ed.) *Constitutions of Nations.*

in civil society. With all the freedom which he has in a state of nature, says John Locke, the natural force of the individual is scarcely adequate to protect him against or to redress injury or injustice that may be done to him in that state; he is therefore driven by necessity into society with others in order to avail himself of the protection of the collective, organised force of the society.[58] What this means is that an organised force is inseparable from the concept of the state, and is as indispensable to the adequacy of the form of government in a state as is a system of legislated law and a machinery for executing it, both of which rest for their effectiveness on force. "For if there is no power to enforce the will of the sovereign, then there is no government, no state, no security."[59] And without security, says Thomas Hobbes, there would be no industry, no technological development, "no arts, no letters, no society, and which is worse of all, continual fear, and danger of violent death, and the life of man, solitary, poor, nasty, brutish and short."[60]

Traditionally, the collective force of society is organised in the form of an armed force and a police. The police is, historically, a later creation than the army. Rome's first police force of 300 men under a municipal police commissioner was only established in 27 B.C. by Augustus, but an organised police force had existed in the city-state of Sparta (Greece) before 500 B.C.

The Roman state presents a remarkable example of the way the collective force of a society may be organised to form an army. The state in Rome may perhaps without impropriety be described as more a military than a civil organisation. Every citizen between 16-60 years of age was liable to military service, and was ineligible for political office until he had served at least ten years in the army. The entire citizenry was organised in military formations called "centuries", originally consisting of one hundred men each. Every male citizen, whether in active military service or not, must belong to one century or another according to his rank or financial standing. An assembly of centuries, the Centurial Assembly, in effect, an assembly of the whole people, was "the broad base of both the Roman army and the Roman government".[61] Among other things, it chose the magistrates — the consuls, the censors, the praetors,

---

[58]   John Locke, *Second Treatise of Civil government* (1960), pp. 350-355.
[59]   Thomas Hobbes, *Leviathan* (1651), edited by Michael Oakshort (1960), p. 82.
[60]   See Rodes *et al, op. cit.,* p. 24.
[61]   Will Durant, *The Story of Civilisation,* III, (1944), p. 26.

the quaestors etc. — and decided on war or peace and legislative measures upon proposals presented to it by the magistracy or the Senate. (In ancient Sparta too, "every citizen was trained for war, and was liable to military service from his twentieth to his sixtieth year."[62])

The Head of State in Rome, by whatever title called, was, first and foremost, the commander of the army. In war, he had to lead the army in person. Every one of the great Roman rulers was, first and foremost, a military commander leading the troops in person in the field of battle — the Scipios, Cato, the Gracchi, Marius, Sulla, Pompey, Caesar, Octavian Augustus, Trajan, Marcus Aurelius Antoninus, Caracalla, Constantine, etc. It was this essentially military basis of the Roman State and the martial spirit thereby instilled in the Roman people perhaps more than anything else, that accounted for its rise to world mastery.

It must not be thought that the Roman army was just a citizens' army. On the contrary, it was a professional organisation — well-trained, superbly organised and highly skilled. Over the years, as the Roman state expanded by colonisation and by territorial conquests, the army grew in numbers, reaching a total combined strength, for both the land and sea forces, of about 450,000 by 180 A.D.[63] But recruitment into it remained, for reason of ensuring the patriotism of its members, restricted, in theory, to Roman citizens, both indigenous Romans and other citizens, even when a legion was recruited from the most distant province (all natives of Italy were born citizens of Rome and Roman citizenship was liberally distributed among the natives of provinces to the extent that the greater number of them were citizens.)[64] In practice, of course, the requirement was not strictly adhered to, as the legions did actually contain non-citizen soldiers who only became citizens as a recompense for distinguishing themselves in war, as by winning a victory. Discipline was the watchword of the Roman army and it was instilled in the soldiers by a system of reward for valour or good conduct and punishment for cowardice or disobedience, by a strong sense of concern for the preservation of the honour of the army and by the influence of religion and regular, unremitting exercise and practice.

The relation of the army to the state and to the government in Rome has

62   Will Durant, *ibid*, II, p. 81.

63   Edward Gibbon, *op. cit.*, p. 19.

64   Edward Gibbon, *op. cit.*, pp. 34 and 37.

left important legacies and lessons for us. First, as has just been noted, the Centurial Assembly, as a military organisation, was the broad base of the government, providing for serving soldiers' meaningful participation in government during the Republican era. Beyond this, however, the army, as army, was not involved in government; it was kept out of government, and dutifully accepted its being so kept out. Despite being the base of the Roman State, the army did not, throughout the period of the Republic, attempt to subject the government to itself. Soldiers were forbidden to be quartered inside Rome or to be marched into or to within a certain radius of it. The all-conquering Roman legions were always stationed in the provinces of the Empire outside Rome and outside Italy. Only around 27-23 B.C. was this rule broken by Augustus keeping six cohorts of a thousand soldiers each near Rome and three cohorts within it, which became the Praetorian Guard, i.e. guard of the *praetorium* or headquarters of the commander-in-chief.

The creation of the Praetorian Guard stationed inside Rome in breach of tradition had a tragic consequence for the relation of the army to government. It led to the army's incursion into government. Beginning in 41 A.D. when Claudius was proclaimed Emperor by the Praetorian Guard, the phenomenon was aggravated by a disorderly cycle of assassinations and elevations of Emperors by soldiers. Emperors began to be made and unmade by soldiers with such frequency as robbed the monarchy of prestige and strength, and imperilled the stability of the state. After an assassination of an Emperor, the leader of the Praetorian Guard might then proclaim himself Emperor or someone else might be so proclaimed by the soldiers. Sometimes the choice went to anyone who made the highest bid for the office in the form of donative to each soldier. In this way, we are told, thirty-seven men were proclaimed Emperors by soldiers in the 35 years from 222-257 A.D. and four between 68-70 A.D.[65] "Democracy," observes Will Durant, "passed from the assemblies to the army, and voted with the sword."[66] Rightly had Edward Gibbon described the Praetorian Guard as "the authors of almost every revolution that distracted the empire."[67]

---

[65]   Will Durant, *The Story of Civilisation*, III (1944), pp. 284-5.

[66]   *op. cit.*, p. 260.

[67]   Edward Gibbon, *op. cit.*, p. 629.

The collapse of the imperial prestige caused by this led to the breakdown of "those psychological forces, which time consecrates into habitual and unquestioned authority,"[68] which in turn encouraged revolts and rebellions everywhere within the Empire and invasions from outside by the barbarians of Central Europe (Germany). The army's incursion into government in Rome was of course only one of the many causes in the long process of the decline and fall of the Roman Empire, but it underlines for us in Africa and some other parts of the developing world the cardinal need for avoiding such an incursion and the doom it spells. It also raises for us the issue of the desirability or otherwise of a standing army in peace time, particularly, a standing army quartered inside the capital city. It needs to be said, however, that the army as such never constituted itself the government of Rome, which means that Rome was never ruled by a military government strictly so-called.

Rome's concept of the state as an organisation of force embracing the entire citizenry meant that organised force and its use were a monopoly of the state. It left no room for individuals raising and maintaining private armies of their own which they could march against not only their own private enemies but also against the state itself — a phenomenon that proved to be perhaps the greatest source of weakness in the medieval states, with armies composed mainly of mercenary soldiers. From the chaos, instability and insecurity incident to this medieval phenomenon, the state has again emerged as an organisation possessing a monopoly of organised coercive force within its domain. Hence it has been defined by Hans Kelsen as an order regulating and monopolising the use of force.[69]

The state retained its character as essentially a military organisation up to the 19th century. Like the Roman rulers mentioned earlier, the medieval kings and those of the 16th, 17th, 18th and early 19th centuries, of whom Napoleon was a notable example, were first and foremost military commanders. The state could not shed its military character so long as war and territorial conquests remained the chief object of the relations between nations. Today, war looms less in the activities of the state while territorial conquests, as an object and instrument of international relations, have virtually yielded place to the principle

---

[68]   Will Durant, *op. cit.*, p. 629.

[69]   Hans Kelsen, *The General Theory of Law and State* (1945), English edn (1961), p. 190.

of the inviolability of each state's territory insofar as it is able to maintain and police its territory effectively. In consequence, the police in modern times have come to loom in importance more than the armed forces as representing the state as an organisation of force. They (the police) are the state's primary instrument for the enforcement of its laws, the maintenance of order and for the maintenance of its authority as the government generally. The armed forces get involved in suppressing insurrection and in restoring order only if and when called upon to do so by the government in aid of the police, subject to such conditions as may be prescribed by law.

The comparatively recent phenomenon of the army seizing the state, overthrowing its constitution and establishing itself as the government of the country, i.e. a military government, is, from what is said above, a tragic desecration of the long-established relation between it and state/government. Happily, the phenomenon is confined in its incidence to Latin America, Asia, the Middle East, the Balkans, and Africa.

Relation of the Army to the State and Government

With the state ceasing to be essentially a military organisation, and the army no longer commanded by the head of state personally, it becomes a matter of some disputation whether the relation of the army is to the state and its constitution directly or to the government in power. Is the army's duty of obedience owed primarily to the state and the constitution or to the government in power whose orders and decisions in all matters, military or otherwise it must therefore carry out? Is the army an organ of the Constitution and thus independent of the government in power or is it an instrument of the latter and subject to its paramountcy and control?

Each of the two viewpoints on this topic has its adherents among various countries, armies, political leaders and military commanders in the world. The principle of the supremacy of the civil government over the military is most strongly maintained in Britain and the U.S. as a tradition of government administration accepted both by the people and the armed forces. In certain other countries, however, the conception of the army as an institution in direct relationship to the nation and the state has found expression in its portrayal as "the purest image of the state" by General Von Seeckt, German War Minister; as "the last bastion of the Spanish nationhood" by General Franco, the Spanish dictator; as "the synthesis of the nation" by Peron, the Argentine dictator; or as "the custodian of the national interest."[70] Such a view of the army is irreconcilable with democracy which (except as may otherwise be provided in the Constitution) conceives all significant governmental powers as residing in the people, and as legitimately exercisable only by persons duly mandated by them in a free and fair election or by others acting in the name of, and responsible to, the people's duly mandated representatives.

Popular Acceptance as the Basis of the State's Legitimacy

Force or might alone does not bestow legitimacy upon the state. The doctrine that might makes right or that "power legitimates itself,"[71] once popular since it was explicitly adumbrated in the writings of Machiavelli and Hobbes in the early 16th and mid-17th centuries respectively, has become discredited. Although of supreme importance in the life of society, security, which is relied upon as its rationale, is not a justification for this doctrine. The justification must have a moral or spiritual basis; power or might cannot be its own justification.

Legitimacy concerns the moral right to wield power over others, the latter is what is called authority. Authority refers to the moral basis of power, it is "the mother of power,"[72] serving therefore to sanctify and legitimate it. Power without authority, that is to say, power not based on, and not sanctified by, authority, is illegitimate, and its exercise over others is morally wrongful.

Authority thus implies a moral relationship whereby society has come to recognise and accept that "a person or body of persons has the moral right to demand obedience," and society a corresponding moral duty to obey him or them. Power based on might or force alone does not confer legitimacy on government, or, in Rousseau's pithy but pointed words, "the strongest is never strong enough to be always the master unless he transforms might into right and obedience into duty."[73] Might must be transformed into a moral right and obedience into a moral duty to legitimate government and the exercise of power by it.

---

[70] S.E. Finer, *The Man on Horseback: The Role of the Military in Politics* (1962), pp. 35-39.

[71] Rodes *et al, op. cit.*, p. 24.

[72] S.E. Finer, *The Man on Horseback: the Role of the Military in Politics* (1962), p. 19.

[73] J.J. Rousseau, *The Social Contract*, Book 1, chap. 3; reproduced in Harry K. Girvetz, *Democracy and Elitism: Two Essays with Selected Readings* (1967); see the discussion on the subject in Christopher Pierson, *op. cit.*, pp. 22-27.

As a moral force, authority or the moral right to exercise rule over others can only spring from society; it must rest on social acceptance or recognition of a title to rule derived from long-continued tradition, convention or some widely accepted myth or belief, such as the belief or myth of the divine right of kings to rule because they were supposed to represent God's will on earth,[74] or the sacredness of the person and authority of certain kings, or, to use examples from Africa, the belief or myth in African societies that the power of the traditional chief is derived from the ancestors whose spirit he incarnates or the belief or myth among Ethiopians that the royal house was descended from King Solomon and that its title to rule was divinely ordained by reason of Solomon being the chosen and anointed of God, as the sacred book, the Bible, tells us. So it is also in a theocracy, as the states established by Mohammed and his early successors were; a theocracy being a state ruled by a religious leader claiming to be, and accepted by society as being, divinely directed. A divinely ordained right to rule is pure myth, there is nothing like that, yet popular acceptance of or belief in it gives it reality as a moral basis for the king's title to rule. However, if and when it ceases to be accepted or believed by the society, the moral authority derived from it also ceases. Tradition resting on popular acceptance therefore holds the key to governmental legitimacy.

Religion and the State

Historically, the authority derived from the doctrine of a divine right was sanctified not only by its acceptance by the governed but also by its acceptance by the Christian religion as part of its own doctrine. Christianity's acceptance of it had its origin in Saint Paul's letter to the early Christians in Rome in which he enjoined them to accept the legitimacy of the power of the Roman Emperors:

> Let every person be subject to the governing authorities. For there is no authority except from God and those that exist have been instituted by God. Therefore he who resists the authorities resists what God has appointed and those who resist will incur judgement. (*Romans* 13:1-2.)

The doctrine, thus sanctified by popular acceptance and by the precepts of the Christian Church, was further sanctified by the fusion of the state with religion. In ancient Greece and Rome, as everywhere else in antiquity, church

---

[74] Hannah Arendt, *On Revolution* (1963), p. 156.

and state were one.[75] Ancient Rome was a classic example. There, right from its founding in 753 B.C. down to the early 4th century A.D., religion (i.e. paganism) and the state were fused in one inseparable union. "Religion was part of the structure and ceremony of government."[76] Its priests were functionaries of the state, with the ruler as the chief priest or *pontifex maximus.* Its temples and shrines were built and owned by the state. Religious ceremonies and rituals were a state affair.

The conversion of the Roman state to Christianity in 381 A.D. (until then, the Roman State still remained a pagan state even after Emperor Constantine converted to Christianity in 323 A.D., the first Emperor to do so) brought about a change in the relationship between it and the Christian Church. While Christianity became the religion of the state and the state a Christian state (*respublica christiana*), religion became structurally and functionally separated from the Roman state. No longer were priests functionaries of the state or the Emperor the chief priest, nor religious ceremonies a state affair. In place of the Emperor as *pontifex maximus* of the pagan religion, the Pope had become the *pontifex maximus* of the Christian religion, and its organisational head or chief executive.

And so originated the distinction between civil government and church government, subject, however, to the paramount authority of the Emperor, even in matters of church government. Following the collapse of the Roman Empire in the West in 451-455 A.D., the church had gained ascendancy over the weak states that emerged from the ruins of the fallen empire, and had also secured its independence from the domination of the Emperors of the Eastern Empire (the empire in the East only fell in 1453). The ascendancy of the Church over the states in the West was later overborne in the upsurge of nationalism and the notion of the absolute sovereignty of the state after the Middle Ages.

The emancipation of the state from subordination to the Church while still remaining a Christian state (this was all that secularization meant initially before the new doctrine of complete separation between church and state originated by the American revolutionaries in the Constitution of 1787) had the sad consequence of depriving it the powerful sanction of religion which, together with tradition, had provided the Roman state's source of authority and legitimacy.

---

[75] Will Durant, *The Story of Civilisation,* II, p. 192.
[76] Will Durant, *op. cit.,* III p. 647.

By this emancipation, the monarch, supplanting the Pope and bishop, had become an absolute, independent power, but he did not "receive the sanctity of Bishop or Pope."[77] The loss of religious sanction following upon the emancipation of the state from **the authority** of the church became the ruin of political authority, as the force and sanction of tradition alone proved inadequate to bestow sufficient authority and legitimacy upon the state and its power. The myth of the divine rights of kings served to some extent to fill the gap created by the loss of religious sanction until it too ceased to enjoy popular acceptance. But even while it lasted, the sanction of the myth was a "pseudosolution" which "served only to hide, for some centuries, the most elementary predicament of all modern political bodies, their profound instability, the result of some elementary lack of authority."[78] In the result, the state has continued to be perplexed by the problem of how to found and constitute a new transcendent and transmundane source of authority and legitimacy for its power and laws. Popular consent alone as expressed through the votes at elections has proved inadequate too.

It is in the light of this problem of lack of sufficient authority or legitimacy by government that the absolute neutrality of the state in matters of religion, as laid down in the decisions of the U.S. supreme court, must be viewed. These decisions seem to carry the separation of Church and state rather too far. While state encouragement of religion might well entail some discrimination against non-believers in any religion, we cannot afford to have the state maintain a position of absolute neutrality between religion and irreligion. Religion is much too important in the life of society for the state to keep away completely from involvement of any kind, no matter how necessary and beneficial to the community, upon the principle of absolute separation.

Religious beliefs have through the ages been the main anchor of morality, providing the necessary sanction and helping to transmit it from generation to generation. Such has been the linkage of the one with the other that it is said morality cannot exist without religion. Subscribing to this view, Will and Ariel Durant declare, after an 11-volume monumental survey of the history of civilisation from the earliest times, that "there is no significant example in history,

---

77 Hannah Arendt, *On Revolution* (1963), p. 160.
78 Hannah Arendt, *op. cit.*, p. 159.

before our time, of a society successfully maintaining moral life without the aid of religion," maintaining that the provisional success of the experiment by the communist countries in dissociating the state from religion "owes much to the temporary acceptance of Communism as the religion (or, as skeptics would say, the opium) of the people."[79] They add in a poignant comment that

> If the socialist regime should fail in its efforts to destroy relative poverty among the masses, the new religion may lose its fervour and efficacy, and the state may wink at the restoration of supernatural beliefs as an aid in quieting discontent.

Liberty, democracy and justice are all concepts with high moral content, requiring therefore the aid of religion to secure and maintain them. Hence the age-old maxim that "only a virtuous people are capable of freedom," that liberty is meant only for a moral people, or, as Edmund Burke puts it: "men are qualified for civil liberties, in exact proportion to their disposition to put moral chains upon their appetites; in proportion as their love of justice is above their rapacity." More pungently still, "liberty," says Alexis de Tocqueville, "regards religion as... the cradle of its infancy, and the divine source of its claims. It considers religion as the safeguard of morality, and morality as the best security of law, and the surest pledge of the duration of freedom."[80]

Alexis de Tocqueville was writing in 1835— more than 100 years before the extreme doctrine of separation laid down by the U.S. supreme court in the 1940s; he attributed the strength and resilience of liberty and democracy in the United States largely to the religious and moral character of her people. The character of American civilisation, he wrote, is the product of two distinct elements: "the spirit of religion and the spirit of Liberty". "The settlers of New England", he continued, were at the same time ardent sectarians and daring innovators," adding, in a much quoted passage:

> I sought for the greatness and genius of America in her commodious harbours and her ample rivers and it was not there; in her fertile fields and boundless prairie, and it was not there; in her rich mines and vast commerce, and it was not there. Not until I went to the churches of America and heard her pulpits aflame with righteousness did I understand the secret of her genius and power.[81]

---

[79]   Will and Ariel Durant, *The Lessons of History* (1960)
[80]   Alexis de Tocqueville, *Democracy in America, op. cit.*
[81]   Alexis de Tocqueville, *op. cit.*

Liberty and democracy took root and flourished in the United States because, in the words of Senator Hatch, "the people were virtuous; they were virtuous because they were moral; and they were moral because they were religious."[82]

In an excellent summation of the role of religion in fostering happiness, discipline, harmony and stability in a democracy, Will and Ariel Durant have said:

> To the unhappy, the suffering, the bereaved, the old, it has brought supernatural comforts valued by millions of souls as more precious than any natural aid. It has helped parents and teachers to discipline the young. It has conferred meaning and dignity upon the lowliest existence, and through its sacraments has made for stability by transforming human covenants into solemn relationships with God. It has kept the poor (said Napoleon) from murdering the rich. For since the natural inequality of men dooms many of us to poverty or defeat, some supernatural hope may be the sole alternative to despair. Destroy that hope, and class war is intensified. Heaven and utopia are buckets in a well; when one goes down, the other goes up; when religion declines Communism grows.[83]

They add in another poignant statement that "as long as there is poverty, there will be gods." We might perhaps modify this last dictum to read that as long as there is death, ill-health and poverty, there will be gods. It is the fear of death perhaps more than poverty that induces in men a belief in gods. Certainly, there would be less need for religion if death did not exist. With immortality, man would have been assimilated to a god.

It can thus be concluded that no society in which morality and religion are absent can ever attain and maintain liberty, democracy and justice. Hence, religion needs encouragement by the state to thrive and to be effective in providing an anchor for morality and in fostering the morality-based values of liberty, democracy and justice, and in inculcating among citizens morality, spirituality and piety. A developing country should not indulge in the doctrinaire rigidity of the state completely dissociating itself from religion. Whatever discrimination against non-religionists — agnostics and such others — that may be entailed in the state giving encouragement to all religions on the basis of equality is not really an unfair one, certainly not such as to warrant the state in keeping off

---

[82] Senator Hatch, *The Phi Kappa Phi Journal,* Fall 1984, No. 5.
[83] Will and Ariel Durant, *The Lessons of History* (1960).

religion completely. African countries must not aggravate further the problem of a lack of authority and legitimacy arising from the loss of religious sanction consequent upon the secularisation of the state. There is really no contradiction in a secular state giving encouragement to religion, as by religious prayers at certain public occasions, attendance of the rulers at church services, the use of the Bible or the Quran in swearing oaths, the provision of aid for religious pilgrimages and other religious purposes. But state encouragement of religion must be on the basis that all religions are treated equally, with no favouritism, preference, protection or sponsorship of any kind for one as against the others. That is the command of section 10 of the Nigerian Constitution.

CHAPTER 14

The Character of the State Inherited from Colonialism

The Illegitimacy of the Inherited State

The state in Africa is the illegitimate child of colonialism — "the bastard child of imperialism," as Karl Maier calls it.[1] How to legitimate it must therefore be one of the cardinal goals of decolonisation. The illegitimacy of the state in Africa is a somewhat different issue from, though related to, that arising from the fact that the state and its ways have no root in the life and experience of the peoples of Africa. Legitimacy concerns, rather, the question of the moral basis of the state and its power. It involves the distinction between might or material strength and the moral right to wield it over others; the latter is what is known as authority. Authority refers to the moral basis of power, it is **"the mother of power,"**[2] serving therefore to sanctify and legitimate it. Power without authority, that is to say, power not based on, and not sanctified by, authority, is illegitimate, and its exercise over others is morally wrong.

Authority thus implies a moral relationship whereby society has come to recognise and accept that "a person or body of persons has the moral right to demand obedience," and society a corresponding moral duty to obey him or them. Power based on might or force alone does not confer legitimacy on government, or, in Rousseau's pithy but pointed words, "the strongest is never strong enough to be always the master unless he transforms might into right and obedience into duty."[3] Might must be transformed into a moral

---

[1] Karl Maier, *This House Has Fallen: Nigeria in Crisis* (2000), p. 7
[2] S.E. Finer, *The Man on Horseback: The Role of the Military in Politics* (1962), p. 19
[3] J.J. Rousseau, *The Social Contract*, Book 1, Chap. 3; in Harry K. Girvetz, *Democracy and Elitism: Two Essays with Selected Readings* (1967).

right and obedience into a moral duty to legitimate government and the exercise of power by it.

As a moral force, authority or the moral right to exercise rule over others can only spring from society; it must rest on social acceptance or recognition of a title to rule derived from long continued tradition, convention or some widely accepted myth or belief, such as the belief or myth of the divine right of kings to rule because they were supposed to represent God's will on earth,[4] or the sacredness of the person and authority of certain kings, or, to use examples from Africa, the belief or myth in African societies that the power of the traditional chief is derived from the ancestors whose spirit he incarnates or the belief or myth among Ethiopians that the royal house is descended from King Solomon and that its title to rule was divinely ordained by reason of Solomon being the chosen and anointed of God, as the sacred book, the **Bible**, tells us. A divinely ordained right to rule is pure myth, there is nothing like that, yet popular acceptance of or belief in it gives it reality as a moral basis for the king's title to rule. But if and when it ceases to be accepted or believed by the society, the moral authority derived from it also ceases. Tradition therefore holds the key to governmental legitimacy.

The title of the European colonisers to rule Africa had no such moral basis in tradition, convention or myth; it was grounded purely on conquest by force of arms — sheer might — or cession obtained by undue influence. Conquest does — no doubt — confer a right, but it is a legal, not a moral, right, while the moral right, equally as the legal right, that might have been derived from the treaties of cession was vitiated by the undue influence by which the consent of the ceding traditional African rulers was obtained, and by the fact that the latter could not have consented to what they did not understand. Thus, the state in Africa, as an entirely new geographical and political entity created by colonialism, was branded with illegitimacy by the circumstances of its origin. And given that the state did not exist before as one identifiable geographical and political entity, there could have been no pre-existing tradition, convention or myth upon which the European colonisers could later seek to ground their title. The enormous powers the colonial state wielded over its African subjects simply lacked a moral basis altogether; based

---

[4]　Hannah Arendt, *On Revolution* (1963), p. 156

as it was entirely on might or force, it was power illegitimately wielded. Neither was it legitimated by popular elections or other means of popular participation over a sufficiently long period of time.

So long as the state in Africa remained a colonial state, it and its powers continued to lack legitimacy, so that what was "transferred" to the African successors at independence was power devoid of a moral right to wield and exercise it, for the European imperialists could not at independence have transferred to their African successors any better title than they themselves possessed.

It was thus left to the African succeeding rulers to try to legitimate their inheritance. Regrettably, with a few exceptions, notably Kwame Nkrumah, the implications of the problem appeared not to have been regarded as a matter of serious concern. Remarkably too, Nkrumah alone had consciously tried to do something about it, albeit in his characteristically egoistic style. He tried to transfer to the state and the presidential office, the attitudes inculcated in the people by African tradition towards chiefly authority, to clothe the office in the garb and image of a chief in African traditional society, with all the authority and respect due by tradition to a chief. The president was thus projected as the "chief" of the new nation and was publicly invested with chiefly attributes. Thus, when he attended public rallies in Ghana, Nkrumah used to assume the style of a chief. He sat upon a "chiefly throne under a resplendent umbrella, symbol of traditional rule," and he took "chiefly titles meaningful to all major tribal units in Ghana: *Osagyefo, Katamanto, Kasapieko, Nufeno*, etc."[5] His opening of parliament was also done in chiefly style. His approach was:

> heralded by the beating of *fantom forom* (traditional drums). He was received by eight linguists representing the various Regions and each carrying a distinctive stick. A libation was poured and the President then entered the chamber to the sound of *mmenson* (the seven traditional horns).[6]

Though this is explicable in part by Nkrumah's irredentist aspiration for the revival of the African cultural heritage, the political significance is obvious. It was intended to harness to the presidency the authority of tradition and the

---

5   H.L. Bretton, *The Rise and Fall of Kwame Nkrumah: A Study of Personal Rule in Africa* (1966), p. 80
6   Bennion, *The Constitutional Law of Ghana* (1962), p. 110

legitimacy which it confers. By aligning the presidency with the institution of chieftaincy in the public imagination, it is hoped to inspire public acceptance of the office and respect for its authority. The mysticism of religion in which the authority of the chief is sanctified was also sought to be transferred to the presidential office. Even the attribute of divinity, which also characterises some traditional chieftaincies, had been claimed for Nkrumah as president of Ghana.

What impact, if any, was made on the problem by Nkrumah's invocation of African tradition is not known. It is conceivable that an alien institution with no root whatever in the life and experience of Africans may not be easily legitimated by clothing it in the garb and image of African tradition. No doubt, tradition must form the basis of any effort to legitimate the state and its powers, but it has to be tradition evolved anew in consonance with the character of the institution.

A conscious effort to evolve appropriate tradition must go hand in hand with other means of legitimation, viz: popular participation in government through elections, referenda or plebiscites; social mobilisation aimed, among other things, at creating a public opinion that is politically conscious and alive; political education about the state and its institutions with a view to making them comprehensible to the people; a programme of social welfare services designed to make the state meaningful and relevant in the lives of the people; the development of country-wide associations and institutions that try to integrate people together for joint action in the pursuit of common political purposes and interests, such as professional and trade associations, labour unions, political parties, religious bodies, etc; inculcating among the people an acceptance of the indivisibility and perpetuity of the state, acceptance of the equal interest of all in the state, the right of every citizen to equality of opportunities and equality before the law, a sense of allegiance to the state and attachment to its institutions, a sense of community and of a common destiny. By these means, regularly and uninterruptedly applied and sustained over a sufficiently long period of time, the peoples of Africa may, hopefully, come to recognise and accept the inherited post-colonial state and its instrumentalities as having the moral right to command, and society, the moral duty to obey their commands.

It is sad that the slow and tortuous process of legitimating the state by means of popular elections, referenda and plebiscites has been arrested or, at least, retarded by the frequent occurrence of a prolonged military *interregnum* in most countries of Africa. Given that a military government is not popularly elected but is rather an armed subjugation of the people, involving a seizure of the state by force of arms or threat of it, i.e. rule based on sheer might, military rule is devoid of the legitimating effect of popular elections, even when the elections are rigged. With the ban under military rule of elections, election campaigns, political rallies, public assemblies and processions on public issues, which are all part of the process of legitimating the state in the eyes of the people, it is as if the country was reverted again to its previous condition as a colonial state at the early stage of colonisation when government was administered by colonial officials without elections — Africa's second colonisation, as military rule may be called without too much impropriety.

ı The legitimacy of a government in power at any particular time raises a different but related issue from the legitimacy of the state conceived as government transmuted into a corporation with perpetual succession. It is not intended to go into a discussion of that here.

The Lack of Legitimacy of the Constitution in Africa

The constitution of the state in Africa lacks legitimacy in the eyes of the people, rulers and the ruled alike. Two factors account for this: first, the origin of the constitution in Africa as an alien institution but more importantly as an imposition; and, secondly, the character stamped on it by colonialism as an instrument of repression and autocratic control, rather than as a charter of good governance and of liberty. There is a third major factor of an aggravating kind: the frequent overthrow of the constitution in a military *coup d'etat* followed by prolonged rule under a military absolutism.

The written constitution, as law and a supreme law, was unknown in Africa before the advent of colonialism. It only came with colonisation, the first known written constitution being that of Liberia of 1847. Like the state itself and all its other institutions, the written constitution originated in Africa as an imposition on African peoples by the colonisers. The earliest colonial constitutions by which various African peoples in a given area were constituted into one colonial state were drawn up by officials — lawyers and other experts

— in the metropolis of the imperial power, and just handed down to the colonial territory concerned. It had no greater meaning or significance and commanded no more respect and loyalty for the colonised African peoples than the other colonial laws by which they were governed, because neither the one nor the other had any roots in the culture and life of their African subjects. There is, as has been observed by Hannah Arendt, "an enormous difference in authority (i.e. legitimacy) between a constitution imposed by a government upon a people and the constitution by which a people constitutes its own government."[7] And the difference is still more enormous where the imposition was by a European imperial government upon a colonised African people.

The constitution by which the African countries in the British colonial empire were ushered into independent existence, the independence constitution as it is called, was no different in this respect from the earlier colonial constitutions. It was an imposition and also bore the character of illegitimacy stamped on it by colonialism. Africa's independence is usually spoken of as a revolution, as it certainly is, but it is such, not because the independence constitution in countries in former British Africa was made by the colonised African peoples by virtue of their revolutionary sovereignty as a constituent power; in other words, it was not product of a successful popular revolution against colonial subjugation and rule, like the Constitution of 1787 that bought to a successful end the American revolt against British colonial rule. Nor was it adopted at a referendum organised and conducted by the British colonial authorities, a referendum to adopt a constitution being unknown anywhere in the British dependent empire or even in England itself which does not have and never has had a written constitution.

Rather, the independence constitution in these countries was the product of a further imposition by the British colonisers in their exit from the continent. It was such indeed in a triple sense. First, it derived its force as law from the imperial authority of the departing British colonisers. It was thus not an autochthonous constitution, which may here be defined as one whose force as law derives from an authority indigenous to the country concerned.

Secondly, the process of its making was dominated by the British colonisers. The African leaders participating in the process were hardly free agents, with

---

[7]   Hannah Arendt, *On Revolution* (1962), p. 145

an unfettered freedom of choice; they were more of supplicants than masters of their country's destiny. They were also not specifically mandated in that behalf by the peoples they professed to lead.

Thirdly, the content of the constitution, the form of government it instituted, was dictated, in part, at any rate, by the vested interest of the departing British colonial masters in leaving behind the legacy of their own system of government as a lasting memorial of their imperial glory. African nationalist leaders accepted the legacy, not so much because they really thought it the best for their countries as because they believed it to be the only basis for independence that would be acceptable to British colonial masters. They could not risk jeopardising the much-desired much-longed-for independence upon that point.

It is gratifying to note that the above picture of the independence constitution as an imposition on Africans is not true of countries in former French Africa. They are characterised by a different inheritance in constitution-making, which illustrated rather vividly the powerful force of tradition in human affairs. The notion of the people as a constituent power and the legitimate authority to adopt a constitution is widely accepted in France, unlike in England, so are a referendum and constituent assembly as a means by which the people may exercise that power. With the French, unlike the English, both the notion as well as the means for practicalising it has become a tradition faithfully adhered to. The tradition forms part of Africa's inheritance from French colonialism. Following upon the inherited tradition, most of the countries in former French Africa have had their successive constitutions adopted through a constituent assembly or referendum or both.

It is worthy of note that any question of the independence constitution as an imposition by France was ruled out by the manner and circumstances in which these countries acceded to independence. The 1958 Constitution of France gave the overseas territories the option, exercisable by a resolution of their territorial assemblies, either to remain integral units of the French Republic as they had been up to then, or to become separate, autonomous (though as yet not independent) states within the newly created French community (i.e. separate from the French Republic), with "autonomy ... to administer themselves and manage their own affairs democratically and freely," subject to the authority of the Community in matters within its jurisdiction under the Constitution (arts. 76 and 77). Between 1958 and 1959 all the African territories took the latter option, and transformed themselves from integral units of the French Republic to separate, autonomous states within the Community by the title of republic. They adopted their own separate constitutions either through a constituent assembly (in some territories the existing territorial assembly simply turned itself into a constituent assembly) or through a referendum following the French precedent of 1945, 1946 and 1958 to which their own participation in the process has familiarised them, limited though their participation in the process was, because of the small number of Africans qualified to vote.

Taking advantage of a constitutional amendment of 1960 which permitted an overseas member of the Community to become independent, "by way of agreements," without losing its membership of the Community and the benefits associated with it (Guinea lost its membership by opting for independence in the 1958 referendum), 14 of the African countries acceded to independence in 1960. Morocco, Tunisia and Guinea had previously become independent on 2 March, 1956, 20 March, 1956 and October, 1958 respectively, followed by Algeria in 1962. The little, insignificant Comoros Islands, with a population of 502,000 (1989 estimate) and Djibouti, with a population of 293,000 (1989 estimate) became independent in 1976 and 1977 respectively. In the manner of their making, therefore, the independence constitutions of the countries in former French Africa present a refreshing contract to those of the former British Africa.

The absence of imposition of any kind is further marked by the fact that many of the independence constitutions in these countries departed from the hybrid model of the Constitution of the French Fifth Republic in favour of the American Presidential system. There were no constitutional conferences on the form of government with which the territories should accede to independence. Each decided for itself entirely in its own judgment. France did not involve itself in what was considered an exclusive affair of the countries concerned.

As with the countries in former French Africa, no question of the independence constitution being an imposition by a departing colonising power also arises in the case of the countries that became independent by armed revolt — Algeria, Angola, Guinea-Bissau, Mozambique, South Africa and Zimbabwe — although in none of them was the constitution adopted through a referendum.

Two countries outside former French and British Africa — Liberia and Ethiopia — have applied the process of a referendum in adopting their constitutions. Influenced no doubt by American precedent, Liberia's Constitution of 1847 was approved in convention on 26 July and later approved by the "people" in a referendum. Its 1984 Constitution was submitted to a constitutional assembly elected in conventions throughout Liberia from 12 May to 20 June, 1983, and was later approved in a referendum on 3 July, 1984. Ethiopia's socialist Constitution was approved in a referendum in February 1987.

It follows from what is said above that the question of the democratisation of the constitution is largely a problem of the countries in former British Africa. It is lamentable that these countries should have missed the opportunities that had arisen since independence to democratise their constitutions, not just in the sense of democratising the form of government but, more importantly in this connection, of democratising the process by which the constitution is adopted, so as to make it an emanation of the popular will.

A serious factor in the constitution's lack of legitimacy in Africa is the character stamped on it by colonialism as an instrument of repression and autocratic control rather than as a charter of good governance and of liberty. From the beginning, it was employed by the colonising power and was therefore seen by colonised Africans as an instrument of autocracy or authoritarianism because of the absolute or unlimited power it gave to the imperial government. Constitutionally, the imperial government held in and over the colonised African territory a power which, because it was derived from conquest, cession or sufferance, was at once unlimited and absolute, embracing the sovereignty of the colonised country in its entirety. Part of this power, it delegated to a locally-based colonial government which also wielded it autocratically.

The legacy bequeathed to Africa by this situation had a parallel in what Hannah Arendt calls "the problem of an absolute" that confronted the French revolutionaries after the overthrow of the absolute monarchy in 1789.[8] The problem was one of attitude, a carry-over from life under a centuries-old absolute monarchy, which had produced in the revolutionaries the belief that the only substitute for the absolute monarchy after its overthrow was a revolutionary despotic dictatorship, an absolutism being the only form of government the country was used to. In the result, instability arising from the government's lack of sufficient authority or legitimacy, has ever since been the lot of the French until the adoption by a referendum of the Constitution of the Fifth Republic under Charles de Gaulle in 1958.

On the other hand, the British monarchy against which the American colonists revolted was a limited monarchy. Never having lived under and experienced an absolute monarchy, it was the good fortune of the American revolutionaries that they were not confronted with this problem of an absolute government, as the colonised African peoples, like the French, had been. For, whereas the thirteen American colonies, being colonies settled by English men, were, subject to the legislative supremacy of the British Parliament, governed by local representative assemblies on the same model as in England, which was recognised by law to be their birthright as Englishmen both in England and in their new settlements; the power of the British monarchy in its conquered or ceded African colonies was absolute and unfettered by such limitation. (Only in 1887 was the restriction by the British Settlements Act which empowered the Crown to set up any kind of legislature, representative or not, in a colony settled **after** that date, just as in a conquered or ceded colony or in a colonial protectorate.) The consequence of this is that the attitude of Africans, rulers and subjects alike, to the constitution of the state has been shaped and conditioned by their life and experiences under absolute governments from the beginning of colonial rule to its end. A constitution has come to mean for them simply an instrument of authoritarian rule, not a charter of freedom from arbitrary coercion.

This colonially-induced attitude towards the constitution as an instrument of autocratic control, rather than as a charter of freedom from arbitrary coercion, still persists today more than three decades after independence, and

---

[8]   Hannah Arendt, *op. cit.*, pp. 158-159

is lamentably reflected in the tendency on the part of post-colonial African rulers to use it as an instrument of repression in the game of politics. In countries in former British Africa, the period between independence and 1973 had witnessed no less than 17 constitutional amendments in Zambia, 13 in Malawi, 11 in Kenya, 10 in Tanzania, 6 in Uganda, 5 in Ghana and 4 in Botswana. Whilst the changes effected through the amendments, e.g. the abolition of federalism/regionalism, chiefly power and the justiciable bill of rights, might not in every case have been politically motivated, the circumstances in which many of them were introduced and passed into law seem to suggest that party or personal political advantage might have been the predominating motive. There were certainly cases where no room is left for doubt that this was the case, as the following examples, taken from three Anglophone African countries (Kenya, Zambia and Nigeria) bear out. There was something of a discreditable drama in these abuses of the power of constitutional amendment, which calls for a somewhat extended account.

Kenya became a *de facto* one-party state in 1963 when the opposition Kenya African Democratic Union (KADU) dissolved itself and took its members *en masse* into the ruling Kenya African National Union (KANU). In 1966, a split occurred within the single party. The Vice-President of the party and of the country, Mr Oginga Odinga, two assistant ministers and 18 other members of parliament resigned from KANU and formed a splinter party under the name, Kenya People's Union (KPU). They were joined later by the minister of information. There was a strong indication that many more were to follow. The KANU government was thrown into a state of panic by the prospect that the trickle of resignations might become a flood. To stem this, the Constitution was amended vacating the parliamentary seats by any member of parliament who defected from the party on whose platform he was elected. The national assembly was called to a special emergency meeting and the amendment rushed through in one day after getting the relevant standing order suspended in order to make this possible. The amendment did produce the desired result of halting the spate of resignations. Thirteen of the defectors, faced with the loss of their parliamentary seats, "applied for readmission to KANU and publicly reaffirmed their loyalty to Mr Kenyatta."[9] But, on hearing

---

9   G.F. Engholm and Ali Mazui, "Crossing the Floor and the Tensions of Representation in East Africa," *Parl. Affairs* (1967/1968), Vol. xxi, p. 149

that, under amendment, they would have to seek re-election before they could regain their vacated seats in parliament, ten of them went back to KPU. The defectors then contended that their seats were in fact not vacated, as the amendment did not in its terms purport to be retroactive. Another amendment was rushed through applying the earlier amendment to MPs who resigned from a party before its commencement.

When the ensuing by-election — the "Little General Election" — showed KPU as not completely emasculated as the government had hoped — nine of its members were re-elected — the Constitution was amended yet again to enable the president, at any time he might consider it expedient and without parliamentary approval, to bring the Preservation of Public Security Act into force and to assume the repressive power under the Act to detain any person without trial and to ban any political party. Thereupon 13 officials of KPU were detained under the Act now brought into force by President Kenyatta. The detention hammer fell on Odinga himself in 1969, and was accompanied by the proscription of KPU. Kenya was again restored to the cherished status of a *de facto* one-party state.

The scenario was much the same in Zambia. A constitutional amendment vacating the seat of a member of the national assembly in the event of his resignation from the party on whose platform he was elected had been passed in 1966 in circumstances showing that it was aimed at maintaining the unity of President Kaunda's ruling United National Independence Party (UNIP) against the threat of a split. The threatened split did in fact take place in 1968 when the party's minister of commerce, Mr Nalumino Mundia, and his supporters broke away and formed the United Party (UP). The UNIP government turned to the Constitution again for an answer to this challenge to its monopoly of power and got it amended in 1969 to disqualify a person in detention from being a candidate for parliamentary election, and to vacate the seat of an existing member who had been in detention for a continuous period of six months. In the result, the opposition parliamentary members in detention since the split in 1968, including Mundia, lost their seats. At the same time, their party, the UP, was banned.

In 1971 another split occurred in UNIP. A new splinter party, the United Progressive Party (UPP), was formed under the leadership of former UNIP Vice-President, Mr Simon Kapwepwe. As with Mundia's United Party, the new party was short-lived. It was banned on February 4, 1972, and most of its leaders were detained; some of them as were members of the national assembly lost their seats under the 1966 and 1969 constitutional amendments. In the by-election that followed, only Kapwepwe was re-elected but his seat was vacated by his detention for nearly one year from January to December 1972.

The Simon Kapwepwe challenge was too much for President Kaunda and his UNIP government. Constitutional amendment was seized upon again to deal once and for all with the danger posed. By this latest amendment, UNIP was proclaimed "the one and only political party in Zambia", and the formation of other political organisations as well as any expression of opinion or other activity in sympathy with any such political organisation was prohibited. Zambia thus became a *de jure* one-party state by government fiat and not by the wishes of the people expressed by their votes at a referendum. From the standpoint of the struggle for power, the 1972 amendment was significant, considering that Kaunda had earlier in 1964 assured the people of Zambia that "any disappearance of the Parliamentary Opposition in this country would not be, and I emphasise, would not be an act of the government, but would only be according to the wishes of the people ... as expressed at the polls in any future election".[10] Clearly, the motivation for the amendment was more the preservation not of national unity as was claimed, but of UNIP's monopoly of political power.

The ground for the use of the constitution for this purpose had been laid in advance in Kenya, Zambia, Malawi, Tanzania and Ghana by the abolition or substantial attenuation of the rigid amendment procedure instituted in their independence constitutions, which made it relatively easy to pass the amendments into law. The abolition or attenuation was rationalised on rather tenuous grounds.[11]

In Nigeria, the power of the government to amend the constitution has also been used or rather abused to settle in favour of the ruling party in the struggle for power between it and the opposition parties. As in Kenya and Zambia, there had been a factional split in the ruling party in Western Nigeria,

---

[10] Leg. Ass. Debates, 20 March, 1964 Col. 420; also speech at Chifubu on 17 Jan., 1965 quoted in Colin Legum, (ed.), *Zambia: Independence and Beyond* (1966), pp. 108-109

[11] See B.O. Nwabueze, *Presidentialism in Commonwealth Africa* (1973), pp. 398-405.

one of the regions (now states) of the Federation of Nigeria. Chief Akintola, the premier of the regional government and deputy leader of the party, the Action Group (AG) — the leader was in the federal parliament as opposition leader — broke away from the party and formed a splinter party, which he aligned with the ruling party in the federal government, the Northern Peoples Congress (NPC). The AG, seeking to have Chief Akintola removed as regional premier, got its legislative members, who still formed the majority in the regional legislative assembly, to sign a letter to the regional governor, stating that they no longer had confidence in Chief Akintola, whereupon he was removed by the governor. Reversing the Supreme Court of Nigeria, the Judicial Committee of the Privy Council in London, as the country's final court of appeal at the time, ruled that Chief Akintola's removal was lawful and valid.[12] A constitutional amendment was promptly passed, nullifying retrospectively the decision of the Privy Council. It also provided that the premier could only be removed by the governor on the strength of votes taken on the floor of the assembly. Thus, against the clear decision of the highest judicial authority in the country, Chief Akintola was continued in power through the use of the power of constitutional amendment. As a sequel to this, appeals to the judicial Committee of the Privy Council were abolished when later in the year (1963) a new Constitution was adopted on the occasion of the country becoming a republic.

The repression of opposition through the use of the power of constitutional amendment in the three countries is a tragic illustration of the attitude implanted in Africans, rulers and the ruled alike, towards the constitution as a result of its lack of legitimacy and sacrosanctity, which deprives it of respect and loyalty among the people. The constitution cannot effectively moderate or mediate the struggle for political power unless it is accepted and respected by all as sacrosanct and above that struggle. Africans must decolonise their minds of the attitude which, as in the colonial days, regards the constitution as an instrument of repression and autocratic control rather than as a charter of good government and of liberty.

The constitution's lack of legitimacy and sacrosanctity has been aggravated

---

[12]   *Adegbenro v. Akintola* (1963) 3 ALL E.R. 544

by the tragic frequency with which it has been overthrown by the military. It has been the lot of Africa to have passed, quite rapidly, from one tragic misfortune to another — from the tragedy of colonial autocracy to that of military absolutism. From its first occurrence in Egypt in 1952 and Sudan in 1958, military seizure of the state by means of a military *coup d'etat* has, as at July 2001, engulfed 32 out of the 53 states in Africa. The tally of military coups and take-overs as at this date stands at 83 (exclusive of publicly acknowledged attempted coups) viz: Algeria (3 coups), Benin (6), Burkina Faso (6), Burundi (3), Central African Republic (3), Chad (4), Comoros (4), Congo-Brazzaville (1), Egypt (2), Equatorial Guinea (1), Ethiopia (2), The Gambia (1), Ghana (5), Guinea (1), Guinea Bissau (1), Lesotho (2), Liberia (1), Libya (1), Madagascar (2), Mali (4), Mauritania (5), Niger (1), Nigeria (6), Rwanda (1), Sao Tome (1 - short-lived), Seychelles (1), Sierra Leone (4), Somalia (1), Sudan (4), Togo (2), Uganda (5) and Zaire (now Democratic Republic of Congo) (1).

Military coups and take-overs complicate Africa's legitimacy problem in various ways of which only three need to be noted here. First, military take-over marks a break in governmental legitimacy because it is an armed usurpation, not only of powers of government, but also of the most fundamental attribute of a people's sovereignty: the right, by means of a constitution, to institute a government for itself and to define the extent of the powers exercisable by government over the individual. It is a forcible seizure of the entirety of a country's sovereignty, a second colonisation, as it were, this time by the indigenes of the country.

In the second place, military rule is devoid of the legitimising role of popular participation in government and politics. Voting at elections (even when the elections are rigged), election campaigns, political rallies, public assemblies and processions on public issues and other forms of popular participation are all parts of the process of trying to legitimise the state and its institutions. With all these banned under a military regime, it is as if the country was reverted again to its previous condition as a colonial state. The attitude towards the colonial government might then have been transferred to the military government, notwithstanding that it is now manned and controlled by indigenous functionaries. The people can, therefore, hardly be blamed if they continue to think of the government during military rule in terms of "they", and not of "we", just as in the colonial days.

In the third place, military rule reincarnates and aggravates "the problem of an absolute" noted above. A military government brought into existence following a successful military *coup d'etat* is an absolute one. It derives neither its existence nor its powers from a constitution; no question therefore arises of any constitutional limitations upon its powers. On the contrary, where a constitution is established, either a brand new one or the old pre-existing constitution modified to suit the nature and purposes of a military government, it is subject to the absolute and supreme power of the military government. The military government is the source from which such a constitution derives its authority, and at whose sufferance it must therefore operate. This is the reverse of the position in a constitutional democracy where the government is the creation of, derives its powers from, and must thus operate subject to the limitations of, the constitution.

The subjection of a constitution to the absolute power and sufferance of a military government necessarily reduces it to nothing, and thus deprives it of all respect and legitimacy. And the longer the situation persists, the more the constitution is degraded in the eyes and estimation of the people. Worse still, the persistence of military rule for a prolonged period of time entrenches absolutism in the culture of the people and acclimatises them to it. It is therefore saddening to reflect that Nigeria, the giant of Africa, had been under military rule for about 28 years out of its over 40 years as an independent state.

Powers and Institutions of the State in the Context of the Backward Societies of Africa

The state is a foreign organism lodged by European colonialism in the body of Africa. It is foreign, not just in the sense that it was the creation of alien European Powers, but more so because, not having existed before European colonisation (Egypt, Sudan and Ethiopia excepted), it has no root in the life, culture, traditions, habits and experience of the African peoples. It was forcibly imposed upon backward peoples lacking the necessary foundations of civilization, and unacquainted with its ideological or philosophical foundation and its ways, its organising principles, institutions, procedures, its traditions of government administration, the habits of order, discipline, obedience to law, patriotism, and loyalty, the attitude of the responsibility and accountability of rulers to the whole mass of the people. In the nature and extent of its powers, in particular, the power to make law by legislation, the state transplanted to Africa by colonialism has nothing remotely corresponding to it in pre-colonial days.

Whilst Africans do have, by nature, a deep respect for human life, human dignity and other fundamental values of humanity, yet, in the context of the state system created in Africa by colonialism, their respect for, and observance of, them is overborne by the stakes involved in the power to control and administer the state which are incomparably higher than the stakes in the pre-colonial traditional polity. It is this factor that conditions the attitude towards state power in Africa, inclining Africans, in the no-holds barred and do-or-die struggle for it, to trample on the human rights of opponents and critics, and to repress other democratic values.

There was nothing in the pre-colonial polity remotely like the alien-type state's strong, formidable organisation of force, its enormous power, the array of patronages at its disposal; its vast business interests and pervasive control over the economy; its status as a subject of international law, entitled by virtue thereof to all the rights and powers bestowed by that law on states; and the way people are subjected, in many aspect of their lives and affairs, to coercion or compulsion by means of regulations of a legislative nature, judicial orders or decrees enforced by the organised coercive force of the state, and executive orders; all backed by an overwhelming force at once intimidating, irresistible and awesome in the form of a **standing or full-time** army and police with all their weapons of violence, as well as other law enforcement apparatuses like prisons and prison warders, concentration camps, detention centres, security agents, road marshalls, tax collectors, customs officers, forest guards and so on – a force made all the more awesome still because it is in the exclusive monopoly of the state.

It should not therefore surprise us that the struggle for the control of the state in Africa should be characterised by blatant repressions of human rights, of the Rule of Law and of democratic processes. Nor should it surprise us that the possession of state power should produce in those wielding it, excessive arrogance and intoxication and an inordinate desire to personalise and cling on to it for an indefinite length of time, for life, if possible. The taste of anything good to which one is unaccustomed is often intoxicating, and produces an irresistible passion to fight over it. No explanation of the problem of human rights, democracy and the Rule of Law in Africa is realistic or complete unless it is set in the context of this factor and takes fully into account its impact.

It is not only that the state is totally different from the pre-colonial African polity in the nature of its power and force; the forms, institutions and principles involved in its administration were also unknown and without any basis in the pre-colonial African polity. Save only monarchy, which has become discredited in most parts of the world anyway, neither the democratic, representative form of government, with its institutions of free and fair elections based on universal adult suffrage and political parties, nor constitutional democracy, with its institution of a written constitution as supreme law enshrining a guarantee of human rights, separation of powers, the Rule of Law, nor the socialist form of state, with its institutions and principles of socialist ownership of the means of production and exchange, total rule, socialist legality and democratic centralism has any real basis in pre-colonial African political experience and culture.

Thus, the African rulers who took over the administration of the state from departing colonisers came to their new roles with hardly anything from Africa's past to prepare and guide them in those roles. This has great significance. Statism, whilst no doubt Europe's great gift to Africa, unleashed on it a crisis of institutions. It led to the introduction into the continent of pernicious authoritarian forms and principles of government which no African would have thought of or comprehended, had the state not been transplanted to it by European colonialism: the authoritarian African one-party system, military absolutism/despotism and totalitarian socialist system, all with a crushing impact upon human rights, democracy and the Rule of Law.

The fault for the introduction of these pernicious, authoritarian forms was not entirely that of the African rulers, as is commonly supposed. Here were political leaders groping in an unfamiliar terrain in search of suitable institutional forms for the government of an inherited, sophisticated, alien organism, little understood by them and hardly at all by the mass of the people to be governed under it. Africa is simply passing through an experimental stage, a phase of trial and error, of adaptations of existing systems, during which various forms have been, and are being tried, to be discarded if found unsuitable. When it first forced itself upon the scene, military rule was widely hailed as Africa's salvation, but it has since proved itself to be an unmitigated evil that has desecrated nearly all our values and institutions, so much so that all seem now agreed in exorcising it forever. The totalitarian socialist state too has been exorcised in its birthplace (Russia), having proved itself, after seventy years of experimentation there, to be also an evil system; it is also on its way out in Africa. Africans should take solace in the fact that the rise and decline in the life of the state in the continent is part of "an inevitably cyclical pattern of the history"[13] of all nations.

The experimental phase through which Africa is now passing is one that usually accompanies political transitions throughout history – in the case of Africa, it is a transition from the pre-colonial traditional political system to the modern state system brought to the continent by colonialism. "In most European states," Robert Jackson and Carl Rosberg tell us:

> strong personal rule preceded the successful establishment of impersonal constitutional government. In general, personal regimes may be thought of as typical of transitional periods, when one institutionalised order has broken down and another has not yet replaced it. In early modern European history, good examples of such a transition are the states which emerged out of the late medieval period; during the Renaissance and the civil and religious warfare which followed, the boundaries, structures, and institutions of those states were not yet settled in the minds of people; as a result, absolutism became a widespread system of rule.[14]

The crisis in which Africa has been gripped since independence is thus primarily "a crisis of institutions,"[15] and only secondarily one of human failures. Effective institutions of government are yet to take root and become firmly established as active instruments of governance in Africa. Personal rulers have stepped into the vacuum, but, hopefully, only as a transitional phase. Without appearing to endorse the more wanton repressions and desecrations of the institutions, principles and norms of democracy by Africa's personal rulers,

---

[13]   See Crawford Young and Thomas Turner, *The Rise and Decline of the Zairean State* (1985), p. 406

[14]   Robert Jackson and Carl Rosberg, *Personal Rule in Africa* (1982), p. 5

[15]   Basil Davidon, *The Black Man's Burden* p. 19

we might say with Robert Jackson and Carl Rosberg that:

> there is reason to believe that the contemporary period of African history,
> when state institutions have been weak and the organisations of
> government limited in their capabilities, will be remembered primarily in
> terms of the exceptional politicians who had to contrive and manage
> personal systems of governance in the absence of effective institutions.[16]

While it is engaged in this business of experimentation and until it finds its feet and bearing, Africa needs the patient understanding and sympathy of the international community.

The State in Africa as an Instrument of Organised Violence and of Arbitrary Oppressive Rule

As earlier noted, the state is not only foreign to Africa, but also its powers, marvellous and dazzling, are without parallel in pre-colonial times. This new alien creation was perceived by Africans as the source of the whiteman's power, of his superiority, and of all the mystique surrounding him; he was thought of as the personification, the embodiment, of the state and of all the good things of life – wealth, prestige, grandeur and comfortable living. Slavish imitation of the ways of the whiteman was part of the mentality bred in Africans by colonialism, but more disastrous in this connection was the feeling of lust for the whiteman's power and privileged position. To have the whiteman's power, i.e. state power, and the grandeur, prestige and mystique associated with it, was the dream of the African elite and politician, creating in them a kind of uncontrollable animal passion. The lust of the African elite or politician, as he contemplated the power and privileged position of the white colonialists, "expresses his dreams of possession– all manner of possession: to sit at the settler's table, to sleep in the settler's bed, with his wife if possible"[17] And, says Frantz Fanon, "there is no native who does not dream at least once a day of setting himself up in the settler's place"[18] The envy and lust had produced a preparedness and determination to use fraud and other illegitimate means to try to achieve the dream. Thus, the ready resort to these means by the political class in Africa in the struggle for the control of the state is, to a

---

[16]   *ibid*, pp. 12-13
[17]   Frantz Fanon, *The Wretched of the Earth* (1963), p. 32
[18]   *ibid*, at p. 32

significant extent, an inheritance, a hang-over, from colonialism.

Even more an inheritance from the colonial past is the violence of post-colonial African politics. Colonial rule in Africa was a regime of force, born of violence, maintained by violence, and "legitimised" by force. Its frontiers were the army barracks and police stations. Its driving force lay in the regular, unceasing and ruthless application of violence. "In the colonial countries," writes Frantz Fanon:

> the policeman and the soldier, by their immediate presence and their frequent and direct action, maintain contact with the native and advise him by means of rifle-butts and napalm not to budge. It is obvious here that the agents of government speak the language of pure force. The intermediary does not lighten the oppression, nor seek to hide the domination; he shows them up and puts them into practice with the clear conscience of an upholder of the peace; yet he is the bringer of violence into the home and into the mind of the native.[19]

Living in such a pervasive, ever–present atmosphere of violence, the African became familiarised to it as the awesome reality in his governance. He formed an attitude, a mentality, about the indispensability, even legitimacy, of violence as a weapon in the political struggle to end colonial domination. He came to accept the logic that a system of alien domination by organised force required to be fought and dislodged by meeting force with force; or putting it differently, the violence of colonial rule produced a counter-violence by the colonised people. This readiness to resort to violence, once instilled in the mentality of the people during the colonial era, survives after independence as an established means in the struggle for the control of the state and an inherited method of political succession.

Transplanted to colonised Africa, the state, otherwise a device for the betterment and advancement of society, takes on the peculiar character of an instrument for the domination, oppression and repression of the people, using violence as the vehicle. It is the state as thus characterised, the state as a system of organised violence for the domination and oppression of the people, that African political leaders inherited from the colonialists at independence. The ways of the state in Africa, as handed down by the colonialists, are characterised by oppression exacted by violence. "The native

---

[19] Frantz Fanon *op. cit.*, p. 31

is an oppressed person whose permanent dream is to become the persecutor"[20] – the persecutor of his fellow natives, that is.

In short, the state transplanted to Africa by colonialism and handed down to Africans at independence is so far different in purpose and character from what it is in the place from where it was exported. It has nothing of that beneficient quality as a device for the welfare of the people and for securing justice among them, which characterises and informs it in Europe. The state in Africa is merely a device for the domination, oppression and repression of the people by a regular, systematic application of organised force, irrespective of whether it is controlled by white European colonialists or by black African rulers; it has no concern with or for the progress and development of the people. The challenge of the state in Africa is to rid itself of this character stamped on it by colonialism and to re-orient itself to its true functions and responsibilities in the developed countries.

There was yet another characteristic of the colonial state that formed part of Africa's inheritance from colonialism. Colonial rule was essentially bureaucratic rule with respect to all functions of government, political, administrative and technical; *ipso facto*, therefore, it was dictatorial rule, governed, as bureaucratic rule is everywhere, by authoritarian habits and practices. The colonial governor, as head of the administration, was a professional bureaucrat in the fullest sense of the term, and it was as a bureaucrat that he exercised his functions as chief executive of the government and sole legislature. A significant fact about colonial rule everywhere in Africa is that, even after the establishment of an executive council and a legislative council with an unofficial majority, or with wholly elected members, it never altogether shed its bureaucratic and dictatorial character up to the very end.

At independence and after, the bureaucratic outfit of the government remained mortised to the dictatorial habits and practices of the past while the politicians, who succeeded to the colonial governor's executive power, patterned themselves, consciously or unconsciously, upon his authoritarian methods and practices. There was thus in post-colonial Africa a divergence between the democratic theory enshrined in the constitution and the authoritarian practices inherited from the colonial past.[21] And, as always, practice

---

[20]　Frantz Fanon, *op. cit.*, p. 42
[21]　Basil Davidson, *The Black Man's Burden: Africa and the Curse of the Nation-State* (1992), p. 208

overrode theory. Herein lies part of the explanation for the authoritarianism of post-colonial governments in Africa.

The State in Africa as an Instrument of Exploitation and Unfair Discrimination

European colonialism in Africa was not just rule and political domination of one country by another; it was not just a matter of empire and "the prestige of the flag," of power and jurisdiction over foreign territories, as where the colonising and the colonised country belong to the same race, e.g. the colonisation of one white people (European) by another. As white settler colonialism in South Africa shows, European colonialism in Africa had a dual aspect; it was a system of political domination by one people over another as well as a system of privilege based purely on race. "Privilege is at the heart of the colonial relationship"[22] and race is the basis of the privilege.

Unfair discrimination based on race, that is to say, racism, "is built into the system;" it is "ingrained in actions, institutions and in the nature of the colonialist methods of production and exchange".[23] Symbolising the fundamental relation which united the colonialist and colonised, "unfair discrimination based on race is so spontaneously incorporated in even the most trivial acts and words, that it seems to constitute one of the fundamental patterns of colonialist personality";[24] it was "a *sine-qua-non* of colonial life."[25] The essence of European colonialism in Africa, E.A. Walcker has said, is the fact that it is a "contact between races."[26] It is this aspect of European colonialism in Africa as a system of privilege and unfair discrimination based purely on race that distinguished it, for example, from Roman colonialism in Europe, and from British colonialism in North America, Australia and New Zealand. Quite significantly too, unlike racism by whites against blacks in the United States, the racism of European colonialism in Africa was one against an overwhelming indigenous black majority by a numerically small alien white minority in a dominating position politically, socially, culturally and economically.

[22]   Albert Memmi, *The Coloniser and the Colonised* (1957), Preface, p. xii
[23]   Jean-Paul Sartre, Introduction in Albert Memmi, *The Coloniser and the Colonised* (1957), pp. xxiii-xxiv
[24]   Albert Memmi, *op. cit.,* p. 70
[25]   *ibid,* p. 74
[26]   Quoted in Georges Balandier, *The Sociology of Black Africa* (1970), p. 33

As a dual system of political domination and race-based privileges, European colonialism in Africa rested on two pillars which formed its indispensable foundation: exploitation and oppression. The privileges were established in the first place by systematic exploitation of the colonised, and were maintained by oppression using physical force and violence. Without these two pillars of exploitation and oppression, the system could not exist, nor thrive as it did.

Thus, the concept of the "colonial situation" denotes essentially the racism of European colonial system in Africa. It implies the privileged position of the white colonialist (European) in Africa based purely on his race, as manifested in the use of race as the determinant of access to wealth, land, positions in government and private establishments and to other benefits and opportunities: as the basis of practically all political, social and economic relations and of social status generally; as a criterion of liability to sanctions or punishments; and as a rationale for the exploitation, oppression and cultural domination of colonised black Africans, their reduction to the status of a subject race, inferior caste segregated in a residential area separate from that for European quarters, as it was called, resulting in the creation of two more or less racially exclusive societies within the colony, that Frantz Fanon calls the principle of "reciprocal exclusivity," viz the colonising society and the colonised society , both co-existing in a relation of mutual opposition and conflict. The opposition between the two was manifested not only in their different languages, religions, cultures and way of life but also in the types of food eaten, clothes worn and the types of houses they lived in: their worlds were totally different — world of ease and comfort for the white colonialists and of misery and suffering for the colonised blacks. The colonised were reduced to a subject race in a real, not merely a figurative sense, that is in the real sense of *de facto* and *de jure* subjection to disabilities in the political, social and economic spheres.

Practically all aspects of the existence of the colonised African were permeated by the colonial situation — his thoughts, his passions, his conduct, his economic pursuits and his entire personality.[27] As Frantz fanon puts it:

> when you examine at close quarters the colonial context, it is evident that

---

[27]   Albert Memmi, *op. cit.*, Preface, p. viii

what parcels out the world is to begin with the fact of belonging to or not belonging to a given race, a given specie. In the colonies the economic substructure is also a super structure. The cause is the consequence, you are rich because you are white: you are white because you are rich. [28]

An element of the racism of European colonialism in Africa was bigotry. The European colonialist in Africa was bigoted about the superiority of his race, just as he was in his scorn for the African: to him the inferiority of the colonised African was a self-evident truth. The African's backwardness, existing long before colonisation, was taken as proof of his inferiority. The black man was regarded not only as biologically inferior but also as pathologically indolent, lacking a sense of responsibility, and incapable of leadership and of governing himself, which therefore marked him out for colonisation in order to expose him to the light of civilization, to salvage him from his addiction to poverty and wretchedness, and to protect him against his "evil, thievish, somewhat sadistic instincts." [29] From this, says Albert Memmi, "comes the concept of a protectorate" [30] and the rationale for the severities of repression by the colonial police and army. Worse still, the colonised African was regarded and treated merely as "a function of the needs of the coloniser," an instrument in the pursuit of colonial exploitation, a mere object towards which no obligation was owed.

The colonial state thus epitomised inequity and injustice so iniquitous as to smack of manicheanism, in Frantz Fanon's telling word. Its grievous injustice was made more so not only because the privileged position of the white colonialist was unmerited, based, as it was, on "a qualification independent of his personal merit," but also because it was a usurpation of advantages and opportunities rightly due to the colonised black majority, which therefore deprived it of legitimacy. The white colonialist was" "an illegitimately privileged person, that is, a usurper." [31] He was able to "benefit from plentiful and undemanding labour and servants because the colonised can be (and are) exploited at will and are not protected by the laws of the colony," he was able "easily to obtain administrative positions, because they are reserved for him and the colonised are excluded from them," [32] He adorned himself with glory

[28]   Frantz Fanon, *Wretched of the Earth* (1968), p. 40
[29]   Albert Memmi, *op. cit.,* p. 82
[30]   Albert Memmi, *loc. cit.*
[31]   Albert Memmi, *loc. cit.,* pp. 9 & 52
[32]   *ibid.,* p. 8

and prestige by degrading the Africans and by constantly keeping up the degradation. Colonial racism was thus an iniquitous system that "distorts relationships, destroys or petrifies institutions and corrupts men, both colonisers and colonised."[33]

It is the state as a system of inequity and injustice arising from domination, exploitation and unfair discrimination that Africans inherited at independence. The African elite who took over the mantle of rulership since the departure of the colonial overlords conceived themselves as inheritors not only of the whiteman's arbitrary powers but also of his relation to the state and the people. They regard the state as their personal estate over which they have a right to exercise personal rule, and the people as subjects over whom, as overlords, they have a right to dominate, exploit and treat in an unfairly discriminatory manner. "The so -called state," writes Claude Ake, "is not able to rise above the struggles and conflicts of contending social groups."[34] Thus, the manifold injustices, inequities, exploitation of the masses by the ruling elite and the unfair discrimination between citizens based on ethnicity and political affiliation have their roots in Africa's colonial past: they are part of its inheritance from colonialism.

Unfair discrimination is indeed a pervasive feature in the administration of government in Africa. An ethnic group which is not in the ruling group as well as communities which voted against the government party in the elections or which were otherwise known to have sympathy for the opposition was victimized and discriminated against by the denial of amenities and development projects while those already in existence there were allowed to deteriorate or even to close down completely. As for the individual, opposition means denial of jobs, contracts, distributorships, loans or export licences or licences for carrying on occupations which require a licence or the revocation of one already held. The allocation of rice, fertiliser, land, market stalls and the grant of other patronages at the disposal of the state — all depended upon party membership or support. Political affiliation is not, of course, the only ground on which individuals are unfairly discriminated against. Perhaps even more widespread is discrimination based on religion, ethnicity or place of origin.

---

[33]   *ibid.,* p. 151
[34]   Claude Ake, *Democracy and Development in Africa* (1995), p. 42

The post-colonial state in Africa is administered largely for the benefit of the ethnic group to which the ruler belongs just as the colonial state was a system of privileges for the white colonialists.

All this is a desecration of the principle that rulers and the governed, the high and the low, are equal before the law and are equally protected by the law and equally obliged to obey its rules, without exemptions based on official position held or social status, what Dicey calls " the universal subjection of all classes to one law administered by the ordinary courts." [35] The African rulers, as the new overlords of the country, place themselves above the law, just like the departed colonial overlords. (The latter could not be tried in Africa for offences against Africans.)

The Attitude of Africans towards the State

A more fundamental and disastrous effect of the alien character of the state in Africa is the attitude created in the people towards it. The state was regarded, not as the people's property, but as the whiteman's. It arouses no strong feeling or sense of identification and attachment, but rather alienation. The people feel alienated from it, and think of it, not in terms of "ours" but of "theirs"; "theirs" referred in the past to the whiteman but now to the indigenous rulers who replace the white imperialists.

This attitude of alienation rather than identification has meant that the state is not able to engage the people's devotion and sense of loyalty and service. The colonial government in Africa was founded on the concept of service to the Imperial Government. Power was exercised, not for the service of the people, but for the purpose of their subjugation and exploitation. Its concern was not with the improvement and development of the social conditions of the people but, rather, with the maintenance of law and order to a degree sufficient to facilitate the continued subjugation and exploitation of the people. The European colonial administrators were not servants of the African people: they were our political masters. The power they exercised belonged, not to the people, but to the colonising state by right of cession, implied grant or conquest. Their social relations with the

---

[35] A.V. Dicey, *The Law of the Constitution*, 10th edn, p. 193

people too, were also those of master and servant, characterised by a cult of superiority which was exhibited not only in their attitude and behaviour towards the people but also in their entire lifestyle. They lived in superior quarters, spatially separated from the people, and were accorded superior incomes and other privileges.

It is a matter for argument how far the notion of the welfare of the people as the purpose of government can apply to a government which, like a colonial government, does not derive its power from the people. Can a government which is not a government of the people by the people be one **for** the people in the real sense of the term? Such a government is almost certain to have interests different from those of the people, if not antagonistic to them as in the case of a colonial government whose primary interest is the exploitation of the people for the benefit of its home country.

The colonial approach to state power and the position of the European colonial administrators as masters of the people with superior rights and privileges was part of Africa's political heritage and experience. It is to be expected that an experience that lasted for over half a century might leave its imprint on the outlook and attitude of the people , and that, from the time when Africans began to be associated in the exercise of state power, the indigenous functionaries might take over the colonial approach and pattern themselves on it. That, I believe, is the origin of the absence of a sense of service and trusteeship that pervades public service in Africa. The concept of service as equally that of trusteeship is foreign to the African public servant. He is notoriously discourteous, disrespectful, arrogant, undevoted, self-serving, unresponsive to the needs of the people, arbitrary, nepotic and lacking in fidelity, probity and accountability.

Inefficiency is inherent in a situation where government and its services are regarded as an alien undertaking or even as nobody's business, as something in which the citizen has no personal stake and for whose failure he has no personal responsibility. This attitude pervades all government undertakings and enterprises, whatever their nature, whether they be an activity of a strictly governmental nature or one of a commercial nature: they are both viewed as a " service" not meant to be operated on efficient commercial lines with a view to profit. And so we find the attitudes and outlooks adopted in regard to the strictly governmental functions being transferred to government commercial enterprises. All the waste, corruption, inefficiency, conservatism, red-tapism and the other bureaucratic "traditions and rigidities of the civil service" are simply transferred to government business enterprises. These and other geo-political factors have tended to relegate economic considerations in the decision-making process of government economic enterprises. The effect of these attitudes is manifested particularly in the excessive cost of land acquisition, buildings, other civil engineering works and a medley of fees (consultancy, professional and other fees), which often eats up virtually the entirety of the initial financial allocation for the project.

The spirit of personal involvement and dedication which characterizes employment in the private sector is thus generally lacking. So is the tradition of "personalised accountability." Unlike

> a private sector industrial establishment which is often on its toes to give satisfactory account of its stewardship to the annual general meeting of shareholders who do not often take kindly to nil dividends report at the end of the business year... a wholly owned government industrial establishment has only to improvise alibis and scapegoats to explain away its hard luck stories to the supervising ministry, whose officials have no personal stake in the fortunes of the business, since they can comfortably rely on annual government subventions[36]

All these combine to make the management of government enterprises complacent, inert and inefficient.

The alien character and colonial origin of the state in Africa is also a significant pre-disposing factor in the rampant practice of corruption. As an alien entity, the people are wont to feel that the only interest they have in it is what they can get out of it in terms of material benefits. The attitude is that anyone connected with it should try to get as much from it as possible by plunder or fraud; to do that was considered legitimate, and not morally reprehensible; those who had the opportunity and failed to utilise it to enrich themselves were mocked. The bearing that this absence of loyalty to the interest of the state has on the origin and practice of corruption is illustrated by the fact that whereas the treasurer of a local council might cheerfully make away with its funds and feel no sense of remorse about it, the treasurer of a

---

[36] *Report of the Study Group on Nigeria's Industrial Policy,* Federal Government Press (1984), p. 48

village union dared not, since, if he did, he would incur moral condemnation and possible ostracisation by the village. This shows, as Wraith and Simpkins rightly said, that developing countries have in such matters the same regard for ethical behaviour as the civilised nations, provided their deepest loyalties were engaged.[37] The rampancy, scope and methods of corruption in Africa have of course increased by the creation of new incentives and avenues for it, mainly by political ambition and the desire for the perquisites that come with the control of the state, but its root cause still remains the lack of devotion and loyalty to the state and its interests. Corruption by public servants manifests indeed a lack of a sense of patriotism.

The Absence of the Spirit of the Laws and Institutions of the State

The African peoples are yet to imbibe and assimilate the spirit — the habits, traditions, attitudes and temper — conditioning the institutions and laws of the state. We may here define the state as both a legal order consisting of a body of laws, mostly legislated laws, regularly enforced by a coercive agency (the police and the army) and by courts with compulsive jurisdiction, for the maintenance of peace and order in society, and the regulation of human activities and social life generally, which is the basis of a civilised society as distinguished from one in a state of barbarism; and as a moral order infused with a certain spirit, attitude and character, that is to say, a community habituated to order, obedience to law which guarantees protection for human rights, respect for constituted authority, discipline, public service, public probity, accountability, loyalty, love of country, etc. Thus effective statehood has both material and moral dimensions.

Africans have taken over the first, the material element, together with the forms and ceremonies associated with the state, but are yet to imbibe and assimilate the spirit that in Europe conditions the administration of the state, its power, its organisation of force, its laws, institutions and process. The spirit of the laws and institutions of the state, unlike the laws and institutions themselves, is not an exportable commodity; it cannot be packaged and

---

[37] Wraith and Simpkins, *Corruption in Developing Countries* (1963).

transported. Models of laws and institutions may be packaged and exported from one country to another, but their spirit cannot, because it has no material form, no material existence capable of being packaged for export. Being only a moral quality, it can only grow, it can only be generated from within the society itself, either by the natives themselves or by colonialists living amongst them.

And so it is that, although liberty, democracy, justice, the Rule of law and order are noble concepts enshrined in the constitutions of most African countries, they have yet no reality as living or active principles in the governance of these countries; they do not, and cannot, become such merely by reason of having been enshrined in the constitution. They are more a matter of the spirit, of the heart, resting not only on the formal existence of a constitution that embodies them, but more on attitude, temper, disposition or a moral sense inculcated by precept, example, habit and tradition. "Liberty," writes a great American jurist, Judge Learned Hand, "lies in the hearts of men and women; when it dies there, no constitution, no law, no court can save it."[38] Learned Hand further affirms:

> Civil liberties lie in habits, customs — conventions, if you will — that tolerate dissent ... If such a habit and such a temper pervade a society, it will not need institutions to protect its civil liberties and human rights; so far as they do not, I venture to doubt how far anything else can protect them: whether it be Bills of Rights or courts that must in the name of interpretation read their meaning into them.[39]

That is what distinguishes human laws and institutions from technology. The latter has no spirit that governs and conditions its applications; when it is transferred from one country to another, nothing more is needed for it to function well than a mastery of its operational manuals and mechanism and proper maintenance. Not so with human laws and institutions; they never function well in the importing country unless the spirit conditioning or governing them is also imbibed and assimilated.

A **standing or full-time army** is a good illustrative example of an alien institution imported into Africa by colonialism but without the spirit — the

---

[38] Learned Hand, *The Spirit of Liberty: Papers and Addresses of Learned Hand,* ed. Irving Dilliard (1959), pp. 221-228

[39] Learned Hand, An Address titled "A Fanfare for Prometheus" reproduced in *The Freedom Reader* ed. Edwin Newman (1963), p. 24; also reprinted in Irving Dilliard (ed.) *op. cit.,* p. 221-228.

ethics and traditions — conditioning it in Europe. No doubt, armies existed in pre-colonial Africa, but not the standing or full-time army, except in Chakazulu's Zululand and perhaps one or two other places. Whilst the causes of military interventions in government and politics in Africa are varied and the subject of considerable debate, one cause stands out distinctly as being beyond dispute, viz: the elitist belief of military officers, that, like the civilian elite, they have a right to rule, and therefore to take over when, in their judgment, the state is being mismanaged by the civilians.

With a few exceptions soon to be noted, the army in Africa, as an institution created by the colonial government, was elitist in its organisation, in its command system, its weaponry, its style, rituals, attitudes and aspirations. The military elite share with their civilian counterparts the same attitude towards the state as an instrument of exploitation, and the same aspiration to control and exploit its power, wealth, influence and grandeur for their personal benefit; both the civilian and military elite in Africa are characterised by the same belief that there they have a right to rule. It is part of the colonial heritage that there is a distinctly elitist outlook towards the right to rule the transplant state. As the military elite watch the civilian rulers in the enjoyment of state power and its perquisites after the departure of the European colonialists, the military elite's ambition is intensely aroused.

The army in Europe is reared in the spirit and tradition of non-involvement in politics, but that tradition was yet to be sufficiently imbibed by the African army officers as at the time of independence; in any case, what little of it had been imbibed was, soon after independence, overborne by their elitist ambition to exploit for their personal benefit the state's power, wealth, influence and grandeur. This bears out our thesis in this study, i.e. that the transplantation of an institution from one country to another in no way implies that the spirit or traditions that condition its practical operation would be imbibed in the receiving country; the one is a mechanical process, the other an evolutionary one; the spirit of an institution evolves and grows from within, if at all, but it cannot be imposed from outside. And so we find that the tradition of non-interference in politics is maintained only as long as the command of the army remains in the hands of the expatriate officers, as is the case for some years after independence. The presence in the top command positions of expatriate officers acts as a deterrent to the elitist impulses of the indigenous officers. It operates to stay their hands, but only temporarily. For with the eventual departure of expatriate commanders under the pressure of the policy of Africanisation of the public services, the inhibition is removed, and the indigenous officers' elitist aspirations and belief in their right to determine the political destiny of the country assert themselves.

All what is said above contrasts with the attitude and outlook of the armies in Africa that originated, not as a creation of the colonial government, but as a product of the armed liberation struggle, as in Angola, Mozambique, Namibia and, to a lesser extent, Zimbabwe. These were not, in their origin, elitist armies, but rather revolutionary ones reared in the rigours and hardships of a war to liberate themselves and their countries from colonial exploitation and oppression. "Such armies do not tend to feel the sentiment of military pride and corporate self-identity as much as the regular armies. Furthermore, as liberation armies, their ideology tends, initially at any rate, to favour popular participation in government."[40]

One of the tragedies of colonialism in Africa is that the European colonisers, for their own selfish interests, had pursued a policy of not enabling Africans to imbibe the spirit of the laws and institutions of the state. The period of time during which, reluctantly and grudgingly, the policy was changed and Africans were exposed to the European system of rule was altogether too short for them to have acquired any but a smattering, ill-founded acquaintance with the laws and institutions of the state, and of the spirit conditioning them. Coming to independence without having imbibed the spirit of the laws and institutions of the state under European tutelage, Africans were left to their own devices; they had to try, by their own efforts after independence, to assimilate the necessary spirit as part of their culture. Infusing the African societies with the spirit of the laws and institutions of the state — spiritual development — must therefore form an important part of decolonisation. The problem is regrettably compounded by the attitude implanted in Africans towards the state, its government, constitution and laws — discussed above.

---

40 S.E. Finer, *The Man on Horseback: The Role of the Military in Politics*, (1962), p. 198

The Social Constitution of the State

Perhaps an even more significant factor in the failure of Africa's experimentation with the alien state system in the heterogenous social constitution of the state, with the endemic, in-built conflicts and violence attendant upon that. The character of the colonially-created state in Africa is defined not only by its formidable organisation of power and force, by forms, institutions and principles of government which were totally foreign to pre-colonial African peoples, but equally and also significantly by a social constitution characterised by a large conglomeration of antagonistic, antipathetic and incompatible ethnic or racial groups, with differing characters, cultures, traditions and outlooks. The state in Africa is thus a plural, multi-national state, not a nation-state. Nearly every one of the present 53 states in Africa today originated through the forcible merger of a large number — hundreds in some cases, e.g. 394 in Nigeria — of different ethnic or racial groups, each made up of a still greater number of autonomous communities, each independent of the other. The worst antagonism arose from the whites and blacks being together in one state in South Africa and Rhodesia (now Zimbabwe).

Conflicts and violence are necessarily built into the social fabric of a state so structured, hence the endemicity in Africa of frequent inter-ethnic or inter-racial feuds (e.g. between Buganda and Bunyoro in Uganda or between the Tutsi and Hutu in Burundi and Rwanda). Violent confrontations between a tribe and the common government (e.g. between Buganda and the Uganda government, between the Tiv and the government of Northern Nigeria or between the Ga and the government of Ghana), and other situations of imminent danger of public order or public safety as well as secessions and civil wars, such as occurred in the Congo (Leopoldville), Chad, Nigeria, Somalia, Sudan, Angola, Liberia, Congo (Brazzaville), Ethiopia, Burundi, Rwanda, Uganda, Sierra Leone and Guinea-Bissau.

To these must be added conflicts and violence arising from divisions among new social, religious and economic groups that sprang up in the wake of the advent of the state — violent disturbances by new religions groups, Christians and Moslems (e.g. the schism between Islam and Christianity in Sudan or between different sects within each of the two religions, such as violent disturbances connected with the Lumba Church in Zambia and Moslem fundamentalist sects in Nigeria, Egypt and Algeria); the warfare between political parties for the control of the state; the unrest between emergent economic classes; military revolts or mutinies, of which there had been four occurrences in Tanganyika, Uganda, Kenya and Congo (Leopoldville); and military *coup d'etats*, of which there had been 82 occurences involving 32 countries.

Violent conflicts between all these various groups comprised within the state are thus at the centre of what Ali Mazrui call "Africa's twin-crises of identity and integration."[41]

The process of transforming a backward, traditional society into a modern one has also imposed its own strains. The society is in a state of flux, and change, especially rapid change such as these countries are undergoing, creates tension. The forces of change — the cash economy, the emergence of a new rich class based on trade rather than on land, urbanisation, industrialisation, vast increases in literacy and education — all exert their impact on the situation of tension and stress.

All these factors react upon one another to make the society of the new states into a kind of cauldron, which continually emits vapours of unrest and instability. Now and again, the uneasy equilibrium breaks down, giving rise to violent disorders in which government services are paralysed, the basic necessities of life are imperilled, normal life and activities disrupted, lives and property destroyed and their general security endangered, forcing countless numbers into exile as refugees. Often, the disorders are followed by a formal declaration of a state of emergency. The armed encounters between Bugunda and the Uganda government of Milton Obote gave rise to the abolition of the Constitution and the seizure of absolute power by Obote and to the declaration of an emergency over Bugunda, later extended to the whole country. So also the violent activities of the Lumba church in Zambia, the assassination of President Anwar Sadat of Egypt by Islamic fundamentalists and the ensuing shoot-outs between them and the government security forces in Cairo and other various parts of the country have led to proclamations of emergency. Such too has been the case in many other African countries.

---

41 Ali Mazrui, *Violence and Thought: Essays on Social Tensions in Africa*, (1969), p. 155

Thus, the endemicity in Africa of frequent situations of violent disorders and states of emergency is largely an inheritance from colonialism. They occur not because Africans are, by nature, prone to violence, but mainly because they are the inevitable result of factors and conditions brought about by colonialism.

Violent disorders and formally declared states of emergency necessitate a resort by government to authoritarian measures to deal with them. This is an invariable consequence in all countries of the world. Nearly all modern constitutions confer extraordinary powers, including the power to curtail guaranteed human rights and to suspend democratic processes, in situations of emergency formally declared in accordance with the provisions of the constitution. Even the most constitutional of constitutional regimes finds it necessary to arm itself, under the constitution, with special powers to deal with an emergency. In all countries, it is recognised that constitutionalism has to be limited by the exigencies of an emergency, since an emergency implies a state of danger to public order and public safety, which cannot adequately be met within the framework of governmental restraints imposed by the constitution.

There is a good justification for this. The preservation of the state and society is an imperative necessity, which should override the need for limited government — *salus populi est suprema lex* (the safety of the people is the supreme law.). The liberty of the individual itself:

> depends for its very existence and implementation upon the continuance of the organised political society — that is the ordered society — established by the Constitution. The continuance of that society itself depends upon national security, for without security any society is in danger of collapse or overthrow. National security is thus paramount not only in the interests of the state but also in the interests of each individual member of the state; and measures designed to achieve and maintain that security must come first; and, subject to the provisions of the Constitution, must override, if need be, the interests of individuals and of minorities with which they conflict.[42]

---

42 Per Chief Justice Blagden in *Kachasu v. Att-Gen. of Zambia,* 1967/HP/273; cf Justice Holmes in *Moyer v. Peabody* 212 U.S. 78 at p. 85 (1909)

In situations of danger to public security, it has been said, "men care more for order than liberty."[43]

Accordingly, all constitutions which impose limitations upon government authorise the limitations to be over-stepped in times of emergency. Constitutionalism and the Rule of Law can no more forbid the exercise by government of extraordinary power in situations of imminent danger to public order and public safety than they can prevent their occurrence. The most they can do is to define in explicit terms in the constitution the kinds of situation to constitute an emergency and which must actually exist in an objective, factual sense to warrant the assumption of authoritarian powers by government. But emergency power can be accommodated with constitutionalism if emergency situations are conceived of as an ephemeral aberration occurring once in a long while, and provided that the extraordinary powers for dealing with them are not so sweeping as to destroy or suspend the restraints of constitutional government completely.

To a great extent, therefore, the authoritarianism of African governments since independence is the result of the endemicity of frequent, widespread, violent disorders or other situations of imminent danger or public order or public security caused by factors and conditions brought about by colonialism. It is not a peculiarly African response. What African governments can rightly be denounced for is the tendency on their part to abuse and exploit such situations for their own aggrandisement.

First, an emergency is sometimes proclaimed and authoritarian measures adopted when the situation that actually exists in the country as an objective fact does not amount to a state of emergency within the intendment and spirit of the constitutional provision, as when in 1962 the federal parliament in Nigeria, invoking the open-ended provision in the Constitution, declared an emergency in the whole of Western Nigeria merely on the strength of fighting among the MPs within the chamber of the regional house of assembly, even though the entire region outside the assembly building was quiet and there was no attempt by the members to carry their brawl outside.

Secondly, an emergency regime is often continued in operation long after the situation giving rise to it has abated or been effectively contained.

---

43. C. McIlwain, *Constitutionalism and the Changing World* (1939), p.276.

Thirdly, the amount or extent of interference with liberty, the rule of law and democracy often goes beyond what is reasonably necessary for dealing with the situation.

Fourthly, the extensive, often arbitrary use made of preventive detention statutes by some African countries outside an emergency declared in accordance with the provisions of the constitutions, e.g. Ghana's Preventive Detention Act 1958, is hardly supported or justified by reference to any clear, real and imminent danger to public order or public security; it stems more from the undue intolerance of opposition and a desire to suppress it in order to enhance the rulers' political position.

Fifthly, the abolition or attenuation of the protective constitutional or other legal provisions inherited at independence for restraining security powers or for safeguarding the interests of detained persons cannot be said to be reasonably necessary for maintaining or securing public order or public safety. There can be no justification for detaining a person for more than ten years without any opportunity of a review by an independent and impartial tribunal.

Sixthly, the resort to the authoritarianism of the one-party system is not supportable upon the proffered rationale that the warfare of the political struggle for the control of the state makes it necessary. The real motivation seems to be, to a large extent, at any rate, the ambition on the part of African rulers for personalised power and for an unlimited, indefinite rule. So also Africa's development crisis, the struggle to regain the continent's capacity for development, is not a justification for the repression of civil and political rights by African governments on the false and untenable premise that the enjoyment of civil and political rights is incompatible with the struggle for economic development — that the realisation of economic and social rights is attainable only if civil and political rights are denied or suppressed. Whilst the implementation of economic and social rights impinge, to some extent, on civil and political rights, the impingement is not such as creates an incompatibility between them. It is all a matter of balancing. It is perhaps not unfair to say with Mathews that "the only correlation between economic development and human rights violations is that privileged classes have tended to perpetuate their rule by violating human rights in order to stay in power"[44]

---

44 K. Mathews, "The OAU and Political Economy of Human Rights in Africa: An Analysis of the African Charter on Human and Peoples' Rights 1982," 1987 1st/2nd Quarters, *Africa Today*, p. 96. See also Report of the ICJ Conference on Development, Human Rights and the Rule of Law (1981), Pergamon Press, pp. 53-54; 137-138.

Finally, military take-overs and the regime of military absolutism have no justifiable basis in the endemicity of situations of social unrest and violence in Africa; the real motivation for them is also the personal ambition for absolute political power on the part of military officers in Africa.

INDEX